Awakening Islam

Awakening Islam

The Politics of Religious Dissent
in Contemporary Saudi Arabia

Stéphane Lacroix

Translated by
George Holoch

Harvard University Press
Cambridge, Massachusetts
London, England
2011

Originally published as *Les islamistes saoudiens: Une insurrection
manquée,* © Presses Universitaires de France, 2010.

Library of Congress Cataloging-in-Publication Data

Lacroix, Stéphane.
Awakening Islam : the politics of religious dissent in contemporary
Saudi Arabia / Stéphane Lacroix ; translated by George Holoch.
p.   cm.
Includes bibliographical references and index.
ISBN 978-0-674-04964-2 (alk. paper)
1. Saudi Arabia—History—1932–   2. Religion and politics—Saudi Arabia.
3. Islamic fundamentalism—Saudi Arabia.   4. Islam and state—Saudi Arabia.
I. Holoch, George.   II. Title.
DS244.63.L345   2011
320.5'5709538—dc22   2010040833

This work, published as part of a program providing publication assistance,
received financial support from the French Ministry of Foreign Affairs,
the Cultural Services of the French Embassy in the United States and
FACE (French American Cultural Exchange).

Contents

Awakening Islam

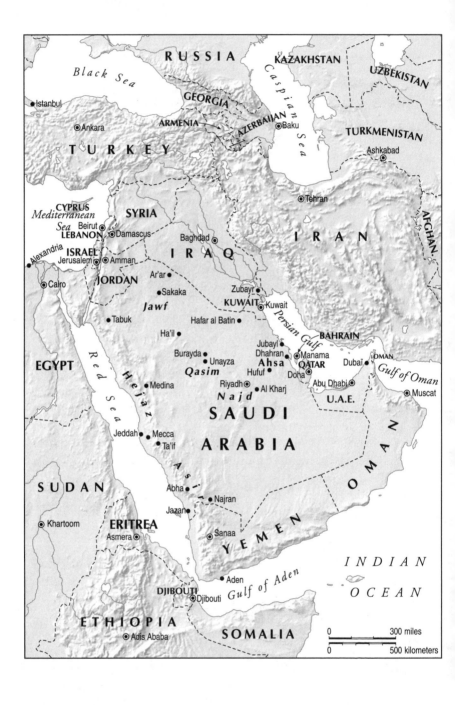

RUSSIA

Black Sea

● Istanbul

KAZAKHSTAN

GEORGIA

◉ Ankara

ARMENIA

AZERBAIJAN ◉ Baku

UZBEKISTAN

Caspian Sea

TURKMENISTAN

● Ashkabad

T U R K E Y

CYPRUS

Mediterranean Sea

Beirut ◉

LEBANON ◉ Damascus

SYRIA

◉ Tehran

● Baghdad

I R A N

AFGHAN.

ISRAEL

● Alexandria

Jerusalem ◉ ● Amman

◉ Cairo

JORDAN

Ar'ar ●

● Sakaka

I R A Q

Jawf

Zubayr ●

KUWAIT

◉ Kuwait

Persian Gulf

BAHRAIN

● Tabuk

Hafar al Batin ●

Ha'il ●

Burayda ● ● Unayza

Jubayl ●

Dhahran ● ◉ Manama

◉

OMAN

EGYPT

Red Sea

Hejaz

● Medina

Qasim

Riyadh ◉ ● Al Kharj

Ahsa

Hufuf ●

QATAR Dubaï ●

● Doha

Gulf of Oman

Abu Dhabi ●

◉ Muscat

N a j d

U.A.E.

S A U D I

Jeddah ● ● Mecca

● Ta'if

A R A B I A

Asir

Abha ●

● Najran

O M A N

S U D A N

Jazan ●

◉ Khartoom

ERITREA

Asmera ◉

◉ Sanaa

Y E M E N

INDIAN

OCEAN

● Aden

Gulf of Aden

DJIBOUTI

◉ Djibouti

E T H I O P I A

◉ Adis Ababa

S O M A L I A

0   300 miles
0   500 kilometers

1

Islamism in a Fragmented Society

Saudi Arabia has remained a persistent blind spot in studies of Islamism.[1] Although all writers agree that the religious influence of the strongly proselytizing Saudi kingdom is a key factor in the emergence and expansion of Islamist movements in the Middle East, there are very few who can describe with any precision the tenor and methods of that influence. The choice is often between caricature and outrageous oversimplification. Saudi Arabia is said to export a retrograde Islam, homogeneous and unchanged since the eighteenth century, when it was revived at the instigation of a preacher from central Arabia, Sheikh Muhammad bin Abd al-Wahhab. In this picture, modernity enters into play only indirectly, through the discovery of oil, which provided a religious idiosyncrasy with the resources for global expansion. The limitations of these descriptions can easily be explained: contemporary Saudi Islam has been the subject of few studies, and they have mostly been based on secondary sources. For both journalists and researchers, Saudi Islam is terra incognita.

The first task is to describe the multiplicity and variability of Islam in Saudi Arabia. To accomplish this, it is necessary to effect a kind of Copernican revolution in the accepted approach: although Saudi Arabia is often considered solely as a power that exports Islam, it also has to be seen as the recipient of influences emanating from most currents of nineteenth- and twentieth-century Islamic revivalism. Those influences introduced modern forms of Islamic activism, as practiced by Islamist movements elsewhere in the Middle East, into Saudi Arabia. The encounter of that activist culture with some of the teachings of Ibn Abd al-Wahhab gave rise in Saudi Arabia to an indigenous Sunni Islamist current that, like the movements that have influenced it, is complex and diversified.

The situation of the Saudi Islamist movement is different from that of Islamism in most Middle Eastern countries because there is no question of combating a secular regime that relies on sources of legitimation other than religion. What is at issue is challenging the monopoly over the divine held by a government based on religion. Islam in Saudi Arabia is therefore a subject of contention, primarily between the regime and the Islamists, but also among the Islamists themselves because of the multiplicity of visions that motivate them. These disputes are sometimes expressed in theological or juridical terms that may appear abstract and remote from everyday realities, but in most cases they are connected to underlying social dynamics, whether vertical conflicts between individuals located at different levels of social hierarchies or horizontal conflicts between agents in different social spheres. In Saudi Arabia, Islam is thus the primary language in which social rivalries are expressed. Hence, far from being a mere study of Islamic politics, the following pages hope to provide the reader with a renewed perspective on the recent social history of the Saudi kingdom.

On August 2, 1990, Saddam Hussein of Iraq provoked a regional and global cataclysm by invading Kuwait. The growing crisis soon produced a collateral victim: the Saudi regime, which was forced to call on foreign troops—chiefly American—to protect its territory against a possible Iraqi attack. The announcement of the arrival of non-Muslim reinforcements in the Land of the Two Holy Places fostered the rise of a formidable opposition campaign against the royal family, carried out by a diffuse but well-organized movement, the Sahwa (short for al-Sahwa al-Islamiyya, "Islamic awakening"). Not only was the kingdom no longer the haven of social peace that observers had described, but it also now appeared vulnerable to a language of protest derived from a resource over which it thought it had a monopoly—Islam.

It is true that a group of millenarian Islamists led by Juhayman al-'Utaybi had seized the Grand Mosque in Mecca in November 1979, but that movement, driven by a very marginal doctrinal vision, had been unable to mobilize more than a small core of a few hundred supporters. The situation was very different in August 1990, when inflammatory sermons in the four corners of the kingdom denouncing the American presence as the stigma of a moral and political failure of the Saudi "system" drew an audience of tens of thousands of young enthusiasts. The protest was soon organized, and several petitions signed by some of the intellectual and religious elite of the kingdom demanded the introduction of radical reforms. For the first time in its recent history, the Saudi system, which until then had seemed invulnerable, was shaken. Disturbances continued until late in 1994 and led to the incarceration of several hundred opposition supporters.

This book will focus on this "Sahwa insurrection" (*intifadat al-Sahwa,* as it is referred to in Saudi Islamist circles). This event affords the most appropriate focal point for the study of Saudi Islamism because it is the only Islamist mobilization of major magnitude in the history of the country, and because, in the trajectory of Saudi Islamism, it represented simultaneously a culmination, a moment of truth, and a foundational break.

The episode marked a culmination for Saudi Islamism because it witnessed the activation of organizations and ideas that had developed over the preceding decades in an Islamist milieu that went back, symbolically, to the early 1950s, when Muslim Brotherhood exiles started settling in the Saudi kingdom. To study the Sahwa insurrection, we thus need to start by putting down on paper a history that has never been written, the history of Islamism in Saudi Arabia. Beyond the mere establishment of facts, I will attempt to provide a substantive history of the practices and views of the Saudi Islamist current.

The Sahwa insurrection was also a moment of truth because it offered a unique opportunity to test the mobilizing potential of Islamism in Saudi Arabia. This book explains how the Islamist movement succeeded in temporarily overturning the logic of social control that in normal circumstances helped maintain the stability of the system, and then why the Islamist mobilization eventually failed. This account will also bring to light certain aspects of Islamist mobilizations (and, to some extent, non-Islamist mobilizations) that are more difficult to observe in contexts other than Saudi society.

Finally, the Sahwa insurrection was a foundational break because it was the event that all later mobilizations of an Islamist bent in the kingdom made into an absolute reference point in an effort to situate themselves in continuity with a "moment" that remains an inexhaustible source of legitimacy in activist circles. Explaining the Sahwa insurrection is therefore a key to understanding the changes that Saudi Islamism has undergone in the early twenty-first century.

The protest of the early 1990s has been the subject of a few studies. For some authors, the explanation of the disturbances that shook Saudi Arabia in the wake of the Gulf War is to be sought in the dominance of a "Wahhabi" religious discourse described as a "double-edged sword," backed by a religious institution fundamentally characterized by its ideological ambiguity.[2] Although explanations of a cultural order have sometimes occupied pride of place in the etiology of Islamism,[3] the place given them in the analysis of the Saudi form of the phenomenon is notable for its disproportionate scale. At a loss in dealing with a relatively prosperous rentier[4] society, lacking in "dangerous classes," some analysts have made the cultural paradigm the principal axis for their interpretation of Saudi Islamism, if not of Saudi society as a whole.

The relevance of the study of Wahhabism to the understanding of Saudi Islamism is unquestionable, but such a study should take into account the complexity and especially the plasticity of the phenomenon. Wahhabism is not, as often portrayed, an unchangeable essence but rather a "tradition" in motion, subject to interpretation and reinterpretation. Indeed, the minimalism—its detractors would say the poverty—of Ibn Abd al-Wahhab's thinking accounts for the proliferation of those interpretations. In that sense Wahhabism determines social phenomena as much as it is determined by them, engendering within itself all sorts of shifting arrangements. More important, the study of Wahhabism does not explain why protest erupted precisely when it did. In the face of this question, some analysts have supplemented their explanatory model by introducing a sociopsychological variable, pointing to the social anomie generated by two factors. The first is cultural and includes the alienation engendered by too-rapid modernization and the exacerbation of anti-American (and, by extension, anti-royal-family) sentiment provoked by the presence of American troops in the Land of the Two Holy Places. The second factor flows from economic causes, such as the relative frustration brought about by the fall in oil income after the 1982 recession.[5] In addition, some writers focused on the charisma of the Islamist opposition figures Salman al-ʿAwda and Safar al-Hawali, who were able to galvanize crowds with appeals that were as much emotional as rational.[6]

Some of these analyses are problematic. Rapid modernization, for example, has been a constant component of Saudi society since the 1960s and was no more likely to foster mobilization in 1990 than at any other moment. Others are correct but could be looked further into. An embryonic dynamic of protest antedated the Gulf War, which operated at most as a catalyst for the mobilization and not as the triggering force. Moreover, although it cannot be denied that the American military presence provoked in the population a diffuse feeling of anger from which the protest was able to profit, its effects on the system—not just individuals alone—need to be specified. Similarly, although the relative frustration caused by the economic recession had undeniable consequences, it did not affect the whole society in the same way, and its effects therefore have to be placed in their proper context.[7] Finally, charisma, as Pierre Bourdieu has shown, has to be understood in connection with social dynamics that are more structural in nature; the prophet, who is the embodiment of charisma, is less the "extraordinary" man than the "man of extraordinary situations."[8]

Beyond the temporal question itself, this sociopsychological interpretive scheme, like its cultural counterpart, is especially unable to answer some deeper questions raised by the Sahwa insurrection. For example, how did the mobilization take hold, and why did it run out of steam? The classic approaches can give only a very partial account of the episode, in part because they are weakened by two problems that have to do with their presuppositions.

First, the two approaches consider mobilizations only as the product of external determinants: an imbalance (cultural or economic) of the system in the case of the sociopsychological approach, an "effect of culture" for the cultural approach. At no point is the strategic dimension of collective action taken into account. The critique of these approaches is at the heart of a whole series of studies that have been published since the 1970s, leading twenty years later to a global theory of collective action, the theory of social movements.[9] For the proponents of this theory, a mobilization is a strategic action that is conducted by groups endowed with a given quantity of material and symbolic resources and that is dependent on a specific context. It lasts over time, often relying on preexisting mobilizing structures and interpretive frameworks. In other terms, frustrations and tensions cannot alone explain "why [and how] men rebel."[10]

Second, the cultural and sociopsychological approaches do not take into account Saudi social complexity. Instead, the cultural approach treats the Saudi cultural corpus as a homogeneous and coherent whole, reducible to a Wahhabism with well-defined characteristics. The sociopsychological approach views the social arena as a unified entity affected by uniform dynamic forces. Both approaches set these "total" entities in opposition to the individual, portrayed as the prisoner of the whims of his psyche. Between the two extremes there seems to exist no place for intermediate structures.

But societies are not uniform entities. They are made up of distinct spheres, each one enjoying relative autonomy; that is, each one is governed, in part at least, by its own logic that cannot be applied to the social world as a whole. To designate these microcosms, the word "field" (champ), promoted by Pierre Bourdieu, seems to have been generally adopted. In Bourdieu's work a field is a configuration of relations among hierarchically arranged positions. In his view, access to dominant positions is a matter of constant struggle among agents whose weapon and goal is "capital," a material or symbolic resource that enables its possessor to "exercise power or influence, thus to *exist* in a particular field, rather than being merely a 'negligible quantity.'"[11] If a field is a competitive arena, it is also the site of an implicit solidarity among players, an "objective complicity underlying all the antagonisms." This complicity is based on the fact that "everyone involved in a field shares a certain number of basic interests, namely, everything that is connected to the field's very existence,"[12] and that sets them in opposition to outsiders. This "field corporatism" is a fundamental obstacle to cooperation between individuals from different fields.

This interpretive grid dividing social reality into fields aims at universal application, but its heuristic value varies from country to country. Its value in the Saudi case is considerable. It should first be pointed out that in a country like Saudi Arabia, the classic divisions of the social arena—state/civil society, government/opposition—are of little relevance. A member of the royal family, for example, who occupies no official function in the state apparatus is endowed merely by his lineage with definite influence on decision making that sometimes exceeds that of a high official who is a commoner. Is he then a state or societal actor? Similarly, where should the religious scholars—the ulema—be situated? They are in many cases both state agents and representatives of society and may, depending on circumstances, be spokesmen for the rulers or for the opposition. To resolve this problem, the princes and the ulema will be considered as agents of specific social fields defined in terms of their governing logic: respectively, the political field and the religious field. These fields are brought together, along with other fields whose agents have some form of power over the social arena, within what Bourdieu calls a "field of power." This theoretical paradigm will make it possible to grasp the dynamics that the classic divisions fail to perceive.

The field concept is especially useful because it is truly palpable in Saudi Arabia, where the field of power has been made up of a set of particularly salient and well-defined fields. To demonstrate this, what is needed is the perspective of history. This return to the past will make it possible to attain a clearer understanding of the concrete form of these fields, their degree of autonomy, and the relations existing among them when the first shoots of Saudi Islamism appeared in the 1960s and 1970s.

The Birth and Development of the Saudi State

The founding moment of the Saudi field of power as it exists today was the pact of 1744 joining the sword of Muhammad bin Saʿud to the religious call *(daʿwa)* of the preacher Muhammad bin Abd al-Wahhab. The former promised to apply the concept of Islam held by the latter, who in turn would legitimate Muhammad bin Saʿud's power. In the heart of Najd, in central Arabia, a state then came into existence—the first Saudi state—dominated by two distinct elites who shared power: a political elite made up exclusively of the descendants of Muhammad bin Saʿud, and a religious elite at first centered around Muhammad bin Abd al-Wahhab and his progeny.

The political arrangement was intended to take the following form: the ulema would interpret the sacred texts, while the princes would govern, that is, would define the ways in which the ulema's interpretations would be applied and would act on behalf of the common good *(al-maslaha al-ʿamma)* in all areas in which the texts turned out to be silent, provided their actions did not contradict any clear *shariʿa* principle.[13] Certain areas gradually became understood as depending exclusively on the princes, such as relations with foreign powers, especially non-Muslim ones. This explains why the traditional Wahhabi ulema did not oppose Saudi Arabia's alliances with the United Kingdom in the early twentieth century and with the United States after 1945. Little by little, two clearly separate spheres took shape: the religious field and the political field, each the respective monopoly of the two elites.

From the beginning, various rules have been observed in order to maintain the appearance of reciprocal autonomy between these fields. Some are formal, such as those having to do with the ritualization of relations between the political and religious fields. For instance, when the Saudi king receives the senior ulema of the kingdom each week, the meeting follows a protocol that confines the participants to their separate functions. No form of collusion is allowed to appear in public. Other rules are more informal: for example, no major Al Saʿud prince has, up to now, sought to become part of the religious field by becoming an *alim* (a Muslim scholar, the singular of "ulema"). Beyond that, autonomy is bolstered by the field-identification process that the agents of the two fields have undergone. This shows up first in the adoption of distinctive status signs:[14] the title *amir* is reserved for members of the ruling family and hence for the agents of the political field, whereas the title "sheikh" *(shaykh)*, given up by the Saudi princes (although it is still used by most of the Gulf ruling families), has become a marker for the agents of the religious field.[15] Dress also plays an important role. The ulema have adopted signs of distinction, for example, by shortening their tunics *(thawb)* or refraining from wearing the *ʿiqal*, the cord holding the *shmagh* (the cloth Saudis wear on their heads). These signifiers were supplemented, beginning in the 1960s, by a more formal process of institutionalization, including the creation of hierarchically organized religious institutions.

The political field is built entirely around the Al Saʿud family, considered the exclusive repository of political competence. Within it, however, competition developed for access to positions of power and the resources they afford. In the 1870s these internal struggles led to the disappearance of the Saudi state, which was finally restored by Abd al-Aziz Al Saʿud, starting with his conquest of Riyadh in 1902. Once he had taken power, he was determined to prevent any future breakup and applied himself to setting up informal regulatory mechanisms intended to guarantee family cohesion. After his death, power was to be exercised collegially by his offspring and would be based on the two complementary principles of consultation *(shura)* and consensus *(ijmaʿ)*.[16] In this system the king would now be just the first among equals.[17] But clans quickly formed among the sons of the founding monarch. In the late 1960s one of these clans began assuming considerable power. It was made up of the seven sons of Hassa bint Ahmad al-Sudayri, among whom were the princes Fahd, Sultan, Nayef, and Salman.[18] The irresistible ascension of the "seven Sudayris" was nonetheless hindered by the presence in power of Faysal (who controlled the executive off and on beginning in 1958, although he did not officially become king until 1964), an authoritarian and much-feared monarch whose position was strengthened by his privileged ties with the religious field. When he died in 1975, the Sudayri clan could finally dominate; even during the reign of Khalid (1975–1982), Crown Prince Fahd was mostly in command, and Nayef and Sultan had taken over the ministries of interior and defense, which they still occupy in 2011. In 1982, after Khalid's death, Fahd officially inherited the reins of power, completing his clan's takeover. This situation explains why, until the mid-1990s, the political field demonstrated unshakable unity, notably in the face of the Sahwa insurrection. The situation changed and the political field was readjusted when, following the stroke Fahd suffered in 1995, Prince Abdallah, an outsider without uterine brothers who had headed the national guard since 1962 and, because he was next in line, had been named crown prince in 1982, was appointed the king's regent, inheriting many of Fahd's prerogatives.

Although the religious field was initially built around the descendants of Muhammad bin Abd al-Wahhab, who bore the name Al al-Shaykh (the lineage of the sheikh), in the nineteenth century it expanded to a small number of other families from Najd. They soon constituted a veritable religious aristocracy, the exclusive guardian and preserver of the intellectual legacy of Muhammad bin Abd al-Wahhab against his detractors. Its members shared a certain number of fundamental points of agreement that were nevertheless the subject of sometimes-virulent interpretive debates, giving rise to a singular theological-juridical tradition.[19] Historically, the upholders of this tradition have used various terms to set themselves apart: *ahl al-tawhid* (advocates of the oneness of God) and *a'immat al-da'wa al-najdiyya* (imams of the Najdi call) in the eighteenth and nineteenth centuries, and then mainly *salafiyyun* (*salafis*, derived from *al-salaf al-salih*, the "pious ancestors" whom they claim to emulate) in the twentieth century. But because numerous other groups have laid claim to the label *salafi* (in particular the ulema I later characterize as "Muslim reformists"), and in order to avoid any ambiguity, I prefer to designate the theological-juridical tradition inherited from Muhammad bin Abd al-Wahhab as "Wahhabi."

The fundamental precepts of Wahhabism are the major teachings contained in the writings of Muhammad bin Abd al-Wahhab, particularly in *The Book of the Oneness of God* and *The Removal of Doubts*.[20] These precepts, derived in part from the medieval jurist Ahmad Taqi al-Din Ibn Taymiyya (1263–1328) and his student Ibn Qayyim al-Jawziyya (1292–1350), were aimed at returning to orthodox Islam, defined as the Islam practiced by the very first generations of Muslims, a society that Ibn Abd al-Wahhab thought had regressed to an age of religious ignorance *(jahliyya)* similar to the one that had preceded the advent of Islam. This implied above all else the purification of the creed *('aqida)* from the innovations *(bida')* that had been incorporated over the centuries and the restoration of the true meaning of the *tawhid* (a term that means simultaneously the oneness, the unity, and the transcendence of God). According to Ibn Abd al-Wahhab, *tawhid* contains three equally important components: the affirmation that God is one *(tawhid al-rububiyya)*, the affirmation that he is one with his names and his attributes *(tawhid al-asma' wa-l-sifat)*, and the oneness of God as an object of worship *(tawhid al-uluhiyya)*. For Ibn Abd al-Wahhab, proclaiming the oneness of God in words is therefore not enough to make one a Muslim; this proclamation must also be expressed in worship, which must be dedicated only to God, with no intermediary. Consequently, Ibn Abd al-Wahhab and his successors constantly denounced certain religious practices that were then widespread in the Arabian Peninsula, such as the cult of saints (at the basis of which is *tawassul*, intercession) and Shiism (which the Wahhabis accused of turning the imams who were descendants of Ali into quasi-divinities), in which they saw forms of associationism *(shirk)*. Wahhabism was first and foremost constituted in opposition to those practices.[21]

Islam, however, is not only creed; it is also law *(shari'a)*. But although Ibn Abd al-Wahhab's positions on creed are clear, his legal positions (on *fiqh*) are much less so, first and foremost because they play a less central part in his work.[22] His position of principle is that the only criterion for the validity of a religious judgment must be the Koran, the prophetic tradition (sunna), and the consensus *(ijma')* of the first generations of Muslims. In theory, that amounts to challenging the jurisprudence of the canonical schools of law (the first principle of which is imitation, *taqlid*) and making interpretation directly from the sacred texts *(ijtihad)* the only pillar of jurisprudence. In practice, however, Ibn Abd al-Wahhab continued to adhere to Hanbali juridical doctrine, which had prevailed in Najd before him, with respect to the rules of exegesis, which also implied a very literal reading of the sacred texts.[23] Most important, Ibn Abd al-Wahhab never expressed an unprecedented legal opinion, at most limiting himself to choosing between various opinions found within the Hanbali school. This contradiction between an asserted ideal of *ijtihad* and a juridical practice largely confined to Hanbalism has been a constant of Wahhabism down to the present.[24] It would later become the source of some of the conflicts that appeared on the margins of the religious field.

Although it occupies a relatively minor place in Ibn Abd al-Wahhab's writings, one principle began to occupy a central position in Wahhabi tradition in the nineteenth century:[25] the principle of "commanding right and forbidding wrong" *(al-amr bi-l-maʿruf wa-l-nahi ʿan al-munkar)* by virtue of which Muslims must encourage their coreligionists to follow the principles of Islam and must admonish them when they stray from the right path. Because this principle has obvious subversive implications if it is used against the political or religious authorities, those authorities have constantly striven to channel its effects. This is how one should understand, for example, the creation in 1926 of an official organization, the Committee for Commanding Right and Forbidding Wrong (Hayʾat al-amr bi-l-maʿruf wa-l-nahi ʿan al-munkar), which in practice plays the role of a religious police force, and which a fragile consensus has considered the only legitimate enforcer of the principle.[26] The members of this committee are often designated by the name *mutawwaʿun*.

The principal dividing line running through Wahhabi tradition is the opposition between "exclusivists" and "inclusivists." Its first outlines showed up on the occasion of the Egyptian conquest of Najd in 1818, when the Saudi ulema split over the attitude to adopt toward the invaders. For the exclusivists under Sulayman bin Abdallah Al al-Shaykh, the grandson of Muhammad bin Abd al-Wahhab, the Egyptians, like the Ottomans from whom they had received their orders, were not true Muslims, and by virtue of the principle of "allegiance and rupture" *(al-walaʾ wa-l-baraʾ)*, the outlines of which were formulated then for the first time, the Wahhabi dogma demanded of an authentic Muslim unconditional loyalty to his coreligionists and a complete break with the infidels. The exclusivists therefore summoned the Wahhabi community to a fight to the death against the Egyptians, and to exile (*hijra*, the hegira of the Prophet) if the Egyptians were to win and occupy the region, which was the case in the northern part of Najd for twenty years, until the restoration of the Saudi state. The inclusivists were less intransigent. Without explicitly distancing themselves from the principle of allegiance and rupture, they interpreted it less rigidly: from their point of view, although the Egyptians were indeed living in sin, and although it was necessary to keep one's distance from them to avoid any harmful influence, that nonetheless did not exclude them from Islam, and it was therefore permitted to live under their rule.

Inclusivists and exclusivists were in conflict in the Saudi religious field throughout the nineteenth century, although the latter were usually in the ascendant. In the early twentieth century Abd al-Aziz Al Saʿud, who had launched the reconquest of the land of his ancestors, made decisive use of the exclusivists, who did not hesitate to proclaim that his combat was a pure jihad designed to restore the Arabian Peninsula to authentic, that is, Wahhabi Islam. Moreover, exclusivist ulema were dispatched to the Bedouin tribes of Najd to instill in their members the spirit of the jihad. The result of this proselytism was the creation of the tribal militia known as the Ikhwan, which soon imposed itself as the prime force of Abd al-Aziz's army. By the mid-1920s, however, the exclusivism of the Ikhwan, whose members were advocates of a "state of permanent revolution"[27] and a jihad without borders, fostered growing conflict with Abd al-Aziz because he was intent on coming to terms with the regional powers, in particular the British, who occupied the neighboring Transjordan and Iraq. In 1929 Abd al-Aziz was forced to turn against the Ikhwan, which he finally crushed with the support of the British.

In the religious field this defeat spelled the waning of the exclusivists, who gradually lost their ascendancy to the more pragmatic inclusivists, who were in a much better position to accept the new constraints of realpolitik. Since the mid-twentieth century the inclusivists have dominated, confining the exclusivists, with rare exceptions, to marginal positions. The year 1954 marked an important stage in this process: Muhammad bin Ibrahim Al al-Shaykh (known as Muhammad bin

Ibrahim), appointed mufti of the kingdom the year before, presided for the first time over a high-level official meeting with non-Wahhabi religious leaders of the Muslim world on the fringes of an Islamic conference held in Mecca. Among those present was the Maliki *shaykh al-islam* of Tunisia, Muhammad al-Tahir ʿAshur, and the Egyptian mufti Hasanayn Muhammad Makhluf.[28] By participating in this meeting, the first among the Wahhabis implicitly recognized the Islamic character of other religious traditions.

Concomitant with his discreet support of the inclusivist Wahhabi ulema, Abd al-Aziz, intent on modernizing his kingdom, made increasing appeals to "Muslim reformists." "Muslim reformism" was a movement of Arab thinkers that had appeared in the late nineteenth century in Egypt and Syria with the ambition of giving the Muslim world the means of catching up with the West. To accomplish this, the reformists, like the Wahhabis, called for a rejection of servile imitation *(taqlid)* and a return to the foundations of Islam, but in their case the return was to be based on a reinterpretation of the sacred texts *(ijtihad)* that relied on some measure of reason. Like the Najdi ulema, the Muslim reformists also showed hostility toward Sufism and popular Islam, although this hostility never took the form of excommunication *(takfir)*, a position they shared with the inclusivists. Through these foreigners whom Abd al-Aziz had invited to staff the nascent administrative services of the kingdom, Muslim reformism established a presence in Saudi Arabia and soon took on the appearance of an "attenuated" variant of Wahhabism as Henri Laoust describes it.[29] It was to this "compromise Wahhabism" that some of the ulema of the Hejaz— traditionally more flexible than their Najd counterparts—adhered after they were integrated into the Saudi state in 1924.[30]

As a result of the power-sharing arrangement previously described, the political authorities now benefited from religious legitimacy. In the 1970s, however, the authorities felt the need for another, "modernizing" source of legitimacy, in imitation of the neighboring secular regimes of Egypt, Iraq, and Syria. This took the form of emphasizing the development *(tanmiya)* of the kingdom and the achievements *(injazat)* it had made possible, particularly the prosperity it had brought to the kingdom's subjects.[31] Although this form of legitimation was first of all used for domestic purposes, its implementation also expressed external political objectives. A modernizing rationale was to serve as a means of promoting the Saudi state in the eyes of the West and as a symbolic response to the "progressive" states in the region that had been quick to place Saudi Arabia among the "reactionary" and "backward" regimes.

To make this modernizing claim effective, the regime had to create a body of "clerics of modernity," counterparts of the ulema or "clerics of tradition," who would be the spokesmen of the kingdom's development and modernization. Hence, under the auspices of the royal family, there came into being a new social type, the *muthaqqaf*, or recognized "intellectual." This birth of the *muthaqqaf* was accompanied and made possible by the emergence alongside the religious field of a second field of cultural production, the intellectual field.

The *muthaqqaf*, as instituted in the 1970s, appeared as the symbolic extension of a new social group that had come into being as a result of the modernizing efforts exerted since the first decades of Abd al-Aziz's rule: the intelligentsia (in the sense of an educated class drawn to Western modes of thinking, which it identified with modernity). The creation of this group was closely connected to the dispatch of Saudi students to foreign schools and universities, at first in Egypt, Lebanon, and Iraq, beginning in the 1940s. This movement was made possible by the Saudi regime's ever-increasing income from oil, large quantities of which had been discovered in the Eastern Province and were now being extracted by an American company, Aramco. For the royal family, the goal of this policy was to train a generation of bureaucrats capable of turning the wheels of a rapidly growing administration.

Once outside the country, many of these students came under the influence of diverse variants of Arab nationalism and leftism, then riding high in the region. In an attempt to remedy these perverse effects, the government decided to shift the flow of students to Western universities, beginning in the late 1950s. However, this did not perceptibly modify the situation. Arab student associations, most of which leaned to the left or gravitated toward nationalist movements and were particularly active on American campuses, played a significant role in the politicization of Saudi students, replacing the influence of Cairo and Beirut.[32]

During the same period Aramco played a significant role in the political socialization of young Saudis. Those who were working for the company rubbed shoulders with Arabs from around the Middle East, many of whom were experienced political activists. They also had access to resources that were unique in the kingdom, beginning with Aramco's library, where, it was said, one could find the works of Karl Marx and socialist theorists.[33]

As a consequence of these developments, by 1953 organizations claiming adherence to nationalism and the Arab Left appeared in Saudi Arabia. Some of these organizations were instrumental in organizing the major strikes that shook Aramco in the mid-1950s. Others were based in Riyadh and Jeddah and made a name for themselves through failed attempts at a coup d'état, such as the Free Officers in 1955 and the Organization of the National Revolution in 1969. In the face of these disturbances, the government first unleashed merciless repression with several large waves of arrests in 1955, 1962, and 1969, when thousands of activists were thrown in jail. In the early 1960s there were also purges of the press and the universities.

But the government knew how to use the carrot, as well as the stick. It made the state's bureaucratic administration, which was continuing its dizzying expansion, into a formidable machine for co-opting the young intelligentsia.[34] The increasing numbers of students who came home with foreign diplomas were systematically integrated into the administration as long as they demonstrated their loyalty.[35] Those with doctorates from foreign universities even obtained top positions. By the late 1960s they occupied most high state offices not reserved for the ulema.[36] This was true even of those who had adopted nationalist or leftist rhetoric while in school, for example, Ghazi al-Qusaybi, Abd al-Aziz al-Khuwaitir, Muhammad Aba al-Khayl, Hasan al-Mishari, Abd al-Rahman al-Zamil, and Ibrahim al-ʿAwaji,[37] who climbed the administrative ladder to the most prestigious positions, becoming, respectively, minister of industry, minister of education, minister of finance, minister of agriculture, deputy minister of trade, and deputy minister of the interior. This generation continued to dominate high public office until the 1990s.

The 1970s witnessed a significant weakening of the leftist and nationalist opposition in Saudi Arabia. Although repression and co-optation undeniably played a role, it is reasonable to think that a structural factor also contributed to this development, namely, the 1973 oil boom *(al-tafra)* that completed Saudi Arabia's transformation into a rentier state.[38] As shown by Giacomo Luciani, it is unlikely that movements motivated by socioeconomic considerations will arise in such a state, so the only protest movements possible are those related to culture or identity.[39] This is precisely what happened in Saudi Arabia: the socioeconomic component inherent in the discourse of all the Saudi opposition groups disappeared almost completely.[40] All that remained was the element of identity, linked to the demand for a way of life that might be characterized as "liberal," not to say—as the Islamists would have no hesitation in doing—"Western." The politically neutered opposition gradually became primarily a cultural opposition, and demands for political liberalization and social justice gave way to demands for societal openness. Nationalists, leftists, socialists, communists, and advocates of Western-style modernization—whose numbers increased with the dispatch of Saudi students to the United States—seemed to overcome their political antagonisms (anti-Americans versus pro-Americans, Arab nationalists versus Saudi nationalists, and so on) to merge into a single "liberal" *(libarali)* movement whose contours remained ill defined. For them, as for their Islamist rivals, who called them "secularists" *('ilmaniyyun),* politics became more a question of lifestyle and values than of social justice or government reform.

Up to this time, the *muthaqqaf* had nonetheless remained a latent category. The preponderant types among the educated population were the intellectual by function, the archetype of whom was the technocrat, and the political activist, who derived his legitimacy from action, not knowledge. This absence of the *muthaqqaf* can be explained in part by the absence under the reign of King Faysal (1964–1975) of the spaces needed for his appearance and recognition, that is, a relatively autonomous field in which to operate. The press had been a promising site of debate for part of the reign of Sa'ud (1953–1964) but had been definitively muzzled in the early 1960s. "We moved from lively and relatively committed opinion journalism to mere information journalism," says a Saudi intellectual. "And even that was a certain kind of information in line with official discourse."[41]

But in the early 1970s spaces for intellectual discussion, at first focused on literary questions, began to appear.[42] Prominent examples included the new "cultural supplements" *(malahiq thaqafiyya)* that some newspapers published and that were not subject to the same censorship as the news. Among them, the supplements of *Al-Riyad* and *'Ukadh* played a very important role, as did the *Al-Mirbad* supplement of the eastern province paper *Al-Yawm,* edited from the outset by Muhammad al-'Ali and Ali al-Dumayni.[43] This development, the first steps of which were taken toward the end of King Faysal's reign, quickened considerably under Khalid (1975–1982) because Crown Prince Fahd, already the de facto ruler, was attempting to make the intelligentsia a favored ally, just as his brother Faysal had relied on religious circles.[44] By opening up a space for it, Fahd offered the intelligentsia an alternative to its aspirations for political participation,[45] assigning it the task of constructing a modern Saudi culture, in line with the economic and social modernization the country was experiencing.

These cultural supplements very soon became a platform for the intelligentsia, who, in addition to defending avant-garde viewpoints in literature and poetry, made use—first implicitly and later more openly—of the freedom allowed by literary discourse to call for a liberalization of Saudi society.[46] Going beyond the dialectic between form and content, the poet Ali al-Dumayni explains how both were from the outset deeply connected:

> The fact of calling into question the classical rules of poetry in the kingdom represents, for many of our poets and critics, the essence of modernity because it challenges established taste, oral cultural authority, and beyond that, the dominant institutions in general, in a struggle around the polarities of authenticity and contemporaneousness, ancient and modern, the constant and the changing, turning inward and openness, clarity and ambiguity—all through the symbolism of a simple poetic act.[47]

Moreover, these liberal men were soon joined by liberal women,[48] whose presence through the pen in this public space represented in itself a challenge to the tradition that confined them to the private sphere. With these female writers, the woman question achieved new prominence.[49] More than just a literary field, an intellectual field had indeed come into being in Saudi Arabia.[50]

Shortly after Faysal's death these new intellectual spaces were joined by "literary clubs" *(andiya adabiyya),* which thereafter were in charge of most cultural activities in the kingdom. In March 1975 a decision was made to establish five of them, in Jeddah, Riyadh, Medina, Mecca, and Taef; they are now found in most large and medium-sized cities in the kingdom. These clubs were under the General Directorate of Youth Affairs (al-Riʾasa al-ʿamma li-riʿayat al-shabab) presided over by Prince Faysal bin Fahd, whose father Fahd had recently become the country's strongman. This choice showed from the outset how important the government considered these clubs to be.

Although the creation of the Saudi intellectual field was guided from above, it is noteworthy that in appearance, it enjoyed a good deal of autonomy and did not seem to suffer from interference from the political field. As in the case of the religious field, the princes of the royal family refrained from claiming the status of intellectuals and systematically remained aloof from debates in the field. Also, the board of directors of a literary club was elected by the club's members—a practice more common in Saudi Arabia than it might appear.[51] Finally, the autonomy of the field was strengthened by the field-identification process undergone by its agents. It manifested itself through the adoption of status signs intended to distinguish the intellectual from his rival in the world of cultural production, the religious scholar: as opposed to the beards of the ulema, intellectuals had well-trimmed mustaches, which became a veritable sign of membership. Similarly, while the ulema usually wore a *shmagh* (red checkered cloth) on their heads, intellectuals tended, unsystematically, to prefer the *ghutra* (white cloth).

By contributing actively to the emergence of the *muthaqqaf,* the government had shaped the intellectual field as it wished and, beyond that, had produced a definition of the intellectual that suited it. In the context of the mid-1970s, this process represented a kind of crowning moment in the political neutering of the intelligentsia. The *muthaqqaf,* herald of Saudi modernization, became the antithesis both of the bureaucrat (because the *muthaqqaf* participated in debate) and of the political activist (because the *muthaqqaf* was loyal to the government).

By the turn of the 1980s, the Saudi intellectual field remained—because of the conditions of its emergence and the prerogatives it was given—intrinsically tied to the liberal intelligentsia, so much so that "liberal" and *muthaqqaf* appeared at the time to be synonyms. This impression was reinforced by the fact that some of the most prominent figures of the intellectual field had been socialized in communist circles, like Muhammad al-ʿAli and Ali al-Dumayni, or Arab nationalist circles, like ʿAbid Khazindar, Ghazi al-Qusaybi, and many others. Aside from a few individuals with Muslim reformist tendencies from the Hejaz, the field did not really contain an Islamic presence. This could primarily be explained by the fact that whereas the foreign members of the Muslim Brotherhood generally refrained from participating in Saudi debates, Saudi Islamism had not yet had time to produce its organic intellectuals. The first Saudi Islamist intellectuals would only enter the scene in the mid-1980s, prompting radical changes in the intellectual field.

Within the field of power, the fields of cultural production—religious and intellectual—rub shoulders with several other fields, the chief one of which is the economic field. Very generally, these fields also have a tendency to develop a strong appearance of autonomy. The economic field, for example, is governed by elected bodies, the chambers of commerce, and, as in neighboring Kuwait,[52] the royal family has traditionally been formally absent from this field.[53] In short, the schema set forth earlier applies well beyond the fields of cultural production alone.

The only exception is the military field. In view of its highly strategic value, the royal family has always stifled the autonomy of the military by exercising direct and very tight control over it. Whereas there have been no princes among the ulema or among the intellectuals, and rarely—at least until recently—any businessman princes, princes among the officer corps have been legion.[54] There is nothing surprising about this. The monopoly of legitimate violence, on which the resilience of the state ultimately depends, implies the unambiguous subordination of the military to the political field. Hence there is nothing particularly Saudi about this exception.

Beyond the field of power, the tendency toward autonomy extends even into the social sphere, where apparently autonomous fields have also been established, sometimes with official sponsorship. For instance, as studies by Amélie Le Renard have shown, Saudi authorities were able from the 1960s to construct the category "women" and a corresponding "field of women," segregated both physically and symbolically from the rest of the social arena but enjoying a large measure of internal autonomy. They thereby gave themselves an effective way of controlling the feminine half of the social sphere by limiting its field of action to issues presumed to be "feminine."[55]

To each of these fields corresponds a specific form of capital its agents possess in variable quantities according to whether they are in a dominant or a subordinate position. In addition, there are basic forms of capital, of value in all fields, flowing from the principles of social classification that govern Saudi society. Those are economic capital, measuring the level of economic resources, and social capital, defined by *nasab* (family lineage).

With regard to economic capital, Saudi society since the boom of 1973 has had the peculiarity of having a relatively large "middle class," if one means by that term those Saudis who live relatively comfortable, though not luxurious, lives.[56] Nevertheless, a segment of the population remains too lacking in economic capital to be included in the middle class. Conversely, the upper bourgeoisie and many of the princes are generally too rich to belong to that class.

As for *nasab,* which determines social capital, it is structured as follows: at the very top of the scale of *nasab* sit the descendants of the great tribes of Najd, divided in order of prestige into two categories: the "Bedouins" *(badu),* a term that in Saudi Arabia designates, in addition to nomads (today only a negligible proportion), members of nomadic tribes settled in the recent past, that is, since the creation of the Ikhwan in the 1910s and 1920s; and the *qabilis* (meaning literally "tribal"), sedentary populations with tribal ancestry. Next come individuals who can prove tribal ancestry, but from a minor Najdi tribe or a "peripheral" tribe, that is, not from Najd. Nevertheless, they are also frequently designated as *qabili*. Finally, at the bottom of the *nasab* ladder are those individuals whose ancestry is socially disreputable. These include Saudis of foreign origin—whether or not they have Saudi nationality—and sedentary populations without tribal ancestors, known as *khadiris*, representing one-quarter of the population of Najd.[57] One of the most visible manifestations of the discrimination of which they are victims is the obstinate refusal of people with tribal ancestry, particularly when they are from Najd, to intermarry with those "without *nasab*." This rule prevails even when the "foreigner" or *khadiri* in question is wealthy.

The example of the Bin Laden family, from the Hadramawt region of Yemen, is a perfect illustration of this paradox. The billionaire Muhammad bin Laden never won the hand of any woman from Najd with a tribal ancestry and usually had to settle for marrying sedentary women from the Hejaz, as well as foreign women, beginning with Osama's mother, who is from Syria.[58] Conversely, the "Bedouin"— often pauperized by the transformations affecting their way of life in the twentieth century,[59] and many of whom crowded at best into *hijras*, sorts of camps set up at the edge of the desert, and at worst into the slums of large cities, following a massive rural exodus in the 1960s and 1970s—continue to enjoy a certain prestige because of their social capital.[60] It is clear, then, that social capital and economic capital are not interchangeable in practice and constitute two parallel and equally vital systems of social classification.

A Fragmented Sociopolitical System

As shown by the developments discussed in the preceding section, the Saudi field of power has traditionally been sectorized, that is, made up of a set of apparently very autonomous fields. This sectorization can be explained by various factors. In some cases—for example, in the first power-sharing arrangement that gave rise to the political and religious fields—it is the result of complex historical processes that, at least initially, do not reflect a political master plan. But sectorization has also appeared, as in the intellectual field and the field of women, as a deliberate strategy of the regime. Splitting the social arena into different social categories, created ex nihilo if necessary, and enclosing each one in a separate social sphere enjoying a certain degree of autonomy within the framework of rules set by the authorities are techniques of social control highly prized by authoritarian regimes. These techniques are found, notably, in corporatist systems,[61] which are widespread in the Middle East.[62] Saudi sectorization is nonetheless distinct from the corporatist model in that relations within various fields and between them and the political field have traditionally been much less formalized. But that has recently begun to change. The institutionalization of those relations since 2000 (with, most notably, the creation of professional associations and a forum for national dialogue) has given rise to a form of "emerging corporatism" that is, in the last analysis, continuous with old practices.[63]

The sectorization of the field of power in Saudi Arabia was also reinforced by the traditionally segmented character of the state. The construction of the Saudi state was entirely guided from above, giving rise, as Steffen Hertog argues, to "a large number of parallel, often impermeable institutions which have grown on oil income, are suffused with informal networks, and coordinate and communicate little."[64] In this configuration, only the royal family, set above the entire system, maintains vertical relations with all the sectors making up the field of power, and horizontal relations between sectors are practically nonexistent.[65] By limiting horizontal relations, the segmentation of the field of power thereby limits the possibilities of interference between fields and in the end reinforces the logic of sectorization.

Until the 1980s the effects of segmentation were easily observable in the world of cultural production. The religious field and the intellectual field were separate from each other because they had arisen apart from each other; they were also relatively closed off from the rest of society because they had been constructed from above. This found expression in the geography of cities: the traveler Amin Rihani mentions the existence in Riyadh of an "ulema quarter" (most likely al-Dikhna) where "if one is seen walking . . . through the street with a swing of the shoulders or a sweep of the garment, he is forthwith reprimanded for his arrogance. If one laughs freely in one's house, some one will soon knock at the door.—Why are you laughing in this ribald manner? No one in that quarter ever dares to miss, except for a reason of sickness, one of the five daily prayers in the *masjid* [mosque]."[66] Although this description dates from 1928, several accounts indicate that the situation in al-Dikhna remained the same thirty or forty years later. This is where the house of Mufti Muhammad bin Ibrahim and the first religious secondary school of Riyadh, the Scientific Institute *(al-ma'had al-'ilmi)*, built in 1949, were located.[67] Moreover, it is where Imam Muhammad bin Sa'ud University would later be built.

Conversely, the al-Malazz neighborhood in the eastern part of Riyadh—where the first Saudi civil servants, many of whom came from the Hejaz, settled in the 1950s—was an oasis of social modernity. Here a liberal lifestyle was prevalent, so much so, as the intellectual Abdallah al-Ghadhdhami recalled, that the residents of nearby al-Dikhna did not hesitate to urge anyone in that "ulema quarter" who regularly failed to show up at the mosque for prayers to move to al-Malazz.[68] It was the site of the first secular institution of higher education, King Sa'ud University, and later of the Riyadh literary club. Moreover, at that time private space was still protected. The intelligentsia could live in their homes as they wished, including, in some cases, drinking alcohol or holding parties, without having to fear a visit from the religious police, who were then far from all-powerful.

This segmentation was not only spatial but also symbolic. Ulema and intellectuals simply were not speaking the same language. While the former dealt with medieval treatises on theology and law, the latter were promoting concepts such as "modernity" *(hadatha)* and "development" *(tanmiya)* unknown to their counterparts. As a result, no debate between the two groups was possible at the time. This singular configuration had important consequences that help explain the system's remarkable stability. Academic orthodoxy long held, as Michael Hudson wrote in 1977, that in Saudi Arabia, "Islamic and customary values have been *harmonized* with modern nationalism and secular values of progress and development,"[69] and "there is little sense of value dissonance on the principles of the Islamic polity."[70] After the call to order brought about by the events in Mecca in 1979, Western scholars became more circumspect, largely abandoning their earlier idyllic vision, although not admitting that there might not be a consensus on the central values of society. Two contradictory perceptions could be found in works on Saudi Arabia: for some writers, the kingdom was on the path to inexorable secularization, and Juhayman al-'Utaybi and his disciples were the expression of a desperate resistance against it,[71] but for others, Saudi Arabia was more than ever living in a situation where religion remained ubiquitous.[72] Both views were partially correct, depending on the sector of the social arena that was the focus of attention, the intellectual or the religious field. Therefore, the reason why social peace was preserved in Saudi Arabia until the 1980s was not the existence of any moral consensus, but rather the segmentation of the Saudi world of cultural production, which limited interactions—and conflicts—between its various components.

A second effect of this segmented configuration was that mobilizations initiated in one sector of the field of power initially had a good deal of difficulty in spreading beyond the boundaries of the field to society as a whole. This can be illustrated by Mufti Muhammad bin Ibrahim's (1953–1969) failed attempts to oppose the policy of modernization that the political authorities were in the process of implementing. Throughout his sixteen years at the head of the religious establishment, Muhammad bin Ibrahim, in his desire to assert the religious field's autonomy, did not hesitate to attack a number of royal decisions. On several occasions, for example, he condemned, in the name of the principle prohibiting the imitation of infidels *(al-tashabbuh bi-l-kuffar)*, the wearing of military uniforms, particularly trousers and caps, although the Saudi army had long been equipped with them.[73] But it was primarily in the denunciation of the "positive laws" *(al-qawanin al-wad'iyya)*, that is, the numerous decrees and regulations that Sa'ud and later Faysal had adopted with the aim of modernizing the judicial and administrative system, that he spoke out. This attitude made Muhammad bin Ibrahim a relatively atypical figure in the Wahhabi tradition, which had tended to leave the political authorities in charge of defining how *shari'a* was to be applied. It was this peculiarity of Muhammad bin Ibrahim that was to make him a posthumous model for the Sahwi ulema.

In 1955, for example, Muhammad bin Ibrahim called for the abrogation of decrees allowing for the creation of a tribunal of commerce and chambers of commerce to settle commercial disputes, going so far as to call the belief in the need for this kind of addition to *shariʿa* "impiety deserving exclusion from the community of the faithful." In 1958 he denounced the secular code for civil servants. In 1966 he denounced the creation of "a committee for the resolution of conflicts," which was equivalent to "governing in spite of what God has revealed." In 1967 he declared the labor code that had just been adopted for workers contrary to *shariʿa*.[74] These are only a few examples.[75] In a short treatise in 1960 titled *Letter on Governing through Man-Made Laws*,[76] he attacked the adoption of positive laws as an act of impiety deserving exclusion from the community of the faithful. The only exception, he argued, was when, "*on a particular issue*,[77] a ruler gives in to a desire or a whim and does not apply revealed law, while remaining convinced that revealed law is the Truth, and acknowledging that he has acted badly and strayed from the right path." In this very limited instance, Muhammad bin Ibrahim goes on, "he is not excluded from the community of the faithful, but has nevertheless just committed a sin even more serious than the major sins [*al-kabaʾir*] of adultery, the consumption of alcohol, theft, and false swearing."[78]

By taking these positions, Muhammad bin Ibrahim argued for a view of religion that infringed significantly on what the political field considered its reserved domain, thereby creating the possibility of conflict. Paradoxically, however, the practical consequences of this attitude were minimal because it did not provoke any notable reaction in society. For this reason, the authorities could tolerate it, and they took no steps to silence Muhammad bin Ibrahim. The mufti's inability to make himself heard can be explained by the enclosure of the religious field within a segmented field of power. Muhammad bin Ibrahim spoke a language that was abstruse for ordinary Saudis, and the religious field had neither the institutional nor the organizational means to escape its isolation and impose its views on society. This would change in the 1980s, when the rise to power of the Sahwa would challenge the segmented character of the field of power.

The apparent autonomy of fields within the field of power serves two purposes. First, it leads to a depoliticization of Saudi elites. This phenomenon has been observed by several authors, some of whom have attributed it to the prevailing consumerism that "move[d] people from the marketplace of ideas to the marketplace."[79] However, there is a structural explanation. As a result of the processes described earlier, the field of power is made up of an assemblage of fields, each of which appears to be separate and self-regulating. This arrangement has the effect of "isolating the center [that is, the political field] from any possible challenge."[80] Consequently, local field logics tend to win out over political ones, and challenges tend to be formulated in the terms of each specific field and to target its dominant figures rather than the political authorities, who operate behind a screen.

Moreover, in the fields that make up the world of cultural production, autonomy fulfills another equally important function because it is essential for the legitimating power of those fields. Indeed, possessing religious or "modernizing" legitimacy does not simply require that the Al Saʿud family set forth a legitimating discourse based on Islam or modernity. To be effective, each legitimacy has to rely on a legitimating apparatus capable of articulating and transmitting the corresponding discourse to the intended audience.[81] In this instance the religious and intellectual fields constitute those apparatuses. The autonomy of those fields is therefore fundamental because endorsement by the ulema or the intellectuals is credible and hence acceptable only if it seems sincere and disinterested. The approval is all the more effective coming from the dominant elites in the field, provided they appear to have reached their eminence because of merit and not merely because the political authorities have supported them.

At the same time, autonomy is a double-edged sword. On the one hand, an autonomous field tends to have its own specific logic and therefore to operate in a closed circle, which makes it in principle inoffensive to the political field. On the other hand, being free from interference from the political field, it might follow its own evolution and, without betraying its autonomy, reformulate its raison d'être by politicizing it. This is what happened in the religious field in the 1950s and 1960s under the impulse of Muhammad bin Ibrahim, although the particularly strong segmentation at the time made it possible to limit the conflagration.

To prevent any deviation, the political authorities therefore have had to set up mechanisms to guarantee their control over the various fields. With this in mind, the political field has always striven to maintain what Michel Dobry calls "collusive transactions" with the dominant elites. The term "collusion," he explains, designates a "more or less shameful, more or less illegitimate (but not entirely) understanding between two parties, two protagonists, at the expense of a third. The transaction . . . means a type of exchange unconcerned with immediate reciprocity."[82] These collusive transactions characterize the complicit relationships that tied the royal family to the dominant elites in various fields and gave rise to a sustained flow of symbolic and material exchanges carried out behind the scenes. In the religious field, the elites in question were the best-known and most respected figures among the ulema; in the intellectual field, they were the dominant intellectuals, notably the ones who controlled the literary clubs (in this case the collusive transactions traditionally went primarily through Prince Faysal bin Fahd, who was in charge of the clubs until his death in 1999); in the economic field, they were the kingdom's principal businessmen, and so on. These exchanges were akin to a form of clientelism, with the difference that clientelism involves by definition an unequal relationship between a patron and a client who see themselves as such. In the case of the religious field, however, although the political field objectively had the upper hand, the ulema saw themselves as enjoying complete equality with the princes and considered their relationship to be based on enlightened mutual self-interest.[83]

The whole challenge for the political authorities consisted of reconciling autonomy with collusive transactions, which in theory represent a serious breach of autonomy. This was possible only through the continuous injection of resources into the machinery of the system. The resources were indispensable for keeping up the collusive transactions tying the regime to dominant elites, who had to remain loyal while policing their respective fields. In particular, this meant preventing any shift of direction in the raison d'être of the field (as had happened with Muhammad bin Ibrahim at a time when resources were relatively small). The influx of resources also enabled the discreet co-optation of rising elites and made it possible to foster competition within the field, giving substance to the specific logic of the field by transforming it into a veritable market logic. For that purpose, great care was taken that the budget allocated to the religious field passed almost exclusively through the dominant elites in the field, who could then distribute it as they saw fit on the basis of internal considerations. The money in question was thus depoliticized, and any challenge over its distribution would be addressed to the elites of the field alone, who served as a lightning rod for the political field. The apparently powerful autonomy the field enjoyed removed any suspicion of political interference. By using intermediaries for distribution, the political field diminished its visible interactions with the rest of the social arena and avoided any politicization of social conflicts. This explains why, as long as petrodollars flowed like water, the political authorities encountered no problems in feeding the system, thereby guaranteeing its resilience.

Ulema and Intellectuals

Historically, the sectorization of the field of power had thus made the Saudi sociopolitical system a well-oiled and theoretically resilient mechanism. How, then, did a powerful Islamist movement, the Sahwa, temporarily succeed in overthrowing this stable edifice? The study of this process is interesting on two counts: first, it tells us a great deal about Saudi Islamism, and beyond that—because studying resistance to power is often the best way to study power itself—about the Saudi system. Second, this study is also guided by a theoretical ambition. Because of the very great prominence of field divisions as a result of sectorization, the Saudi case makes it possible to grasp social dynamics of a more general nature that are less easily observable in other contexts. This is true, for example, of the respective roles and relationships maintained by intellectuals and ulema (that is, elites belonging to the intellectual and religious fields) within Islamist movements, which have never been the subject of detailed study.

Although the role of leadership in a protest mobilization is too often neglected by social movement theory, it is fundamental because "leaders make a difference in converting potential conditions for mobilization into actual social movements."[84] But these leaders have to be endowed with particular qualities. To hope to achieve its ends, a social movement must contain elites with the human and technological know-how indispensable for organizing and managing the mobilization (to cite only a few examples, knowing how to conduct a meeting by bringing together opposing points of view, negotiating with potential partners, explaining demands to the media, organizing a demonstration, recruiting members, and producing and distributing a leaflet),[85] as well as elites capable of "evoking a particular emotional state in people, namely a state of motivation and commitment, often identification, with a leader or with a movement or goal,"[86] which implies that they have the means to make the movement's action and message appear as just and/or necessary in view of the cultural environment in which they operate. The first kind of elite is endowed with what can be named "militant resources" and the second with "legitimating resources." In order for the movement to take hold, these resources have to be present in sufficient quantity; a handful of minor-league legitimating elites will never make a successful movement.

The precise nature of each type of elite (and its corresponding resources) depends on the existing political culture. In a traditional Islamic system, the second kind of elite would refer to the religious scholars charged with *ijtihad* (religious interpretation), and the first kind to the mujahideen given the task of jihad (effort for Islam) in the broad sense, whether their jihad is conducted with the pen or with the sword. In the modern systems of the Muslim world, the place occupied by the Islamic element in political culture is nonetheless variable. In Saudi Arabia, despite government efforts to promote other forms of legitimacy, it remains preponderant. Elsewhere, thanks to the resurgence of Islam since the 1960s, it has regained considerable importance. In this sense, in most Muslim countries the ulema remain the primary possessors of legitimating resources. In contrast, militant resources tend to be the province of laymen with modern education (intellectuals or combatants, depending on the mode of action chosen).

This theoretical approach is empirically relevant. In the case of Iran, for instance, the success of the revolution owes a great deal to the effective collaboration of a portion of the intellectual elite with the fraction of the clergy gathered behind Ayatollah Khomeini,[87] guaranteeing an abundant supply of militant and legitimating resources. Similarly, in Algeria, the impressive initial success of the Islamic Salvation Front (Front Islamique du Salut, FIS) can be explained by successful cooperation between Islamist "technocrats," represented by Abbasi Madani, and Islamist "theocrats," of whom Ali Belhaj was the key figure.[88] The failure of the Islamist uprising that was to have taken place in Egypt following the assassination of President Anwar Sadat on October 6, 1981, could serve as a counterexample. Because it included a significant number of intellectuals and military officers,[89] the al-Jihad group had sufficient militant resources to carry out the assassination of the president, but it included in its ranks only a single ʿalim with a minimum of religious capital, the Azhari sheikh Umar Abd al-Rahman, who, although he was willing to sanction the operation, could not by himself compensate for the group's obvious lack of legitimating resources. Indeed, in this instance the religious field seems to have stood fast as one man against the movement. This, according to Gilles Kepel, was fatal to the movement: "The virulent opposition of the doctors of the law to the radicalized disciples of [Sayyid] Qutb stopped the message of these disciples from passing among the mass of the population and limited it to young circles, among both students and the lumpenproletariat of the bidonvilles."[90]

The difficulty is that intellectuals and ulema operate in different fields located at different sites in the social arena, and each field is strongly corporatist, by virtue of which they are not naturally inclined to join in a single project, even when they share certain ideological points of reference. This split is even more pronounced in the Saudi system, where government policies intensify the logic of sectorization.

There is only one way in which contact and collaboration between ulema and intellectuals can be established: if the barriers between them collapse, or, in the Saudi case, if the system is desectorized.

French sociologist Michel Dobry shows that for this kind of system to go off the rails and a political crisis to break out, mobilizations would have to spring up simultaneously in different significant fields in the social arena. Such a system is able to react to an isolated mobilization arising at any given time in one of its fields through the regulatory mechanisms specific to the field in question, which make it possible to end the mobilization while preventing it from spreading. But in the case of a "multisectoral mobilization," the ability to react tends to decline. If the various local crises become synchronized, the logic of sectorization that governs the system in ordinary circumstances is likely to collapse. In that case the divisions in the social arena become blurred, and there is a generalized loss of field identification, which produces a weakening of field corporatisms.[91] Actors who earlier operated in distinct physical and symbolic spheres can now enter into contact with one another; cooperation across sectors, hitherto unthinkable, becomes conceivable. This is how in France in May 1968 students, intellectuals, and workers—although they belonged to very different social worlds and initially mobilized on distinct grounds—ended up joining hands. In the case of Islamist movements, simultaneous mobilizations in the intellectual and religious fields would then make it possible to conceive of a shift to a situation in which intellectuals and ulema could collaborate. Because mobilizations are collective actions, not actions of isolated individuals, this would also guarantee the availability of sufficient militant and legitimating resources for the movement.

Empirically, certain aspects of this process can be seen at work in Iran and Algeria. In both cases, several years before the outbreak of the political crisis, there was an emergence of separate and simultaneous mobilizations in the intellectual and religious fields. In Algeria in 1982, for example, a clandestine organization of Islamist intellectuals was established in the universities, the Jaz'ara.[92] At the same time, one could observe in the religious field the rise of "neo-Salafi preachers"[93] wishing to "set themselves up as a replacement for the traditional class of the ulema."[94] The political crisis of 1988–1989, in which the system was forced to open up after a series of popular riots, enabled both fields to overcome their mutual antagonism and together establish the

Islamic Salvation Front.[95] Similarly, with Khomeini's rise to power in Najaf beginning in the 1960s, a protest movement in the religious field appeared in Iran, while simultaneously and independently the intellectual field witnessed a growing mobilization of Islamist intellectuals, prominent among whom was Ali Shariʿati. In this instance as well, cooperation between the two groups could not be taken for granted; one needs merely to read the writings of Shariʿati, the anticlericalism of which (in the literal sense of opposition to the clergy, not to religion) is obvious, to be convinced of that.[96] The political crisis, however, enabled the two sides to merge their protests and form the bulk of the battalions of the Islamic Revolution. The same reasoning makes it possible to account for the Egyptian failure. In the years before 1981, one could not see a glimmer of mobilization in the religious field. This may be explained by the fact that the reform of al-Azhar University, carried out under Nasser in 1961, had conferred a particular temporality on the field that, with very few exceptions, produced no ulema who broke with the traditional establishment until the 1980s.[97] It was only then, at a time when mobilization in the intellectual field had already fizzled out, that the religious field began to arouse itself.

At the same time, while the joint presence of ulema and intellectuals is a considerable asset for mobilization, it also has decisive implications for the course the mobilization might take.[98] Ulema and intellectuals, in fact, have largely distinct views of the world, the product of differences in their socialization and their habitus. Their cooperation therefore usually masks muffled, sometimes even unconscious, struggles for control over the meaning and goals of the mobilization.[99] The implications of these struggles are considerable. In the end, they are what determine the direction the movement will take on the ground. The Islamic Republic in Iran, for example, as it was constituted after 1980 may be seen as an expression of the victory of the ulema over the Islamist intellectuals within the revolutionary movement. In addition, these struggles may eventually produce new interpretations of the mobilization, whose meaning becomes openly contested. As the Saudi case will show, if, amid protest euphoria, the movement tends to present a façade of unity, these underlying struggles can assume considerable importance after the fact, when the movement enters its declining phase and its legacy becomes a symbolic resource that everyone is intent on appropriating. In the Algerian case these struggles helped foster the violent conflict that shattered the Islamist movement after 1993.[100]

The insistence on leadership, an aspect of mobilization that is generally neglected in the literature on social movements, should in no way obscure the importance of the other factors emphasized in that literature. Leaders—when they have the necessary militant and legitimating resources—are, of course, essential to get the mobilization organized and to generate a dynamic (in other words, for the mobilization to take hold), and they have a notable effect on the unfolding of the movement. But once the protest dynamic has been created, other variables unfailingly enter into play. Among them is the ability of the movement to rely on solid mobilizing structures, capable of making the support it enjoys visible in case of a test of force with the authorities. It will be seen that in the end, this was precisely the rub in the case of the Sahwa insurrection. Bringing ulema and intellectuals together on the same platform is indeed an indispensable key for initial mobilization, but it is not a sufficient condition for eventual success.

As will be seen in the following pages, the theoretical outline developed here helps shed valuable light on the dynamics that governed the Sahwa insurrection. Moreover, some processes that operated only implicitly in the examples of Egypt or Algeria came to the surface with remarkable clarity in the Saudi case because of the greater prominence of field divisions. The analysis of the Sahwa insurrection will therefore provide the opportunity to make those mechanisms more clearly visible.

Chapter 2 describes the development of the Sahwa and shows how it challenged the segmentation of the field of power. The Sahwa spread its ideology, a blend of Wahhabism and concepts inherited from the Muslim Brotherhood, and built its networks, from the most informal to the most organized (known as *jama'at islamiyya*, or "Islamic groups"), from a base in the Saudi educational system, which it had made its stronghold. In the process it quickly managed to establish itself as a powerful social movement and to permeate virtually all spheres of the social arena. In theory, Sahwi networks and the new language promoted by the Sahwa made it possible to establish contact between previously disconnected realms, such as the intellectual and religious fields. It thereby represented the latent possibility of a unification of ocial space. There were, however, a few limitations to the Sahwa's unifying potential, expressed in particular by the emergence of competing Islamist movements, although those remained a minority, as discussed in Chapter 3.

Moreover, this potential desegmentation was at this stage not enough to break down the sectorization on which social control was based. This was all the more true because at the time the Sahwa did not represent an antigovernment opposition movement, since its Islamist discourse targeted the entire world with the exception of Saudi Arabia, which it considered the only state worthy of being called "Islamic." In the mid-1980s, however, for both demographic and economic reasons, mobilizations bringing together followers of the Sahwa sprang up simultaneously in the intellectual and religious fields, reflecting growing discontent among Sahwi youth in the social arena. Chapter 4 analyzes these evolutions.

The Iraqi invasion of Kuwait and the resulting American military presence in Saudi Arabia precipitated the "Sahwa insurrection," whose developments are analyzed in detail in Chapter 5. The diverse forms of discontent were politicized and converged; the multisectoral mobilization that had been germinating for several years blossomed into a full-scale political crisis. In this context the logic of sectorization collapsed. The Sahwa, whose cohesion was ordinarily limited by the strength of divisions between fields, was able to establish unity. Above all, the weakening of field corporatism made previously unimaginable cross-sectoral cooperation possible. Sahwi intellectuals and Sahwi ulema joined forces and combined resources: the mobilization could get organized and take hold. The protest dynamic created was so powerful that representatives of Islamist movements that had historically been rivals of the Sahwa even contributed their support.

The "Sahwa insurrection" that resulted seemed to be the expression of an unprecedented consensus and appeared to have sufficient resources to succeed, but the movement lacked one essential element: solid mobilizing structures on which it could rely to keep the protest going. Even before repression came down from above and countermovements supported by the government arose from below, the movement was doomed to failure. This explains the great ease with which the authorities crushed the protest in September 1994, as Chapter 6 shows.

Participation in the movement by individuals who were from very diverse fields and social circumstances and consequently had somewhat different aims and worldviews made the meaning of the mobilization a matter of muted struggle among the various protagonists. As Chapter 7 shows, this rivalry adumbrated the lines of confrontation that arose among the various self-proclaimed heirs of the Sahwa, beginning in the late 1990s. Most important, it will be shown that these struggles over the meaning of the Sahwa insurrection, which reached their climax in 2002–2003, masked the inability of all participants to revive the mobilization effectively in a context in which sectorization had recovered its powers. Hence, far from imperiling the system, "Islamo-liberals," "neojihadis," and the ulema of the "new Sahwa" remained above all prisoners of the logic of the specific field to which they belonged. As a result, everything indicates that the cycle of mobilization initiated in the mid-1980s is reaching its end.

2

The Development of the Sahwa

When the situation became difficult for the Muslim Brotherhood . . . they found refuge in the kingdom, which welcomed
and protected them, and, after God, guarded their lives. . . .
After they had spent a few years among us, we realized that
they needed work, so we found ways for them to support
themselves: some of them became teachers, others university
professors—we opened the doors of schools and universities
to them. But unfortunately, they had not forgotten their earlier affiliations, and they began to recruit people, to create
movements, and they rose up against the kingdom!

Prince Nayif, Saudi interior minister, November 2002

The Muslim Brotherhood—Egyptians and non-Egyptians—
played an essential role in the development of the kingdom,
particularly in the areas of moral education, general education, and Islamic culture. Since the time of King Faysal—
blessed be his name—they have served the kingdom! They
played a considerable role in the creation of institutes and
universities, and in teaching, writing, and the establishment of educational programs for the children of the kingdom at a time when no one else in Arabia was able to take
on that task!

Lashin Abu Shanab, member of the guidance council of the
Muslim Brotherhood in Egypt, November 2002

The 1960s and 1970s witnessed the development in Saudi Arabia of a
vast social movement practicing a modern form of Islamic activism

that until then had been absent from the country's political land-scape. This movement was called the Islamic Awakening (al-Sahwa al-Islamiyya), or simply the Sahwa. Relying on the state's own institutions, it soon managed to gain a hold over an entire generation of young Saudis. At the same time, more highly structured networks were developed within the Sahwa. Taking advantage of an extremely favorable political climate, it soon became a central element of the Saudi social fabric.

The Muslim Brotherhood and Saudi Arabia

Although the Sahwa quickly succeeded in assuming a native color-ation by incorporating key elements of Saudi religious culture into its language and conduct,[1] its principal originators were the exiled Muslim Brothers, who came from social and political contexts completely foreign to Saudi Arabia.

The movement of the Muslim Brotherhood was established in Egypt in 1928. Its founder, Hasan al-Banna (1906–1949), a disciple of the more conservative faction among the Muslim reformists, led by Rashid Rida, wanted to establish an organizational framework to promote and implement his masters' ideology. From the outset the movement had a dual purpose: to fight against foreign occupation and to work for the establishment of an Islamic state that would apply *shari'a*. The movement grew rapidly in Egypt and the rest of the Middle East, where it began to establish branches by the late 1930s. The Brotherhood provided crucial support to the Egyptian revolution of July 23, 1952, that brought Gamal Abdel Nasser to power. But although it hoped to see a new political arrangement emerge that would favor it, the move-ment soon became the principal victim of the military regime. In De-cember 1954, after an assassination attempt against Nasser that the Brotherhood was accused of fomenting, it faced a terrible wave of re-pression. It suffered a second ordeal when it was accused of conspiracy in 1965.

It was in the concentration camps that Nasser set up for the Broth-erhood that the movement's thinking developed in decisive ways. There, Sayyid Qutb (1906–1966), imprisoned from 1954 to 1964, wrote his voluminous commentary on the Koran, *In the Shade of the Koran,* as well as what an entire generation of Islamists considered his major work, *Milestones.*[2] In that work he asserts that "the whole world is living in a state of *jahiliyya*" (in Islamic historiography, the age of "ignorance" preceding the advent of Islam), which is based on "opposition to God's domination of the world and to the characteristic of the divine, namely, sovereignty [*hakimiyya*]." The sovereignty of God will be restored only when there is a pure Islamic state, based on *shariʿa* alone. To overcome the material obstacles barring the path to that goal, a vanguard *(taliʿa)* must act (that is, use "movement," *haraka*).[3]

Although the concepts Qutb uses remain relatively undefined, there is no doubt that his doctrine radicalizes the positions taken by al-Banna. Al-Banna had never described his society as a modern *jahiliyya,* nor had he ever called for anything other than *daʿwa* (preaching), in the belief that in order to win power, it was necessary to begin by winning hearts. By the early 1970s, after the trauma of the Nasser years, supporters of the traditional reformist line, known as "Bannaists," and supporters of the revolutionary line, known as "Qutbists," competed for control of the movement in the Middle East.

The Brotherhood's concern with Saudi Arabia was of long standing. Hasan al-Banna had shown increasing interest in the country by the late 1920s. Almost annually he went on a pilgrimage to the holy cities,[4] and he took advantage of these trips to strengthen his ties with notables in the Hejaz who were favorable to his ideas and, through them, with Saudi officials who assured him of their support.[5] But this support did not mean that the authorities were favorably disposed to the movement taking root in the kingdom. According to a well-known anecdote, in October 1946, at a time when the Brotherhood was becoming established in most countries of the Middle East, Hasan al-Banna asked King Abd al-Aziz for permission to open a branch of the organization in Saudi Arabia. Because this violated the prohibition of activity by political parties on Saudi territory, the king rejected his request,[6] reportedly saying: "What good would that do? Here, we are all brothers, and we are all Muslims."[7]

During the same period other Egyptian Brothers traveled to Saudi Arabia, but they were few in number and taught there for short spells before returning home. The situation changed when authoritarian nationalist regimes came to power in the Middle East beginning in the 1950s. Fearing the growing popularity of the Muslim Brotherhood throughout the area, those regimes subjected the movement to harsh repression. For many of its members, emigration became the only means of survival. Following the Nasser regime's first wave of repression in 1954, many Egyptian Brothers found refuge in the Gulf States, particularly Saudi Arabia, which even granted some members Saudi nationality.[8] After the United Arab Republic joining Egypt and Syria was established in February 1958, Syrian members of the Brotherhood were threatened by Nasser, and many of them also took refuge in the Saudi kingdom. The dissolution of the United Arab Republic in 1961 reduced pressure on the movement in Syria, but the lull was of short duration. After the Baathist military coup of 1963, repression of the Brotherhood resumed. In Iraq the coup d'état by General Abd al-Karim Qasim in July 1958 marked the beginning of persecution of the Brotherhood there as well, and members left the country in large numbers.

A second wave of emigration, primarily of Egyptian members, to Saudi Arabia took place in the 1970s, in a very different political context. Nasser's death in 1970 and Sadat's succession produced an easing of relations between the Egyptian government and the Islamist movement, and most imprisoned members were released in 1971. Hence emigration was now driven more by economic than by political considerations. The oil boom had opened exceptional career opportunities, and Muslim Brothers, who had solid networks in the kingdom, were particularly well placed to seize them.

From the earliest days of their emigration until the late 1950s, the Brothers in Saudi Arabia generally occupied minor positions and remained politically inactive. As the geopolitical context changed and regional rivalries increased, the position of the Brotherhood changed as well, and it became a pivotal player on the Saudi stage. In 1957 hitherto-cordial relations between King Sa'ud and Nasser suddenly deteriorated. The episode marked the onset of the Arab cold war that remained intense until the late 1960s between a "progressive" bloc leaning toward the Soviet Union, with Nasser as its self-appointed leader, and an "Islamic" bloc led by Saudi Arabia that favored American interests. The Yemeni revolution of September 26, 1962, that brought to power an ally of Nasser, Abdallah al-Sallal, on the southern border of the kingdom was under these conditions a point of no return.

It was during this period of increasing tension that the Islamic bloc was organized around what official Saudi discourse designated as the principle of "Islamic solidarity" *(al-tadamun al-islami)*. The creation of the bloc was spurred by Prince Faysal (who was intermittently in charge from 1958 on, although he did not officially become king until 1964). Faysal understood the necessity of not surrendering the ideological arena to a master of propaganda like Nasser. To confront Nasser's pan-Arab socialism, he had to make Islam, the kingdom's chief symbolic resource, into a counterideology, but the very traditional Wahhabi ulema were quite incapable of engaging in a political debate of this magnitude. Thus the members of the Muslim Brotherhood in Saudi Arabia were increasingly brought into the anti-Nasser propaganda apparatus and became its core by 1962.[9] No one but these experienced Islamists, sometimes themselves Nasser's victims, was in a better position to denounce the "ungodliness" of his secular government and to use Islam as a weapon against it.

To perfect this ideological counterattack, Faysal strove to provide those involved with the same resources that Nasser was using to broadcast his message. To counter Sawt al-ʿArab (the Voice of the Arabs), Nasser's propaganda radio station that had successfully penetrated even rural areas of Saudi Arabia, where it was very popular, he established Sawt al-Islam (the Voice of Islam).[10] Against the Egyptian press, which described the Saudi monarch as "an agent of imperialism," the Saudi press responded by presenting Nasser as an "Egyptian Stalin."[11] Often understood merely as an expression of Faysal's modernizing tendencies, the decision in 1962 to establish the first Saudi television network, which began broadcasting in 1965, must also be seen as an element in this propaganda competition.

In addition to this media counteroffensive, two institutions emerged to complete the anti-Nasser apparatus. One was the Islamic University of Medina, established in 1961 as a competitor to al-Azhar University in Egypt, which Nasser had brought under his control with the great reform in 1961 officially aimed at "modernizing" it, and with which he hoped to give religious legitimacy to his propaganda.[12] When King Sa'ud declared in May 1961 that the operation of the Islamic University would rely on those individuals "who have been driven from their country after having been robbed, abused, and tortured,"[13] he clearly identified the Muslim Brotherhood as key players. The other important institution the Saudi government created to counter Nasser's influence was the Muslim World League, established in 1962. Here the Muslim Brotherhood held a less central position than in the university because the aim of the league was to be a forum for representatives of all countries and movements belonging to the Islamic bloc. Nonetheless, it was represented by two influential figures: the Egyptian Sa'id Ramadan, Hasan al-Banna's son-in-law, and the Jordanian Kamil al-Sharif. The league also included figures from movements close to the Brotherhood, such as the Pakistani Abu al-'Ala Mawdudi, the founder of Jamaat-e Islami.

An Educational System at the Service of the Brotherhood

The Arab cold war allowed the discourse of the Muslim Brotherhood to gain a foothold in Saudi Arabia, but primarily as one intended for export and directed to the outside world. Beginning in the mid-1960s, this changed when the discovery of radical cells declaring adherence to Arab nationalist and leftist ideas in major Saudi cities persuaded Faysal that the fight against them needed to go beyond external propaganda. The members of the Brotherhood were now asked to direct their activities within the kingdom, notably through the media, where they had taken positions since the early 1960s, but also from other platforms, such as lectures and public seminars.

At the same time, the 1960s and 1970s were marked by a vast program of institutional modernization in Saudi Arabia, notably in the area of education, made possible by the influx of petrodollars. However, the kingdom was sadly lacking in elites able to participate in this process because the Wahhabi ulema had little knowledge of modern matters, and members of the young intelligentsia, whose ranks were still sparse, were usually assigned to administrative tasks and purposely kept away from educational institutions. Under these circumstances the Brotherhood, which counted many university graduates in its ranks, seemed to be ideal candidates. Moreover, Faysal had adopted the mantra of "Islamic modernization," a concept that was in many respects close to the views of the Brotherhood.[14] The Muslim Brotherhood would then to be for Faysal what the Muslim reformists had been for his father Abd al-Aziz, but in a context where resources were immeasurably larger.

In the early stages of the establishment of the Saudi educational system, the Brotherhood played only a minor role. When the kingdom's first university, Riyadh University (soon to become King Sa'ud University), was founded in 1957, very few Brothers worked there. Located in the "liberal" neighborhood of al-Malazz, it even gained a reputation as a haven for the intelligentsia.[15] This was particularly the case because the very existence of some divisions, such as the Faculty of Commerce, remained controversial in the eyes of the ulema. By the early 1970s, however, the university had fallen back into line as the number of Brothers on the faculty increased in both science divisions and the Faculty of Education, which became their stronghold. At this time as well, specifically in 1971, the university's purportedly liberal president, Abd al-Aziz al-Khuwaitir, was replaced by a more conservative figure, Abd al-Aziz al-Fadda.[16]

At the Islamic University of Medina, founded in 1961, foreign activists made up the bulk of the faculty from the outset.[17] Muslim reformists were most heavily represented in the early 1960s, but the proportion of Muslim Brothers constantly increased in the course of the decade.[18] Among the well-known Brothers who taught at Medina University in this period were the Syrian Muhammad al-Majdhub and the Egyptian Ali Juraysha.

But it was at King Abd al-Aziz University in Jeddah and its annex in Mecca that became Umm al-Qura University in 1981 that the Brothers were virtually in the majority from the beginning. Among the Syrians on the faculty were three of the most illustrious figures in the movement: Muhammad al-Mubarak,[19] who chaired the *shari'a* department from 1969 to 1973, as well as Ali al-Tantawi[20] and Abd al-Rahman Habannaka, both of whom taught in the same department. Among the Egyptians were Muhammad Qutb, Sayyid Qutb's brother, who was appointed a professor in the Faculty of *Shari'a* of Mecca after his release from prison in 1971; Sayyid Sabiq, author of the celebrated book *The Jurisprudence of the Sunna*,[21] a still largely unchallenged legal reference work for the Brotherhood, who chaired the department of legal studies in Mecca and later graduate studies as a whole;[22] and Muhammad al-Ghazzali, who chaired the department of *da'wa* and the fundamentals of religion *(usul al-din)* until the mid-1980s.[23] The Palestinian Brother Abdallah 'Azzam, who would become the leading proponent of Arab jihad in Afghanistan, also made a strong impression when he taught a semester at King Abd al-Aziz University in 1981.[24]

The Brotherhood had an equally significant presence at Imam Muhammad bin Sa'ud University (known as Imam University) in Riyadh, founded in 1974. Among the Egyptians were the first representative of the Brotherhood in the kingdom, Manna' al-Qattan, who climbed the rungs to become head of graduate studies,[25] and Muhammad al-Rawi, who chaired the exegesis *(tafsir)* department.[26] The Syrian Brotherhood was well represented in the persons of Abd al-Fattah Abu Ghudda[27] and Muhammad Abu al-Fath al-Bayanuni.[28] A Muslim Brother from Sudan, Zayn al-'Abidin al-Rikabi, former editor of the journal of the Kuwaiti Brotherhood, *Al-Mujtama'* (literally "society"), also played a prominent role beginning in the mid-1970s. On the basis of his long experience as a journalist, he helped establish the university's Faculty of *Da'wa* and Communication. He even became the chief adviser to Abdallah al-Turki, president of the university and himself a former member of the Saudi Brotherhood.[29]

A significant number of the most renowned members of the Muslim Brotherhood were thus teaching in Saudi Arabia in this period. This explains why the leadership chose Mecca to hold in 1973 its first meeting to restore the movement's advisory council since the repression of the 1950s. This was the first step toward establishing an "international organization" *(al-tandhim al-duwali),* which was set up in the late 1970s; its existence was made official in 1982.[30] Although the presence of these illustrious Brothers in the kingdom's universities was emblematic, it should not obscure the fact that since the late 1960s, hundreds of the movement's grassroots militants had permeated the various levels of the Saudi educational system, where they taught all subjects, religious and secular. They made up the bulk of the personnel in the religious secondary schools, called Scientific Institutes *(ma'ahid 'ilmiyya)*, of which there were thirty-seven in the kingdom in 1970.[31] Some of these Brothers later achieved notoriety, including the Syrians Muhammad Surur Zayn al-'Abidin, who taught in Scientific Institutes in Ha'il, Burayda, and the Eastern Province from 1965 to 1973; Muhammad al-'Abda, who taught at the same time in Ar'ar and al-Rass; and Sa'id Hawwa, future ideologue of the Syrian Muslim Brotherhood, who taught in Hufuf and Medina from 1966 to 1971.[32] During that time Sa'id Hawwa wrote the books that made him famous when he returned to Syria, particularly the short work *Soldiers of God*,[33] which later became an essential reference for Middle Eastern Islamists.[34] Members of Qutbist groups with no direct connection to the Brotherhood were sometimes also present, as in the case of the Egyptian Umar Abd al-Rahman, the future mufti of the assassins of President Sadat, who came to teach in a Saudi Scientific Institute in the 1970s.[35]

The Brotherhood's members affected the Saudi educational system not only as teachers but also by acting as a major force in reconfiguring it and in redefining the curricula. In this way they introduced into the system the essential elements underlying their ideology and view of the world.

When the Islamic University of Medina was created in 1961, an advisory council was set up on which, along with a majority of Muslim reformists, sat an influential Brother, the Syrian Muhammad al-Mubarak, known as an expert in Islamic education because of his leading role in the foundation of the Faculty of *Shari'a* of Damascus in 1955.[36] Other members of the Brotherhood were also consulted informally, among them Mahmud al-Sawwaf, former leader of the Brotherhood in Iraq, and the Syrians Ali al-Tantawi[37] and Muhammad al-Majdhub.[38]

In 1964 the Saudi authorities called on Muhammad al-Mubarak to set up the curricula for the Faculties of *Shari'a* and Education in

Mecca. In the latter faculty he was the originator of a new discipline, "Islamic culture," defined by one of its specialists as "the science of the totalizing character of the Islamic conception of the world with respect to values, systems, and ideas, and the critique of the humanist legacy they contain."[39] A few years later he taught two courses in Islamic culture in that faculty: Contemporary Islamic Society and The System of Islam.[40]

In the late 1960s the rapidly developing but still very heterogeneous educational system called for the adoption of a national educational policy that would bring about its unification, but the control Mufti Muhammad bin Ibrahim exercised over the religious component of the educational system blocked any initiative along those lines. His death in 1969 made it possible to move forward on the issue. To produce its broad outlines, King Faysal had already established a group of experts in a subcommittee on education in 1965. The rapporteur of the subcommittee, which included a number of Brothers, was the Egyptian Brother Manna' al-Qattan, who was also already the representative of the movement in Saudi Arabia.[41] The subcommittee's work led to the adoption in 1970 of the text known as *Educational Policy in the Kingdom of Saudi Arabia*, which is still the primary document concerning education in the country. It defines the purpose of education as "conveying the understanding of Islam in a just and comprehensive manner,"[42] as "creed, religious practice, conduct, *shari'a*, government, and system."[43] At the individual level, "That requires inculcating in [the student] an Islamic epistemology so that his conception of the universe, the individual, and life emanates from a total Islamic vision."[44] This consciously totalizing conception of Islam owes more to the thinking of the Muslim Brotherhood than to traditional Wahhabism.[45]

To carry out these objectives, "religious sciences will occupy a central place at every level of primary, intermediate, and secondary education,[46] and in all branches, and Islamic culture will be a central subject at all levels of higher education."[47] As seen with Muhammad al-Mubarak, who introduced the concept to Saudi Arabia, the conception of Islamic culture is closely connected to the modern vision of the Muslim Brotherhood. Islamic culture, indeed, became the Brothers' preferred subject.[48] Consequently, its prominence in the educational system, as ratified by the new educational policy, only widened the scope of the Brotherhood's influence. Osama bin Laden, for example, although he was an economics student, allegedly came into contact with his earliest political influences, Muhammad Qutb and Abdallah 'Azzam, in the required Islamic culture course.[49]

This new educational policy also enabled the Brotherhood to promote another of its obsessions, the Islamicization of the sciences, particularly the social sciences.[50] One of the proposals set forth in the document calls for "giving to the sciences and to the various fields of knowledge . . . an Islamic orientation . . . so they may take their inspiration from Islam."[51] Thus, for example, King Abd al-Aziz University in Jeddah offered courses in Islamic economics taught by one of the first alleged Saudi Muslim Brothers, Muhammad Umar Zubayr. An entire department of Islamic economics was established in 1976. Later, departments of Islamic psychology and Islamic sociology were established at Imam University, both bastions for the Muslim Brothers and their Saudi followers.[52]

Outside Islamic culture and Islamicized sciences, their strongholds, a significant number of Brothers also taught, among the religious sciences, exegesis of the Koran and Islamic jurisprudence (fiqh). One subject, however, always remained outside their control: creed ('aqida). This was traditionally the exclusive prerogative of the Wahhabi ulema, and under no circumstances would they delegate its teaching. The only exceptions were the Egyptians of the pro-Wahhabi association Ansar al-Sunna al-Muhammadiyya, whose members were considered sufficiently close to the Saudi religious establishment to be granted that distinction.

A study of the annual catalog for 1977–1978 (Hijri 1397–1398) of the Faculty of Fundamentals of Religion of Imam University is very enlightening in this regard. The teaching committee of the department of creed included eleven members, nine of whom were Wahhabis from Najd, while the remaining two were Egyptians known for their fervent pro-Wahhabism (and probably with ties to Ansar al-Sunna al-Muhammadiyya). The teaching committee of the exegesis department, however, presented an entirely different picture: it was headed by the Egyptian Muslim Brother Muhammad al-Rawi and included eight other members, most of whom were Syrian or Egyptian, often close to the Brotherhood.[53]

The 1970s thus witnessed the establishment in Saudi universities of two centers of attraction and influence: a Wahhabi center with creed as its bastion and a Muslim Brotherhood center focused on Islamic culture but extending its sway to most other departments. The hold of the Brothers, followed by that of their Saudi disciples, soon became so great that they even managed to penetrate the Wahhabi sanctuary of creed. Safar al-Hawali tells how a Syrian member of the Brotherhood, Muhammad Amin al-Masri, as head of graduate studies in the Faculty of *Shari'a* in Mecca, "made strenuous efforts to introduce the study of contemporary schools of thought [*al-madhahib al-fikriyya*] into the creed curriculum. God wished that this subject be taught by one of the figures of contemporary Islamic thought, Professor Muhammad Qutb, may God protect him."[54] Qutb thus found himself in the highly unusual position for a Brother of being affiliated with the department of creed. In the 1980s some of the Sahwi ulema, in particular Safar al-Hawali, a student of Muhammad Qutb, were in turn given that honor, teaching the same course on "contemporary schools of thought."

The text of the 1970 *Educational Policy* also established a very strong, almost symbiotic connection between *ta'lim* (education in the intellectual sense) and *tarbiya* (education in the moral and ultimately religious sense, conveyed through Islamic socialization). Education thus was viewed as a matter not only of transmitting knowledge but also primarily of producing "good Muslims." In the end, learning was to be dedicated to that goal alone. This was indicated by the article defining the role of education as "transmitting to the student the indispensable ideas, feelings, and capacities for him to bear the message of Islam."[55] In addition, the aim was to stimulate in the student a form of social activism by "teaching him to identify cultural, economic, and social problems in society and preparing him to contribute to their solution."[56] To develop this side of *tarbiya*, a whole series of extracurricular Islamic activities was put in place, often at the instigation of the Muslim Brothers and their disciples. These activities were considered complementary to the education acquired in schools and universities because they were a way of putting into practice the principles that had been inculcated, of making them alive.

The first stages of this development go back to the 1960s, when committees for raising Islamic consciousness (lijan al-taw'iya al-islamiyya) were set up in various parts of the kingdom to coordinate the Islamic activities organized by teachers in primary and secondary schools.[57] This led to the establishment of a high commission for the same purpose,[58] which unified the activities of the committees.[59] The secretary general of the commission was the Saudi Muslim Brother Hamad al-Sulayfih,[60] who was also partly behind the creation in 1972 of the World Assembly of Muslim Youth (al-Nadwa al-'alamiyya li-l-shabab al-islami, known as WAMY). Although the activities of the WAMY extended far beyond Saudi Arabia, it actively helped establish extracurricular activities of all kinds in the kingdom.

For the youngest students, circles for the memorization of the Koran (halaqat tahfidh al-qur'an) were set up as complements to modern schools. An official document recounts that in 1962 a Pakistani sheikh named Muhammad Yusuf Sethi, who had established several hundred of these circles in his native country, suggested to notables and ulema in Mecca that the same idea should be adopted in the Saudi kingdom.[61] The first Charitable Association for the Memorization of the Koran (al-Jam'iyya al-khayriyya li-tahfidh al-qur'an al-karim) was established in Mecca, and it was soon imitated in other cities in the kingdom. In Riyadh, for example, a similar association was established in 1966 with the help of a local sheikh, Abd al-Rahman al-Faryan. The number of circles attached to these associations grew quickly: in 1971 there were 48 of them in Riyadh and 17 in the rest of Najd.[62] Beginning in the late 1970s, these groups experienced exponential growth.[63] In 2003 the kingdom counted 104 associations for the memorization of the Koran, supervising 27,987 circles for the memorization of the Koran.[64]

In the early 1970s the range of activities of Islamic tarbiya broadened, notably with the gradual Islamization of student activities. Those activities went back to the 1940s and 1950s and at first were indebted mostly to the Anglo-American model that had been imported into the Middle East through Egypt. Islamic activism soon started spreading through primary- and secondary-school clubs *(andiya tullabiyya)*[65] and, in universities, through cultural, social, and sports committees *(lijan)*.[66] Islamization also reached the scouting movement (*al-kashshafa* or *al-jawwala*), which had been in existence in the kingdom since 1943, when the first scouting group was established in the School for the Preparation of Study Missions (Madrasat tahdir al-bi'that) in Mecca.[67] When the Brotherhood entered the picture, its model of scouting, which had experienced its glory days in Egypt in the 1940s, attained dominance.[68] Activities with a religious purpose, such as campaigns to assist pilgrims, became preponderant.[69]

Beginning in the mid-1970s, camps (*mukhayyamat* or *marakiz*) were set up, usually in the desert, where youth could gather on weekends and during summer school vacations.[70] The camps, divided into "families" named after heroes of Islamic history, included a mixture of sporting and religious activities, similar to the ones the Brothers had organized through their scouting organization in Egypt.[71] It is therefore no surprise that the first of these camps were established by Saudi scouting organizations.[72] The practice was gradually taken up by other organizations, such as the committees for raising Islamic consciousness and the university committees, and then by institutions such as the universities and the WAMY.[73] In time, summer camps came to represent the archetype of *tarbiya* organizations. In 1990 there were thirty summer camps in the city of Riyadh alone, while Imam University organized fifty-five of them around the kingdom.[74]

Activities carried on in the framework of these organizations were of several kinds. Some were purely religious, such as Koran recitation contests. Others involved sports, such as footraces or soccer games. Still others joined play to ideology: "Islamic chants" *(anashid islamiyya)*, for example, with themes ranging from "the greatness of Islam" to "the Palestinian resistance," that were learned by heart and sung a cappella by the group (musical instruments were considered prohibited according to Wahhabi jurisprudence). Other activities had intellectual aims, such as editing a magazine discussing Islamic subjects. Sometimes there were also small exhibitions on the "wounds of the *umma.*"[75] They were intended to sensitize young Saudis to the misfortunes of their coreligionists elsewhere in the world.

One particularly significant activity was theater. In committees for raising Islamic consciousness or in summer camps, young participants were often asked to stage episodes in the contemporary history of the Muslim world that were considered traumatic. One young Islamist recalled participating in a play on "the expulsion of the Muslims from Palestine," depicting Palestinians driven off their land by a cruel and domineering David Ben-Gurion.[76] Other plays took Andalusia as a subject, with similar ideological purposes. Through theater, young participants were to experience vicariously, mentally if not physically, the sufferings of the Muslim world. The purpose was to introduce and naturalize frameworks for the interpretation of the world produced in very different contexts and to integrate them into a new identity that was in the process of gestation, that of the Sahwa. In this process certain feelings, beginning with sadness and disgust at the misfortune of coreligionists, played an essential role. They were sometimes expressed in spectacular ways. It was not unusual for an audience at a play evoking the suffering of its "brothers" to break collectively into sobbing.[77]

The Emergence of the Sahwa

Saudi Arabia in the 1960s thus experienced a massive influx into the local religious field of an exogenous tradition, that of the Muslim Brotherhood, and the establishment of institutions that were largely in its service in both form and content. This transplantation was the source of a vast social movement that produced its own counterculture and its own organizations and, through the educational system, soon reached almost all the fields of the social arena.

Locally, the social movement was known as al-Sahwa al-Islamiyya (Islamic Awakening), or simply the Sahwa. This notion was not specifically Saudi but applied more generally to the widespread Islamic resurgence that had taken hold in the Muslim world since the 1960s. In the Arab world the phenomenon was closely linked to the rise of

Islamist movements, particularly the Muslim Brotherhood. In Saudi Arabia, one of the countries where it was a driving force behind the resurgence, the taboo against political organizations meant that any explicit public reference to the Brotherhood was banned. The term "Sahwa," less politically charged, therefore prevailed as the name for the movement resulting from its influence.

The Sahwi counterculture was defined by adherence to an ideology and to certain practices that ran, at the time of their emergence, against the preponderant social norms. The ideology of the Sahwa is located at the juncture of two distinct schools of thought with different views of the world: the Wahhabi tradition and the tradition of the Muslim Brotherhood. Like the Muslim reformist tradition from which it derives, the tradition of the Muslim Brotherhood is primarily political and was constructed, in its Bannaist version, against the "imperialist West," and in its Qutbist version, against the "godless regimes" of the Middle East. The Wahhabi tradition, in contrast, is primarily religious and was constructed against the *bida'*, that is, the impurities that were supposed to have grown up around the original dogma of the pious ancestors. Historically, its principal enemy was not the West nor the political authorities but the non-Wahhabi groups within Islam, beginning with the Shiites and the Sufis.

The concerns and priorities of the two traditions were thus totally distinct. This made them formally complementary and laid the groundwork for the emergence of the Sahwa through the intermediary of the educational system that, though dominated by the methods and thinking of the Muslim Brotherhood, maintained creed as a Wahhabi preserve. Ideologically, the Sahwa could be described as a hybrid of Wahhabism and the ideology of the Brotherhood. On theological questions connected to creed and on the major aspects of Islamic jurisprudence, the Sahwis adhered to the Wahhabi tradition and considered themselves its faithful heirs. But on political and cultural questions, their view of the world tended toward that of the Muslim Brotherhood, although it was partly reformulated in terms derived from the Wahhabi tradition.

Within the Sahwa, both Bannaist and Qutbist tendencies were initially represented, but the latter soon came to dominate. There is indeed a close ideological affinity between Qutbist thinking and the Wahhabi tradition, both of which are based on the same Manichaean opposition between Islam and *jahiliyya*. More prosaically, the preponderance of Qutb's ideas is connected to the fact that the Brothers who flocked to Saudi Arabia in the 1970s, soon overtaking by their numbers the ones already present, had frequently been socialized in Qutbist circles.

Beyond internal disputes, several figures are considered the intellectual fathers of the Sahwa ideology, the outlines of which became clear in the course of the 1970s: Muhammad Qutb, who played a prominent role in its theoretical development, which led some disciples to call him the "sheikh of the Sahwa";[78] Abd al-Rahman al-Dawsari, who was the first to encourage the move from theory to practice and became known by some as the "precursor of the Sahwa";[79] and Muhammad Ahmad al-Rashid, whose writings broadly influenced the ways the movement acted and organized itself. In addition, the Kuwaiti journal *Al-Mujtama*ʿ had a strong influence on the beginnings of the Saudi Sahwa.

Muhammad Qutb was born in Musha in Upper Egypt in 1919. He grew up in the shadow of his brother Sayyid, who was thirteen years his senior and whom he described as the person in his life who had the greatest influence on him: "He supervised my education and my intellectual development, he was for me a father, a brother, and a friend."[80] Muhammad studied at Cairo University, graduating with a degree in English literature in 1940. Like his brother, he grew close to the Muslim Brotherhood in the late 1940s, and both were arrested and tortured in 1954. But Muhammad, who was much less implicated, was soon released from the prison where Sayyid remained for ten years.[81] In 1965 he was one of the first Brothers to suffer from the new wave of repression unleashed by the government. The Egyptian authorities accused him—most probably mistakenly—of being at the head of the Brotherhood's secret organization.[82] He was released by Sadat in 1971, after six years in prison and the death by hanging of his brother in 1966. A few months later he left for Saudi Arabia, where he was appointed professor at the Faculty of *Shariʿa* in Mecca (this faculty became the core of Umm al-Qura University in 1981).

Little known at the time for his own intellectual work, Muhammad Qutb arrived in Saudi Arabia as the intellectual heir of Sayyid.[83] In his writings from then on, he attempted to mediate between the conceptual apparatus forged by his brother and the precepts of the Wahhabi tradition: the opposition between *jahiliyya* and *hakimiyya* (divine sovereignty) that was the driving force behind Qutbism was viewed as parallel to the opposition between *jahiliyya* and *tawhid* (the oneness, unity, and transcendence of God) propounded by Ibn Abd al-Wahhab. Muhammad Qutb's purpose was to establish an equivalence between the full application of *shari'a*, which was at the core of the Muslim Brotherhood's demands, and the purification of creed, the central concern of the Wahhabis. As he explained in *The Jahiliyya of the Twentieth Century*:

> There is no difference between the question of creed and the question of *shari'a*: either there is government according to God's revelations [*al-hukm bima anzala Allah*], or *jahiliyya* and *shirk* [the association of God with other entities]. For the knowledge of the Truth of God and just belief in Him imply granting sovereignty [*hakimiyya*] only to Him as they imply directing adoration [*uluhiyya*] only to Him. . . . *'Aqida* [creed] and *shari'a* are the two sides of a single question, they emanate from a single source and lead to a single end. This source and this end are belief in God and submission [*islam*] to Him.[84]

Going so far as to redefine the foundations of Wahhabism in the light of notions developed by Sayyid, he stated that in addition to the three forms of *tawhid* described by Ibn Abd al-Wahhab, there is a fourth, which he called *tawhid al-hakimiyya* (the unity of sovereignty), meaning that God alone must be sovereign, and therefore that the application of *shari'a* can brook no obstacles.[85] This new concept is perfectly orthodox, Qutb explains, because it derives directly from the *tawhid al-uluhiyya* (the oneness of God as an object of worship); it therefore adds nothing to the teaching of Ibn Abd al-Wahhab but merely makes his thinking explicit. The "unity of sovereignty" would soon come to occupy a prominent position in the theoretical apparatus of the Sahwa.

In addition to making himself the leading theorist of the Wahhabi-Qutbist hybrid, Muhammad Qutb tried to mask those elements of his brother's legacy that were incompatible with the political and religious environment of his adopted country. In particular, that involved sweeping Sayyid's very first works under the rug,[86] such as *Artistic Representation in the Koran* (1945),[87] whose references to art and music were considered incompatible with Wahhabi norms, and especially *Social Justice in Islam* (1949),[88] whose arguments laid the groundwork for the theory of Islamic socialism, which was later given real substance by the Syrian Brother Mustafa al-Siba'i in *The Socialism of Islam.*[89] In the Saudi political context of the 1970s, such leftist positions had obviously become untenable in the face of a government that proclaimed itself the champion of conservative Islam. Moreover, in *Social Justice,* Sayyid Qutb attacked the Umayyad dynasty and its hereditary power in extremely violent language. This could not fail to outrage both the Wahhabis, who rejected any challenge to the role of the first generations of Muslims, and the Saudi regime, which also made heredity the principle for the transmission of its power.

Sayyid Qutb's controversial writings were neutralized in two ways. First, new editions of *Social Justice in Islam* published by Dar al-Shuruq in Cairo were revised to eliminate the most problematic passages and terminology.[90] Second, Muhammad Qutb reiterated to anyone who would listen: "This is the first book [Sayyid] wrote after first having been interested in literature and literary criticism, and it does not represent his thinking at maturity. . . . He did not advise that it be read. . . . The books he recommended not reading are all those that preceded *In the Shade of the Koran,* including *Social Justice.*"[91] The result of this process was that the Qutbist strain that took root in Saudi Arabia was what could be called late Qutbism, from which all left-leaning influences had been removed. What was left, then, was essentially *In the Shade of the Koran* and *Milestones.*

Muhammad Qutb, moreover, produced explanations of these two books intended to attenuate their revolutionary implications. He wrote unambiguously: "The situation of the *da'wa* today is practically identical to the situation of the Muslim community during the Mecca period. . . . Under these circumstances, resorting to violence does not help the *da'wa.*"[92] Consequently, the path to follow was now that of *bayan* (speech, as opposed to the "movement," *haraka,* advocated by

Sayyid Qutb) and *tarbiya* (moral education).[93] In addition, Muhammad Qutb, like the majority of the Sahwa at the time, refused to call into question the Islamic character of the Saudi state, qualifying the passages in *Milestones* where Sayyid had written that there were currently no Islamic states on earth. But despite these precautions, the subversive potential of Qutbism remained largely intact.

Muhammad Saʿid al-Qahtani, a professor at Umm al-Qura and a prominent student of Muhammad Qutb (who directed his thesis), continued the work of cross-fertilization begun by his teacher in a book that had a significant influence on the nascent Sahwa: *Allegiance and Rupture in Islam* (*Al-walaʾ wa-l-baraʾ fi-l-islam*), published in 1984. Its originality lies in the reformulation of the fundamentals of Qutbist ideology in terms that, although they had become common in Wahhabi discourse, were still considered distinctive markers of Wahhabi exclusivism. Al-Qahtani thus establishes an equivalence between the pair *hakimiyya/jahiliyya* and the pair *walaʾ/baraʾ*: applying the Law of God, he explains, means declaring allegiance to the *umma*, while advocating *jahiliyya*, notably by subscribing to "contemporary schools of thought" such as nationalism, Nasserism, secularism, and the like, means pledging allegiance to the infidels.[94]

In addition, al-Qahtani redefines the notion of allegiance and rupture to make it a weapon directed not only against "heretical Muslims," as in traditional Wahhabism, but also against the West and its civilization. This usage was adopted and amplified by the neojihadis of the late 1990s. Although it never enters into the details of the exclusivist body of doctrine, aside from surface correspondences, *Allegiance and Rupture in Islam* nonetheless significantly helped rehabilitate Wahhabi exclusivism in Sahwi circles. This facilitated alliances that were established in 1993 and 1994 between the Sahwa and the rejectionists, ardent disciples of the exclusivist school.

Abd al-Rahman al-Dawsari was born in 1913 in a merchant family from the Qasim region that had been settled in Kuwait for ten years.[95] He attended the Mubarakiyya School, the first modern school in the emirate, where he was taught by Muslim reformist sheikhs.[96] He later moved toward the Muslim Brothers, among whom he admired Hasan al-Banna and later Sayyid Qutb,[97] although he never officially joined the organization. When the Brotherhood supported Nasser's revolution in 1952, al-Dawsari definitively distanced himself from the movement. In his view, "This revolution is a continuation of the revolution of Mustafa Kemal Atatürk the Freemason; behind it lie America and Freemason circles."[98] The word "Freemasonry" *(al-masuniyya),* hitherto absent from the Saudi lexicon, became al-Dawsari's trademark. It represented for him a unifying principle bringing together all the "enemies of Islam"—Judaism, secularism, communism, and nationalism, as well as materialism, existentialism, and others—in a vast conspiracy against the entire *umma.*[99] Although all these elements are connected, al-Dawsari explains, priority must be given to the battle against the inner enemy, the "hypocrites" *(munafiqun),* "nationalists, offspring of Jewish Freemasonry and students of colonization, who are more harmful to Muslims than what is known as the state of Israel."[100] This priority is justified by strategic considerations because the hypocrites "are the ones who enable the existence and resiliency of Israel and give Muslims the experience of torture,"[101] as well as by the simple need to purify the Muslim creed from those "modern schools" that, just like the medieval "Kharijites, Mu'tazilites, Qadirites," and others, deviate from correct dogma.[102] Using this twofold political and dogmatic justification, al-Dawsari links the concerns of the Muslim Brotherhood to those of the Wahhabis. In doing so, he carries out a transfer of the hostility of the Wahhabis against their traditional enemies, Islamic groups whose creed is seen as deviant, to the traditional enemies of the Muslim Brotherhood, secularists, communists, and the like.

In 1961 al-Dawsari left Kuwait and moved to Riyadh, not far from the Qasim region, his family's original home. According to some accounts,[103] he had just been jailed in Kuwait for stirring up public opinion against the constitution of the newly independent emirate, which he denounced as a violation of the supremacy of *shari'a.* King Faysal is said to have bowed to pressure from Mufti Muhammad bin Ibrahim and to have negotiated al-Dawsari's release on condition that he settle permanently in Saudi Arabia. In the same year al-Dawsari gave up his business activities to devote himself full-time to preaching.[104] He was thereafter very active in the Saudi religious field, where he had two kinds of influence. The first was ideological, because he actively contributed to spreading an early form of political consciousness in religious circles, thereby creating an environment suitable for the Sahwa's influence. Also, at a time when the world of cultural production remained highly segmented, he was the first sheikh to attack untiringly the "deviations" of Saudi liberals among the intelligentsia and in the nascent intellectual field. His second kind of influence related to his methods. He engaged in a veritable jihad through the pen, sending a letter to the editor of the respective newspaper for every article in the press in which he detected a violation of Islam. Some of these letters were published in the newspaper in question or in the magazine *Al-Da'wa,* the organ of the official religious institution, but most of them piled up in editors' desk drawers.[105] At the same time, al-Dawsari was traveling throughout the kingdom, visiting mosques, summer camps, government departments, and schools to denounce the "Masonic peril" he thought threatened the country.[106] He did not mince words: for example, when asked to give a lecture at the Institute of Public Administration of Riyadh, a bastion of the Saudi intelligentsia, he began his talk by stating: "I am speaking to you from one of the havens of world Freemasonry in Riyadh," and went on to violently attack the institute's programs.[107]

Abd al-Rahman al-Dawsari succeeded in exercising significant influence in the Saudi religious field until his death in 1979, even rubbing shoulders with the highest authorities of the Wahhabi religious establishment.[108] He was able to do this primarily because he had a major advantage over the Muslim Brothers in exile: he was of Najdi origin and was thereby seen as legitimate in a religious field in which lineage still carried great weight. Because of his origin, he could allow himself to launch fierce attacks against Saudi liberals, whereas Muslim Brothers, as immigrants, were generally reluctant to get involved in the internal affairs of their host country. All of this made him the "precursor of the Sahwa."[109]

Muhammad Ahmad al-Rashid, the pseudonym of Abd al-Mun'im Salih al-'Ali al-'Izzi, was born in Baghdad in 1938. He joined the Iraqi Muslim Brotherhood in 1953 and began the study of religious sciences. Predisposed to the Hanbali tendencies of the Baghdad branch of the movement, he turned to the few sheikhs in Iraq who were carrying on the pro-Wahhabi Muslim reformist tradition inherited from Mahmud Shukri al-Alusi, notably Abd al-Karim al-Shaykhali. Al-Rashid thus came to mix Wahhabi religious culture with the Brotherhood's political culture. A dedicated supporter of clandestine activism, he resisted the successive waves of repression that struck the Iraqi Brothers in the 1960s until, weary of the battle, he fled to Kuwait in 1972.[110] From then on he contributed regularly to the magazine *Al-Mujtama'*, where he began to work out his vast theory of *da'wa*, which he titled "For a Renewal of the Jurisprudence of *da'wa*." He left Kuwait in the 1980s and thereafter divided his time between the United Arab Emirates, Malaysia, and Switzerland. After the fall of Saddam Hussein in 2003, he is reported to have returned to live in Iraq.[111]

Muhammad Ahmad al-Rashid's essential contribution to Sahwi ideology was to theorize Islamic activism in accordance with the presuppositions of the Wahhabi tradition. Two of the five books he devoted to the subject even became part of the basic Sahwi library. The first, *The Point of Departure,* is a demonstration of the legitimacy of organized political action, relying on jurists such as Ibn Taymiyya and Ibn Qayyim al-Jawziyya, who are recognized and accepted by the Wahhabi tradition.[112] The second, *The Journey,* is a veritable treatise on political activism that deals with three complementary subjects: the movement's "external policy, defined by the nature of relations between the movement and governments, parties, and other groups, that might take the form of warfare, truce, alliance, support, or a call for assistance"; its "internal policy, which establishes the form of the organization, determines the requirements for becoming a member or an emir, and the rights and duties of preachers"; and its "educational policy, which determines how preachers are trained . . . notably on the moral level."[113] Deeply affected by the experience of repression in Iraq, al-Rashid discusses extensively the forms of clandestine organization and the political strategies that should be adopted in an authoritarian context. It is not at all surprising, therefore, that the book was banned in Saudi Arabia,[114] but according to a former member of the Saudi Muslim Brotherhood, "It circulated clandestinely everywhere, and some bookstores we knew even sold it secretly."[115]

Al-Mujtamaʿ, the magazine that made al-Rashid's work known, was published in Kuwait from 1969 on by the Association of Social Reform (Jamʿiyyat al-islah al-ijtimaʿi), the local branch of the Muslim Brotherhood. This magazine played a major role in the intellectual development of the Sahwa. Ismaʿil al-Shatti, its editor from 1979 to 1991, explains: "Saudi Arabia was our primary market; we sold a large number of copies there, even in official circles. Universities, schools, and government departments were regular subscribers." Although contributors included influential theorists such as al-Rashid and Muhammad Surur Zayn al-ʿAbidin, the magazine's principal role was to offer readers "Islamic news" by keeping them informed about the "misfortunes" of the Muslim world, which it presented from an ideological angle.[116] This was how, in al-Shatti's view, *Al-Mujtamaʿ* helped politicize the Saudi religious field. It should be added that although the magazine was established at the initiative of the Bannaist wing of the Muslim Brotherhood, when Ismaʿil al-Shatti assumed the editorship, it moved closer to the Qutbist wing,[117] which made it more in step with the spirit of the Saudi Sahwa.

In addition to the ideology that distinguished the Sahwis within the religious field, they adopted a set of very specific social practices. Those practices were intended to "politicize everyday life" in order to establish the group and delineate its place in the social arena.[118]

The Sahwis viewed Islam as a total system that should govern every detail of daily life, including ways of dressing and speaking and forms of social behavior. The Sahwis thus adopted a very strict code of conduct that they considered an emanation of the Islamic norm. In the process they borrowed widely from the practices of Wahhabi ulema, but although these practices had hitherto been the preserve of a small religious elite, the Sahwa made them a model applicable to everyone.

On certain questions, Sahwis even sought to distinguish themselves from traditional ulema by showing greater intransigence.

Relying on various hadiths, most Sahwis, for example, asserted that it was forbidden *(haram)* to wear a tunic coming below the ankle and to trim one's beard. In contrast, the Wahhabi ulema thought wearing a long tunic was merely reprehensible *(makruh)* when it was not done out of vanity and allowed beards to be trimmed if they grew larger than a fist.[119] Like the Wahhabi ulema, but much more forcefully, the Sahwis also opposed wearing the *'iqal* (the cord holding the *shmagh* or the *ghutra,* the cloths Saudis wore on their heads).[120] Sahwi women wore their long black dress *('abaya)* on the head, not the shoulders, gloves to conceal their hands, and socks inside their shoes. Some of these practices were designed primarily to reinforce the group's separateness in the social arena rather than to conform to some preexisting religious norm. This was true for wearing the *shmagh* or the *ghutra* without an *'iqal,* which was not in response to an explicit prohibition but to a much vaguer legal principle: wearing an *'iqal* would be "contrary to what is most appropriate" *(khilaf al-awla).*[121]

In their conversations the Sahwis adopted "Sahwi speech" that immediately identified them in social settings. For example, they endeavored to blend their dialect with classical Arabic. They frequently used religious formulas such as "may God help you" *(Allah yu'inak)* "may God bring you success" *(Allah yuwaffiqak),* and "fear God" *(Ittagallah).* Their discussions concerned both religious prohibitions (their Wahhabi side) and the situation of Islam and Muslims (their Brotherhood side).[122]

Their singular identity was constructed and reinforced through action. The various extracurricular activities described earlier played a key role in this process. This was particularly true of the summer camps, which enabled the Sahwis to give their charges the sense of belonging to a group and sharing values and a worldview that set them apart from the rest of society. The fact that the camps were generally held in the desert reinforced this feeling of separateness by adding the physical to the moral.

The Sahwi identity in the process of formation suffered, however, from a fundamental ambiguity. It was in revolt, of course, but the revolt was against an abstract reality—the "infidels" *(kuffar)* and the "hypocrites" *(munafiqun)*—with no precise embodiment on Saudi territory. Therefore, when Sahwis, following the teachings of the Brotherhood, evoked the suffering of Muslims, they were careful to specify that they were talking about the suffering of all Muslims around the world except those in the Saudi kingdom. Deprived of flesh-and-blood enemies, the Sahwa emerged primarily as a movement of "rebels without a cause."

The *Jamaʿat* as Vanguard of a Countersociety

By the late 1960s organized networks had sprung up within the Sahwa, the members of which were distinguished from the mass of Sahwi sympathizers by a greater commitment to serving the cause. With a unique capacity for mobilization, these networks were the backbone of the Sahwa.

The Sahwa community can be described as being made up of three concentric circles. The third and largest included everyone brought up in the Saudi school system reformed by the Brotherhood and thereby socialized, willingly or not, in a Sahwi intellectual environment. Although individuals in this circle had all been affected by the Sahwa's ideology and worldview, many of them had not adopted its practices. Apart from a few exceptions, they represented an entire generation of young Saudis who sometimes identified themselves as the "Sahwa generation" *(jil al-Sahwa).*

The second, smaller, circle included those who, in addition to having gone through the educational system, had chosen to participate in extracurricular activities, through which they established the fraternal bonds that gave substance to the identity of the Sahwi movement. For many, that meant an Islamic commitment *(iltizam),* expressed in the adoption of the Sahwi practices described earlier. The Sahwis identified the members of this second circle as the "committed" *(multazimun).*

The first and smallest circle included the committed who, when participating in extracurricular activities, had been recruited—often unknowingly—into one of the Sahwa's organized networks. They then took regular classes in small groups known as circles *(halaqat)* or families *(usar)* that inculcated the specific ideological body of doctrine of the network to which they now belonged.[123] These networks were generally known in Islamist parlance as *jama'at tarbawiyya* (*tarbiya* groups),[124] *jama'at da'wiyya* (*da'wa* groups), *jama'at al-maktabat* (library groups, referring to the area of the mosque where books were kept, known to be a place where those groups liked to meet), or simply *jama'at* (sing. *jama'a*). The members of this inner circle were known as "affiliates" *(muntamun)*, meaning members of a *jama'a*.

Technically, there were two main *jama'at* in the Sahwa. The first of them was made up of four loosely connected subgroups, also referred to as *jama'at*, which all claimed affiliation with the Muslim Brotherhood (al-Ikhwan al-muslimun). The members of the other main *jama'a* were referred to as "Sururis" *(al-sururiyyun)*. These five networks (the four Brotherhood groups and the Sururis) were organized hierarchically and were headed by an advisory council. In addition to the young affiliates, they brought together thousands of officials from the educational system and the administration and managers from the private sector.[125] Most of them had been recruited when they were young and had ascended the rungs of the *jama'a*, where they now occupied senior positions. Although the *jama'at* were overwhelmingly male, they did have female sections, more developed among the Brothers than among the Sururis.[126]

Aside from a few fleeting references,[127] no work of scholarship or journalism has dealt with these *jama'at*, although they have existed for nearly forty years. They have always been a significant taboo in Saudi politics, and none of their known leaders has ever publicly acknowledged their existence. Even recently, Salman al-'Awada, when asked by a reporter whether he was a Sururi, answered with a pun and changed the subject.[128] But in the last few years some mid-ranking members and young activists of the *jama'at*, whether still affiliates or dissidents, have timidly begun to speak out. Given the great secrecy under which the *jama'at* were established and the resulting near absence of written documents concerning them, this attempt to retrace their history is mostly based on personal interviews with those insiders, as well as with non-Saudi Islamists who played a role on the regional level. As will be seen in the next chapters, shedding light on the *jama'at* allows us to introduce an essential variable without which it would not be possible to adequately understand and explain the dynamics behind Islamist mobilizations in Saudi Arabia.

Most accounts trace the origin of the Sahwa's organized networks to Manna' al-Qattan, who was born in 1925 and was one of the earliest Brothers to settle in Saudi Arabia, in 1953. In the early 1960s, when the Egyptian Brother Ali 'Ashmawi traveled to Saudi Arabia, he was told that the Brothers in Saudi Arabia had chosen al-Qattan as their leader, or, as 'Ashmawi asserts, that al-Qattan had imposed himself as the person in charge. Al-Qattan seems to have been so completely unknown outside the kingdom at that time that when 'Ashmawi told a fellow Egyptian Brother that al-Qattan was the local leader, he exclaimed: "Who is this Manna' al-Qattan? Strange things are going on over there."[129] At that time the role of Manna' al-Qattan was primarily that of mediator between the Saudi government and the Egyptian "central office" of the Brotherhood. Under his aegis, and apparently with the blessing of King Faysal, the various branches of the movement in exile in Saudi Arabia had reconstituted themselves with the primary aim of providing logistic and financial support to militants who had remained on the ground.[130] But, as King Abd al-Aziz had done with Hasan al-Banna, Faysal did bar al-Qattan from establishing a Saudi branch of the Brotherhood.

The nature of Manna' al-Qattan's role in the creation of a network of Saudi Brothers is a matter of debate. 'Ashmawi believes that it was a direct one,[131] but in the view of many, al-Qattan merely had a good deal of influence on the men who became the first Brothers in the kingdom. This is the version adopted by Isma'il al-Shatti, a leading figure in the Kuwaiti Brotherhood and very knowledgeable about the Saudi networks: "Saudis in any case would never have agreed to be led by a non-Saudi," he argued.[132]

The first *jama'a* of the Saudi Brotherhood was apparently created by Hamad al-Sulayfih. Born in Najd in 1938, he was one of the first graduates of the Faculty of *Shari'a* of Riyadh in the late 1950s, and he went on to become a high official in the Ministry of Education, where he was the first person put in charge of supervising the activities of the committees for raising Islamic consciousness.[133] Already under the influence of al-Qattan, who taught at the faculty, al-Sulayfih was reportedly also impressed by the ideas and the personality of the Egyptian Brother Saʿid Ramadan, Hasan al-Bannaʾs son-in-law, who frequently traveled to Saudi Arabia. In the late 1960s al-Sulayfih decided to see more of the world and secured appointments as educational attaché in Iran and then in Pakistan. He therefore asked one of his subordinates, Abdallah al-Turki, born in the Sudayr region in 1940 and also a graduate of the Faculty of *Shariʿa* of Riyadh, to take over his embryonic network. When he returned to Saudi Arabia, he gave up his first plan and created another *jamaʿa,* which became famous in Saudi Islamist circles as the Brothers of al-Sulayfih (Ikhwan al-Sulayfih).[134]

Al-Sulayfihʾs first *jamaʿa* that had been turned over to Abdallah al-Turki soon came under the leadership of another graduate of the Faculty of *Shariʿa* and a student of al-Sulayfih and al-Qattan, Saʿud al-Funaysan, born in Zulfi in 1942. Al-Turki, who had just been appointed president of Imam University, wanted to distance himself from any potentially compromising activities.[135] The group now under al-Funaysanʾs leadership was closely tied to a small informal religious institute in Riyadh, which served as its base and recruiting structure, and where the groupʾs members often took courses. Located in the conservative neighborhood of al-Dikhna, the institute was called Dar al-ʿilm (The House of Religious Knowledge).[136] Saudi Islamists, as a result, often called the group the *jamaʿa* of Dar al-ʿilm, or more prosaically, the Brothers of al-Funaysan (Ikhwan al-Funaysan).[137] When al-Funaysan was transferred to Imam University in the late 1970s (where he became head of the Faculty of *Shariʿa* in 1982), his *jamaʿa* established a powerful base there and was then sometimes known as the Brothers of Imam University.[138]

These two first *jamaʿat* related to the Brotherhood were soon joined by a third, known as the Brothers of Zubayr (Ikhwan al-Zubayr), after the town of the same name southwest of Basra in Iraq. Families from Najd fleeing frequent famines and wars had moved to this fertile oasis since the seventeenth century.[139] In the late nineteenth century Zubayr became a base for the inclusivist Wahhabi ulema, who had been driven out by the domination of the exclusivists over the Saudi religious field.[140] Only inclusivists would have sought refuge in a town known as the site of the tombs of prestigious "saints," namely, companions of the Prophet, including Zubayr, from whom the town derived its name.[141] In 1922 Zubayr was annexed to the Hashemite Kingdom of Iraq, thereby becoming part of a politically turbulent country. The various movements active in the region set up bases there, but the ambient conservatism ensured that the Muslim Brotherhood met with the greatest success. In the late 1940s a group of notables and ulema, among whom was Rashid al-Faqih, father of the Saudi opposition figure now living in exile in London, Sa'd al-Faqih, created the Association to Combat Vice (Jam'iyyat mukafahat al-radhila).[142] It formed the core of the Association of Social Reform (Jam'iyyat al-islah al-ijtima'i), the local branch of the Muslim Brotherhood established in 1952 and banned following the 1958 coup d'état. The persecuted members of the Brotherhood joined the great wave of emigration of the inhabitants of Zubayr to Kuwait and Saudi Arabia that had begun in the 1930s and 1940s and had become significant with the first signs of oil wealth.[143] The two countries had decided to offer citizenship under certain conditions to Zubayris who requested it. In Saudi Arabia a commission was set up to examine requests, two of whose members were illustrious Brothers from Zubayr, Abdallah al-'Aqil and Umar al-Dayil. The emigration of the Zubayr Brothers had fundamental consequences for the two countries that received them. In Kuwait they played a key role in the 1963 creation of the Association of Social Reform, the principal organ of the Kuwaiti Muslim Brotherhood, which bore the same name as the association they had established in Zubayr eleven years earlier.[144] In Saudi Arabia they simply recreated their Zubayr organization, making it the third Muslim Brotherhood *jama'a* active in the kingdom.[145] Recruitment was for a long time limited to individuals from Zubayr and their descendants before being opened to all Saudis in the 1980s.[146] Among the better-known figures of this *jama'a* was Sa'd al-Faqih (before his exile to England).

In the late 1960s a fourth group of Muslim Brothers appeared, based in the Hejaz (the three others had been concentrated in Najd), known as the Brothers of the Hejaz (Ikhwan al-Hijaz). According to some accounts, its founder was named Ali al-Tchadi.[147] Other accounts stress the role played by Muhammad Umar Zubayr, a Saudi born in the Hejaz in 1932 who became president of King Abd al-Aziz University in 1971. The World Assembly of Muslim Youth (WAMY) that had been created with the help of al-Sulayfih was quickly taken over by the members of this fourth *jama'a*, who made it their base and one of their primary recruiting organizations. The extent of the control exerted by the Brothers of the Hejaz over the WAMY is illustrated by the story an interviewee tells of an individual belonging to another *jama'a* in the Muslim Brotherhood who was appointed to a key post in the association and was forced to resign under pressure.[148] The *jama'a* of the Brothers of the Hejaz spread rapidly throughout the kingdom, particularly in the eastern and western provinces, where it met with great success, and to a lesser extent in Najd, so that in the late 1980s it was the principal Muslim Brotherhood *jama'a* in the country.[149] The strong presence of the Saudi Brothers in the two provinces of the Hejaz and the Ahsa' can also be explained by the long familiarity of their populations with the movement's ideology. In the Hejaz this was the result of traditional relations with Egypt, as well as of the long-standing Muslim reformist presence. In the Ahsa' it came from the region's strong commercial and family ties with neighboring Bahrain,[150] where Muslim reformists and then the Brotherhood had been very active since the 1920s. The names of 'Awad al-Qarni and Sa'id al-Ghamidi are frequently mentioned as prominent Brothers of the Hejaz.[151]

Although these four *jama'at* of Saudi Brothers claimed the same affiliation, they never succeeded, despite numerous attempts, in establishing formal unity.[152] According to some Saudi Brothers, this fact was what troubled the Egyptian supreme guide of the Brotherhood, Mustafa Mashhur, when he wrote his little book *The Unity of Islamic Action in a Single Region*.[153] But there were many bridges between groups. For instance, in the mid-1980s there was reportedly a coordinating council comprising the principal leaders of the Brotherhood *jama'at,* except that of al-Sulayfih.[154] Most accounts stress the high degree of cooperation among the various *jama'at,* particularly in the organization of student activities.[155] For the Brothers, this insistence on displaying a united front was in response to another consideration: the increasing power of a dissident and then competing *jama'a,* the Sururi *jama'a,* which appeared from the early 1980s to be a growing threat to their position in the marketplace of Islamic activism in Saudi Arabia.

One significant question concerning those *jama'at* is that of the link between the Saudi Brothers and the parent organization in Egypt and the other branches of the movement, brought together in the late 1970s within the international organization. At the individual and informal level it is clear that ties were long standing and numerous through organizations such as the WAMY, controlled by the Saudi brothers, and to a lesser extent through the Muslim World League. But formally it seems that these ties have never been given official status. Among the thirty-eight members of the supreme advisory council of the international organization of the Brotherhood in the 1980s, the Kuwaiti Islamist Abdallah al-Nafisi notes the presence of a Saudi directly appointed by the supreme guide and two others chosen in the name of regional representation. He goes on to say that the "Saudi emissary" (meaning the one appointed by the guide) was a naturalized Egyptian.[156] As for the two remaining Saudi representatives, they also were, according to Isma'il al-Shatti, who long represented Kuwait in the international organization, naturalized Brothers who remained officially connected to the branches of their native countries: Manna' al-Qattan and Abdallah al-Aqil, a historic member of the Muslim Brotherhood from Zubayr, who was based in Kuwait but had been granted Saudi citizenship. Al-Shatti adds that al-Sulayfih may sometimes also have been present, but because of his personal connections and never explicitly as a representative of his *jama'a.*[157] More recently, in July 2009, Egyptian authorities accused 'Awad al-Qarni of being a member of the international organization, a charge he has vehemently denied.[158]

An even thornier issue is that of the *bay'a* (oath of allegiance) that the members of the movement are theoretically obliged to pledge to the supreme guide. According to various accounts, the oath seems never to have been required of members of the *jama'at* in Saudi Arabia. The subject was so sensitive that the foreign Brothers who had been naturalized as Saudi citizens, considering themselves already bound by a *bayʿa* to the king of Saudi Arabia, refused to take another. This provoked dismay and sometimes anger among their comrades from other countries, who nonetheless accepted the fait accompli because of the strategic importance of Saudi Arabia for the movement.[159]

According to most available accounts, the second major Saudi *jamaʿa*, the Sururi *jamaʿa*, came into being in the late 1960s, that is, around the same time as the Brotherhood *jamaʿat*.[160] The term "Sururi" comes from the name of the Syrian Muhammad Surur bin Nayif Zayn al-ʿAbidin (known as Muhammad Surur), born in the Hawran in 1938,[161] who had been active in the Syrian Muslim Brotherhood since the mid-1950s.[162] From the early 1960s, when he was a middle-rank member, he started expressing strong criticism of the movement. Politically, he adhered to the still minority Qutbist line of Marwan Hadid, who advocated immediate armed struggle.[163] Religiously, he asserted that "to carry out *daʿwa*, one must be in agreement with the creed and the methodology of the pious ancestors."[164] In his view, this was not true of the Brotherhood, including the Damascus branch under ʿIsam al-ʿAttar, which, although reputedly more intransigent on the question of creed than the Aleppo and Hama branches, he criticized for its inclusivist and pragmatic tendencies.[165] In 1965 he decided to leave Syria and move to Saudi Arabia. There he at first taught mathematics and religion in the Scientific Institutes of Haʾil, Burayda (where one of his students was allegedly Salman al-ʿAwda),[166] and finally the Eastern Province.[167] In 1968, weary of "trying to reconcile [his] new convictions with [his] membership in the movement," he left the Brotherhood for good.[168]

He then decided, he explains, to adopt a new form of Islamic activism in harmony with Wahhabi theological precepts.[169] This was the origin of the Sururi *jamaʿa* in the Qasim region, where Muhammad Surur was based at the time. According to most accounts, however, although Surur was the instigator and, for some, the spiritual guide, he never really held the reins of the *jamaʿa*.[170] Surur hints at the same thing when he explains that when he began this "new activism," he had decided not to occupy the role of leader because he did not consider himself an *ʿalim mujtahid* (a sheikh sufficiently knowledgeable to be capable of religious interpretation) and because he was afraid to "burden this project of reform and renewal with the responsibility for [his] past errors."[171] A Saudi secondary-school teacher named Falah al-ʿItri therefore assumed leadership of the *jamaʿa*,[172] which became known in Islamist circles as the *jamaʿa* of Falah. Most foreign Brothers, unaware of the Saudi religious scene's internal dynamics, considered it to be a new Brotherhood *jamaʿa*.[173] But rivalry with the Saudi Brothers in the kingdom began from the outset. Muhammad Surur explains: "After leaving [the Brotherhood], I had to suffer harassment and hostility from my [former] associates. I do not think that anyone in the Muslim world has suffered as much from his brothers and former companions as I."[174] This is confirmed by the account of a young activist in the Saudi Brotherhood: "The movement veterans told us that the disputes with Surur and his *jamaʿa* had started almost from the beginning. No one understood where he got his money. Some said that he was getting funds from enemies of the *umma*."[175] In 1973 Muhammad Surur was asked to leave Saudi Arabia after reports were received denouncing his activities as subversive.[176] He then went to Kuwait, where he took advantage of the confusion outside Saudi Arabia about his allegiance to join the Muslim Brotherhood magazine *Al-Mujtamaʿ*. He gradually lost direct contact with the Saudi *jamaʿa* he had inspired and even tried to found a new movement, based in the Salimiyya neighborhood of Kuwait City, but the plan failed.[177] Ironically, it was not until the late 1970s, when Muhammad Surur was already far away, that the Saudi Brothers, especially in Riyadh, began to use the term "Sururi" to designate the *jamaʿa* of Falah.[178] Founded in the Qasim region, where it had established a monopoly in the sphere of Islamic activism, it had quickly spread to the capital, where it came up against competition from various groups of the Brotherhood. According to a former middle-rank member of the Sururi *jamaʿa*, "The term 'Sururi' was used [by the Saudi Brothers] in a disparaging manner. Giving the movement the name of a Syrian was intended to emphasize its foreign origin."[179]

Despite its polemical origins, the term "Sururi" soon became the *jamaʿa*'s most common designation also because its members refused to adopt a specific name, which would have amounted to acknowledging their status as a movement. They were satisfied with identifying themselves by vague names such as "the young" *(al-shabab),* "the pious" *(al-salihun),* or "the good" *(al-tayyibun)*[180] while distinguishing themselves from the Brothers, whom they called "comrades from the other side" *(al-zumala' al-akharun).*[181] As a young man who had been successively a Sururi and a member of the Brotherhood explained: "When you are with the Brothers, there always comes a moment when they explain to you that now you are in a *jama'a,* that you have obligations and duties. To leave, you have, for instance, to write a letter to the head of your study group. But in the Sururis it is very different. They never talk about the *jama'a.*"[182] This refusal by the Sururis to admit their status does not come merely from security considerations but is primarily ideological. In the traditional Hanbali-Wahhabi view, the fact of organizing into a *hizb* (party) or a *jama'a* (group) poses a problem because it contributes to dividing the community of the faithful, whereas there should be only one party, the party of God. This is also in part what motivates members of the Saudi Brotherhood to remain silent publicly about its existence.

The considerable mobilizing power of the *jama'at* was not affected by their clandestine character. This was because they were very cohesive and their leaders enjoyed a high degree of loyalty, largely derived from the groups' modes of socialization. Recruits, to begin with, were often very young, particularly those who joined through the circles for the memorization of the Koran or the committees for raising Islamic consciousness that were active in schools. By intervening in the primary socialization of children, the *jama'at* gave themselves the means to exercise deep influence. Young people later joined study groups and were expected, on pain of expulsion, to attend one or more discussions a week led by the member in charge of the group, the *murabbi* (educator), sometimes also called emir. Sometimes young members were assigned homework, such as a review of a book approved by the *jama'a,* which would be the subject of a debate. On weekends and during vacations, members of the group, under the supervision of their emir, would go to a camp together or take part in similar activities. These repeated experiences made it possible to bind the group around the emir, who exercised absolute authority. His orders, which sometimes came from his hierarchical superiors in the *jama‘a,* could not be questioned.[183] This situation sometimes approached a cult of personality: the emir set himself up as a model for his disciples to imitate.

In part voluntarily, because they felt some distrust of the surrounding world, and in part unwillingly, because their appearance and behavior tended to marginalize them, those young Islamists gradually found themselves disaffected with their society. Recounting his experience as a young Sahwi affiliate in a unique autobiographical novel, Muhammad al-Muzayni describes the magnitude of the break between the Sahwa and the rest of the social world:

> Under the influence of these austere teachings, we lost feeling for the everyday pleasures. . . . The details of people's faces disappeared, and our relations with them became brittle and superficial. From our point of view, they were all the same, there was no difference between a friend and a distant acquaintance, and that was even true for our close relations and our family. The idea of hanging on to our religion seemed to us the same as hanging on to burning coals. We felt the heat of the fires glittering in people's eyes. And we burned ourselves in that heat for the simple reason that we were alone in our short clothing that provoked ridicule and criticism from people who crossed our path, locked into the silence with which we responded to those faces that displayed expressions of surprise at seeing a *mutawwa‘* [someone showing the external signs of religiosity] who was someone other than the imam of the mosque.[184]

In this situation of near alienation, the study group and, more broadly, the *jama‘a* became all the more indispensable.

The use of incentives made it possible to strengthen even further the members' attachment to the *jama‘a.* A first kind of incentive was made up of the feelings the members were encouraged to develop. Some were positive. Muhammad al-Muzayni explains, "We always wanted to create bonds of love between ourselves, and we emphasized these ties by expressions like 'I love you in God,' or, as a form of introduction, 'your brother in God'."[185] Others were negative. Abdallah Thabit, author of a fictionalized autobiography with the theme of Islamist radicalization in Saudi Arabia, emphasizes the importance of fear "of the torments of hell and of death."[186] In the face of that fear, the *jamaʿa* seemed to be a "lifeline" in a directionless world.

Another sort of incentive was material in nature. The account of a Brother from the Eastern Province provides a good illustration: "At King Fahd University of Petroleum and Minerals [in Dhahran], the Brotherhood controls student housing. The competition is stiff for rooms on campus, because most students come from other regions of the kingdom. But anyone who belongs to the Brotherhood or joins up is certain to get what he needs."[187] Many accounts confirm this clientelistic use of the resources at the disposal of the *jamaʿat*. Because they enjoy real material benefits, their members are less likely to leave for fear of losing them.

It should be noted that at the periphery of the Sahwa, among those who did not belong formally to any *jamaʿa*, the authority exercised by the *jamaʿat* has traditionally been greater than one might expect. Because of the authoritarian character of a country where any other form of social organization, aside from the family and the tribe, is prohibited, there are few influences in competition with the *jamaʿat*. It is therefore not surprising to observe that the orders given by *jamaʿat* leaders not only induced nearly complete obedience among members but also had significant influence on the second and, to a lesser extent, the third circles of the Sahwa rotating around them.

A Favorable Context

Although the Sahwa was at first partly the product of foreign influences, it thus acquired an endogenous character by producing its own identity and its own organizations. In the favorable context of the 1970s, it experienced spectacular growth. The explanation lies primarily in the religious field, which provided the resources the Sahwis needed to conquer the social arena.

To understand what might have incited the Wahhabi ulema to provide such decisive support to the Sahwa, it should be recalled that since the 1950s the ulema had been suffering at the sight of a society that was becoming increasingly influenced by Western mores. This was at that time one of the main reasons for Muhammad bin Ibrahim's fierce opposition to a whole series of laws adopted by the government. But the segmented nature of the social arena had limited the capacity of a religious field lacking any real social infrastructure to mobilize people in its name. It was partly to compensate for this structural weakness that Muhammad bin Ibrahim, once he had moved into the inclusivist camp, was happy to accept the exiled activists of the Muslim Brotherhood, in whom he saw welcome reinforcements.

When he died in 1969, the major Wahhabi ulema changed tactics, not strategy. In the wake of his death, the government did all it could to limit the future capacity of the religious field to serve as a counterpower. An "official religious institution" *(al-mu'assasa al-diniyya al-rasmiyya)* was established, and its rules were set by the political field. The personal and informal were replaced by the collegial and bureaucratic. The title of mufti was abandoned, and various newly created organs shared the prerogatives until then jealously guarded by Muhammad bin Ibrahim. The chief one is the Committee of Senior Ulema (Hay'at kibar al-ʿulamaʾ), made up of three entities:[188] the Council of the Committee of Senior Ulema (Majlis hay'at kibar al-ʿulamaʾ), whose members (seventeen at the time of the council's creation) are appointed by royal decree and which issues fatwas on the major questions of society and on political issues directly affecting the regime;[189] its counterpart, the Permanent Committee for Research and Fatwas (al-Lajna al-daʾima li-l-buhuth wa-l-iftaʾ), which issues fatwas on personal matters;[190] and the General Office for the Management of Scientific Research, Fatwas, Preaching, and Guidance (al-Riʾasa al-ʿamma li-idarat al-buhuth al-ʿilmiyya wa-l-iftaʾ wa-l-daʿwa wa-l-irshad), which ensures "coordination among all the associations and organizations of preaching in Saudi Arabia."[191] Thus was established something akin to an organized hierarchical clergy, a relatively rare occurrence in the Sunni world. Most of its members belonged to the same "religious aristocracy," the vast majority of whom came from a string of villages in Najd, referred to by Nabil Mouline as the "Najdi crescent," who had dominated the religious field since the nineteenth century.[192] These great ulema families had traditionally arrogated to themselves the monopoly of Wahhabi religious knowledge, and they controlled—and blocked others from—its transmission networks.

Despite this reorganization, in order not to appear to be interfering with the autonomy of the religious field, the government had to make sure that the appointments it made appeared to respect the existing hierarchies within the field. For example, a figure like the influential Abdallah bin Humayd, one of the last exclusivists and a reputed critic of the government, was appointed to the Council of the Committee of Senior Ulema and then in 1974 became head of the Supreme Council of Justice (al-Majlis al-aʿla li-l-qadaʾ). The government nonetheless had various means to neutralize strong ulema. Collegiality made it possible to compensate for them with weak ulema. One such sheikh was Sheikh Abd al-Aziz bin Baz, born in 1909, vice president of the Islamic University of Medina since its founding in 1961, who was heavily handicapped by a *khadiri* genealogy, extremely rare among major Wahhabi ulema. In the case of Ibn Baz, the government even went so far as to promote his rise behind the scenes. It was widely reported that in the early 1940s Ibn Baz had demonstrated his independence by standing up to King Abd al-Aziz, whom he had criticized for having allowed American companies to set up shop in Saudi Arabia. As a result, he had earned a short prison term before repenting.[193] This "heroic deed," whether true or exaggerated, helped endow Ibn Baz with strong religious capital, indispensable to attain a high position in the field. After his appointment to the Council of the Committee of Senior Ulema in 1971, in 1975 he was appointed president of the Permanent Committee for Research and Fatwas and then to that of the General Office for the Management of Scientific Research, Fatwas, Preaching, and Guidance.[194]

Although the case of Ibn Baz is emblematic of the ways in which the construction of sacred authority can result from profane processes, it was not the only example of political intervention in the religious field. The essential activity of the royal family consisted of the distribution of resources. With the sudden influx of petrodollars engendered by the oil boom, it now had the means to tighten the collusive transactions that tied it to the dominant figures in the religious field. Much more effectively than in the past, when it had been unable to prevent repeated criticism from Muhammad bin Ibrahim, it could now provide abundant resources to the "senior ulema" and through them to the religious field as a whole, while co-opting anyone who rose to prominence there. This distributive function became an essential aspect of the General Office for the Management of Scientific Research, Fatwas, Preaching, and Guidance, which received the largest part of the budget allocated to the religious field and distributed it according to its own judgments. Autonomy was thereby apparently preserved, but it created no risks for the political authorities.

This reorganization of the religious field, coupled with the sudden influx of resources, produced a radical change. Whereas Muhammad bin Ibrahim had chosen independence, the "senior ulema" now preferred to systematically ratify royal decisions. The position of Ibn Baz on positive laws was emblematic of this change. Although Muhammad bin Ibrahim had not hesitated to make their adoption a red line separating believers from unbelievers, Ibn Baz added a much more restrictive condition before *takfir* could be pronounced, known as the condition of legalization *(shart al-istihlal)*.[195] This meant that there was a major act of impiety *(kufr abkar),* which alone merited excommunication, only when the government went directly against *shari'a* by making lawful what God's law had explicitly prohibited. Confronted with this contradiction with his master in an interview in a Kuwaiti magazine, Ibn Baz had no recourse but to answer: "Muhammad bin Ibrahim was not infallible. He was an *'alim* like the others, who was sometimes right and sometimes wrong. He was neither a messenger nor a prophet."[196]

Although these ulema no longer allowed themselves to take on the state, they nonetheless maintained undivided domination over the religious field, and the government continued to delegate control over it to them. Unlike the situation at the time of Muhammad bin Ibrahim, when religious infrastructures remained lacking, the religious field now enjoyed sustained development made possible by the dazzling growth of oil revenue, the annual amount of which was multiplied by seventy between 1970 and 1980.[197]

In this context, with colossal resources now at their disposal, the ulema of the official religious institution organized their resistance, so to speak, by acting directly on society. For example, they began to encourage, morally and financially, all initiatives, as long as they were not incompatible with Wahhabi norms, that were likely to strengthen the presence of Islam and, beyond that, their own presence in the social arena. With their blessing, Islamic associations, organizations, and circles proliferated in a largely deregulated field. "Saudi Islamist movements were practically acting in the open," according to Nasir al-Huzaymi, who was active in this period. "During the hajj [pilgrimage to Mecca], each one had its own camp and organized its own campaigns. I even remember a speaker from al-Jamaʿa al-Salafiyya al-Muhtasiba [al-Huzaymi's group] announcing over a microphone the opening of the movement's campaign, explicitly identifying it."[198] Former Sururi Sulayman al-Dahayyan says, "If you just pronounced the word 'Islam,' everything was possible."[199] The result was the establishment of what the Islamist intellectual Mazin al-Mutabaqqani described as "a veritable Islamic civil society."[200]

The emergence of this "Islamic civil society" was also made possible by the great freedom of tone and action that reigned in the religious field because the "senior ulema" in charge of policing it turned out to be incapable or unwilling. Mazin al-Mutabaqqani, writing about the late 1970s, observes:

It can be said with great certainty that no period of the Saudi regime was as marked by freedom of expression in the mosques and freedom of assembly as that period. I remember that in Jeddah alone there were about ten orators who delivered very vehement Friday sermons. No authorization from the Ministry of the Hajj and the *Waqfs* [religious endowments] or from any other government body was necessary. In the great mosque of Medina, it even happened that individuals stood up after the Friday prayer and started to criticize social morality, as well as the government in a subtle way. [Al-Mutabaqqani is probably referring here to preachers of al-Jamaʿa al-Salafiyya al-Muhtasiba, the first group to attack openly the "deviations" of society and then the government.][201]

In this lively environment the official religious institution acted as a kind of Vatican of the religious field, actively supporting all its legitimate agents—those who did not challenge the bases of the Wahhabi tradition—and always striving to remain aloof from their internal disputes. At the head of this Vatican sat Ibn Baz, a veritable Wahhabi pope whom all the participants in the Saudi religious field called *al-walid* (our father). He was known to have good relations with all movements in the field,[202] whether the Muslim Brotherhood and the Sahwa, the Ahl al-Hadith,[203] or even the Tabligh, a pietist and proselytizing movement from the Indian subcontinent that had grown exponentially in Saudi Arabia in the 1970s.[204] In turn, all these movements claimed support from Ibn Baz in their disputes, exhibiting fatwas and *tazkiyat* (recommendations) in which he had praised their merits.[205] The same thing applied, to a lesser degree, to the man considered his de facto second in the Wahhabi religious institution, Sheikh Muhammad bin ʿUthaymin.

Despite this proliferation of groups, the fact remains that because the Sahwa enjoyed a special position at the heart of the system, it was in the best position to benefit from the patronage of the official religious institution. In this context extracurricular activities experienced dazzling growth. Similarly, the *jamaʿat* were able to extend their grip on the Saudi social arena without hindrance.

The Unifying Potential of the Sahwa

The fact that the Sahwa's earliest base was the educational system had a decisive consequence. Because Saudi graduates were distributed throughout nearly all fields, the Sahwa was able to establish a presence throughout Saudi society. Above all, the considerable resources it received from the religious field following the oil boom of 1973 enabled it to develop its networks further and make its presence more felt everywhere. In the process, although it had been built up initially on the margins of existing norms, it soon imposed a new norm, through which it tended to homogenize the social arena. This occurred at every level. For example, the ubiquitous presence of Sahwis blurred the boundaries that had existed between "religious" and "liberal" neighborhoods, unifying space in a conservative mode. This led to the prohibition of cinemas, an increased presence of the religious police, who no longer hesitated to violate private space, and, more symbolically, the disappearance of female singers from Saudi television.[206] The Sahwa also imposed a new language that, like Islamist discourse everywhere else, represented a bricolage[207] of the language of the intelligentsia with that of the ulema, which it combined and transformed.[208] As a result, the rise to power of the Sahwa called into question the logic of segmentation that had long been dominant in the field of power and in Saudi society as a whole.

But this process had its limits. Desegmentation did not at this stage mean desectorization. The latent unification of the social arena came up against the vitality of the logic of the field. Even though the agents of the Sahwa may have shared the same ideological reference points, the fields to which they belonged imposed their rules on them. Sahwi ulema and Sahwi intellectuals (in the sense of educated laymen) did not act according to the same rationale and for the same stakes.[209] Similarly, although the *jama'at* were in principle transsectoral, in routine circumstances they operated in a very decentralized fashion. This was particularly true for the fundamental distinction between religious and lay members, who continued to be socialized in entirely separate ways. This separation was strengthened by the division in the Saudi school and university system between religious and secular institutions.

Further, although it is possible to describe the fundamentals of a Sahwi culture, it would be mistaken to think that those fundamentals were received uniformly. Because of the difference between the backgrounds, dispositions, and worldviews of Sahwi sheikhs and that of Sahwi intellectuals, they did not see their commitment in a completely identical way. For intellectuals, the Sahwi message, like Islamism elsewhere in the Arab world, tended to state an implicit challenge to the authority of the ulema. Men of religion have little place in the work of Qutb, who thought that "they don't understand the true spirit of the Koran."[210] But for the sheikhs, whether or not they belonged to the Sahwa, the ulema were still the "heirs of the prophets" *(warathat al-anbiya')*. The indispensable preeminence of the ulema was even a recurrent theme in the writings of Sahwi ulema.[211] This in itself might suggest that they felt it necessary to justify their authority to the rest of the Sahwa. There is what amounts to a paradox here: although the Sahwa constituted a latent principle of unity, it had to bow to field rules. In this case the rise of the Sahwa even strengthened field corporatism by offering to each side new discursive tools for asserting its superiority. The *jama'at* were also seen in distinct ways. For the ulema, they were akin to traditional networks for the transmission of religious knowledge, but some intellectuals saw them as a form of embryonic political organization.

Although the Sahwa represented an unprecedented principle of unity of the social arena, in routine circumstances it was thus unable to escape from the logic of sectorization. These intrinsic problems were soon joined by an extrinsic threat. Although it laid claim to a monopoly of Islamic activism, the Sahwa's position was soon challenged by new actors arising at its margins.

3

Resistance to Sahwa Ascendancy

In the face of Sahwa control over some of society's central institutions—particularly the educational system—and the movement's growing visibility, pockets of resistance sprang up in the religious sphere. In the name of a regenerated Wahhabism freed from Muslim Brotherhood influence, students of Sheikh Muhammad Nasir al-Din al-Albani formed a current known as Ahl al-Hadith and conducted a counteroffensive that soon took on the form of a violent challenge to the Saudi government with the 1979 takeover of the Grand Mosque in Mecca, perpetrated by a radical Ahl al-Hadith faction. At the same time, the last upholders of the exclusivist school of Wahhabism still active in Saudi Arabia, such as the Ikhwan of Burayda and a few isolated sheikhs in Riyadh, opened a second front against the rising power of the Sahwa. Finally, with the Afghan jihad of the 1980s, other Islamist rivals of the Sahwa came on the scene—the jihadis, whose influence was growing steadily.

Ahl-al-Hadith

Muhammad Nasir al-Din al-Albani,[1] the son of a Hanafi sheikh, was born in Albania in 1914. In 1923, after a secular government came to power following the dissolution of the Ottoman Empire, his family decided to leave the country and settle in Damascus. Nasir al-Din learned Arabic and the craft of watchmaking, and his father taught him the basic tenets of religion in strict accordance with the tradition of Hanafi jurisprudence. His education might have stopped there had he not shown as an adolescent a great appetite for reading. Taking advantage of the free time his profession left him, he spent long hours at *al-maktaba al-zahiriyya,* the first public library in Syria, which had been established in the early 1880s by one of the precursors of Muslim reformism, Tahir al-Jaza'iri.[2] He thereby learned about Islam from books rather than through the intermediary of the ulema.[3] In his twenties al-Albani was further influenced by Muslim reformism through his reading of the journal *Al-Manar,* the main vehicle for the movement's ideas. During the same period he frequented the salons of Muhammad Bahjat al-Bitar, a student of Jamal al-Din al-Qasimi, the leading figure of reformism in Syria.[4]

Primarily known for its modernizing tendencies, Muslim reformism was also characterized by its promotion of a certain form of *salafi* orthodoxy in creed and religious practices. Consequently, al-Albani's socialization in Muslim reformism prompted his hostility to Sufism and, more broadly, to popular Islam. But this hostility quickly took more radical forms and approached Wahhabi attitudes, as in his first book,[5] *Warning to Those Who Kneel Not to Mistake Tombs for Mosques.*[6]

At the legal level, also, al-Albani adopted and hardened the positions of the Muslim reformists: their calls for the rejection of *taqlid* (imitation of existing jurisprudence) in his case took the form of a categorical rejection of the four canonical legal schools *(madhahib).* To make a revival of *ijtihad* (interpretation of texts) possible, Muslim reformists, starting with the editor in chief of *Al-Manar,* Rashid Rida, had pointed to the need for a critical reappraisal of the hadith. However, they had not made it a central point of their doctrine because they continued to give reason and independent judgment a leading juridical role.[7] Even their critique of the hadith included, in addition to a technical critique of the *isnad* (the chain of transmission of the hadith, which comprises the names of all those who transmitted it), a reasoned critique of the *matn* (the content of the hadith).[8] Here as well, al-Albani's approach was inspired by but moved away from that of his teachers. Claiming adherence to the medieval school of the *ahl al-hadith* (advocates of the hadith), sworn enemies of the *ahl al-ra'y* (advocates of opinion), he asserted that the use of reason must at all costs be banned from the juridical process. To that end, hadith, which provides answers to problems with no solution in the Koran without calling on human reason, had to be placed at the heart of the process. The starting point for this was untangling the authentic *(sahih)* from the weak *(da'if)* in a body of hundreds of thousands of narratives. This was the subject of the science of the hadith *('ilm al-hadith)*, which al-Albani made the prime religious science, overriding law *(fiqh)*, which he saw as merely a corollary of hadith (he called it *fiqh al-hadith*).[9] But this science of the hadith had to be protected from the interference of reason. The critique of *matn* should therefore remain formal, that is, linguistic or grammatical. Only the *isnad*s could really be challenged, and studying them would make it possible to determine the authenticity of any particular hadith. For al-Albani, the most important discipline within the science of hadith was thus the "science of critique and fair evaluation" *('ilm al-jarh wa-l-ta'dil)*, which evaluated the morality and thereby the reliability of the transmitters; for this reason, it was also known as the "science of men" *('ilm al-rijal)*.

A final major difference between al-Albani and his reformist teachers was his extension of the critique to the whole body of hadith. Rashid Rida, for example, was reluctant to go that far, believing that a hadith *mutawatir* (with several chains of transmission) was beyond criticism.[10] In contrast, al-Albani did not hesitate to declare as weak certain hadiths from the two canonical collections of al-Bukhari and Muslim.[11]

Al-Albani became famous in Syria in the 1950s for his knowledge of hadith, which he began to teach informally in 1954.[12] By 1960 his popularity had begun to worry the government, and he was put under surveillance, even though he avoided taking any political positions.[13] He was therefore happy to accept the teaching position he was offered the following year in the newly established Islamic University of Medina. His name had been suggested by Sheikh Abd al-Aziz bin Baz, who was then vice president of the university. Ibn Baz was in a unique position within the Wahhabi establishment to understand and appreciate al-Albani. He had been a student of Sa'd bin 'Atiq, one of the few Saudi ulema who had traveled to India in the 1880s to study with the sheikhs of the Ahl-e Hadith movement, whose calls to reject *taqlid* and make hadith the heart of the Islamic corpus somewhat anticipated the positions upheld by al-Albani.[14]

For al-Albani, the battle with the more traditional Wahhabi was only beginning. As soon as he arrived in Medina, his presence provoked vigorous polemics in Saudi religious circles, which were still dominated by unacknowledged supporters of the Hanbali school of jurisprudence, beginning with Mufti Muhammad bin Ibrahim Al al-Shaykh. To make matters worse, al-Albani took the provocative step of asserting that although Muhammad bin Abd al-Wahhab was *salafi*—in conformity with the pious ancestors—with respect to creed, he was not *salafi* in matters of law *(fiqh)* because he was a Hanbali, and what is more, he had only vague knowledge of the hadith, demonstrated by the fact that one of his letters included a notoriously weak hadith.[15]

Al-Albani's attacks on the founding sheikh and his calls to conduct *ijtihad* outside the framework of the legal schools were direct challenges to the authority of the Wahhabi ulema, but these ulema were in an awkward position because Wahhabism had been characterized from its inception by an ambivalence between the theoretical aspiration to fulfill the duty of *ijtihad*—an aspiration that al-Albani did not hesitate to take advantage of—and a juridical practice that represented a continuation of the Hanbali school. Moreover, al-Albani's religious authority was difficult to challenge because his conception of the creed was impeccably Wahhabi. On several occasions fatwas by al-Albani created a scandal in the religious establishment. The Mufti, who refused to lower himself to respond to someone he still considered merely a second-rank scholar, deputized one of his principal assistants, Isma'il al-Ansari, to refute the Syrian sheikh.[16] But al-Albani was growing increasingly popular. The ulema of the kingdom were forced to wait for him to commit a serious mistake before they could get rid of him. The opportunity finally arose when, after a reappraisal of the authenticity of certain hadiths accepted by the Hanbali school, al-Albani argued, in a book titled *The Veil of the Muslim Woman*,[17] for women's right not to cover their faces. Saudi religious figures of all tendencies could not accept a position contrary not only to the Hanbali-Wahhabi legal tradition but even more to all the existing customs of Najd. Mufti Muhammad bin Ibrahim therefore found it easy to justify not renewing al-Albani's contract, and he was forced to leave the kingdom in 1963.[18] Al-Albani was arrested in Syria in May 1967 and then was released along with all political prisoners in June. The following year his protector, Ibn Baz, invited him to head the graduate division of the Faculty of *Shariʿa* of Mecca,[19] but the maneuver failed "because of opposition from the [Saudi] authorities,"[20] which indicates that he was still a controversial figure. He was imprisoned again a few years later in Syria for a period of eight months[21] and then left the country for Jordan in 1979.[22] Saudi Arabia partially rehabilitated him in 1975 by appointing him a member of the supreme council of the Islamic University of Medina.[23]

Although al-Albani taught for a relatively short time in Saudi Arabia,[24] his ideas had a lasting influence. They encouraged greatly renewed interest in the study of hadiths and their authenticity, and this interest spread to all segments of the religious field. As a former Islamist explained, "It had become a quasi-dictatorship of the hadith. When a sheikh quoted a hadith in a sermon or a lecture, he could be interrupted at any time by one of his students asking him: 'Has this hadith been authenticated? Has al-Albani verified it?' That could not help but strengthen the antipathy the ulema of the religious establishment felt toward al-Albani."[25] Indirectly and perhaps against his will, al-Albani also influenced the Sahwa, whose representatives saw in his appeals for a revival of *ijtihad* a way of legitimating political positions that diverged from the official line. But al-Albani always occupied a secondary position in Sahwi writings because his most ardent disciples were the Sahwa's sworn enemies.

Those self-proclaimed disciples of al-Albani adopted the name Ahl al-Hadith in reference to the medieval school that he had claimed to follow. By relying on al-Albani's positions for legitimacy, they broke both with the traditional Wahhabi religious establishment and with the Sahwa.

Al-Albani had denounced Wahhabi attachment to the Hanbali school and had put himself forward as an advocate of a regenerated

Wahhabism purified of elements contrary to the doctrine of the pious ancestors. By adopting these ideas, the Ahl al-Hadith were not challenging the spirit of Wahhabism, which they claimed to be defending, but rather the legitimacy of the institution that had made itself its guardian. However, this critique of the legal methodology of Wahhabism did not generally imply a critique of its social prescriptions—the prohibition of photography, music, and tobacco, for instance—which the Ahl al-Hadith mostly shared. Al-Albani's opposition to obligatory wearing of the *niqab* (which covers women's faces) should not lead one to think that the Ahl al-Hadith were much more liberal in social matters than the Wahhabis.

More than the Wahhabi religious establishment, with which relations remained relatively cordial thanks to Ibn Baz, the Ahl al-Hadith's nemesis was the Sahwa movement, which, like it, was an outsider in the Saudi religious field and had begun to really flourish in the early 1970s. The Ahl al-Hadith justified that opposition by referring to al-Albani's positions, particularly with respect to the Muslim Brotherhood, which they identified with the Sahwa, and with respect to political activity.

In 1966, at a time when Islamists of all tendencies, as well as figures of the Wahhabi religious establishment like Ibn Baz, were paying homage to the martyrdom of Sayyid Qutb, who had just been executed at Nasser's orders, al-Albani was one of the few sheikhs who dared express open criticism. He attacked Qutb's conception of creed, in which, he argued, he detected signs of the doctrine of the "oneness of being" *(wahdat al-wujud)*,[26] defined by the Andalusian mystic Ibn 'Arabi (1165–1240) and identified with Sufism.[27] Elsewhere al-Albani attacked the Brotherhood's founder Hasan al-Banna, denouncing his "positions contrary to the sunna" and insisting on the fact that al-Banna was not a "religious scholar" *('alim)*.[28]

These attacks derived from al-Albani's major criticism of the Brotherhood (and by extension, of its emulators in the Sahwa), that its members were more interested in politics than in religious knowledge and creed. In his view, the order of priorities should have been the opposite. He therefore adopted the following motto: "In the present circumstances, the good policy is to abandon politics."[29] At the same time, as he explained in a 1977 lecture, "All Muslims agree on the need to establish an Islamic state, but they differ on the method to use to achieve this goal. [For me], only Muslims' adherence to *tawhid* can dissipate the causes of disputes so that they can march toward their goal in unified ranks."[30] In this spirit he developed his theory of *da'wa*, which he called *al-tasfiya wa-l-tarbiya* (purification and education). He explained: "I call *tasfiya* the purification of Islam from everything foreign to it that corrupts it. To do that, it is first necessary to purify the sunna of all the forged and weak hadiths that it contains and then to interpret the Koran in the light of this now-authentic sunna and the notions and conceptions inherited from the pious ancestors." As for *tarbiya*, al-Albani sees it as consisting of "inculcating in young people the authentic Islamic creed drawn from the Koran and the sunna." The radical difference between this approach, which favors creed over politics and the individual over the state, and the approach advocated by the Muslim Brotherhood was spectacularly illustrated in a fatwa from al-Albani that called on the Palestinians to leave the occupied territories of Gaza and the West Bank because they were no longer in a position to practice their religion properly there, and between creed and land, it was creed that should come first.[31]

The Ahl al-Hadith made these positions taken by al-Albani into an ideological paradigm leading to a much more systematic anti–Muslim Brotherhood and anti-Sahwa argument. At a time when the Brotherhood was at the height of its power, the attacks by al-Albani and his disciples produced a vigorous response. In the 1970s the Brotherhood adopted "a boycott of [al-Albani's] lectures and of everything associated with his *da'wa*," and several accusatory articles were published in the Brotherhood's journal *Al-Mujtama'*.[32] By the 1980s al-Albani's stance was no longer tenable because he was hoping to establish himself as one of the most respected religious authorities in the Muslim world and needed to appear as less confrontational. He therefore attempted to moderate his positions, saying about Sayyid Qutb, for example, "Yes, it is necessary to refute [Qutb], but with restraint, and without excess.... Yes, it is a duty to refute him.... But that does not mean that we should show hostility toward him, or forget that he has some virtues. The important thing is that he is a Muslim and an Islamic writer, according to his own understanding of Islam ... that he was killed in the name of *da'wa*, and that the men who killed him are the enemies of God."[33] However, this did not affect the position of the Ahl al-Hadith, who stuck to al-Albani's earlier stances.

The Ahl al-Hadith also adopted a certain number of practices that distinguished them in the social arena. Most of these practices were based on fatwas by al-Albani that were contrary to the Hanbali-Wahhabi consensus. For instance, the Ahl al-Hadith tended to follow the injunctions about prayer that al-Albani had collected in a short book that had created a scandal when it was published, *The Characteristics of the Prophet's Prayer*.[34] Among other things, al-Albani argued for the need to add "and his blessings" *(wa barakatuhu)* after pronouncing the ritual "peace be with you and the mercy of God" *(al-salam 'alaykum wa rahmatullah)* with which Muslims end their prayer, and for authorization to wear shoes while praying inside a mosque. Likewise, in his form of prayer the position of the hands differed from the one that had been recommended by centuries of Hanbali-Wahhabi jurisprudence. Because of the conspicuousness of these ritual differences, the appearance of the Ahl al-Hadith provoked disputes in the mosques of Medina and other Saudi cities where the movement had taken root. This sometimes led followers to assemble in mosques under their control. These mosques did not have a *mihrab* (a niche inside the mosque indicating the direction of Mecca), because the Ahl al-Hadith considered it a *bid'a* (blameworthy innovation).[35]

With regard to dress, like the Sahwis but even more intransigently, the Ahl al-Hadith prohibited the wearing of the *'iqal* (cord fastening the *shmagh* or the *ghutra*, cloths Saudis wear on their heads). For the tunic *(thawb)*, they demanded that it come down only to midcalf ("four fingers below the knee"), largely to distinguish themselves from the Sahwis, who wore it at ankle length. Some followers of the Ahl al-Hadith pushed the imitation of the Prophet so far as to wear their hair long, again distinguishing themselves from the Sahwis, who considered it in the interest of their movement to be well groomed.

The Ahl al-Hadith began to coalesce in the 1960s in Medina. They were especially found in a religious institute called Dar al-Hadith (the House of the Hadith) that had existed since 1931 but had been attached in 1964 to the Islamic University of Medina, where it functioned as the department of hadith until an official department was established in 1976.[36] Al-Albani often lectured there in the 1960s, and some of his students, among them Ali al-Mazru', taught there. With the increasing influence of the Ahl al-Hadith, there were vigorous disputes between al-Albani's disciples, who were already seen as "revolutionaries" of the hadith, and supporters of a more traditional conception of the study of the hadith, such as the president of the institute, Umar Falata. Al-Albani's influence soon reached the other principal place where the hadith was taught in the Hejaz, the Dar al-Hadith al-khayriyya (the Charitable House of Hadith) in Mecca.[37] Small groups inspired by the Ahl al-Hadith also appeared in Riyadh and Burayda with their own leaders, who were often imams from a mosque.[38]

The development of the Ahl al-Hadith soon confronted a major obstacle. Despite their growing presence in the hadith institutes of Medina and Mecca, they never controlled those institutions, which remained in the hands of traditional specialists in the study of the hadith. Unlike the foreign members of the Muslim Brotherhood and their Sahwi disciples who dominated the educational system, the Ahl al-Hadith had no organizational base for the mass diffusion of their message. Partly to overcome this situation and to make their action more effective, some followers of the Ahl al-Hadith started considering the creation of an organization. They thereby hoped to follow the example of the Tabligh (to which some of them had previously belonged),[39] whose members were very actively engaged in proselytism in Saudi Arabia at the time and were, along with the nascent Sahwa, one of their major rivals.

Al-Jama'a al-Salafiyya al-Muhtasiba and the 1979 Events

The emergence of the Ahl al-Hadith in Medina resulted in a notable increase in vigilantism in that city.[40] Indeed, al-Albani's young disciples thought that it was their duty to remedy the failings of the committees of *mutawwa'un* (religious police) theoretically in charge of enforcing the Islamic injunction of "commanding right and forbidding wrong." They even showed particular zeal, not hesitating to destroy posters representing human beings. These actions led to repeated clashes with the inhabitants of Medina, who were not used to being called to order in this way.[41]

In 1965 the authorities finally cracked down on these practices. A small group of Ahl al-Hadith followers who had attacked a store displaying female mannequins was arrested for destruction of private property. Two foreign students at the Islamic University of Medina who were implicated, Abd al-Rahman Abd al-Khaliq from Egypt and Umar al-Ashqar from Jordan, were deported. Both later became famous. Abd al-Khaliq founded the major *salafi* movement in Kuwait, the Society for the Revival of Islamic Heritage (Jam'iyyat ihya' al-turath al-islami), and al-Ashqar became one of the most prominent ideologues in the *salafi* wing of the Jordanian Muslim Brotherhood.[42]

This incident gave those among the Ahl al-Hadith who were considering setting up an organization a decisive argument. They asserted that only by institutionalizing their action within a framework connected to the official religious institution would they be guarded against such misadventures. Six of them, including Juhayman al-'Utaybi, decided to establish the "*salafi* group" *(al-jama'a al-salafiyya)*. They went to see the vice president of the Islamic University of Medina, Sheikh Abd al-Aziz bin Baz, to tell him of their plans and to offer him the position of guide of their group. Already in his papal role, Ibn Baz accepted their proposal after suggesting that they add to their title the adjective *muhtasiba* (practicing *hisba*, which is closely associated with commanding right and forbidding wrong), which they agreed to do. Ibn Baz probably insisted on this because of the fierce debate then going on about the legitimacy of collective action in the light of Wahhabi norms. As in the case of the *jama'at,* the more traditional scholars believed that the creation of groups or parties resulted in fragmenting the community and was thus a potential source of dissension *(fitna)*. By calling itself *muhtasiba,* the new organization was hoping to appear to be performing the same function as the religious police (whose official name, the Committee for Commanding Right and Forbidding Wrong, relates it to the same duty of *hisba*), which was considered acceptable by Wahhabi ulema.

Ibn Baz appointed a vice guide to take charge of the group's everyday activities, Sheikh Abu Bakr al-Jaza'iri, of Algerian origin. Al-Jaza'iri had been a professor at Dar al-Hadith and later at the Islamic University of Medina since the 1950s and was known for his unwavering loyalty to the political and religious authorities. An administrative council of five members was set up at the head of al-Jama'a al-Salafiyya al-Muhtasiba (JSM), including al-Jaza'iri and four of the founding members. The members of the new organization called each other *ikhwan* (brothers).

Although the group was established in the 1960s, it seems that it was only in the early 1970s that it began to experience rapid growth. It was then that it set up headquarters in a two-story building in Medina built for that purpose, located in the lower-class neighborhood of al-Harra al-Sharqiyya. The building, administered by a Yemeni student at the Islamic University of Medina named Ahmad al-Mu'allim, was called the House of the Ikhwan (Bayt al-ikhwan). From then on it was the site for daily classes in the science of hadith and weekly lectures addressed to the members of the JSM.[43] Among the lecturers were ulema formally affiliated with the JSM, notably Abu Bakr al-Jaza'iri, Ali al-Mazru', and Muqbil al-Wadi'i, as well as sheikhs close to the group, like the Pakistani Badi' al-Din al-Sindi, who belonged to the Ahl-e Hadith, and the Egyptian Sa'd Nada, a member of Ansar al-Sunna al-Muhammadiyya.[44] According to some accounts, al-Albani also delivered lectures when he came to Saudi Arabia on the occasion of the hajj.[45] The House of the Ikhwan contained a small mosque with no *mihrab,* where, far from prying eyes, the members of the movement could perform the ritual gestures prescribed by the Syrian sheikh.

In time the movement expanded, and its organizational structure grew more complex. Other Houses of the Ikhwan modeled on the one in Medina were set up in the major cities of the kingdom. In 1976 the movement had branches in Mecca, Riyadh, Jeddah, Taif, Ha'il, Dammam, and Burayda.[46] Each of them was headed by an emir. In Medina the JSM had grown so much that other houses were built to accommodate the members of the movement. At some point the JSM even controlled entire neighborhoods, where, for instance, one could no longer find anyone selling or smoking tobacco. Within the Medina headquarters, several sections were set up to share the tasks. One, headed for a time by Juhayman al-ʿUtaybi, was in charge of arranging members' trips to the various branches of the JSM, another of receiving guests, and a third of organizing preaching tours for missionaries who went into the countryside to spread the group's message and recruit new members.[47] Branches of the movement were also set up in other Gulf countries, particularly in Kuwait, where the JSM had many followers.[48]

The increasing visibility of the JSM in Medina and in other cities from the mid-1970s on revived tensions both with the Wahhabi ulema and with the advocates of a more traditional conception of the hadith. The trigger was a 1976 fatwa by Ali al-Mazruʿ authorizing believers to continue eating after the first call to prayer of the day during Ramadan, on the grounds that this indicated only the time of prayer and not sunrise. This opinion, contrary to the Hanbali jurisprudence upheld by the Wahhabi ulema, provoked their anger, and al-Mazruʿ was barred from teaching in the Mosque of the Prophet in Medina.[49] During the same period Muqbil al-Wadiʿi was summoned by two of the highest religious authorities in Medina—ʿAtiyya Salim, a judge on the city's tribunal, and Umar Falata, who had become assistant secretary general of the Islamic University of Medina—to be questioned about twelve of the JSM's religious practices that they considered problematic. The point of no return was reached in the late summer of 1977 when a small group of ulema led by Abu Bakr al-Jazaʾiri, who had gone over to the views of the Wahhabi ulema, and Muhammad al-Subayyil, one of the imams of the Grand Mosque of Mecca, went to the House of the Ikhwan in Medina to try to persuade the group to abandon its "heterodox" religious practices. A meeting was held on the roof of the building that led to a particularly violent verbal confrontation between Juhayman al-ʿUtaybi, whose charisma had for some years made him the real leader of the JSM, and al-Jazaʾiri, the titular vice guide.[50] The clash ended with a massive rallying of the group's members, particularly the youngest, to Juhayman's rejection of compromise, while al-Jazaʾiri proclaimed the return of the House of the Ikhwan to the Hanbali-Wahhabi norm. Driven out of their headquarters, Juhayman and his followers moved to Juhayman's house. When the other branches of the JSM learned of the split, they declared their allegiance to Juhayman.[51]

This first schism marked the start of an important development within what remained of the JSM. Since its creation the JSM had essentially been a pietist movement, concerned primarily with individual religiosity and ignoring the state and politics. However, its new leader, Juhayman al-ʿUtaybi, had very definite views on the legitimacy of the Saudi state. He was born in the first half of the 1930s in the *hijra* of Sajir, where members of the tribe of ʿUtayba who had joined the Ikhwan Bedouin army during the period of King Abd al-Aziz's conquests had settled. His father had fought alongside Sultan bin Bijad, one of the legendary leaders of the revolt that the first Ikhwan had launched against the Saudi monarch, angered by his willingness to adopt the rules of realpolitik to transform his chiefdom into a modern state. In Sajir, Juhayman had grown up with tales of glorious battles won by his ancestors and their betrayal by the king who had founded the modern Saudi state. He thought of himself as the heir of the first Ikhwan, whom he defended vigorously both in his discussions with other members of the JSM[52] and in his writings. "We wish to clear from all suspicion our Ikhwan brothers who conducted jihad in the name of God by being faithful to him, while this state and its malevolent ulema described them as Kharijites, so that there are people today for whom the question is so confused that they do not even ask God to grant them his mercy," he declared in one of his letters.[53] This identification with the first Ikhwan had shaped his political consciousness and made him a determined opponent of the power of the Al Saʿud.

His rise to power in the JSM had led to an initial politicization of the movement, but in 1977 the JSM was by no means a force in opposition to the Saudi state. However, Juhayman's criticisms of the government, particularly on the question of the rate of interest adopted by Saudi banks, which he identified as usury *(riba)* that was prohibited by religious texts,[54] gave the ulema of the official religious institution and the members of the Sahwa an ideal pretext to urge the authorities to curb an increasingly troubling competitor.[55] Accused, wrongly according to most accounts, of arms possession and planning an insurrection, the JSM was the target of a first wave of arrests in December 1977, affecting about 150 people, among whom were some of the major figures in the movement, including Ali al-Mazru‘, Muqbil al-Wadi‘i, the future Mahdi Muhammad al-Qahtani, and Badi‘ al-Din al-Sindi.[56] They were released a little more than a month later,[57] thanks to the intercession of some ulema of the official religious institution, with Sheikh Ibn Baz in the forefront.

Warned of imminent arrest by an informer, Juhayman managed to escape. This was the beginning of a long period of wandering in the desert regions of Najd that lasted until November 1979. During this time the police were constantly on his trail, and he came close to being arrested on several occasions, but every time he managed to escape with the help of Bedouins who supported his cause or were nostalgic for the first Ikhwan, with whom they identified him.[58] From his internal exile Juhayman remained in close contact with the JSM, continuing to lead it more than ever. At this time a real cult of personality started to grow up around him.[59] While he was on the run, he was continuously surrounded by a small group of loyalists who acted as intermediaries with the rest of the movement. They took charge of transmitting his orders to the secret meetings regularly held in remote locations, which Juhayman did not attend for security reasons.[60]

The now-unchallenged control of the JSM by Juhayman accelerated the politicization of the movement's discourse in the form of an increasingly marked opposition to the Saudi state. This development went hand in hand with the radicalization of some members of the movement following the first arrests, which had shocked the ranks of the JSM and indeed the religious field as a whole. It was the only time since the first Ikhwan in the 1920s that religious activists had been subjected to a repression until then reserved for nationalist and leftist militants. At the same time, the JSM paradoxically came out of the ordeal with renewed self-confidence, particularly in relation to its perennial rival, the Muslim Brotherhood. In the words of a JSM activist quoted by former member Nasir al-Huzaymi, "No one is now better than anyone else; just as the Muslim Brothers endured repression [in their countries of origin], some of us have also endured repression in the name of *da‘wa*."[61]

The twelve letters the movement published between mid-1978 and early 1979 are the best source for studying the discourse of the JSM during this period.[62] After cross-checking sources and an intertextual study of the letters, it seems clear that they appeared in three groups of one, seven, and four letters. Although they are known as the "Letters of Juhayman," only eight of them bear his signature. He had difficulty writing because he had left school at the end of primary school and was probably dyslexic. For this reason, he dictated the content of those eight letters to the future Mahdi Muhammad al-Qahtani and to Ahmad al-Muʿallim, who wrote them down. Of the four remaining letters, one is signed by al-Qahtani, another by a Yemenite named Hasan bin Muhsin al-Wahidi, and the last two by "one of the students of religion" (ahad talabat al-ʿilm), a pseudonym for another Yemenite, Muhammad al-Saghir.[63] Somewhat surprisingly, the letters were printed in Kuwait on the presses of the left-wing newspaper Al-Taliʿa (The Vanguard) that the JSM had been able to contact through the family connections of one of its Kuwaiti members, Abd al-Latif al-Dirbas. The paper's owners, delighted to make their contribution to the struggle against the "reactionary regime" of the Al Saʿud, even agreed to bill the JSM at cost.[64]

The distribution of the first letter, titled Clarification Concerning the Community of the One God Designated as Guide of the People,[65] in which Nasir al-Huzaymi participated, occurred simultaneously in the major cities of the kingdom on August 31, 1978. The second group of letters, known as the Seven Letters, was printed and distributed a few months later, on the occasion of the hajj, in November 1978. After several months the four final letters were printed and distributed.[66] Some of these letters were submitted to Ibn Baz by members of the movement, and according to Juhayman, he approved their general content, limiting his criticism to the fact that Saudi Arabia was specifically targeted.[67] The first letter was even shown to him before publication, and his remarks, received after printing, were stamped onto each copy before distribution.[68]

The distribution of these letters gave rise to a second wave of arrests of members of the JSM. Muqbil al-Wadiʿi says that he was accused of being the author of the letters, which he denied vehemently. Like the other members of the movement who had been rounded up, he spent three months in prison, after which the Saudis were released and the non-Saudis were given deportation notices.[69] Thanks to the intercession of Ibn Baz, al-Wadi'i was given an extension to defend his master's thesis at the Islamic University of Medina. Two months later, with his degree in his pocket, he had to leave Saudi Arabia and settled in northern Yemen, in the small town of Dammaj, where he established a religious institute he named Dar al-Hadith.[70]

The first of the "Letters of Juhayman" is the least politically explicit because it does not directly concern the Saudi state, but rather is intended to situate the followers of Juhayman in relation to the other components of the religious field. Juhayman explains that this field is divided into three main groups. The first considers that "the foundation of religion is to combat the worshipers of tombs . . . and to struggle against Sufism and innovators" (he is referring here to the Wahhabis). A second group "says the same thing as the first, but adds that it is also necessary to combat the blind attachment to the schools [of jurisprudence] and calls for a purification of the hadith from what has been added on, which is its major preoccupation" (here he is speaking of al-Albani and the Ahl al-Hadith). The third group "devotes itself to refuting communism and . . . concentrates its efforts on the control of important positions in governments with the aim of seizing power" (here he is describing the Muslim Brotherhood). He adds, following the anti-Brotherhood line of the Ahl al-Hadith, that this third group "does not act in the manner of the Prophet, relies on ideas, has adopted the principle of hiding behind many curtains, and hastens to betray anyone under whose power it finds itself." As for the first two groups, "What [they] do . . . is unquestionably right, but [the problem is] that they attack individuals who have no power, while they remain silent in the face of attacks on the religion of God committed by the powerful." In Juhayman's view, the JSM has to distinguish itself from all these groups, including the Ahl al-Hadith, from which it originated, by sticking to the strict application of the principle of the "community of Abraham" *(millat Ibrahim)*, according to which, following the example of the prophet Abraham in the Koran, the believer must dissociate himself completely from the infidel, whether his impiety is the result of his religious or his political practices.[71] In other writings he associates this principle with that of allegiance and rupture, central for the proponents of the exclusivist school within Wahhabism.[72] Although this school probably influenced Juhayman, he nonetheless remained faithful to the spirit of the Ahl al-Hadith in his writings by refusing to base his argument on anything other than verses of the Koran and especially hadiths and, consequently, refraining from quoting the writings of Sulayman bin Abdallah Al al-Shaykh and his disciples. That is, he integrated into his ideology certain elements of the Wahhabi exclusivism of the nineteenth century while at the same time endeavoring to go beyond it.

This identification with the exclusivists might suggest that Juhayman was decreeing *takfir* (excommunication) against the Saudi regime, which he accused "of making religion a means of preserving its interests in this world, of putting an end to jihad, of pledging allegiance to Christians (America), and of spreading evil and corruption among Muslims."[73] But in his letter titled *The State, Allegiance, and Obedience,* he explicitly denounces *takfir* of rulers[74] and shifts the debate to another area, the legitimacy of the state. In other words, refusing to frame the debate in terms of individuals, he formulates it in terms of institutions. In his view, both the actions and the non-Quraysh origins of the Al Sa'ud make the oath of allegiance *(bay'a)* that unites the Saudi government with its people null and void *(batila)*.[75] Obedience is therefore not owed to it and should even be forbidden when its policies contravene divine law.[76] For the committed Muslim, this implies keeping a distance from a state seen as illegitimate, which means refusing to occupy any office in its institutions and remaining apart from the "corrupt" educational system, even more so because it is controlled by the Muslim Brotherhood and the Sahwa.[77] As a consequence, around this time most of the JSM members who were still students at the Islamic University of Medina or elsewhere abandoned their studies, and those who were employed by the state resigned their positions. The same distinction between individuals and institutions appears in Juhayman's view of the ulema. He was extremely critical of the official religious institution but refused to implicate individual ulema, showing particular consideration for Ibn Baz, whom he respected to the end.[78]

This refusal to declare *takfir* may explain the compensatory messianic tendencies of Juhayman. How can one hope to put an end to the prevalent "corruption" if one refuses to excommunicate the rulers, a necessary condition for their overthrow, except by relying on divine intervention? The question of the Mahdi (the Islamic equivalent of the Messiah) and the end of days had certainly been a matter of interest in the JSM since its creation, but it did not become central in the movement's discourse until the summer of 1978, under the influence of Juhayman.[79] The *Seven Letters* were published and distributed in late 1978, and the first of them was devoted entirely to this theme. In it Juhayman presented all the hadiths on the subject of the Mahdi that he considered authentic and tried to connect them to recent historical events in the Arabian Peninsula (the conquests of King Abd al-Aziz, the defeat of the first Ikhwan, and the overthrow of Sharif Husayn, in particular), in order to demonstrate the imminence of the end of the world.[80]

During the same period Juhayman declared that a dream had confirmed to him that his companion Muhammad al-Qahtani, the former imam of al-Ruwayl Mosque in Riyadh who had joined the movement several years earlier, was the Mahdi. He had the attributes described in the corresponding hadiths: he was named Muhammad bin Abdallah, like the Prophet; he called himself *sharif*, claiming therefore to be a descendant of the Prophet;[81] and his physical appearance conformed to the descriptions of the Mahdi. For these reasons, the idea that al-Qahtani was the Mahdi had long been common among his small circle of disciples in al-Ruwayl Mosque.[82] When Juhayman adopted this position, it became the official line of the JSM.

But Juhayman's messianic rhetoric did not have unanimous support in the movement. Among the skeptics, some, like Nasir al-Huzaymi, left the JSM for good, while others, out of loyalty to the group or because they were captives of Juhayman's charisma, decided to stay. It was the small core that emerged from this final split that carried out the armed seizure of the Grand Mosque of Mecca on November 20, 1979.

The rise of messianism in the JSM was accompanied by a growing militarization of the group, seemingly justified by the inevitability of a conflict with the forces that, according to tradition, would oppose the coming of the Mahdi. In late 1978 JSM members began to collect weapons smuggled from Yemen.[83] Then, during the months before the attack, they trained in the use of weapons in the countryside near Mecca and Medina.[84] Finally, they set a meeting in Mecca in October 1979 during the pilgrimage, a few weeks before the beginning of the fifteenth century of the Hegira.

Taking inspiration from a hadith quoted by the compiler Abu Dawud that predicts the coming of a religious reformer *(mujaddid)* at the beginning of every century, Juhayman chose the first day of the year 1400 (November 20, 1979) to storm the Grand Mosque and consecrate al-Qahtani as the Mahdi between the corner of the Kaaba containing the black stone *(al-rukn al-aswad)* and the footprint of the prophet Abraham *(maqam Ibrahim)*, as tradition required. For Juhayman and his followers, this act was to mark the beginning of the reign of the Mahdi, a prelude to the end of the world. This explains the relatively small quantity of provisions (dried milk, dates, and bread for a week)[85] that the two hundred to three hundred attackers had hidden in the mosque's basement a few days before the attack, because they thought that they would have to defend themselves only until the prophecy was realized.

Of course, nothing of what tradition promised actually happened. Only a few days after the beginning of the siege, al-Qahtani was killed by the Saudi forces massed around the building. Juhayman did everything possible to prevent news of his death from spreading among his followers for fear of undermining their morale.[86] As a result of this, some militants believed that the Mahdi was still alive years after the siege, even though his lifeless body had been shown from every angle on Saudi television. It took two weeks for the Saudi forces, with the logistical assistance of a team from the French National Gendarmerie Intervention Group (GIGN) under the command of Captain Paul Barril, to restore control over the mosque.[87] Sixty-three of the rebels arrested by the Saudi authorities, those against whom there was proof that they had fired on the security forces, were executed, and the others were sentenced to long prison terms.[88] A wave of arrests ensued that affected most of those who had had any contact with the JSM in the months or years preceding the siege, including Nasir al-Huzaymi, who spent seven years in prison. Within a few weeks the Saudi branch of the JSM was almost completely dismantled. The few members who managed to escape took refuge in the desert regions in the north of the country, among the same Bedouins who had helped Juhayman when he was on the run, or in Kuwait and Yemen, where the JSM still had solid bases. Al-Albani, denounced as the one who had inspired Juhayman, was persona non grata in Saudi Arabia for several years.[89]

The saga of the JSM and the tragedy of Juhayman's Ikhwan had decisive effects on the evolution of Islamism in Saudi Arabia. It led first to a split among the Ahl al-Hadith, the outlines of which had begun to appear in 1977. Some Saudi followers of the Ahl al-Hadith, sometimes designated in the lexicon of the religious field as the revolutionary Ahl al-Hadith *(ahl al-hadith al-thawriyyun)*,[90] preserved the radical legacy of Juhayman while mostly underplaying his embarrassingly unorthodox messianism. Within the Saudi Islamist family, they constituted what might be called the rejectionist Ahl al-Hadith (or simply rejectionist) branch to emphasize the fact that its primary ideological position was rejection of the legitimacy of the Saudi state and withdrawal from society.[91] Rejectionists were organized in autonomous and very close-knit communities,[92] sometimes centered in apartments re-creating the environment of the House of the Ikhwan in Medina. An example was the community of Bayt Shubra (the house of Shubra, named after the Riyadh neighborhood where it was located) in the early 1990s, whose members included Mishari al-Dhayidi, Abdallah bin Bijad al-ʿUtaybi, and Fahd al-Shafi.[93] Others were located in the desert, far from the corruption of cities, such as the community of the *hijra* of Bahra, whose members included two future leaders of al-Qaeda in the Arabian Peninsula, Saʿud al-ʿUtaybi and Saʿud al-Qahtani. Because these communities refused to have any interaction with the state, they tended to derive their livelihood from commerce, particularly in dates and incense, looked on with particular favor because the Prophet himself was a merchant.[94]

Because most of the ulema of this tendency in Saudi Arabia had been killed or arrested after the siege of Mecca, the young men who joined the rejectionists—a few dozen in the early 1980s and a few hundred by the end of the decade—often went abroad to study, particularly to Kuwait, where the local branch of the JSM was still active, with ulema such as Jabir al-Jalahma and Abd al-Latif al-Dirbas.[95] Others went to Pakistan to study with Badiʿ al-Din al-Sindi,[96] who had been deported from Saudi Arabia because of his ties to the JSM, and, more often, to Yemen, where Muqbil al-Wadiʿi had made the Dar al-Hadith institute he had established in Dammaj a base for the rejectionist Ahl al-Hadith.[97]

Beginning in the very early 1990s, many of these rejectionists came under the influence of Abu Muhammad al-Maqdisi (whose real name was ʿIsam Barqawi), a Palestinian sheikh born near Nablus in 1959 and raised in Kuwait, where he was socialized first in Qutbist and then in JSM circles.[98] Al-Maqdisi made a name for himself in Islamist groups in the mid-1980s with a book titled *The Community of Abraham*.[99] Based in part on the foundational letter by Juhayman, *Clarification Concerning the Community of the One God Designated as Guide of the People*,[100] the book offers an original synthesis of the ideas of the JSM with the core elements of Qutbism. Al-Maqdisi adopts Juhayman's concept of the community of Abraham and, like him, associates it with the principle of allegiance and rupture. But unlike Juhayman, he does not hesitate to declare *takfir* against "those rulers who do not govern according to God's revelation."[101]

Most important, al-Maqdisi preserved from his time with the JSM undying hatred for the regime of the Al Saʿud. His most famous book, *The Manifest Evidence of the Impiety of the Saudi State*,[102] applies the concept of the community of Abraham to the Saudi case. Well versed in the Wahhabi tradition, he included many quotations from the works of exclusivist ulema of the nineteenth century. He thereby helped revive a legacy that the inclusivist turn taken by the Saudi religious establishment had obscured, but he also subverted its meaning. Hence in this work exclusivist anathemas are hurled not just against "miscreants"—Sufis, Shiites, and others of the "impious"—as they traditionally were, but also against the "un-Islamic rulers," referring to the Al Saʿud. Under the influence of this book, many rejectionists adopted against the Saudi state the practice of *takfir* that they had previously condemned and developed a growing interest in studying the exclusivist heritage that they had neglected because they considered it too "Hanbali." Al-Maqdisi even came to Saudi Arabia to see his disciples in person in the early 1990s, making a notable visit to Bayt Shubra.[103]

Contrary to the rejectionists, the majority of the Ahl al-Hadith—particularly the few ulema who had managed to reach an institutional position in the Saudi system, notably at the Islamic University of Medina, like Rabi' al-Madkhali—submitted to the Saudi authorities and, anxious to avoid any identification with their rejectionist cousins, thereafter demonstrated unstinting loyalty. Many of those who adopted this position were former sympathizers of the early forms of the JSM, like Falih al-Harbi[104] and Rabi' al-Madkhali himself.[105] In the wake of the events of 1979, they had to clear themselves of the suspicion that weighed on everyone who had ever had ties to the movement. To do this, they also swept under the rug the criticisms of Wahhabism in Ahl al-Hadith discourse and concentrated primarily on opposition to the Sahwa. To indicate their political preferences, these individuals will be called the loyalist Ahl al-Hadith.

Despite their different positions, the ties between loyalist and rejectionist Ahl al-Hadith members always remained ambiguous, if only because they shared the same body of writings and the same anti-Sahwa terms of reference. It is therefore not surprising that in the 1980s Muqbil al-Wadi'i, who was denouncing Saudi Arabia from his native Yemen, and Rabi' al-Madkhali, who considered it a model Islamic state, maintained more than cordial relations. It was also not uncommon for individuals to move from one group to another, for example, Yusuf al-Dayni, a loyalist who converted to rejectionism in the early 1990s.[106] Similarly, in the Afghan jihad, a warlord like Jamil al-Rahman was able to secure support from both camps.

The consequences of the events of 1979 were not limited to the Ahl al-Hadith alone. Before those events the Saudi government had been convinced that danger could come only from the intelligentsia and had granted great freedom to religious actors. The occupation of the Grand Mosque of Mecca was therefore a terrible shock. The authorities concluded that they had to take action, discreetly but firmly, to weaken all informal groups operating at the margins of the religious field. To exclude independent preachers, beginning in 1982 it was required that every mosque orator have an official authorization from the Ministry of Hajj and *Waqfs*. Although this ministry was subject to government orders, it was headed by a cleric, which made it possible to preserve the illusion that this was a measure of self-regulation taken by the religious field.[107] Along with the JSM, a collateral victim of this policy was the Tabligh, which was targeted by an official ban in the early 1980s that was ratified, again to preserve the illusion of autonomy, by certain dominant authorities in the religious field.[108] Another movement that had been treated with consideration by the government, the Ikhwan of Burayda, was also affected.

As a result, "institutional" Islam strengthened its dominance over the Saudi religious field. This heavily benefited the Sahwa, which greatly increased its influence. For instance the authorities further encouraged the proliferation of extracurricular activities connected to Sahwi circles, particularly the summer camps, because they alone "made it possible to attract and control young people in a society where there is nothing else for them."[109] The geopolitical situation also favored the Sahwa. In the context of the Islamic cold war that had been raging between Riyadh and Teheran since the establishment of the Islamic Republic in 1979, only the Sahwis were able to present a sophisticated response to the revolutionary discourse of Khomeini's followers. They played the role that their predecessors in the Muslim Brotherhood had played in the past against Nasser. They thereby became indispensable to the regime, which offered them an ever-increasing number of opportunities.

The Last Bastions of Exclusivist Wahhabism

Alongside the Ahl al-Hadith and their offshoot the JSM, a second front against the increasing dominance of the Sahwa over the Saudi religious field arose at the same time from the last bastions of the exclusivist school of Wahhabism, whose followers were now a minority compared with the inclusivists. Two of those bastions were the community known as the Ikhwan of Burayda and a group of sheikhs in

Riyadh, the most famous and influential of whom was Hamud al-Tuwayjiri.

The community known as the Ikhwan of Burayda originated in the early decades of the twentieth century. At that time the dominant religious positions in Burayda were occupied by the Al Salim family, whose rise was a reward for their unshakable loyalty to the Al Saʿud during the troubled times that had preceded Abd al-Aziz's conquest of the Qasim in 1906.[110] Umar Al Salim, then the leading figure in the family, was also an eminent representative of the exclusivist school of Wahhabism. In that capacity he actively participated in the ideological indoctrination of the first Ikhwan fighters and even became a judge of one of the first and largest of the *hijras* (camps where the Ikhwan settled), al-Artawiya.[111] But when the Ikhwan rebelled, rather than supporting the men who claimed to be his disciples, Umar Al Salim again chose loyalty to the Al Saʿud. This earned his family continued dominance over religious affairs in Burayda despite the obvious contradiction between his exclusivist commitment and the new inclusivist line defended by Abd al-Aziz. It was not until Umar Al Salim died in 1943 that the family's local monopoly and that of the exclusivist school began to significantly decline.

Thanks to the efforts of a student of Umar Al Salim, Fahd al-ʿUbayd, born around 1910, the exclusivist school nonetheless managed to maintain an informal presence in Burayda in the guise of a small group known as the Ikhwan of Burayda (Ikhwan Burayda).[112] Like Al Salim in his time, these Ikhwan combined unfailing loyalty to the Saudi government with uncompromising exclusivism that went along with great distrust of technological modernity, notably the telephone, television, and even audiocassettes with religious content. As a result, although they acknowledged the legitimacy of the royal family and did not hesitate to pray for its safety, the Ikhwan of Burayda ordered their followers to keep a distance from everything connected to the Saudi state, whose truly Islamic character they called into question. They insisted on not receiving pay from the state, devoting themselves to commerce in imitation of the Prophet, particularly in dates, a trade that was flourishing in the Qasim. They likewise refused to send their children to Saudi public schools because they taught geography and

English, subjects that they saw as tarnished with impiety and that did not take sufficient heed of the principle of allegiance and rupture *(al-wala' wa-l-bara')*. To remedy the situation, in the early 1960s rich members of the Ikhwan established a school where the teaching exclusively followed their principles, known as the private scientific school *(al-madrasa al-'ilmiyya al-ahliyya)*.[113] In 1980 some of the Ikhwan who had been living in the center of the town took a further step and decided to come together in al-Khubaybiyya, a western suburb of Burayda reserved for them where they could live as they liked.[114]

Just as surprising as the existence of this group of a few hundred diehards in the city of Burayda was the great indulgence the authorities showed toward them from the very beginning. This was not simply a matter of laissez-faire and respect for the autonomy of the religious field; in the case of the Ikhwan of Burayda, the Saudi government knowingly took exceptional steps to allow them to maintain their specific character. The authorities, for example, gave them special identity cards without photographs in order not to offend their beliefs. Also, state schools allowed former students of the private scientific school—which did not hand out diplomas, because learning there was to be pursued "for the love of God" *(li-wajhillah)* and not "to gain advantages in this world" *(li-ajl al-dunya)*—to continue their studies in the general system after a brief test of their knowledge.[115]

The Ikhwan of Burayda saw the increasing power of the Sahwa beginning in the late 1970s and particularly in the 1980s as both a godsend and a threat. It was a godsend because the growing presence of religion in the public sphere that accompanied the Sahwi upsurge gave rise to renewed interest in a group that was being marginalized. As former member Mansur al-Nuqaydan explains, in the 1970s the Ikhwan of Burayda had been reduced to a few dozen members, primarily sheikhs. In the 1980s their ranks grew considerably, reaching as many as five hundred, mostly young men, by the end of the decade. However, the growing dominance of the Sahwa was also seen as a threat because of the remarkable hostility between the two groups. In the view of the Ikhwan of Burayda, the Sahwis—whom the Ikhwan called *al-khuluf* (latecomers, as opposed to the *salaf,* the first)—neglected *'ilm* (religious science) and did not pay enough attention to creed. For example, they thought that the works of the Sahwa's major ideologues, Sayyid and Muhammad Qutb, among others, were full of distortions of the true Islamic norm embodied by Wahhabi exclusivism. The Ikhwan of Burayda therefore tried to oppose the Sahwi upsurge by fighting on two fronts, ideological and organizational.

Several of their sheikhs wrote and distributed refutations of Sahwi ideology and those who inspired it. One of these sheikhs was Abdallah al-Duwaysh, born in 1953 and considered by the early 1980s a leading scholar in the movement. In a refutation of Qutb's *In the Shade of the Koran,* he denounced the supposedly rationalizing tendencies of the Egyptian ideologue and, as al-Albani had done, "his adherence to the dogma of the oneness of being [*wahdat al-wujud*]."[116] These attacks created a stir in Sahwi circles in Burayda and provided one of their rising stars with an opportunity to make a name for himself. He was Salman al-ʿAwda, a young sheikh born in 1956 who had been socialized from his earliest years in Sururi circles, where he had allegedly been taught by Muhammad Surur Zayn al-ʿAbidin and Abd al-Rahman al-Dawsari in person. In 1988 al-ʿAwda was awarded a master's degree in sunna by the annex of Imam University in Burayda and later taught there.[117] In 1985 he wrote *Muslims between Extremism and Laxity,*[118] in which he denounced the "extremists" who rejected technological modernity, particularly electricity and automobiles, in an indirect but obvious reference to the Ikhwan. Abd al-Karim al-Humayd, one of the most austere of the Ikhwan sheikhs (he was known for living in a dried-mud house and traveling only on horseback), felt particularly targeted and answered with an "insult poem" *(hijaʾ).*[119] Abdallah al-Duwaysh took up his pen to write *The Considered Refutation in Response to the One Who Speaks of Extremism,*[120] in which, point by point, he denounced al-ʿAwda's accusations, which he attributed to the Sahwis' incurable ignorance of true religious science.

The Ikhwan of Burayda also opposed the expansion of the Sahwi organizational apparatus, particularly the proliferation of circles for the memorization of the Koran, arguing that they were a blameworthy innovation because nothing of the kind existed in the time of the Prophet. Hence in the mosques the Ikhwan controlled, such as the Great Mosque of Burayda directed by Sheikh Abdallah al-Qarʿawi, they categorically refused the establishment of these circles.[121] An emblematic episode in this conflict came in 1986 with the distribution of several pamphlets denouncing the practices of these circles, particularly the annual ceremony of awarding diplomas conducted by the Charitable Association for the Memorization of the Koran of Burayda. The president of the association, the respected sheikh Salih al-Bulayhi, was attacked by name. Although these pamphlets were anonymous, their authors, among whom were Sulayman al-'Alwan, a young Ikhwan sheikh expert in the hadith, and Mansur al-Nuqaydan, were found and arrested on a personal complaint by al-Bulayhi to the governorate of Burayda.[122]

This unprecedented arrest of members of the Ikhwan of Burayda illustrates the complete transformation that was taking place in the relationship between the group and the Saudi government. It also reflects the ascendancy of the Sahwa over Saudi state institutions and the great suspicion, in the aftermath of the events of 1979, aroused by any informal religious group. In the mid-1980s the Saudi state ended the special treatment the Ikhwan had enjoyed until then. They were now subject to the logic of the religious field alone and were placed at the mercy of the Sahwa, which was much more powerful than they. In 1985 the Sahwis secured the dismissal of the imam of the Great Mosque of Burayda, Abdallah al-Qar'awi.[123] The Ikhwan then suffered a severe blow in 1987 when, using the arrest of al-Nuqaydan and al-'Alwan as a pretext, the local authorities closed the private scientific school, which became a regular public school, required to follow the national curricula.[124]

Although the Ikhwan of Burayda were the most visible manifestation of the persistence of exclusivist Wahhabism in 1980s Saudi Arabia, they were only a part of the phenomenon. Various sheikhs, based primarily in Riyadh, also continued to follow the line set by the most famous Wahhabi ulema of the nineteenth century. The most influential of these sheikhs was Hamud al-Tuwayjiri, born in 1916 in al-Majma', where he was the student of one of the last great exclusivists of the twentieth century, Abdallah bin Humayd, who died in 1982.[125] In 1963 Hamud al-Tuwayjiri made a name for himself with a famous letter, a veritable exclusivist profession of faith, *The Masterpiece of the*

Companions on What Is Said about Allegiance, Love, Hatred, and Repudiation. In it he rejected any "allegiance to the enemies of God, namely, the apostates, the hypocrites, the Jews, the Christians, the Zoroastrians, and the other infidels," and warned against "becoming their friend, praising them, treating them peaceably, giving them precedence in meetings, and anything that glorifies them in word or deed."[126] Other books of his vehemently attacked any imitation of infidels *(al-mushabaha bi-l-kuffar)* and the use of modern technology.[127] Not surprisingly, Hamud al-Tuwayjiri was also one of the first Saudi ulema to attack Sayyid Qutb and the Muslim Brotherhood[128] and to denounce the methods of the Sahwa, particularly the use of Islamic chants and theater.[129]

In the 1970s their shared opposition to the Sahwa and a worldview not devoid of similarities brought these Wahhabi exclusivists together with the JSM.[130] Members of the "Ikhwan of Medina" (as the JSM was known in Burayda) in their early days often went on study trips to the Ikhwan of Burayda, and Hamud al-Tuwayjiri's book *The Precious Gift Offered to All about What Has Been Written on Sedition, Combat, and the Signs of the End of the World,*[131] which, quite unusually for a Wahhabi, deals with the question of the Mahdi, was one of Juhayman's points of reference.[132]

However, dissension soon broke out between these exclusivist Wahhabis and the JSM. It first derived from the attachment of the former, in accordance with Wahhabi tradition, to Hanbali jurisprudence. The disagreement appeared clearly when Juhayman wrote:

We wanted to study with ulema, and for that purpose we looked for ulema who rely on the Koran, the sunna, and nothing else, and who do not allow themselves to be turned away from the truth by fear or desire. So we went to see the sheikhs of the Qasim [the Ikhwan of Burayda], but we found them to be mere readers, not ulema. For they defend the *madhhab* [the Hanbali school of law], and what the supporters of the *madhhab* have said, and ignore what goes against it, even if that is the application of the sunna. And with regard to sunna, they have no scruples about teaching weak or forged hadiths.[133]

Another reason for dissension was the loyalty of the Ikhwan of Burayda to the royal family, which was completely incompatible with the political positions taken by Juhayman. From 1977–1978 on, relations between the JSM and the exclusivists, particularly the Ikhwan of Burayda, significantly deteriorated, the latter in the end choosing to remain loyal to the Saudi state. Their loyalty initially protected them from the wrath of the authorities after the Mecca episode. A few years later, however, they were subjected to repression by the political authorities, as noted previously. The ensuing feeling of betrayal provoked the radicalization of some followers of the group. In many cases those radicalized Ikhwan joined the rejectionist trend, as happened with Sulayman al-'Alwan, who later became a neojihadi sheikh, and Mansur al-Nuqaydan, who became associated with the community of Bayt Shubra.

The Jihadis as Additional Rivals

The Soviet invasion of Afghanistan in 1979 provoked anger and indignation throughout the Muslim world, including Saudi Arabia. A few years later the conflict started attracting hundreds and then thousands of Arab Islamists, among whom were many Saudis who wanted to join what they saw as a legitimate jihad. With their commitment, a new form of internationalist Islamism came into existence in Saudi Arabia, jihadism, but from the outset it came up against the essentially "nationalist" conception that the Sahwis had of Islamist activism. Moreover, the jihadis in the kingdom relied on a powerful network, the development of which was seen by the Sahwa as a challenge to its hold over Saudi youth. For all these reasons, despite appearances, jihadism was constructed more in opposition to than in cooperation with the Sahwa.

From the start of the Soviet invasion of Afghanistan, the Saudi Sahwa expressed its unanimous support for the Afghan people and for the resistance being organized under the various mujahideen factions. A large spontaneous collection of donations sprang up in the kingdom, particularly around mosques, and it became formalized in 1981 when the state created the High Committee for the Collection of Donations for Afghanistan (al-Hay'a al-'ulya li-jam' al-tabarru'at li-afghanistan), overseen by Prince Salman.[134] Jihad against the Soviets gradually became one of the favorite themes of Sahwi sermons, which constantly called for solidarity with the "Afghan brothers."

In the mid-1980s serious divergences began to appear. These were the result of the activism of the Palestinian Muslim Brother Abdallah 'Azzam, who was born in 1941 and held a doctorate from al-Azhar University in Cairo. Ever since he had moved to Islamabad in 1981, 'Azzam had made himself the herald of a jihad in which he saw a unique opportunity to bring the Muslim world out of its long-standing lethargy by giving a new direction to the Islamist movement.[135] In 1982 he began publishing a series of motivating articles in the magazine *Al-Mujtama'*, widely read in Saudi Arabia, in which he recounted the divine favors accorded to the martyrs *(karamat al-shuhada')* of the Afghan jihad and called on young Arabs to "join the caravan."[136]

With the writing in 1984 of his major book titled *The Defense of Muslim Territories Is the First Individual Duty*,[137] 'Azzam took a decisive step. In it, speaking as a religious scholar, hence in the form of a fatwa, he proclaimed that defensive jihad *(jihad al-daf')* in Afghanistan—understood primarily in military terms—was an individual duty *(fard 'ayn)* for all Muslims. He thereby broke with classic Islamic jurisprudence that considered jihad an individual duty only for the inhabitants of a country under occupation and presented it as a collective duty *(fard kifaya,* which does not imply the participation of everyone) for the rest of the *umma.* 'Azzam even made it the first of all duties, before the five pillars of Islam, notably prayer. It also applied to adolescents, who in this particular case did not need their parents' consent, and to members of an Islamist movement, who did not need the approval of their leadership.[138] To put it plainly, any capable Muslim, wherever he might be, ought to join the fight to avoid committing the gravest of sins.

In the introduction to the book, 'Azzam boasted of support from various religious authorities, some of them linked to the Muslim Brotherhood, such as the Syrians Abdallah 'Alwan and Sa'id Hawwa, while others came from the heart of the Wahhabi religious institution, like the sheikhs Ibn Baz and Ibn ʿUthaymin. As evidence of the support of Ibn Baz, ʿAzzam asserted that the sheikh had promised to write a preface for his fatwa once ʿAzzam had abridged it, but that did not happen because he had not had an opportunity to see the sheikh again.[139] It is likely that Ibn Baz, keen to maintain his papal position, preferred to provide discreet support to ʿAzzam while not officially coming out in his favor. Indeed, in the various public fatwas he issued about the conflict in Afghanistan, Ibn Baz always cautiously adhered to the line set by classic jurisprudence.[140] As for Ibn ʿUthaymin, he merely said that ʿAzzam's letter "ought to be presented to the [General Office for the Management of Scientific Research] for examination," which did not imply approval of its contents.[141]

ʿAzzam's fatwa quickly became a source of vehement disputes in the Islamist field in general (so much so that ʿAzzam's membership in the Muslim Brotherhood was suspended),[142] and in the Saudi religious field in particular. The vast majority of Sahwi sheikhs refused to see the jihad in Afghanistan elevated to the rank of "first individual duty for every Muslim," believing, in the words of Salman al-ʿAwda, that "donating the price of an airline ticket is better than going there."[143]

The reasons offered for this Sahwi refusal were officially of two kinds. First, the Afghans were "bad Muslims" because they belonged to the Maturidi school (close to the Ashʿarite school, which allows some room for reason, earning denunciation from the Wahhabis) in matters of creed, followed the Hanafi school of jurisprudence, and were inclined toward the practice of Sufism. This was the opinion of a rising star in the Sururi wing of the Sahwa, Sheikh Safar al-Hawali, born in 1950 in al-Baha in Asir, a professor in the department of creed in Umm al-Qura University. In the mid-1980s he delivered a lecture titled "The Notion of Jihad" in response to ʿAzzam. In it he explained that "the problem [of the Afghans] is not a problem of territory [ard] and land [turab], but a problem of tawhid." Hence tawhid, not jihad, should be the primary individual duty. This was all the more true because "a mujahid in Afghanistan or elsewhere who knows tawhid and the truth of faithfulness to God is worth a hundred, or a thousand, or perhaps even three thousand, because that is one of the reasons for victory if

God wills it." Hence, al-Hawali concluded, "Jihad by the sword is probably the type of jihad that has the least value. . . . Anyone can play a role in it, in contrast to jihad by preaching, where very few can be useful. The essential jihad on which we should concentrate our efforts, and without which any jihad is futile, consists of bringing people together, training them, educating them."[144] This position taken by the Sahwa fostered a lively debate in jihadi circles. For instance, the principal religious scholar of the Egyptian group al-Jihad, Abd al-Qadir bin Abd al-Aziz, wrote a short book in 1990 explicitly targeting al-Hawali, in which he endeavored to demonstrate that *tawhid* and jihad were compatible.[145]

To justify their rejection of 'Azzam's ideas, the Sahwis also developed a geopolitical argument. As Safar al-Hawali put it, the Afghan conflict was nothing more than a vast operation aimed at putting Muslim blood at the service of American interests and objectives.[146] At a more general level, the Sahwis were primarily "nationalists" attached to the Arabian Peninsula, the cradle of Islam (Salman al-'Awda called it the "peninsula of Islam," *jazirat al-islam*), and they believed that it should be the principal focus of their activities.[147] As Safar al-Hawali said in his response to 'Azzam: "If we consider that the first duty of our era—*tawhid*—has been accomplished and we move on to another duty, which is to rid Muslim countries of the enemies of religion who are occupying them, what is the first place where we should start? The Arabian Peninsula. . . .[148] Because countries differ in their importance just as enemies and duties differ."[149] It was thus primarily on this point that the Sahwis came up against the internationalism of the jihadis. But that was not the only reason for the differences between the two groups.

The two official arguments put forth by the Sahwis to justify their refusal to urge young Saudis to go to fight in Afghanistan were joined by an unstated reason. The Sahwis were worried that their disciples would free themselves from networks under their leadership and join a new network outside their control that was taking shape around 'Azzam.[150]

Along with his calls to "join the caravan," by October 1984 'Azzam had established in Peshawar, on the Pakistani border with Afghanistan, the Bureau of Services *(maktab al-khadamat)* intended to provide logistical help to candidates for jihad.[151] The money needed for its operation was provided by Osama bin Laden, a rich Saudi of Yemeni origin born in 1957, who had first been active in the *jama'a* of the Brothers of the Hejaz, but had recently come under the influence of 'Azzam.[152] While the Arab fighters were at first divided among the training camps of the various Afghan factions, an important step was taken in 1986 when Bin Laden came out of the shadow of his mentor to set up his own camp, the Den of the Companions (Mas'adat al-ansar), intended exclusively for training Arabs.[153] Separate training for Arabs thereafter gradually became the rule. It is clear that repeated criticism by the Sahwa had had an impact, and that this was intended as a way of "protecting" Arabs from the Afghan environment.[154] In addition, as 'Azzam's former right-hand man Tamim al-'Adnani suggests, Bin Laden may have already had a plan to set up an independent force of Arab mujahideen, so he thought that "jihad could be useful to us, to train us, more than we could be useful to it. It was as though his priority was to benefit from the jihad rather than to help it."[155]

Recruitment on Saudi territory began very informally when a few figures based in the Hejaz joined 'Azzam's enterprise.[156] In addition to Osama bin Laden, they included Wa'il Julaydan, a Medina businessman, and Sheikh Musa al-Qarni, a professor at the Islamic University of Medina and a former activist in the Saudi Muslim Brotherhood.[157] Each of these pioneers then returned to preach among his friends and family, assembling a small group of disciples who followed him to Afghanistan.[158] It is particularly telling that the Den of the Companions was initially made up of Bin Laden and four of his childhood friends, all of whom came from Medina.

But by the end of 1986 recruitment was beginning to be organized more systematically, with small groups of individuals generally gathered around a sheikh who, usually after having gone to Afghanistan, encouraged and assisted potential candidates for the jihad.[159] The candidates received support from certain institutions, including the Saudi Red Crescent and the International Islamic Relief Organization (Hay'at al-ighatha al-islamiyya al-'alamiyya),[160] but also from the Saudi government, which provided through Prince Sultan 75 percent of the cost of an airline ticket for anyone who wanted to join the fight.[161] In addition, this was a period when Abdallah 'Azzam and Osama bin Laden were enjoying growing popularity, which enabled them to travel frequently to Saudi Arabia to give speeches encouraging young men to join them, while jihadi magazines such as *Al-Jihad,* which 'Azzam began publishing in 1984, had a growing readership.

One of the primary targets of the jihadi recruiters was the young Sahwis who, despite the reluctance of their leaders, were predisposed by their training to back the Afghan cause with enthusiasm. After all, Sahwi circles had praised, in obviously theoretical terms, the virtues of jihad and had often spoken about the wounds of the Muslim world. The testimony of a young Sahwi who became a jihadi illustrates how recruitment took place in a summer camp:

> When I was in the camp, I heard that young jihadis [*shabab al-jihad*] were talking in one of the units. At that time I was wild about news of the jihad and those who were in it. . . . But the leaders of the camps and of the *da'wa* groups [the *jama'at*] were afraid that the young jihadis would approach the young Sahwis [*shabab al-da'wa*], who would adopt the behavior of the jihadi movement. For the idea of going to Afghanistan was foreign [to those leaders]; the only thing that interested them was gathering donations, clothing, supplies, but nothing more. But some young jihadis managed to get into the camp and recruit among the young men who were there; they took some of them with them to Afghanistan.[162]

It was among the young members of the network of the Saudi Muslim Brotherhood, to the dismay of their leaders, that the jihadi recruiters seem to have had the greatest success.[163] There are several possible reasons for this. Despite the relative harmonization that took place in the course of the 1980s, the Muslim Brothers still represented the least rigorist element of the Sahwa and were thus less likely than the Sururis to be concerned about the nature of the Afghans' creed. Moreover, the pioneers of the Afghan jihad had all belonged to the Muslim Brotherhood, 'Azzam in Jordan and Bin Laden, Samir al-Suwailim (known as Khattab, future leader of the jihadis in Chechnya),[164] and

Musa al-Qarni in Saudi Arabia. Al-Qarni, before leaving the Brother-hood to join the jihad, had even held the particularly coveted position in Sahwi networks of dean of student affairs at the Islamic University of Medina.[165] It is therefore likely that personal connections played a role. This explains why the vast majority of Saudi jihadis came from regions where the Brotherhood was solidly established, primarily the Hejaz, followed by the Eastern Province and to a lesser degree, the northern region bordering on Jordan. The Qasim, an exclusive bastion of the Sururis, in contrast, had negligible representation.[166]

Attempting to take advantage of the existing dynamic, in August 1988 Osama bin Laden secretly established in Peshawar an organiza-tion named al-Qaeda (al-Qa'ida, the base). It adopted the rather vague program "to lift the word of God and to make His religion victori-ous."[167] Al-Qaeda thereafter sought to impose itself as the backbone of a close-knit jihadi network defined primarily by a shared identity, the fruit of common experiences and influences, and based on personal connections developed in Pakistan and on the Afghan battlefield.[168] This process of constructing a jihadi identity was facilitated by the separate training of Arabs beginning in 1986. From then on, the Arab jihadis no longer thought of themselves as regular mujahideen but as the Arab ansar (al-ansar al-'arab), who, like the first converts in Me-dina at the time of the Prophet (those who were historically known as the ansar), were entrusted with making themselves the vanguard of an Islamic army that, according to 'Azzam, would fight "until all other lands which formerly were Muslim come back to us and Islam reigns within them once again. Before us lie Palestine, Bukhara, Lebanon, Chad, Eritrea, Somalia, the Philippines, Burma, South Yemen, Tashkent, Andalusia."[169] In Saudi Arabia this common identity was reinforced by the welcome extended to fighters returning from Afghanistan, who were treated as national heroes until the late 1980s, and by their grow-ing stigmatization in the early 1990s that led to the first repressive measures (interrogations, short periods of imprisonment, and the like) taken against them.

Beginning in the late 1980s, the jihadis were subjected to new influ-ences in the "great breeding ground of world Islamism" that Peshawar had become.[170] They came into contact with movements that made the fight against Arab regimes an absolute priority, like the radical Egyptian Islamist organizations al-Jihad and al-Jamaʿa al-Islamiyya that had been reorganized in Pakistan after the release of their members who had been sentenced in the trial of President Sadat's assassins.

The year 1989 marked a turning point in this evolution. First, Abdallah ʿAzzam, father and guarantor of jihadi ideology in its classic form, was assassinated, most probably by radical Egyptian Islamists.[171] Second, Abu Muhammad al-Maqdisi took up residence in Pakistan.[172] There he wrote his famous book *The Manifest Evidence of the Impiety of the Saudi State*,[173] published in mid-1990, a few months before the Gulf War, which met with some success among the Saudis in Peshawar. Although the jihadis maintained the primacy of their internationalist commitment for a few more years and, at least in appearance, kept silent about their hostility to the royal family,[174] the influence of al-Maqdisi and the Egyptian radicals prepared the way for them eventually to join the opposition to the Saudi regime after 1993.

The late 1980s also witnessed a comeback of the Ahl al-Hadith current, which had been severely weakened after the events of 1979 and the ensuing repression. This reversal was made possible by the positions its members took on the Afghan jihad. Whether they were loyalists or rejectionists, the Ahl al-Hadith thought, like the Sahwa, that *tawhid* came before jihad, and that priority had to be given to the purification of the creed. But while the Sahwa, without becoming involved on the ground, supported the Afghan resistance, the Ahl al-Hadith refused to endorse movements that in their view were only offshoots of the Muslim Brotherhood and were therefore not much better than the Communists they were fighting.

This stance of the Ahl al-Hadith was greatly appreciated by the Saudi government, which, although it could not yet say so openly, was growing increasingly suspicious of the Afghan jihad, which it knew was marked by the increasing influence of radical Islam hostile to the regimes of the Middle East. Some observers even argue that the split between Bin Laden and ʿAzzam was encouraged by the Saudi government because it feared that it did not have sufficient control over the Palestinian.[175] But Bin Laden's rise to power changed nothing in the situation because he quickly laid claim in turn to an autonomy that the authorities of the kingdom found intensely displeasing. This convergence between the regime's unofficial position and the line taken by the Ahl al-Hadith enabled the movement to return to favor. The loyalist Ahl al-Hadith began their rehabilitation and were discreetly given access to platforms and positions of influence, while the rejectionist Ahl al-Hadith, headed by the Yemeni Muqbil al-Wadiʿi, entered into a kind of temporary truce with the Saudi government. But cooperation between the two sides did not stop there.

The Ahl al-Hadith had long-standing contacts in Afghanistan with a sheikh from Kunar, born in 1934,[176] who had studied with Ahl-e Hadith ulema in Pakistan[177] and was using the pseudonym Jamil al-Rahman (his real name was Maulavi Husayn). When he returned to Afghanistan in the 1960s, he became known for his *salafi* tendencies. In 1965 he established an association named Jamaʿat al-Daʿwa ila-l-Kitab wa-l-Sunna (Group Preaching for the Koran and the Sunna),[178] intended to purify local Islam of the "blameworthy innovations" connected to Sufism and Hanafi jurisprudence. With the onset of the Afghan conflict, he joined the Hizb-e Islami, the faction of Gulbuddin Hekmatyar, where he was in charge of education.

In the second half of the 1980s Jamil al-Rahman decided to declare his independence. According to Musa al-Qarni, "Some Gulf merchants, Saudis and Kuwaitis, came to see him and said to him: 'Sheikh Jamil al-Rahman, you are a *salafi*, how can you fight with Hekmatyar? . . . How can you conduct jihad under the banner of a Muslim Brother? . . .' They then promised him money and support on condition that he leave the Hizb and form an independent command."[179] Thereafter, his Jamaʿat al-Daʿwa ila-l-Kitab wa-l-Sunna (which Muqbil al-Wadiʿi eloquently described as the "Ahl al-Hadith of Afghanistan")[180] became a satellite of the Ahl al-Hadith, and unofficially of the Saudi government, on Afghan soil. In addition to abundant donations from rich merchants close to the Ahl al-Hadith or the royal family, it received complete support from Nasir al-Din al-Albani,[181] as well as from loyalist Ahl al-Hadith leaders like Rabiʿ al-Madkhali[182] and, which at first may seem more surprising, from rejectionists like Muqbil al-Wadiʿi.[183]

Most important, Jamil al-Rahman began to welcome Saudi fighters, who, to protect them from evil influences, were ordered "not to visit competing *madafat* [guest houses tied to the various factions]; if they disobeyed, they faced exclusion and the cessation of their monthly stipend—which, thanks to Saudi financing, was far higher than the salaries paid to volunteers in other guest houses."[184] These fighters belonged to both loyalist and rejectionist Ahl al-Hadith groups.

Yet, despite the efforts made to keep them away from the rest of the jihadi scene, the inevitable occurred. Many fell under the influence of Abu Muhammad al-Maqdisi, who, because he had come from the JSM, relied on a body of writing and a methodology with which they were familiar.[185] They also made contact with jihadi networks, opening the way to an association between the two groups that would mark the early 1990s.[186]

The support Jamil al-Rahman received from Saudi Arabia also gave him substantial resources. In October 1988 he "liberated" the whole of the governorate of Kunar, which then became a veritable "*salafi* emirate."[187] Two months later, in December 1988, he began to publish a magazine, *Al-Mujahid,* which had a large readership in Saudi Arabia.[188] The entry of this new faction onto the Afghan stage upset the precarious existing balances, particularly because Jamil al-Rahman obstinately refused to cooperate with the other groups, whose deviations in creed he denounced. The war against Hekmatyar, who was supported by the Sahwa, raged on. Jamil al-Rahman paid for it with his life; he was assassinated, most probably by a Hekmatyar supporter, in December 1991.[189] This increase in danger in Afghanistan was both cause and effect of a parallel escalation in tensions in Saudi Arabia between Sahwis and Ahl al-Hadith loyalists in the wake of the Gulf War.

The Limits of the Sahwa's Grip

At a time when the Sahwa had imposed an increasing presence throughout most fields of the social arena, the emergence of the Ahl al-Hadith and jihadi movements, as well as the resurgence of Wahhabi exclusivism, represented a clear challenge to its monopoly on Islamic activism. With respect to their social bases, the Sahwa's challengers shared a common characteristic. Many of their members were déclassé (they were rich in social capital but economically poor) or discriminated against (poor in social capital, whatever their economic status). The déclassé were primarily "Bedouins" *(badu),* endowed with high social status but major losers economically and politically in the construction of the Saudi state. As for the discriminated against, they were individuals whose ancestry *(nasab)* was socially discredited: Saudis of foreign origin, whether or not they had Saudi nationality, and settled populations of nontribal ancestry, known as *khadiris.*

An analysis of the makeup of the JSM clearly brings out these categories. From information provided by Nasir al-Huzaymi and various written sources, it is possible to determine the profile of a sample of 35 members of the movement: 18 of them were "Bedouins" from the tribes of Harb (5), Shammar (5), ʿUtayba (3), Lihyan (3), and Banu Tamim (1) and from an unidentified tribe (1); 8 were foreigners (with or without Saudi nationality) from Yemen (6), Egypt (1), and Iran (1); 2 were *khadiris;* and one individual came from Najran on the Yemeni border, a region looked down on by Saudis of the interior.

Among the movement's ulema, foreign residents, particularly Yemenis (notably Muqbil al-Wadiʿi, Ahmad al-Muʿallim, and Hasan al-Wahidi) were overrepresented. In a society in which mobility in the religious field had traditionally depended on membership in certain networks for the transmission of knowledge controlled by a veritable religious aristocracy that came from the "Najdi crescent," it is not surprising that these ulema found the Ahl al-Hadith stance attractive, because it called into question the body of texts on which the legitimacy of the dominant sheikhs was based, as well as the very criteria of legitimacy within the religious field. Indeed, because every hadith was suspect and could be subject to criticism, the Ahl al-Hadith attributed only relative importance to transmission within established networks. For them, a great scholar was one who had memorized—in books—an important number of hadiths and biographies of transmitters and could analyze them to validate or invalidate the authenticity of narratives. It was thanks to this symbolic coup that al-Albani, a total outsider, of Albanian origin and largely self-taught in matters of religion, was able to impose himself successively in the Syrian and Saudi religious fields.

In the case of the Ikhwan of Burayda, it is necessary to draw a distinction between the veterans of the movement, who were mostly settled individuals of tribal origin (*qabilis*), and new recruits who joined starting in the mid-1980s. Among the latter, there was a large proportion of *khadiris*.[190] With regard to the jihadi network, it is clear that the socially discriminated-against groups were at first well represented. To mention only two examples, Osama bin Laden is from Hadramawt in Yemen, while one of the first sheikhs to join him, Musa al-Qarni, comes from the region of Jazan on the Yemeni border. It is also noteworthy that most jihadis came from the Hejaz and the Eastern Province, where socially discriminated-against groups are well represented, whereas Najd—the heart of the Saudi social fabric, where social capital is concentrated—was little represented. To the victims of discrimination in the Saudi social arena, the internationalism of jihadi ideology might at first have seemed a means of escaping from the implacable rules imposed by the social classifications operating in the kingdom. This changed, however, after the early years of the Afghan jihad. By 1987 the "Afghan cause," which was widely publicized and had official support, more easily attracted fighters from other segments of the population.

The fact that the rivals of the Sahwa included a large proportion of individuals who were déclassé or discriminated against points, in a mirror image, to the limits of the Sahwa movement. Because it largely depended on the education system, the movement included primarily members of the urban middle classes, who were the most educationally favored. In rural areas[191] and among the most destitute, where access to education (especially higher education) was reduced, Sahwi presence was also reduced. Also, it is edifying to note, as Sulayman al-Dahayyan bluntly states, that "the Sahwa is a movement dominated by the *qabilis*."[192] This is an assertion that is difficult to verify empirically because there are obviously no statistics covering the Sahwi membership. Nonetheless, it is clear that although the leaders of the movement came from all regions of the kingdom (particularly from the south and the Hejaz, which was unquestionably a remarkable innovation compared with the traditional Wahhabi ulema, the vast majority of whom were from Najd), there were very few among them of nontribal ancestry.[193] Thus by blocking the advancement of those who did not have the "right" pedigree, the Sahwa seems in the end to have reproduced the constraints of social capital in its ranks.

Regardless of their unquestionable symbolic importance, these movements of resistance to the Sahwa did not represent a real threat to Sahwi control on the ground. Because its position inside the system gave it the advantage of constantly growing resources, and because the proportion of the educated population was increasing exponentially in a society in which the urban middle classes were also constantly growing because of rapid urbanization and increases in wealth,[194] the Sahwa remained by far, and even more after 1979, the principal force of Saudi Islamism.

4

A Sacrificed Generation

In the mid-1980s the well-oiled mechanism to which the Saudi system owed its resilience began to experience malfunctions, due primarily to the economic recession brought about by a sudden drop in oil income. This occurred at the very time at which the first generation educated in the school system reorganized by the Muslim Brotherhood, the Sahwa generation, reached adulthood. This provoked Sahwi "uprisings" in various fields where Sahwis found themselves in subordinate positions and now had no hope of rising. To legitimate their action, they were led to transpose the interpretive frameworks they had learned from their Islamist socialization onto Saudi terrain. The "rebels without a cause" had finally found their cause. This laid the groundwork for a major political crisis, which broke out on a large scale when, on August 7, 1990, King Fahd called on American troops to protect the country from Saddam Hussein's alleged ambitions, a step that catalyzed the ensuing mobilization.

Sahwi Rivalries for Control of the Social Arena

To understand what precipitated the crisis, it is necessary to analyze more thoroughly the structural mechanisms that explain the remarkable quietism the Sahwa demonstrated until the mid-1980s. In Saudi Arabia the field of power (as well as to some extent the social arena) has traditionally been made up of a set of largely autonomous fields. Each field was divided among various groups that fiercely competed against each other. The Sahwa, which was present in many of the fields, was one of those groups. The struggles in which it was initially engaged were with rival Islamist movements, particularly the Ahl al-Hadith. But following the weakening of non-Sahwa Islamism after 1979, the struggle was at its most intense within the Sahwa itself, pitting against each other the two principal *jamaʿat,* the Muslim Brotherhood and the Sururis, in the various fields where they were to be found, primarily religion and education.

At the time of the *jamaʿat's* emergence, some ideological differences existed between the Saudi Muslim Brotherhood and the Sururis. At the root of the Brotherhood networks were individuals close to the line of Hasan al-Banna, such as Hamad al-Sulayfih, Abdallah al-Turki, and Muhammad Umar Zubayr, all students of Mannaʿ al-Qattan, as well as the vast majority of the Brothers from Zubayr. Muhammad Surur, on the other hand, was from the outset, even before his departure from Syria, an admirer of Sayyid Qutb. In other words, the Saudi Brothers and the Sururis represented at first the Bannaists and the Qutbists, respectively, of the Saudi religious field. But this did not last; the rise of Qutbism among the Brothers outside the kingdom, joined to its greater theoretical compatibility with the Wahhabi tradition, led in the 1970s to a harmonization of the Sahwa on the Qutbist line, as redefined most notably by Muhammad Qutb.

Despite this, a continuing divergence remained between the various *jamaʿat* with respect to the position to be adopted toward any Muslim whose creed (*ʿaqida*) went against Wahhabi dogma, primarily Shiites and Sufis. For most Sururis, who implicitly adopted the old exclusivist line, *takfir* was called for, while for the Brotherhood, faithful to the more inclusivist line of their counterparts throughout the Middle East, although any divergence from orthodoxy was extremely blameworthy, it did not necessarily imply exclusion from the community of believers. It is not surprising, therefore, that the individuals selected to represent the kingdom in meetings with Iranian ulema, notably through the Muslim World League, were almost systematically Brothers and never Sururis.[1]

The 1979 Iranian revolution was a shock for Saudi Arabia, which felt directly threatened. This was the beginning of a new Middle Eastern cold war pitting the two Islamic great powers in the region against each other. Under these circumstances the kingdom did not hesitate to provide moral and financial support to Saddam Hussein's Iraq in his war with Iran that began in the following year. The Saudi-Iranian cold war was also a propaganda war. Radio broadcasts and newspaper articles in Arabic emanating from Teheran called for the export of the Islamic Revolution, attempting to attenuate its specifically Shiite character and presenting it as a universal model. In response, the Saudi regime denounced the sectarianism of the Islamic Republic and encouraged a revival of anti-Shiism, which the rise of inclusivism among the Wahhabis, while not eliminating it, had muffled. The denunciation of the Shiite peril became a commonplace of Saudi religious discourse, echoed in chorus by all components of the religious field, including both Muslim Brothers and Sururis. With that, the last major point of difference between the two *jama'at* practically disappeared in the 1980s.[2]

However, this did not stop the Sururis from constantly denouncing the Saudi Brotherhood's supposed lack of rigor with regard to creed. Accordingly, the Sururis tried to attribute to the local Brotherhood the responsibility for controversial positions taken by thinkers tied to the movement outside Saudi Arabia. For example, when Muhammad al-Ghazzali, who was considered close to the Brotherhood, published *The Prophetic Sunna between Jurists and Traditionists*,[3] in which he denounced Wahhabi attitudes toward the woman question and the Muslim Other, he provoked an uproar in Saudi Islamist circles. In a book titled *Serene Dialogue with Sheikh al-Ghazzali*,[4] Salman al-'Awda, a Sururi, replied by accusing al-Ghazzali of distorting Sunni Islam by relying too much on reason. In the grammar of the local religious field, these accusations were primarily intended to embarrass members of the Brotherhood in the kingdom. Other attacks in the same period targeted the ideologue of the Syrian Muslim Brotherhood, Sa'id Hawwa. Although he was politically in line with Sahwi norms because he was a convinced Qutbist, Hawwa, like most Brothers from his birthplace, Hama, had strong connections to Sufism. His book *Our Spiritual Education* was at the root of the polemic.[5] The dispute was particularly embarrassing for the Saudi Brothers because some of Hawwa's books had traditionally been read in their study groups and were sold in their bookstores. With their Wahhabi credentials thereby in question, the Brothers had to dissociate themselves from the Syrian ideologue. In the course of a few months in the mid-1980s his books disappeared from their bookstores[6] and from the curriculum of their study groups.[7]

Following the same logic, the Sururis in the 1980s sought to achieve intellectual autonomy from the Brotherhood. Until then, with very few exceptions, both referred to the same body of established texts, books by Muhammad Qutb (and to some extent by Sayyid Qutb), as well as the magazine *Al-Mujtama'*, along with the classics of Wahhabism. That changed in 1986 when the Islamic Forum (al-Muntada al-islami) was established in London. According to a former Sururi, it became "the principal think tank of the *jama'a*."[8]

The Islamic Forum began publishing a political and religious monthly, *Al-Bayan*, which within a few years became basic reading for all the Sururi circles in Saudi Arabia. Its columns featured a whole new generation of ideologues and thinkers linked to the *jama'a*, most prominently the founder of the journal, the Syrian Muhammad al-'Abda, an early Sururi and a close friend of Muhammad Surur. Other regular contributors included Muhammad al-Duwaysh, a major theorist of *tarbiya* (moral education) in the Sururi movement; Abd al-Aziz al-Julayyil, a former pharmacist and founder of one of the main Sururi bookshops of Riyadh, al-Tayyiba; and Abd al-Aziz al-'Abd al-Latif, a well-known professor of creed at Imam University. The prominence given to someone like al-'Abd al-Latif was in fact an outcome of the Ahl al-Hadith's criticism of the Sahwa for lacking *'ilm* and neglecting issues of creed. The Sururis, and to a lesser extent the Brothers, now strove to bring to the fore ulema acceptable by Wahhabi standards. In addition, *Al-Bayan* brought in non-Saudi thinkers, which demonstrates the extension of the Sururi network beyond the kingdom's borders.

Among them were two substantial figures, the Egyptian Gamal Sultan and the Sudanese Ja'far Shaykh Idris, both Islamist critics of the Muslim Brotherhood in their respective countries because of their stronger adhesion to Wahhabi precepts. The writings of Gamal Sultan, particularly those denouncing non-Islamist and non-*salafi* Islamist currents of thought, had so much influence in Saudi Arabia that the Sahwi journalist Nawwaf al-Qudaymi called Sultan "the godfather of Sahwi thought."[9]

But although *Al-Bayan* played an essential role in providing the Sururis with an ideological output of their own, its content did not diverge greatly from traditional Sahwi ideology and was thus not far from the worldview of the Saudi Brotherhood. The apparent battle of ideas between Brothers and Sururis was thus primarily the reflection of a much more material conflict, with the existential stake of control over the resources of the Saudi religious field and eventually of the social arena. This stake was all the higher because the Sahwa's various fields of activity, particularly religion and education, experienced sustained expansion into the 1980s, made possible by an increasing injection of petrodollars. The Sahwa constantly increased its presence in all those fields.

Seizing control of institutions was a goal of the highest importance for the *jama'at*. This involved large institutions like the charitable associations for the memorization of the Koran that supervised the circles of memorization at the regional and municipal levels, the offices of the Ministry of Education that were in charge of student activities in each district, and the deanships of student affairs that coordinated extracurricular activities in each university. It also involved local institutions, such as the mosques (and the "libraries" and circles for the memorization of the Koran that they housed), the committees for raising Islamic consciousness, and, more widely, all the associations that made up the student activities sector in schools and universities.

The large institutions were essential targets for conquest because of the significant resources that passed through them, and because whoever controlled them could take command of the local institutions under their jurisdiction by appointing members of his *jama'a* to them.[10] These local institutions were of great importance for the perpetuation of the *jamaʿa* because they were the principal recruiting structures. This was especially true because the recruiting capacity of a *jamaʿa* was more dependent on the number of grassroots organizations and institutions it controlled than on its effective power of attraction. Adhesion to a *jamaʿa* was usually not the result of a conscious choice made in an open religious market. A young man became a Sururi (or a Brother) because the circle for the memorization of the Koran or the library of the mosque in his neighborhood was controlled by Sururis (or Brothers). Similarly, the membership of the leader of the committee for raising Islamic consciousness in the school attended by a young man who decided to get involved in Islamic activism was likely to determine his affiliation. This logic was particularly implacable because a young man who joined a *jamaʿa* was not immediately aware of that fact, and when he did realize his membership, group pressure made it too late to turn back. The *jamaʿat* did everything possible to maintain the captive character of their markets. According to a former Sururi, "The Musa bin Nusayr summer camp was the camp reserved for our study circle and a few others. But we did not have the right to register at Nahawand camp, for example, even though it was much closer to where we lived!"[11]

In principle, the university, where all *jamaʿat* were present, should have been an exception to this rule. In Riyadh's King Saʿud University, for example, the Brotherhood controlled the scouts *(al-jawwala)*, while the Sururis controlled the committees *(al-lijan)*.[12] Each *jamaʿa* organized activities and offered services intended to attract students. But the deck was often stacked there as well. Several accounts indicate that students who already belonged to a *jamaʿa* were ordered by their emir when they entered the university to join a particular group and engage in certain activities so that they remained in the bosom of the *jamaʿa*.[13]

The best way for the *jamaʿat* to ensure control over institutions was thus to build solid networks of patronage and clientele that enabled them to work behind the scenes to promote their members to key positions. In time, some institutions became the monopoly of a *jamaʿa* well established enough to deny access to others. The example of the

World Assembly of Muslim Youth has already been mentioned; it was controlled by the Brothers of the Hejaz, who made sure that no other *jama'a* gained a foothold.

This situation sometimes created tensions. "At the Charitable Association for the Memorization of the Koran in Jeddah," one witness recalls, "the Brothers had always been in control, with each president systematically appointing his successor from within the *jama'a*. In the late 1990s the Sururis complained about this monopoly and demanded that elections be held to choose the president. One of them finally won, and the association changed hands."[14] There were also attempts to break monopolies at the local level, with varying degrees of success. One interviewee recounts how Brothers sought to gain a foothold in a school in Burayda, a city where the Sururis enjoyed a monopoly:

A friend, head of a secondary school in Burayda, told me this: "One day, X, a young chemistry teacher in the school and a recent graduate of King Fahd University of Petroleum and Minerals [where the Brotherhood was in the majority], came to see me. He said to me: 'I want to create an association for *tarbiya islamiyya* [Islamic education].' I replied: 'Why do you want to create an association for *tarbiya islamiyya*, since we already have one?' 'The existing association is for *taw'iya islamiyya* [raising Islamic consciousness],' he answered. 'Mine will be different.' I gave him my permission, because in my view the more the better. [The witness explains that the head of the school was of Islamist inclination but not affiliated with any *jama'a*.] A few days later, a delegation of Sururis came to see me and said: 'Why did you authorize X to create a new association for *tarbiya islamiyya*?' I replied: 'Do not worry, he is a good man.' They answered me: 'No, he is a Muslim Brother. We have had an eye on him for some time and we forbade him to get into any activity.' I finally had to give in to their objections, and his association could not be established."[15]

As this anecdote illustrates on a small scale, the impossibility of challenging the control of one *jama'a* over the existing institutions of a key sector sometimes impelled members of the competing *jama'a* to try to build their own institutions from the ground up. This is what happened in the humanitarian field, long considered the preserve of the Muslim Brotherhood, which controlled the World Muslim League (although its members were not just Saudi Brothers), as well as the International Islamic Relief Organization (Hay'at al-ighatha al-islamiyya al-ʿalamiyya). To secure a position in this essential sector of Islamic activism, the Sururis encouraged the creation in 1992 of the al-Haramayn Foundation (Mu'assasat al-haramayn).[16] It experienced remarkable growth until it was closed down in 2004 under pressure from the American authorities, who accused it of supporting terrorism.[17]

All of this was made possible because the resources provided were significant and the different fields involved were constantly expanding, enabling them to absorb new entrants. As a consequence, the members of the Sahwa, particularly those in the *jamaʿat,* were much too busy competing for control of the available resources and positions to think about changing the rules of the game. This explains why, at this stage, the rapid development of the Sahwa had no visible effect on the stability of the system.

The Sahwa Generation and the Effects of Recession

The economic recession that struck the kingdom from 1982 onward radically changed the situation. It resulted from a fall in Saudi oil production, combined with a significant decline in the price of a barrel of crude.[18] The country's oil revenues consequently fell from $109 billion in 1981 to $70 billion in 1982 and gradually declined further, reaching the low point of $16 billion in 1986.[19] Given the central role of oil production in the Saudi economy, gross domestic product (GDP) fell by 35 percent between 1982 and 1986, strongly affecting the kingdom's budget, which declined from $91 billion in 1982 to $45 billion in 1986. The Saudi economy then entered a period of stagnation, with a GDP that remained close to its 1986 level and a budget that decreased even further to about $37 billion in 1988 and 1989.[20] The crisis lasted until 1990–1991, when the Gulf War induced a partial recovery of oil prices and, by extension, Saudi revenues.

The 1980s were marked by the growing presence of the Sahwa in all fields of the social arena. This coincided with the advent of a new generation, the product of the Saudi educational system as it had been reshaped in the late 1960s under the influence of the Muslim Brotherhood. The fact that this generation called itself the "Sahwa generation" (*jil al-sahwa*) indicates the strong sense of common identification of its members. Although this feeling was stronger in the two core circles of the Sahwa—the committed (*multazimun*) and the affiliates (*muntamun*)—because it was reinforced by shared day-to-day practices, it also affected a significant portion of individuals in the broader third circle who, although they had not embarked on religious activism, had been socialized in the same social and intellectual environment.

For these students and recent graduates, prospects were much less promising than those of their predecessors. In the early 1970s anyone returning with a doctorate from the United States could hope to become a high official, perhaps even a minister, within a few years. Although graduates of American universities retained advantages in the early 1980s, they had become plentiful,[21] and each of them had to make his own way with difficulty. The "miracles" of the 1970s, which remained alive in collective memory, were part of the past. As for most graduates of Saudi universities, they had little prospect but to find positions as minor officials in an already-bloated bureaucracy because the private sector, which in any event was still in its infancy,[22] had become accustomed to hiring foreign workers in their place for reasons of cost and productivity. This was true for graduates not only of religious universities but of secular universities as well, who enjoyed little extra advantage.[23]

During the recession this phenomenon increased alarmingly. The expansion of the bureaucracy, which had grown constantly since 1970, experienced an unprecedented slowdown[24] at the same time at which the regime was attempting not to tighten quotas in the universities,[25] so they were continuing to produce increasing numbers of graduates. Steffen Hertog describes the situation:

"Most employees were forced to stay on the same level of seniority for many years. The times of rapid bureaucratic mobility for young educated Saudis had largely passed, with a demoralizing effect on latecomers. From the mid-80s on, individuals got stuck on the lower- to mid-level of the civil service. Rapid mobility was followed by great immobility."[26] The private sector, whose activity depended very largely on state contracts, was also experiencing a serious crisis and offered no better prospects.[27]

Hence an entire generation endowed with a strong sense of shared identity saw its aspirations hindered. The resulting frustration was even stronger because this generation had come of age in a society marked by the effects of the oil boom and experiencing exponential enrichment, and so its expectations were particularly high. Blocked as they were, these young people developed a powerful resentment against the preceding generation, embodied by the intelligentsia, who dominated almost all government administrations. But what might appear to be a routine conflict of generations took on a decisively ideological coloration in the Saudi context, as the young Sahwis mobilized the interpretive frameworks inherited from their Islamist socialization to develop their own reading of the conflict.

The views then prevalent in the Sahwa depicted the previous generation, in the words of a leading Sahwi sheikh, as "the generation of defeat, secularism, and Westernization . . . on whose ruins was erected the blessed generation of the Sahwa," the first to have "awakened" religiously.[28] A young Sahwi who entered a ministry at a low level in the mid-1980s explained: "This experience opened my eyes. All my superiors were secularists ['ilmaniyyun], who smoked and lived disordered lives. Except for a few young men like me who had recently joined at low levels, no one wore a beard. How could we the pious [salihun] be under the orders of men like that?"[29]

To counter the "secularists," the Sahwis could rely on a substantial library of ideological texts inherited from early theorists such as Muhammad Qutb[30] and Abd al-Rahman al-Dawsari and constantly developed by contemporaries like Safar al-Hawali.[31] But these teachings had largely remained at the level of abstraction, with no concrete expression in the Saudi context, save for the isolated activism of al-Dawsari, who was later considered a precursor for that reason. This body of ideological texts was made operational in the 1980s. Under its tutelage the Sahwa generation soon saw itself as the collective victim of a vast "secular-Masonic plot." The country, they claimed, had been taken hostage by the intelligentsia, organized in clandestine networks, which had only one objective, to eradicate Islam in the kingdom.[32]

One piece of evidence for this control was alleged to be the high number of former leftists and Arab nationalists occupying important positions at the head of the Saudi state.[33]

A leaflet distributed at the time of the Gulf War illustrates how the Sahwis viewed this "secularist conspiracy":

> The United States succeeded in establishing among those who have studied in America a complete organization of secularists who are loyal to them and whom they have infiltrated into all the organs of the state. Among them are ministers, vice ministers, and heads of administrations. America had to use trickery to achieve its ends. It asked each individual it enrolled to join the opposition to the government by adhering to Arab nationalist or Marxist positions. Then, once they had received their degrees, it asked the government to hire them to gain their loyalty and [illegible]. After that, it used them to combat the ulema and the Islamists and to secularize the country. The examples are numerous, including Dr. Ibrahim al-ʿAwaji, Dr. Sulayman al-Salim, Hisham Nazir, Dr. Hamad al-Marzuqi, Ahmad Zaki Yamani, Dr. Ghazi al-Qusaybi, and many others. . . . There is even a special group in the government apparatus that the American government considers an integral part of its policy agenda and that it is prepared to protect whatever the costs. Its members include Muhammad Aba al-Khayl, the minister of finance, whom America enrolled for its purposes when he was a student at the University of Baghdad, and Dr. Muhammad al-Tawil, president of the Institute of Masonic Administration, whom it recruited when he was studying public administration at the University of Pittsburgh.[34]

As this document shows, various personalities and institutions were the focus of Sahwi hostility. At the top of the list was Ghazi al-Qusaybi, a former leftist and a modernist *(hadathi)* writer who had become minister of industry in 1975 and minister of health in 1982, whom the Sahwis saw as embodying the whole "secularist domination" over the Saudi state. In 1979 al-Qusaybi had been the target of a fatwa from Ibn Baz[35] calling on him to repent after he had told *Newsweek,* in a fashion typical of the Saudi intelligentsia: "If you don't take into account our aspiration for a better life after 3000 years of inhuman existence, you cannot understand what is happening today in Saudi Arabia."[36] For the conservatives, this was an outrageous comment because it implied in substance that before the advent of the oil age and going back to the birth of Islam, the country had been living in darkness. In the second half of the 1980s Ibn Baz's fatwa was photocopied in industrial quantities by Sahwis and distributed in universities and ministries.[37]

An institution was also presented as playing a major role in the alleged secularist conspiracy, the Institute of Public Administration, founded in 1961 with the aid of the Ford Foundation and already described in the late 1970s by Abd al-Rahman al-Dawsari as "one of the sanctuaries of world Freemasonry in Riyadh." Its successive presidents, Muhammad Aba al-Khayl and Muhammad al-Tawil, did have an Arab nationalist past and were known as leading liberals. But Sahwi attacks against the institute went beyond the personality of these two individuals. A Sahwi university professor who taught there for a time describes "the institute [as] the staging ground for the secularists, their Trojan horse to seize power. Otherwise, how can you explain the importance it has acquired, although it does not even have the status of a university and does not award doctorates? It is the heart of the secularist organization, whose members all have a link to the institute in one way or another."[38] These accusations were constantly repeated by Sahwis in publications distributed in thousands of copies (the university professor mentioned a fifty-page pamphlet on the "secrets" of the institute) and in sermons recorded on cassettes. Muhammad al-Tawil even tells of having been summoned by Ibn Baz, who had been alerted by the Sahwis, to prove that the institute did indeed contain a mosque.[39]

The Modernism Dispute

Although these attacks may have been vehement, it was the intellectual field that soon became the major site of confrontation between the Sahwa and the liberal intelligentsia. Unlike the fields in which the Sahwa had a presence from the beginning and where the *jamaʿat* were active, the intellectual field was initially relatively quiescent. There were debates between advocates of literary realism and advocates of romanticism, but they were not very passionate, notably because the resources available provided amply for the small number of active intellectuals. Almost all actors in the field came from the liberal intelligentsia, apart from a small minority of Muslim reformist intellectuals from the Hejaz and of traditional *udaba'* (men of letters), who had resigned themselves to their subordinate position. Moreover, the intellectual field had succeeded in preserving its autonomy, and episodes of interference from the religious and political fields were rare and isolated.

In the early 1980s modernism *(hadatha)* became the dominant intellectual current. This term, which had been found in the Arab intellectual lexicon outside Saudi Arabia since the first decades of the twentieth century, at first designated a break with a literary tradition seen as fossilized and the adoption of new narrative and poetic modes. But literary criticism was also implicitly social criticism, and calls for the modernization of literature for many writers implied calls for social modernization. Modernism therefore imposed itself as a natural expression of the aspirations of the intelligentsia and thereby as an extension of the intellectual tradition on which the field was founded. In this context the modernist became the quintessential intellectual. This situation was summarized a few years later by the modernist theorist Abdallah al-Ghadhdhami, paraphrasing Shakespeare: "To be a modernist intellectual or not to be an intellectual."[40]

Literary clubs and cultural supplements throughout the country celebrated the supporters of a break with ossified literary—and, implicitly, social—norms. Of non-Saudi Arabs, there was talk only of the poet Adonis, the playwright and essayist Salah Abd al-Sabur, and the thinker Muhammad ʿAbid al-Jabiri, and of Europeans, Roland Barthes and Jacques Derrida. The Saudis who had made a name for themselves since the 1970s were also numerous, including the poets Ali al-Dumayni, Muhammad al-ʿAli, and Abdallah al-Sikhan and the novelists ʿAbid Khazindar, Rajaʾ ʿAlim, and Saʿd al-Dawsari. The same years witnessed the advent of a Saudi school of literary criticism, represented primarily by Abdallah al-Ghadhdhami and Saʿid al-Surayhi.

The critics were the most controversial of all because they made explicit—they were the first in Saudi Arabia to use the word "modernism"[41]—the break implicit in the literary output of poets and novelists. Naturally, then, they were the source of scandal.

In 1985 Abdallah al-Ghadhdhami, then vice president of the literary club of Jeddah, published a work of literary criticism considered by many the manifesto of Saudi modernists, *Sin and Expiation: From Structuralism to Deconstruction*,[42] inspired largely by Western theorists, particularly Roland Barthes. Pursuing the modernist argument to its logical conclusion, he advocates a literary modernity not merely in form, as do the proponents of free verse in poetry, but a real modernity of content, both methodological and epistemological. Otherwise, the book is very technical and full of the jargon of literary studies, which makes it anything but intelligible for the general public.

The publication of this book, however, marked the onset of a formidable controversy in intellectual circles and eventually in the entire social arena that would put an end to the modernist movement and lead to its general condemnation. What explains the magnitude of this controversy, provoked by what could have been seen as just an obscure treatise of literary criticism? This is especially puzzling because, despite what its author says,[43] the book said nothing new beyond what was already in vogue in the Saudi intellectual field.[44] According to Sa'id al-Surayhi, "Modernism always meant for us more than a simple movement of literary renewal; it was a veritable project for social modernization."[45] Two years earlier, in 1983, al-Surayhi had published *The Poetry of Abu Tammam: Between Classic Criticism and the View of New Criticism*,[46] which makes arguments very similar to those of al-Ghadhdhami. Al-Surayhi's work had provoked some criticism at the time, but the debate, of no great magnitude, had been limited to the intellectual field.[47]

If the reactions to the publication of al-Ghadhdhami's book were that vehement, this was because the structural conditions of the intellectual field and the social arena had changed. In the early 1980s the Sahwa movement had reached a level of development that enabled it to produce its own "organic intellectuals." Born mostly in the 1950s, they were among the first products of the Saudi school system re-created by the Muslim Brotherhood and therefore represented the older members of the Sahwa generation. They were also the first Sahwis to receive higher degrees, master's degrees or doctorates, from which they expected a minimum of recognition.

Depending on their training, they fell into one of two groups: ulema who specialized in religious sciences and lay intellectuals who were specialists in the human sciences (literature, sociology, psychology, and so on) or physical sciences (mathematics, physics, medicine, engineering, and the like). Although the former obviously found their place in the religious field, the latter found themselves paradoxically doubly excluded. Ulema, Sahwi or not, who because of their field corporatism had a strong sense of caste, barred their access to the religious field because of their secular education. At the same time, the intellectual field remained the preserve of the heirs of the liberal intelligentsia and continued to be based on a definition of the intellectual that left no place for these new entrants. Worse, the intelligentsia seemed to relegate them, because of their ideological attachment to Islam, to a religious field that rejected them.

These "Sahwi intellectuals" were not the first Islamist claimants to the status of intellectual in Saudi Arabia. Before them had come the foreign members of the Muslim Brotherhood living in the kingdom. But they had been more interested in the debate in the rest of the Arab world, generally in their country of origin, than in Saudi Arabia, which they considered off limits. There had also been the small group of Muslim reformists from the Hejaz. In fact, it was primarily among the latter that the few Saudis were found who in the late 1970s joined the calls for the creation of an "Islamic literature" *(al-adab al-islami),* which led to the establishment in November 1984 of the League of Islamic Literature (Rabitat al-adab al-islami). But their role was minor, since the majority of founders of the league,[48] including those based in Saudi Arabia, came from other countries in the Muslim world, and their decision to support the creation of a counterinstitution rather than trying to enter the existing intellectual institutions must be seen as an acknowledgment of their inability to dismantle the established modernist monopoly.

The Sahwi intellectuals adopted a much more aggressive approach. Beginning in the 1980s, they openly challenged the intelligentsia's control of the intellectual field, calling into question the definition of modernity that established the Saudi intellectual as a category. To do this, they began to impose their presence in places where it had previously been unthinkable.

Literary clubs—particularly those in Jeddah, Riyadh, and Abha, which were then considered the three major ones and the main modernist strongholds—became targets for conquest by Sahwi intellectuals. They made a dramatic entrance, as al-Ghadhdhami, then a member of the administrative council of the Jeddah club, relates: "In 1980 we had a dreadful time filling the hall for lectures. I even remember once when we were hosting a senior Egyptian professor and to avoid embarrassment, we had to bring in laborers from the neighborhood by promising them there would be something to eat! But starting in 1985, everything changed; we went from an empty hall to an audience of a thousand all at once!"[49] But the audience was certainly not the one al-Ghadhdhami had hoped for. According to a Sahwi intellectual, "Whenever there was a lecture by a modernist intellectual, a large number of us came to attend. Once he had finished speaking, several of us spoke up to give our point of view. We had to do that because we were not on the platform!"[50]

The yearly national festival of heritage and culture (al-mahrajan al-watani li-l-turath wa-l-thaqafa) in Janadriyya saw similar developments. Created in 1985 at the initiative of Crown Prince Abdallah's chief adviser, Abd al-Aziz al-Tuwayjiri,[51] incidentally known for his Arab nationalist inclinations, and organized under the aegis of the National Guard, it combined horse racing and exhibitions about the "popular traditions" of the Saudi kingdom with high-level intellectual debates open to the public. Symbolically, the festival set tradition, reduced to its expression in folklore, against a modern and universal Saudi culture, consecrating Saudi Arabia as one of the major intellectual centers of the Arab world. This was in line with the process initiated in the mid-1970s by the creation of the Saudi intellectual field, whose purpose was to endow the regime with modernizing legitimacy. It is noteworthy that it was now Abdallah, previously considered an inveterate conservative, who put himself forward as the promoter of this modernizing legitimacy after its initiator Fahd, now king, who had been visibly shaken by the events of 1979, concentrated his efforts exclusively on religious legitimacy. This shift in legitimating register explains why King Fahd in 1986 adopted the title of "Servant of the Two Holy Places" *(khadim al-haramayn al-sharifayn)*, which was meant to bring to the fore the services the kingdom rendered to the pilgrimage and to pilgrims.

In an unprecedented step for Saudi Arabia, the most celebrated Arab modernist intellectuals were invited to Janadriyya, including the thinkers Muhammad ʿAbid al-Jabiri and Mohammed Arkoun, the poet Abd al-Wahhab al-Bayati, and the writer Sunʿ Allah Ibrahim.[52] They rubbed shoulders with the cream of the Saudi intellectual field, represented by such names as Abdallah al-Ghadhdhami, Saʿid al-Surayhi, and Aziz Diaʾ. Despite the presence of some traditional *udabaʾ* (men of letters), the image projected by Janadriyya was of a festival to the glory of modernism. The Sahwi intellectuals, who were kept away, were furious. At the second festival, in 1986, there were many of them in the audience. They were very clearly distinguishable from the liberals by their appearance—bushy beards and short tunics *(thawb)*—as well as by their attitude. According to a reporter assigned to cover the event, the *mukabbirun* (those who cry out "Allah akbar") gradually outnumbered the *musaffiqun* (those who applaud—a gesture the Sahwi considered non-Islamic).[53] The Sahwi presence was so large that "there were soon entire halls full of *mutawwaʿun* [individuals wearing the external signs of religiosity] facing a platform where four terrorized *hadathiyyun* [modernists] were seated."[54] The technique was similar to the one used in the literary clubs: the Sahwis were silent while the speaker was talking and then monopolized the floor, with one intervention after another to "correct" what he had just said. Some did it, in the eyes of their peers, with brilliance and attained some reputation in the Sahwa. This was the case for Saʿid bin Zuʿayr, born in 1950, a professor in the Faculty of *Daʿwa* and Communication at Imam University, and for Muhammad al-Masʿari, born in 1946, professor of physics at King Saʿud University, neither of whom had been well known beforehand. Al-Masʿari even confessed with feigned embarrassment that the recording of one of his most trenchant interventions was wildly popular in Sahwi circles.[55]

The cultural supplements of Saudi newspapers were not spared from the conflict, although things happened in a slightly different way. Almost all the supplements were in the hands of the modernists, notably *Al-Mirbad*, the supplement to the newspaper *Al-Yawm*, edited by Shakir al-Shaykh, who was close to al-Ghadhdhami, as well as the supplements to ʿUkadh, run since 1981 by Saʿid al-Surayhi,[56] and *Al-Riyad*. Similarly, the literary pages of the major magazines at the time, such as *Al-Yamama, Iqraʾ,* and *Al-Sharq,* held to an uncompromising modernist line. As a result, the strategy the Sahwi intellectuals used at Janadriyya and in the literary clubs was ineffective. Opponents of modernism could inundate the cultural and literary supplements of the major newspapers and magazines with angry letters, but they were never published.[57]

Soon, however, the interests of the Sahwi intellectuals coincided with those of a small newspaper in Mecca on the verge of bankruptcy, *Al-Nadwa,* which had a weekly cultural supplement called *Al-Jiyad* (literally, "the best ones"). Sensing the potential benefits, in 1985 the owners decided to make their paper a platform for antimodernism.[58] The first antimodernist articles in the paper were written by a resident of Mecca named Muhammad al-Milibari.[59] Indefatigable, in three years he wrote more than thirty articles on al-Ghadhdhami's book, all—as al-Ghadhdhami mischievously pointed out—without knowing its content in detail because he forbade the reading of it.[60] Al-Milibari called modernism a "war on Islam"[61] and identified it with other Sahwi anathemas such as "Freemasonry, communism, secularism [and] the fifth column."[62] With his writings, al-Milibari opened the way for other Sahwi intellectuals who eagerly took the plunge. *Al-Nadwa* became their stronghold and the symbol of the resistance to modernism. At the same time, sales of the newspaper increased exponentially.[63]

The growing interest of the Saudi public in this apparently very elitist debate was facilitated by the increasing involvement of Sahwi ulema, who thereby were helping bridge the gap between the intellectual field and the broader social arena. At first silent, they took hold of the debate in 1987 and began to make it a subject of their sermons. The resulting attacks from the religious field on the intellectual field were unprecedented in magnitude and laid the groundwork for the desectorization that would characterize the coming crisis.

At the turn of 1988 the kingdom's mosques were echoing with in-flammatory sermons,[64] in which modernists were accused by name of impiety, and al-Ghadhdhami was called "the rabbi of the modern-ists," "the prophet of deconstruction," or simply "'Abd al-Shaytan al-Ghadhdhami."[65] A cassette recorded by Sa'id al-Ghamidi, an alleged Brother of the Hejaz, became the symbol of the antimodernist strug-gle. According to al-Ghadhdhami, "There was not a single person in Saudi Arabia who did not listen to it or have it in his hands."[66] Sa'd al-Faqih swears that "60,000 copies of it were distributed at King Sa'ud University alone, and they went like hotcakes."[67] This was the cassette that provided the material for a book titled *Modernism in the Light of Islam*, written by another alleged Brother of the Hejaz, 'Awad al-Qarni, which also became widely popular,[68] partly because al-Qarni had persuaded Ibn Baz to write a preface in which he approved the book's content. In its pages al-Qarni describes modernism as a vast conspiracy[69] and explains that the conflict between Islamists and modernists "is a pure conflict of creed [*'aqida*]."[70] He further ex-plained in an interview: "I did not react to modernism by considering it a mere literary affair. For modernism is a school of thought that came into the Arab world to spread certain specific ideas, and litera-ture was just a pretext. . . . Besides, two clearly identifiable groups stand behind modernism: what remains of the leftists, and the supporters of some Western schools of thought like existentialism or even liberal-ism. They are the ones who assembled in a single entity that they called 'modernism.'"[71]

Al-Qarni put himself forward as the defender of "authenticity" *(asala)* against "Westernization" *(taghrib)*, tracing the origins of modernism to European thought of the nineteenth century, marked in his view by profound atheism and depravity.[72] The disciples of al-Ghadhdhami could well deny this connection and try to give their movement indigenous credentials by claiming the legacy of two He-jazi writers of the early twentieth century, Muhammad Hasan 'Awwad and Hamza Shahata,[73] but nothing could stop the powerful antimod-ernist feeling that was taking hold of Saudi society.

The popular reaction surprised even one of the men responsible for the escalation, Sa'id al-Ghamidi. "When he recorded his cassette," al-

Faqih explained, "he did not think that the issue would take on such importance. Before leaving for a short trip to Egypt, he left a copy at his neighborhood Islamic recordings store. What a surprise when he came back ten days later and found out that tens of thousands of copies of the cassette were already in circulation!"[74] But the fact that the Sahwi ulema had brought the dispute into the social arena is not enough to explain the magnitude of the reactions it provoked. The primary reason for the intense popular interest was the fact that the combat of the Sahwi intellectuals echoed that of the youth of the Sahwa generation because both of them had come up against what they saw as the domination of the "secularists." It was these young men who constituted the bulk of the mobilization against modernism.

The Quarrel of the Ulema

Similar social dynamics simultaneously affected the religious field. As with intellectuals, the 1980s witnessed the emergence of a new social type, the "Sahwi ulema." These were mostly individuals born in the 1950s, socialized from their earliest years in Sahwi circles, brought up in the Saudi school system, and graduates of the religious faculties of Saudi universities, from which many had received master's or doctoral degrees. This career, they thought, made them legitimate actors in the Saudi religious field. Indeed, they had often succeeded in making a place for themselves on its periphery. They taught in religious faculties of Saudi universities, were influential in the area of extracurricular activities, and occupied midlevel posts in various institutions in the field, such as the committees for commanding right and forbidding wrong and Islamic charitable associations.

But the heart of the religious field remained desperately out of the reach of these Sahwi ulema. They had no access to leadership positions in most Islamic institutions, to the General Office for the Management of Scientific Research, Fatwas, Preaching, and Guidance, to the Supreme Judicial Council, or to the highest body, the Council of the Committee of Senior Ulema, where the traditional Wahhabi ulema were unquestionably in control.[75] The members of this last group were the ones who received all the honors, while the Sahwi sheikhs were relegated to a decidedly secondary place in religious protocol. The resulting resentment was further intensified by the fact that the traditional Wahhabi ulema continued to represent a closed religious aristocracy from which the Sahwis felt excluded because most of them did not belong to the "right" networks. Now that the creation of a religious educational system had partially democratized access to ʿilm previously monopolized by the traditional ulema, the Sahwi ulema wanted access to the highest positions of the religious field to be democratized as well.

The situation remained stable as long as the religious field was experiencing continued expansion and the Sahwi ulema—as part of the competition among the jamaʿat with which many of them were affiliated—were busy dividing the new resources made available, which also enabled new entrants to find a place. In these circumstances the Sahwa was very careful to deal tactfully with the traditional Wahhabi ulema. To clearly indicate their subordination, the Sahwis went so far as to refrain from issuing fatwas in the legal sense of the term, instead referring systematically on general questions of fiqh to the opinions of the "senior ulema."[76] For the same reason, they generally called themselves duʿat (plural of daʿiya, "preacher") rather than ʿulamaʾ (ulema). By presenting themselves as a complement rather than an alternative to the official religious institution, they not only preserved its authority but also shared with it the fruits of their success. One observer explained the magnitude of that contribution: "In the 1970s Ibn Baz had only a few dozen students in his classes. In the 1980s, at the Sahwa's peak, there were thousands of them."[77]

But as in other areas, the situation changed in the mid-1980s because the ever more numerous Sahwi ulema were becoming a force that could not be ignored, and because the recession had blocked the expansion of the now-congested religious field. It was then that the "peripheral" Sahwi ulema took the unprecedented step of launching a low-intensity war against the "central" ulema, the traditional Wahhabi sheikhs.[78] In this conflict divergences between Brothers and Sururis became secondary, and the Sahwa more or less reestablished its unity.

To strengthen their presence in the Saudi social arena, the Sahwi ulema first set themselves apart by adopting a technique that, like much of what derives from modern technology, was looked on with suspicion by the most intransigent Wahhabi ulema: recording their sermons on cassettes, whose wide distribution was ensured by a network of specialized stores for "Islamic recordings" *(tasjilat islamiyya)*. In a lecture delivered in 1990, Salman al-ʿAwda claimed that there were sixty or seventy of them in Riyadh alone, and that sales ran as high as 200,000 copies for each sermon.[79] These stores were divided between Brothers and Sururis, and their affiliation was apparent in the choice of authors on sale. On their shelves could also be found unaccompanied Islamic chants that were greatly appreciated by Sahwis but were denounced by the Ahl al-Hadith and some Wahhabi ulema.

The advent of the "Islamic cassette" *(al-sharit al-islami)*, as al-ʿAwda called this new phenomenon, represented a major innovation in the Saudi religious field. Mansur al-Nuqaydan provides an account of his first encounter with the new medium in his hometown of Burayda:

> In 1984 the first Islamic recordings store in the city that sold sermons and Islamic chants opened its doors. Before that, all one could find were cassettes of readings from the Koran by prestigious sheikhs like Abd al-Basit Abd al-Samad or al-Manshawi. They were sold in the same general music stores where you bought cassettes of [the singers] Oum Kalthoum and Abd al-Halim Hafiz. Soon after the first Islamic recordings store opened, I went there on my bike and stopped to get some. The cassettes available then were primarily those by Abd al-Rahman al-Dawsari, Ahmad al-Qattan, and Abd al-Hamid Kishk.[80]

The three names mentioned by al-Nuqaydan encompass the entire history of the Islamic cassette in Saudi Arabia. Abd al-Hamid Kishk, "the great tenor of the Islamicist movement" in Egypt in the 1970s,[81] was the first to popularize this new technique in the Arab world, where his cassettes were widely distributed. The Kuwaiti Ahmad al-Qattan, a member of the Wahhabi-leaning wing of the emirate's Muslim Brotherhood, inherited the technique of the recorded political-religious sermon from Kishk,[82] but he developed its content along lines more compatible with Wahhabi norms and more acceptable in the Gulf countries, leading a prominent Saudi journalist to call him "the Kishk of the Gulf."[83] Al-Qattan claims as his students some of the most famous Saudi preachers, including ʿAʾid al-Qarni and Abd al-Wahhab al-Turayri.[84] Abd al-Rahman al-Dawsari, finally, was the very first Saudi to have made cassette recordings of his sermons, in the late 1970s.

The Islamic cassette, which soon became a trademark of the Sahwa, enabled these ulema to achieve considerable popularity, extending well beyond Sahwi circles and the religious field. It became a vital tool in the social desegmentation brought about by the rise of the movement. It is what allowed the modernism dispute to spread beyond the exclusive salons of the intellectual field to society as a whole. But the Islamic cassette was primarily exploited by the Sahwi ulema in a struggle they considered much more existential because it was taking place in their own field, and on it depended their position in the field—their struggle with the traditional Wahhabi ulema. The Sahwi ulema were, however, always careful to distinguish between the official religious institution, embodied by a figure like Salih al-Luhaydan, head of the Supreme Council of Justice, bête noire and frequent target of the Sahwis, and its two charismatic leaders, Ibn Baz and Ibn ʿUthaymin, whose papal role placed them above disputes and who were usually exempt from criticism.

The first of the two main foci of the Sahwi ulema's critique was the principle of *fiqh al-waqi*ʿ (meaning both "the understanding of reality" and "the *fiqh* of reality"). The medieval jurist Ibn Qayyim al-Jawziyya (1292–1350), a disciple of Ibn Taymiyya, highly valued by the Wahhabis, defined it as follows:

> Neither a mufti [that is, any person who issues fatwas] nor a judge is in a position to issue a correct opinion if he does not possess two types of understanding. The first consists of understanding the reality [*fiqh al-waqi*ʿ] to which the opinion relates . . . with the help of connections, indications, and indexes. The second type corresponds to the understanding of what should be done with respect to this reality and therefore to the understanding of the judgment of God as it is estab-

lished in His book by the voice of His prophet in the face of that reality. After that, it is only a matter of making the two coincide.[85]

Abundantly quoting Ibn Qayyim, the Sahwi ulema in the second half of the 1980s more and more openly claimed a monopoly over *fiqh al-waqi'*. By doing so, they were hoping to bring to the fore what they considered their superiority over the traditional ulema.

Around this time one of these young Sahwi ulema, Nasir al-'Umar, born in Burayda in 1952, who held a doctorate in the sciences of the Koran from Imam University, where he taught, delivered a lecture titled "*Fiqh al-waqi'*." In it he explains what he and his peers concretely understood by that notion: "A science making it possible to understand current situations, notably the factors acting on societies, the forces dominating states, the ideas designed to undermine faith, and the legitimate means of protecting the *umma* and making it advance now and in the future."[86] For al-'Umar, *fiqh al-waqi'* requires of the ulema, in addition to their mastery of religious sciences, that they possess vast knowledge of "the social sciences such as history, as well as of contemporary political science and the media." He goes on, "If they neglect one of these disciplines or anything else they might need, that will have negative consequences for their understanding of reality and their evaluation of events, and hence for the opinions they express."[87] To achieve their goals, they will have to rely on a certain number of carefully selected sources. Al-'Umar suggests to the practitioner of *fiqh al-waqi'* that he read historical studies, because "whoever does not understand the past does not understand the present";[88] political works, for example, "memoirs of contemporary politicians," "books on international relations, political economy, the functions of an ambassador, and so on"; and finally, "books dealing with the secrets of politics and the role of international organizations, like *The Game of Nations*[89] and the works of Machiavelli."[90] To these, al-'Umar adds books by Islamist writers such as *Our Contemporary Reality* by Muhammad Qutb,[91] *Does History Repeat Itself?* by Muhammad al-'Abda,[92] and the famous pamphlet by Muhammad Surur Zayn al-'Abidin, *Here Come the Zoroastrians*,[93] in which the Syrian sheikh presents the Iranian revolution as the starting point for a strategy of Shiite domination of the Middle East.[94] Finally, the practitioner of *fiqh al-waqi'* needs to follow the media attentively and regularly because "it is no exaggeration to say that someone who stops following the news for six months needs a long time to get back in touch with the present."[95]

Most important, al-'Umar explains that *fiqh al-waqi'* is the most important subject today at every level: for the *umma* in general because its "future depends on the reach of *fiqh al-waqi'* and the attitude that will be adopted toward it";[96] and more specifically for the religious field, "because secularists are conspiring against the ulema, trying to damage their image in the eyes of the masses by using . . . what might look like a contradiction in fatwas or a weakness in *'ilm.*" The only remedy for that is for "the fatwa to be based on reality . . . to pull the rug out from under the feet of the slanderers."[97]

The Sahwi ulema thus presented themselves as saviors of the religious field and of the whole *umma* because they were—so they claimed—the only true holders of *fiqh al-waqi'.* This set them apart from the traditional Wahhabi ulema, against whom they launched constant attacks in their sermons and writings. It is true that this criticism was never direct and never named names, as, for example, when Salman al-'Awda declared that "one of the things for which many ulema of our age can be criticized is that they live in isolation from the reality surrounding them."[98] However, things were entirely different in the closed study circles of the Sahwi ulema, where they did not hesitate to make their thinking explicit to their listeners. According to Yusuf al-Dayni, who frequented Sahwi circles in the late 1980s: "In the study circles we were told that the ulema of the Wahhabi religious institution were, of course, very learned in *fiqh,* but that they lacked awareness, that they did not understand reality. For a purely religious question, it was recommended that we see them. But for any political or intellectual question, we were told to turn to the *du'at* [the 'preachers,' that is, the Sahwi ulema]."[99]

Ancillary to the Sahwi critique on the theme of *fiqh al-waqi'* was the widespread accusation that the traditional Wahhabi ulema "were swamped by minor details" *(al-ighraq fi-l-juz'iyyat)* at the expense of "totalities" *(kulliyat).* This critique was presented in a famous lecture by Salman al-'Awda in which he attacked, again implicitly, "certain ulema" for focusing only on the ritual aspects of the religion and forgetting its political, social, and economic implications.[100]

The question of *irja'* was the second focus of the Sahwi offensive against the traditional religious institution. The term *irja'* (from *arja'*, to postpone one's judgment) literally designates the attitude of not taking sides. Historically, the Murjites (*murji'a,* those who, in the eyes of orthodox Islam, were guilty of *irja'*) were the Muslims who, during the first civil war in Islam among Shiites, Sunnis, and Kharijites in 657, refused to side with any of the factions. Because this, in practice, implied the refusal to rebel against authority, whatever its nature, the notion of *irja'* was associated from the beginning with the idea of political quietism. The term then developed a more general sense, designating anyone who judged a believer (and by extension a ruler) solely on the basis of his declared faith rather than by his actions or even his respect for ritual obligations.[101] It was traditionally understood as derogatory; in medieval writings cataloging "deviant sects" *(firaq)* in Islam, *irja'* always occupied a prominent position.

In the mid-1980s the denunciation of *irja'* became a recurring motif in the discourse of Sahwi ulema. The first issue of the magazine *Al-Bayan,* published in 1986, had a long article titled "*Irja'* and the Murjites." Its arguments were found in more detailed form in the doctoral dissertation of Safar al-Hawali, defended the same year, titled "The Phenomenon of *Irja'* in Islamic Thought." In this dissertation, which was written under the supervision of Muhammad Qutb in the department of creed of Umm al-Qura University,[102] al-Hawali explains at the outset that he intends "to study *irja'* as an intellectual phenomenon [*dhahira fikriyya*], not as a historical sect [*firqa ta'rikhiyya*]," because by considering only the latter, "we would not be able to discover the truth of our contemporary reality, which is dominated by the thinking of *irja'*." He adds: "The most disastrous aspect of this is that certain orientations of Islamic *da'wa*, whose essential purpose is to bring people back to the truth of faith, in creed and in deeds, adhere to this sterile way of thinking and preach along its lines."[103]

As is customary in this kind of writing, the "orientations" just mentioned are never explicitly identified in the course of al-Hawali's long argument. To grasp the real meaning of the text, it is therefore necessary to consider the way in which it was read in Sahwi circles at the time. Interviews have shown that several groups were particularly targeted.[104] First came the Muslim Brotherhood, accused sometimes of being too conciliatory toward established authority and sometimes—as in the case of some of the more liberal thinkers close to them, such as the Egyptian Fahmi Huwaydi[105] and the Sudanese Hasan al-Turabi—of making too many concessions to the "secularists." Because al-Hawali was affiliated with the Sururi *jama'a*, it is probable that with these attacks he was trying to embarrass the Saudi Brothers. The Ahl al-Hadith were another of his targets, in keeping with their ongoing conflict with the Sahwa. A particular focus was al-Albani, whose application of *takfir* was denounced as too restrictive, particularly in the case of Muslims who did not pray, whom al-Albani out of principle refused to excommunicate.[106] However, beyond al-Albani and the Ahl al-Hadith, it was primarily the Wahhabi ulema of the official religious institution who were seen as guilty of *irja'*. The Sahwi sheikhs denounced their constantly quietist attitude toward the regime, which they countered with the principle of the unity of sovereignty *(tawhid al-hakimiyya)*, by virtue of which the ulema could not remain silent before the rulers when *shari'a* was violated, because the faithful application of *shari'a* is an integral part of *tawhid*. Above all, with this principle, they were challenging the traditional separation of powers between the ulema and the princes and the idea that certain spheres could be managed autonomously by the political authorities.

Around the time when his thesis was published as a book and began to be widely distributed, al-Hawali started giving a series of weekly lectures in the Prince Mit'ab Mosque in Jeddah in which he commented on one of the most important works in the Wahhabi corpus, *The Profession of Faith of al-Tahawi* [Al-'aqida al-tahawiyya] by the medieval jurist Ahmad al-Tahawi.[107] When he came to the question of "government in spite of what God has revealed" and of what to do in the face of such a government, al-Hawali set out the opinion of al-Tahawi—which largely echoed the quietist opinions of Ibn Baz, Ibn 'Uthaymin, and the sheikhs of the official institution—before distancing himself from it. To do that, he had to find the support of an authority of a rank equal to that of the ulema he was challenging. He therefore announced that for this part of his commentary, he would rely on a "rare text," the *Letter on Governing through Man-Made Laws*[108] by the former mufti Muhammad bin Ibrahim Al al-Shaykh, who had a much more intransigent position on the question.[109] This text had been practically forgotten because, given its potentially subversive character, the government had decided not to reprint it after its author's death in 1969.[110] By making it the subject of several of his lectures, al-Hawali made it known in Sahwi circles. Photocopies of it soon began circulating and became highly valued.[111] The Sahwi ulema thus made Muhammad bin Ibrahim into a counterauthority whom they opposed to the official Wahhabi ulema of their time.

Although these positions of Safar al-Hawali and other Sahwi ulema, in the spirit of the struggles stirring the religious field, were primarily aimed at discrediting the traditional Wahhabi ulema, they also had obvious, though still latent, political implications. Indeed, the accusation of *irja'* directed against the official religious institution was based on the principle of the unity of sovereignty, which was used here for the first time concretely in the Saudi context. This laid the ground for subsequent challenges to the political authorities. Similarly, in the climate of the late 1980s, the positions of Muhammad bin Ibrahim appeared eminently subversive. A few years later this would facilitate the movement of the Sahwi ulema into open opposition to the regime.

The mid-1980s were thus marked by the simultaneous appearance of Sahwi mobilizations in the religious and intellectual fields, in tune with a broader mobilization of the youth of the Sahwa generation in the social arena. The synchronization of these mobilizations can be explained by two preexisting variables, the economic recession and the entry onto the stage of a new "political generation," that together and in relatively similar ways affected all areas of society. In each case, however, the mobilization took place according to the logic of the field in which it was operating. Hence, for some, the "enemy" was primarily embodied by the traditional Wahhabi ulema, while for others, it was "secularists" or their modernist associates.

The end of the decade, however, was marked by the first signs of a desectorization of the social arena. This is what was at work when the Sahwi ulema went outside their field to lend a hand to Sahwi intellectuals, or when the intellectual field became a sounding board for social frustrations. But for the moment, the political field had succeeded in remaining apart from the effects of the nascent mobilization. That was about to change, giving the emerging crisis an entirely different dimension.

5

The Logic of the Insurrection

The mobilizations that sprang up in the religious and intellectual fields, echoing growing discontent in the social arena, were aimed primarily at denouncing a social order—transfigured into a moral order—that the Sahwis considered unjust. The responsibility for the existence of that order was at first attributed by some to mysterious "plots" hatched by "secularists" to seize control of the state. Initially the royal family was never directly attacked.

Little by little, however, the rhetoric began to change. The royal family was transformed from the victim of those "groups that had confiscated the state" to the principal supporter of their intrigues. The Saudi government became the enemy and was openly attacked. The last vestiges of sectorization disappeared, giving way to the unification of the social arena. This enabled ulema and intellectuals to start acting together, sharing their legitimating and militant resources. It was now possible for the protest to get organized and gain momentum even though, because of the diversity of its actors' worldviews, its meaning and goals would remain contested.

Toward the Politicization of Social Dynamics

Sahwi ideology contained in embryo the fundamentals of a discourse of political opposition, and most of the figures who inspired it—including Muhammad Qutb, Abd al-Rahman al-Dawsari, and Muhammad Ahmad al-Rashid—had been opposition figures in their countries of origin. But in Saudi Arabia the Islamist discourse underlying Sahwi ideology had been subject to some adjustment, for example, when Muhammad Qutb amended the work of his brother Sayyid to eliminate elements that might be seen as subversive by the government. Moreover, the Sahwis had traditionally, at least in appearance, upheld the Islamic character of the Saudi state. In the late 1980s and early 1990s some of them adopted a much more ambiguous position. Although they never openly rejected the legitimacy of the Saudi regime (as the rejectionists and later the jihadis did), they were intent on pointing out its limits, making the principle of the unity of sovereignty *(tawhid al-hakimiyya)* a sword of Damocles suspended over the regime with the aim of pushing it to embark on radical reforms.

According to some accounts, the beginnings of the break between the Sahwa and the Saudi regime go back to the late 1970s. Starting in 1976, violent confrontations raged in Syria between the armed branch of the Muslim Brotherhood and the Baathist regime of President Hafez al-Assad. Wishing to preserve its historic ties to Syria, Saudi Arabia chose to maintain an apparently neutral position.[1] This attitude provoked anger among the Syrian Brothers in Saudi Arabia, who saw it as a betrayal.[2] This anger was conveyed to the Saudi Sahwi networks, over which the Syrians had had significant ascendancy since the time of Muhammad Surur Zayn al-ʿAbidin. Among the young Sahwis stirred by the cause of the Syrian insurrection was Osama bin Laden,[3] then a member of the Saudi Muslim Brotherhood, who worked to gather donations for the insurgents.

Although Sahwi resentment at the official Saudi position in the Syrian crisis was genuine, it nonetheless was kept private. It was only in the late 1980s that public declarations hostile to the political authorities started to take place. These challenges launched against the royal family came first from Sahwi intellectuals, confined to the periphery of an intellectual field that remained the monopoly of the modernists. At first convinced that they were the victims of a "secularist plot" aimed at seizing control of the Saudi state, they gradually adopted the idea that the royal family—which, it was now pointed out, had ultimate control over the press and the literary clubs—was the source of their misfortunes. Antisecularist rhetoric gradually became antiregime rhetoric. Sahwi intellectuals took advantage of the relative freedom of expression afforded to them by the Janadriyya festival to include in their speeches messages that were "subtly hostile to the Saudi regime."[4] Muhammad al-Mas'ari observed, "Janadriyya was transformed into an intellectual earthquake that shook . . . Saudi Arabia. And perhaps future days will show that it was one of the decisive factors in the destruction of the . . . Al Sa'ud."[5]

The latent conflict between Sahwi and traditional Wahhabi ulema was similarly transformed into a conflict with the political authorities, because the Wahhabi religious institution was now gradually seen as nothing but an appendage of the royal family. At that point antiregime rhetoric crept into the religious field, where the most provocative positions were taken by what a member of the Saudi Brotherhood called "kamikaze preachers." He describes them as follows:

> We were generally informed by other *shabab* [youth—a term often used by the Sahwis when talking about each other] a few hours in advance that a preacher was going to deliver a political sermon in a particular mosque. This type of sermon was very popular. A number of us would go to the designated place and listen to the preacher in question. Afterward he was usually dismissed by the authorities and we never saw him again. Sometimes a recording of his sermon had been made, and it continued to circulate on cassette.[6]

In the most extreme cases the sermons denounced "the collusion of the regime with the enemies of the *umma*," whether the United States or the "secularists," and the practice of usury *(riba)* in Saudi banks. But usually they were stinging attacks on the United States and did not necessarily contain a direct allusion to Saudi policies.

The references to the United States were relatively new in Sahwi discourse. Previously the Sahwis had thought that just as the Muslims had sided with the Christian Byzantines against the "atheist" Persians—because, as Nasir al-'Umar wrote, "the victory of the 'people of the book' [ahl al-kitab] is a sign of the victory of Truth over Lies and makes possible the victory of Muslims over the 'people of the book' afterward"[7]—the cold war required implicit support for the United States until the USSR collapsed. The shift first came from external causes, such as perestroika, interpreted as a harbinger of Soviet weakness, and the onset of the Palestinian intifada in 1987, which provoked anger against Israel while having the indirect effect of exposing America's unshakable support for the Jewish state. But the internal causes were perhaps even more significant. The aim was to attack the political authorities in a way that would be most damaging to them, by more or less explicitly associating the royal family with the policies of its main foreign ally. Hence by the late 1980s verbal attacks on the United States often had to be understood as veiled criticisms of the regime.

An emblematic indication of the rise of Sahwi contentiousness was the publication in December 1989 of the first issue of the monthly *Al-Sunna,* edited by the Center for Islamic Studies, located in Birmingham, England. The center had been established in the mid-1980s by Muhammad Surur Zayn al-'Abidin, right after he had arrived from Kuwait, where the radical tenor of his anti-Shiite positions—set out in *Here Come the Zoroastrians,* which he had signed with the pseudonym Abdallah al-Gharib in an attempt to protect himself[8]—drew pressure from the authorities, who wished to mollify the Shiite minority in the emirate.[9] Like the Islamic Forum, with which it had close relations based on Surur's personal and intellectual connections to Muhammad al-'Abda, the Center for Islamic Studies saw itself as a Sururi think tank. And like *Al-Bayan, Al-Sunna* soon became required reading for Sururi circles in Saudi Arabia.[10]

Despite the strong ties between them, the difference between *Al-Bayan* and *Al-Sunna* was considerable. While *Al-Bayan* systematically avoided anything that might appear subversive in the eyes of the Saudi regime and limited itself to abstract considerations, *Al-Sunna* did not hesitate to attack the royal family when it thought that necessary. It would do so in a rather vehement way after the call for American troops in August 1990. According to Muhammad al-Mas'ari, "This duality of positions was necessary for the Sururis, who were then hesitating about the attitude to adopt vis-à-vis the regime. At the same time, Muhammad Surur was independent enough that the Sururis in the kingdom did not have to pay the price for his attacks."[11]

One result of the uncompromising line adopted by *Al-Sunna* was that the few Saudis who ventured to publish articles in it usually used pseudonyms—Salman al-'Awda, for example, signed an article with the pseudonym Abu Mu'adh al-Khalidi.[12] An exception, however, was Muhammad al-Hudayf, born in 1950 and then a student in the United Kingdom, who contributed regularly to the journal under his own name until he returned to Saudi Arabia in 1992[13] and earned some renown in Sahwi intellectual circles. But in general, *Al-Sunna* had to count on non-Saudi intellectuals sympathetic to Sururism, including the Egyptian Gamal Sultan, who also wrote for *Al-Bayan*. Another effect of the critical tone *Al-Sunna* adopted toward the Saudi regime was that from its very first issue it was prohibited from entering the kingdom. That did not prevent the Sahwis from smuggling it into the country every month and making large numbers of photocopies that were distributed outside mosques and in universities. When those participating in the distribution were caught red-handed, they were arrested, like the Saudi opposition member now exiled in London, Kassab al-'Utaybi, who says that he was jailed three times for this very reason.[14]

In 1988 and 1989, confronted with growing signs of unrest, the political authorities had begun to take steps involving a careful mixture of regulation and coercion; the steps were taken by sector, an indication that the royal family wanted to maintain at all costs the divisions of the social arena. In the religious field, the proliferation of remarks hostile to the United States, and indirectly to the Saudi regime, was so great that on December 21, 1988, a circular from the Ministry of Hajj and *Waqf*s (in charge of mosques) noted that "some mosque orators call in their sermons for the destruction ... of the Jews, the Christians, and other religious groups, identifying the states by name," and then explained that "that is not what the Koran has taught us, for the

Koran contains no particular names of states," and called for an end to this practice.[15] In addition to sermons, two other methods the Sahwis used to spread their message were targeted. On August 11, 1988, a circular from the Ministry of Hajj and *Waqf*s prohibited the spontaneous distribution or posting on walls of mosques of posters containing "religious advice" *(nasiha)* and "guidance" *(irshad)*.[16] In November 1989 the authorities raided the Islamic recordings stores in Mecca and other cities in the kingdom. Some employees were arrested and then released after promising to stop selling cassettes with subversive content. A large quantity of material was also confiscated.[17] According to some sources, a high-level meeting was organized in January 1990 by Prince Salman, the governor of Riyadh, attended by representatives from the Ministry of the Interior, the Ministry of Information, and the Ministry of Hajj and *Waqf*s. The group recommended increasing the pressure on preachers and owners of Islamic recordings stores to avoid any further disorder.[18]

But as the Saudi regime was beginning to intervene in the religious field to attempt to put an end to the first signs of protest of the Sahwi ulema, in the intellectual field the regime was siding with the Sahwi intellectuals in their battle with the modernists. Until 1988 the regime had been careful to preserve at any cost the autonomy of the intellectual field by refraining from interference in the disputes between Sahwis and modernists,[19] but the increasing pressure of the Sahwis at Janadriyya and in the literary clubs, which was causing growing tensions, placed it in an embarrassing position. The involvement of the Sahwi ulema in 1987 broadened the scope of the conflict, which spilled into the social arena. In early 1988 ʿAwad al-Qarni persuaded Ibn Baz to write a laudatory preface for *Modernism in the Light of Islam*. The leading figure of the Wahhabi establishment called the book an "invaluable work" that had "made it possible to lift the veil on these modernists and bring to light their nefarious intentions."[20] This unusually open support from Ibn Baz for one side in the conflict radically changed the situation for the regime.[21] Afraid of seeing its religious legitimacy sacrificed on the altar of an increasingly controversial modernizing legitimacy, it was obliged to react. To calm the waters in the religious field, the princes decided to drop their support for intellectuals who were, in the last analysis, much less vital to them than their historic partners, the heirs of the religious cofounder of the Saudi state.

In September 1988 the Saudi Ministry of the Interior consequently ordered the Saudi media to stop publishing anything about modernism.[22] Within months numerous intellectuals classified as modernists working for the cultural supplements of Saudi newspapers were transferred[23] or simply fired.[24] This produced radical changes in editorial lines. To mention only one example, the magazine *Iqra'*, whose literary pages had until then celebrated Abdallah al-Ghadhdhami, Ali al-Dumayni, and ʿAbid Khazindar, now published a column by the modernists' sworn enemy, Muhammad al-Milibari,[25] along with reviews of works of "Islamic literature" and articles by one of the first Sahwi female intellectuals, Suhayla Zayn al-ʿAbidin.[26] Moreover, the modernists were subjected to increasing harassment. Al-Ghadhdhami was put under so much pressure at King Abd al-Aziz University in Jeddah, where he was teaching, that he was forced to ask for a transfer to King Saʿud University in Riyadh. Saʿid al-Surayhi was refused his doctorate because of the impiety his dissertation allegedly contained.[27]

At the same time, the gates of Saudi cultural institutions were opened wide for the Sahwa, which finally moved from the audience onto the platform. At the literary club of Riyadh, the invited speakers were now Muhammad Qutb, Ahmad al-Tuwayjiri, or Tawfiq al-Qusayyir.[28] The club in Jeddah, which had historically been considered the main modernist bastion, held seminars on religious themes.[29] But the most spectacular change occurred at Janadriyya, where Abd al-Aziz al-Tuwayjiri had personally supervised the selection of speakers from the outset.[30] The task was now turned over to the Faculty of *Daʿwa* and Communication of Imam University,[31] the faculty that had been established a few years earlier with the help of the Sudanese member of the Muslim Brotherhood Zayn al-ʿAbidin al-Rikabi, and where the Sahwis had an overwhelming majority. Beginning in 1988, Sahwi intellectuals occupied pride of place in the program. Saʿid bin Zuʿayr and Muhammad al-Masʿari now even chaired some debates.[32] The program also featured Sahwi ulema: ʿAʾid al-Qarni and Safar al-Hawali were among the participants at the spring 1989 session.[33] Foreign guests included increasing numbers of prominent Islamist intellectuals, like the Tunisian Rashid al-Ghannushi, the founder of the Ennahda movement, and the Algerian Abbasi Madani, cofounder of the Islamic Salvation Front (FIS), who both attended in 1989.[34] The program also contained religious lectures delivered by Ibn Baz and Ibn 'Uthaymin.[35]

The Gulf War Crisis as Catalyst

When Saddam Hussein invaded Kuwait on August 2, 1990, the Saudi regime feared that the Iraqi army would continue its advance, penetrate into Saudi Arabia, and seize the Eastern Province of the kingdom, where the oil wealth is concentrated. In the face of this threat, the royal family, which had reached a unified position after some internal debates, determined that it had no choice but to call on an international force led by the United States to protect the country, which would also serve as a rear base for the liberation of Kuwait. The first American soldiers stepped onto Saudi soil on August 7, 1990, and on August 9, after a complete news blackout of several days, King Fahd publicly announced that the appeal to foreign soldiers was a necessary measure, but that their presence would be temporary.[36] It was not long before the facts contradicted him. After the liberation of Kuwait in late February 1991, the United States maintained its bases in Saudi Arabia, arguing for the necessity of preserving a military presence close to Iraq in order to enforce United Nations resolutions.[37]

These events are of considerable importance, but for reasons that partly differ from what has been previously asserted. The Gulf War has generally been looked at as representing the source of a "crisis of legitimacy" for the Saudi regime, of which the rising power of Islamism was the consequence.[38] It is true that the Gulf War caused delegitimization, but the dynamics at work were far more complex. Indeed, when the Saudi government called on the Americans, the Sahwa was already at the height of its influence, and local mobilizations had been occurring for several years in two key fields, the religious and the intellectual, which were the regime's "reservoirs of legitimacy."[39] Moreover, the incipient politicization of each field had begun to provoke tensions between them and with the authorities. Thus by August 1990 the legitimacy of the regime had already been affected.

To try to defuse the approaching crisis, the government had no choice but to counterattack on both flanks of its legitimacy by urging its allies in the religious and intellectual fields to take up the defense of its positions. The Wahhabi religious institution had to respond to criticism from the religious field (that is, the Sahwi ulema), while the liberal intellectuals were called on to react to criticism from the intellectual field (that is, from Sahwi intellectuals inside the country and from Islamists abroad). By adopting this scheme, the regime hoped to enforce the divisions of the social arena by providing responses by sector while minimizing any visible interaction that the political field might have with other fields.

In the religious field, the Council of the Committee of Senior Ulema held a special meeting on August 13, 1990, and issued a fatwa in which it "support[ed] the actions decided on by the leader—may God grant him success—to call upon qualified forces possessing equipment provoking fear and terror in those who would like to commit aggression against this country."[40] The next day the president of the Supreme Council of Justice, followed by the judges of the Final Court of Appeal, issued a similar opinion.[41] In short, all representatives of traditional Wahhabism and of the official religious institution lined up behind the political authorities.

The Saudi regime also decided to mobilize its supporters in the intellectual field, the very men it had sacrificed to the Sahwis a couple of years earlier. In return, the Sahwis, who had gained a foothold in the Saudi media in the late 1980s, now disappeared once more, replaced by many liberal voices who justified the position taken by the regime. The most emblematic among them was the former minister Ghazi al-Qusaybi. Al-Qusaybi was the typical intellectual bureaucrat who never lost an occasion to stress that he had "put every moment of his life at the service of the development *(tanmiya)* of the country, including the building of schools, hospitals, factories, and roads."[42] Beginning in the autumn of 1990, he published a daily column in *Al-Sharq al-Awsat* under the title "In the Eye of the Storm," defending the official Saudi position and utterly condemning its opponents. Al-Qusaybi's favorite targets were those he called "Saddamist fundamentalists" *(al-usuliyyun al-saddamiyyun)*, meaning all the Islamist intellectuals of the Middle East who, like the Tunisian Rashid al-Ghannushi, the Algerian Abbasi Madani, and the Sudanese Hasan al-Turabi,[43] had denounced the call on American forces, thereby in al-Qusaybi's view implicitly siding with the Iraqi dictator. But although those foreign activists were his first targets, the spectrum of his attacks soon expanded to include the Sahwa.

The Sahwi ulema, who had definitively broken free from the confines of the religious field despite the regime's attempts to maintain sectoral divisions, reacted vehemently in both the religious and the intellectual debates. Not hesitating to transform their latent conflict with the traditional ulema that had been brewing since the late 1980s into open warfare, they directly challenged the decision to call on foreign troops to protect the kingdom and denounced the religious authorities' support for the move. Safar al-Hawali was the first to speak on this subject in an improvised speech on August 19, 1990,[44] and then in a study submitted to the Committee of Senior Ulema that was subsequently published in London under the title *Leading the Ulema of the Umma out of Confusion*. Brandishing the principle of *fiqh al-waqiʿ*, he asserted that the fatwa by the Council of the Committee of Senior Ulema authorizing the call on foreign troops was mistaken because of its complete ignorance of reality *(waqiʿ)*. Basing his argument on Western analyses and newspaper articles, al-Hawali claimed that the American military presence in the Gulf constituted primarily the realization of a long-range American plan to seize the region's resources. As a result, the fatwa of the "senior ulema" was erroneous because "the reality is not at bottom a call for assistance *[istiʿana]*," as the committee had argued to justify its decision. But al-Hawali went further by challenging the very legality, with regard to *shariʿa*, of calling on the infidels for aid.[45] He was thereby taking a position not only with respect to the understanding of reality, over which the Sahwis had long claimed a monopoly, but also with respect to basic issues of *fiqh*, which represented an unprecedented challenge to his elders. Al-Hawali went on to point out the inherent contradictions in the positions of the senior ulema. Had not Ibn Baz himself, at the height of the Arab cold war, when Nasser called on Soviet experts for assistance, definitively condemned this practice?[46] This contradiction was widely commented on in Sahwi circles and became the subject of various sermons starting in late August 1990, all of which challenged the validity of the August 13 fatwa. This fostered the idea that these "senior ulema" were in fact only "palace ulema" producing fatwas on demand.[47]

The articles by liberals, particularly those by al-Qusaybi, provoked even more vehement attacks from the Sahwi ulema, first because the rules of decorum between men of religion did not apply, second because al-Qusaybi—the "theorist of secularism," as he was referred to in Sahwi circles[48]—had been a bête noire of the Sahwi ulema since the 1980s, and finally because al-Qusaybi, openly breaching sectoral boundaries, had in his articles assumed the right to speak about religion, for instance, stating that fatwas were changeable by nature and had to adapt to modern circumstances.[49] For the Sahwi ulema, this "exploitation of religion for secularist purposes,"[50] a flagrant violation of their special preserve, was a genuine casus belli. The first sheikh to react was ʿAʾid al-Qarni, in a speech titled "Arrows in the Eye of the Storm," in which he went so far as to threaten reprisals against his "secularist" enemies, especially al-Qusaybi: "What would happen if the sword of the ruler protecting the *tawhid* fell on their heads, if it crucified them after Friday prayers and picked up their heads?"[51] This speech was followed by two sermons by al-ʿAwda and al-ʿUmar,[52] equally vehement and very widely distributed.

But far from retreating, al-Qusaybi answered these three preachers with a vitriolic book titled *Until There Is No More Fitna*. The title, explicitly referring to a verse of the Koran frequently quoted by the Islamists,[53] indicates something of its tenor. Accused of encroaching on the ulema's special preserve, al-Qusaybi answered by upping the ante, copiously quoting Ibn Taymiyya and Ibn Qayyim while conversely calling on the Sahwi ulema to "stick to their field of specialization," that is, to respect the divisions of the social arena and not step outside the religious field. Moreover, he accused them of wanting more than anything to come to power.[54] To the "secularist conspiracy" imagined by the Sahwis al-Qusaybi counterposed an "Islamist conspiracy"[55] that he claimed was designed to install an Iranian-style regime where the ulema would be the rulers.[56] With this book, the conflict between Islamists and liberals took on a more radical dimension.

Sahwi reactions were not long in coming. In late 1991 the sheikh and Sahwi ideologue Muhammad Saʿid al-Qahtani and two intellectuals of the same tendency, Walid al-Tuwayriqi and Saʿid bin Zuʿayr, co-authored a book titled *Secularism Laid Bare: Al-Qusaybi, Poet Yesterday and Preacher Today,*[57] which set al-Qusaybi's "libertine" poetry alongside his writings on Islam. But Sahwis were particularly surprised by al-Qusaybi's resistance to their attacks: *Until There Is No More Fitna* was widely distributed—"by the boxful," al-Hawali said in one of his sermons[58]—and was reprinted only four months after publication.[59] Increasingly it was pointed out that the media in which he and other "secularists" wrote were the property of Saudi princes, including the newspaper *Al-Sharq al-Awsat,* owned by Faysal bin Salman, son of the governor of Riyadh. Because of the color of its pages, the Sahwis called it the "manure green" *(khadraʾ al-daman)* newspaper, and they frequently launched calls to boycott it.[60] It was only a short step from that to the conclusion that al-Qusaybi was acting on orders from the royal family—Prince Salman, according to some, or even directly from King Fahd, according to others[61]—and the Sahwis did not hesitate to take this step. The "secularists," they declared, were nothing but agents of the Saudi government, revealing its true face.

The counterattack by the royal family had thus had the opposite of its intended effect. Support of the dominant elites of the religious and intellectual fields for as controversial a decision as the call on American troops laid bare the mechanisms of the collusive transactions that linked those elites to the political authorities. In circumstances in which they had already been the targets of Sahwi mobilizations for several years in their respective sectors, the consequences were dramatic. Rather than limiting their attacks to the religious institution and the liberal intellectuals, Sahwi ulema and intellectuals now targeted those they considered ultimately the ones truly responsible for the intrigues of their opponents, the princes of the royal family. The politicization of the sectors and their rationales begun in the late 1980s was now fully accomplished.

On November 8, 1990, an incident of an unprecedented kind in Saudi Arabia added a significant catalyst to the crisis. Forty-nine Saudi women driving in fifteen cars paraded down ʿUlaya Street in Riyadh to demand the right to drive. They were arrested, and some of them spent the night at the police station and had their passports confiscated; those who taught at the university were suspended and did not recover their positions until two years later.[62] Most of these women had received degrees in the United States in the 1980s and were connected to the liberal current that the Sahwis considered the driving force behind the "secularist conspiracy." Several of them, such as Fawziyya al-Bakr and ʿAziza al-Maniʿ, the chief organizers of the demonstration, had become known for their outspoken writings on the condition of Saudi women. Their decision to demonstrate seems to have been the result of coordination among different liberal circles.[63] Convinced that the presence of thousands of female American soldiers driving military vehicles into the cities of the kingdom offered them a unique opportunity to change mentalities, these liberals had decided to make their demands heard.[64]

This incident had a colossal effect, "even more important than the whole question of the call on American troops,"[65] on the development of the protest. The Sahwis saw it as evidence, as Nasir al-ʿUmar declared, that "the secularists or more precisely the hypocrites [*al-munafiqun*]—to use the religious term—have begun to close ranks and to weave their plots at the very moment when many of us had imagined that they had turned tail in defeat. They have begun to speak again, but, worse than that, they have acted."[66] The impact of the incident was even greater because the account presented in Sahwi circles seemed wide of the facts.[67] According to the rumors, the parade of cars had left from the diplomatic quarter; the women were wearing makeup and were "not veiled," which in Sahwi terms meant that they were wearing only a headscarf, not a *niqab* covering the face; one of them was even said to have thrown her headscarf to the ground and to have trampled on it.[68] Moreover, Sahwi leaflets accused Prince Salman of having given his prior approval to the demonstrators, as the women were said to have insolently repeated to the officers from the Committee for Commanding Right and Forbidding Wrong who had raced to the scene of the incident.[69] According to the leaflets, Salman was alleg-edly using the demonstration to divert the Sahwis' attention from the royal family by turning it to the "secularists."[70] If that had really been the goal, it was an obvious failure because all the incident did was to increase the pressure on the political authorities. Ibn Baz's fatwa and the communiqué from the Ministry of the Interior[71] issued shortly there-after to reiterate the ban on women driving did nothing to remedy the situation. Hence the event's only result was to strengthen the identifi-cation the Sahwa believed existed between its historic rivals in the re-ligious and intellectual fields and the political field. The last vestiges of the logic of sectorization were swept away.

A Heterogeneous Opposition Front

The transformations that occurred in the wake of the Gulf War led to a considerable intensification of the crisis and prompted a significant shift in the logic that it followed. As a result, the Sahwi protest took on a new character, with the collaboration of elites from various fields forming an opposition front to the political field. These individuals belonged to three main groups with relatively distinct worldviews: the Sahwi ulema; the *munasirun* (supporters), a term designating the few traditional Wahhabi ulema who supported the movement; and the Sahwi intellectuals. Although they appeared to share a common pro-gram, their differences meant that it would have to coexist with the particular emphases of each group in a relationship of constant ten-sion. At the heart of this relationship lay the definition of the meaning and goals of the protest.

The first of these groups was the Sahwi ulema. Although they be-longed to the religious field, the particularities of their discourse and methods conferred on them, at least in comparison with the tradi-tional Wahhabi ulema, an unquestionable modernity. This appeared particularly in their political conceptions, which contrasted with the nonexistent or totally quietist views of their elders in the religious establishment. Safar al-Hawali's geopolitical analyses illustrate this specificity very well. Like al-Hawali, Salman al-'Awda was known for having developed one of the most sophisticated political discourses among these ulema. Moreover, because of his earlier controversy with Sheikh Muhammad al-Ghazzali, he already enjoyed a solid reputation in Sahwi circles. On August 28, 1990, a few weeks after the call to foreign troops, al-'Awda delivered a lecture titled "The Causes of the Collapse of States," in which he presented a relatively coherent vision of domestic politics, emphasizing what a state should not do if it wanted its legitimacy to endure. Drawing on the *Prolegomena* of the medieval thinker Ibn Khaldoun (1332–1406), he described twelve causes likely to lead to the collapse of a state, among which were the moral and economic corruption of its governing apparatus, the oppression imposed by its leaders, and the absence of consultation *(shura)* in decision making. The oppositional tenor of the discourse was clear when al-'Awda warned against "any weakening of the foundation on which the state is built," continuing, in a bold allusion to the Saudi regime:

> Some states were founded on the basis of religion, to protect and propagate it, to implement the principle of commanding right and forbidding wrong, and to apply *shari'a*. . . . As long as a state [like this] remains faithful to its foundation and to the purpose for which it was built, it cannot fail to remain powerful, respected, and unconquered, because it has the support of its population. But if it moves away from its founding rationale . . . it loses the reason for its existence, and its first supporters abandon it . . . while it shows itself unable to win new support, which causes its collapse.[72]

If questions of a strictly political order occupied the Sahwi ulema, they represented only one aspect of a discourse that was above all distinguished by its totalizing character. Thus moral and religious questions, like those related to the purity of the creed, also continued to be priorities for the Sahwi ulema. To some extent, religion and morals were even seen as the root cause of all events. This explains why Safar al-Hawali concluded his long demonstration that the American presence in Saudi Arabia was the implementation of an old plan to control the resources of the Gulf by proclaiming that "the real explanation for this catastrophe, as God has shown in His Book ... is that what has stricken us is nothing but the product of our faults, our sins, and our rebellion against the Law of God."[73] The solution, he explains elsewhere, is

> for us to remind people of the presence of God, create bonds between them and Him ... teach them the return to the Koran and tell them: build mosques, end the corruption that fills the shopping centers, command right and forbid wrong, repent. .... For if you change what is in you, you will see that God will have Saddam overthrown by a military coup or something of the kind, then you will see that God will cause the disappearance of America—which is the greatest and most dangerous enemy—by whatever means seems good to Him, and He will come to our aid against it.[74]

In light of the previous passages, it is difficult to agree with Mamoun Fandy's assertion that "Hawali is writing as a strategic thinker rather than a theologian."[75] Strategic thinking for him is merely a detour to reach conclusions largely within the realm of religious morality. As central as the political register may be in Sahwi thinking, it does not represent for these ulema an end in itself. Ideologically the Sahwi ulema, with their hybrid worldview, were thus located halfway between the two other groups that were to take part in the reform effort: the *munasirun,* whose view of the world was based mostly on traditional Wahhabism, and the Sahwi intellectuals, chief among whom were the so-called enlightened Sahwi intellectuals, whose conceptions were essentially political.

In the wake of Saddam Hussein's invasion of Kuwait, the most prominent of the Sahwi ulema, about thirty of them, decided to meet regularly to coordinate their efforts. These sessions, at first informal, were institutionalized in March 1991 with the establishment of a "monthly forum" *(al-muntada al-shahri),*[76] also called the "council of preachers" *(majlis al-duʿat);* the inevitable Sheikh Ibn Baz, still playing his papal role, agreed to be honorary president.[77] This forum was set up independently of the *jamaʿat* and the divisions to which they led in Sahwi circles. It contained side by side preachers of Sururi tendency such as Salman al-ʿAwda, Safar al-Hawali, and Nasir al-ʿUmar, others linked to the Brotherhood, like ʿAwad al-Qarni and Nasir al-ʿAql, and independents like ʿAʾid al-Qarni. In this sense the council of preachers embodied, in the religious field, the recovered unity of the Sahwa in the face of the crisis. Some *munasirun* also sometimes attended the meetings.

Above all, the establishment of an institution of this kind expressed the growing pretensions of the ulema of the Sahwa to constitute themselves as an independent religious authority, hence necessarily in competition with the official religious institution. The Sahwi ulema (who were increasingly claiming the title of "ulema," in addition to their traditional label "preachers," *duʿat*) no longer hesitated to claim the right, jealously guarded by the traditional Wahhabi ulema, to issue fatwas. During the three and a half years of its existence, which ended with the mass arrests of September and October 1994,[78] the council of preachers issued a dozen joint fatwas on events in Saudi Arabia and the Muslim world. Some, like the one in the spring of 1992 in which the sheikhs expressed their satisfaction at the overthrow of the Communist government of Najibullah in Afghanistan,[79] or the one in which, a few months earlier, they called for a halt to disputes between Islamists in Saudi Arabia and elsewhere after the assassination of Jamil al-Rahman,[80] were relatively consensual. Others were much less so.

For example, a fatwa was issued in the form of an open letter to Sheikh Ibn Baz in the wake of the Madrid conference between representatives of Israel and various Arab countries in the fall of 1991.[81] After the Saudi regime had suggested that it was disposed to participate in the peace process, the Sahwi ulema resolutely came out against any normalization of relations with the Jewish state and for a continuation of the jihad. In the summer of 1993 another joint fatwa implicitly denounced the Saudi government's "lack of support" for the Bosnian cause.[82] And when the Yemeni Socialist Party in May 1994 declared the secession of South Yemen, which had merged with the North in May 1990, the Sahwi ulema drafted a vehement manifesto.[83] They denounced the Saudi regime's policy of discreetly supporting the secessionists in order to weaken the new Yemeni regime, as well as a June 1994 fatwa from Ibn Baz in *Al-Daʿwa* calling for a reconciliation between the two sides,[84] without making any distinction between them, "as though the communists had become Muslims and should no longer be fought with jihad!"[85] This direct challenge to the elderly sheikh marked a certain radicalization of the opposition.

To strengthen their claims to authority, the Sahwi ulema also organized demonstrations of strength in the religious field, like the first great "competition for the memorization of the sunna" *(musabaqat al-sunna al-nabawiyya)*[86] organized by Salman al-ʿAwda in Burayda in October 1992. This event drew delegations from all the cities of the kingdom, including most of the rising stars in the Sahwa—Sururis, Muslim Brothers, and independents alike. It was arguably the first Sahwi gathering of this magnitude.[87] Also among those invited were the traditional *munasirun*. The event lasted for several days, included a series of lectures and seminars (with such figures as al-Hawali, Ibn Zuʿayr, and al-ʿUmar) in the various cities of the Qasim, and attracted an unusually large audience: al-ʿAwda estimated it as at least fifteen thousand.[88]

Even more than a demonstration of strength, this meeting was intended to be a demonstration of *ʿilm*. To claim religious authority, the Sahwa needed to shed the stigma its enemies had applied to it of being more interested in politics than in religious science. In these circumstances the decision to organize a competition for the memorization of the sunna was especially meant as a challenge to the Ahl al-Hadith, who had made the hadiths their field of choice and the essence of all religious knowledge.

The *munasirun* (literally, the "supporters," plural of *munasir*) were the second group to take part in the protest. The term, used in certain Islamist circles at the time, designated the traditional Wahhabi ulema who, unlike their peers who made up the bulk of the official Saudi religious institution, had chosen to ally themselves with the young Sahwi activists and to support the nascent opposition. The role of the *munasirun* was essential for the Sahwis because they granted unquestionable Wahhabi legitimacy to the movement, and their presence alone made it possible to oppose openly the ulema of the official religious institution. At the same time, the *munasirun* had a worldview that differed greatly from that of the Sahwis. Because of their traditional training, political questions were largely foreign to them, and the focus of their criticism was almost exclusively on moral and social questions.

There are various explanations for the support these sheikhs offered to the opposition. First of all, the group included traditional Wahhabi ulema who believed that they had not received the honors they deserved from the official religious institution. The example of Hamud al-Shuʿaybi is a good illustration of this. This old blind sheikh had been born in 1927 in Shaqra, in the heart of the Najdi crescent, from the Banu Khalid tribe, which was well represented among the major Wahhabi ulema.[89] He was one of the first students at the Scientific Institute of Riyadh, where he was taught by the most prominent sheikhs of the time, including Muhammad bin Ibrahim and Muhammad al-Amin al-Shanqiti, to whom he was very close. He began teaching courses on creed at the same institute in 1955 and then joined Imam University on its foundation. There he taught some of those who would become major figures in the official religious institution, including Salih al-Fawzan and Abd al-Aziz Al al-Shaykh, both members of the Council of Senior Ulema (Al al-Shaykh even became the kingdom's mufti in 1999).[90] However, despite his age, his origins, and his experience, al-Shuʿaybi was never invited to join the highest bodies in the religious field. He was especially jealous of Muhammad bin ʿUthaymin, who also taught at Imam University. Unlike al-Shuʿaybi, Ibn ʿUthaymin, one year younger, had been promoted to the Council of the Committee of Senior Ulema, where he was seen as second after Ibn Baz. At the university Ibn ʿUthaymin, considered a real star, taught only two courses, which were always heavily attended, while al-Shuʿaybi received no special treatment and had to give six courses at which students were not particularly assiduous. This personal hostility to Ibn ʿUthaymin, reflecting a broader feeling of marginalization, seems to have been one of the primary reasons that al-Shuʿaybi joined the protest.[91]

The same factor showed up in the careers of two other *munasirun,* Abdallah bin Jibrin and Abd al-Rahman al-Barrak. Like al-Shuʿaybi, Ibn Jibrin, born in 1933, came from the Najdi crescent—the town of al-Quwayʿiyya—and from the Banu Zayd tribe, well represented among the Wahhabi ulema. He too was educated at highly reputed institutions by the greatest ulema of the time, including Muhammad bin

Ibrahim. By the 1960s he was teaching in various scientific institutes and, from 1975 on, in the department of creed of Imam University. In 1982 he was appointed fatwa officer (*ʿadu iftaʾ*) in the General Office for the Management of Scientific Research, Fatwas, Preaching, and Guidance;[92] in other words, he was a minor official[93] whose prerogatives were purely administrative and was not a member of the prestigious Permanent Committee for Research and Fatwas,[94] much less, as has sometimes mistakenly been written, a member of the Council of the Committee of Senior Ulema.[95] His growing popularity in Sahwi circles, with which he had established contacts, contrasted with the frustration of a man who believed that he was not rising quickly enough in the religious field. This frustration probably lies behind his support for the opposition. Abd al-Rahman al-Barrak, also born in 1933, came from a social background less prized in the religious field than that of Ibn Jibrin or al-Shuʿaybi. He was born in al-Bukayriyya, in the Najdi crescent, but was according to some indications a *khadiri*[96] (other sources indicate that he came from the Subayʿ tribe),[97] for which he compensated by a very close association with Ibn Baz.[98] He was one of the first students of the Scientific Institute of Riyadh in 1952, where he was taught by the most prominent sheikhs in the kingdom. He lectured there in turn from 1959 to 1962 and then joined the department of creed at Imam University on its creation, a post he held until 2000.[99] However, al-Barrak was always kept in a subordinate position in the official religious institution. Like Ibn Jibrin and al-Shuʿaybi, it was his alliance with the Sahwa in the 1980s and 1990s that brought him to the front of the stage.

A second category of *munasirun* consisted of two traditional ulema whose children played a major role in the Sahwi protest movement and drew their fathers in at their side. They were Abdallah al-Masʿari, former president of the Claims Court (Diwan al-madhalim) and father of the Sahwi intellectual Muhammad al-Masʿari; and the exclusivist Hamud al-Tuwayjiri, father of the Sahwi sheikh Abdallah al-Tuwayjiri. Al-Tuwayjiri's joining was particularly surprising because he was at first strongly opposed to the Sahwa. Aside from his son's influence, his great age and illness, which means that he may have had only a fragmentary awareness of the events around him (he died in late 1992), could explain what seems to have been a genuine reversal. As for Abdallah al-Mas'ari, the fact that after being close to King Faysal, he had been shunted aside and removed from his position at the Claims Court in 1975 probably contributed to his radicalization.[100]

Three other ulema became *munasirun* for less obvious reasons. Abdallah bin Qu'ud, born in 1925, was able, despite his *khadiri* ancestry, to join the Committee of Senior Ulema in 1977.[101] For him to achieve this, the unconditional support of Ibn Baz, to whom, like al-Barrak, he was very close, seems to have been decisive.[102] However, Ibn Qu'ud was dismissed in 1986, something unprecedented in the committee's history, "following his refusal to sign certain fatwas."[103] It is difficult to determine whether his inclination to dissent was the source or the result of that decision. In any event, in the early 1990s Abdallah bin Qu'ud brought unfailing support to the Sahwi movement of protest. Although Abd al-Mushin al-'Ubaykan was born in 1952 and thus was younger than the other *munasirun,* he is universally described as a traditional Wahhabi sheikh, which means that at the crucial period when the Sahwa was establishing its presence in the education system, he was able to pass through the mesh of the Sahwi net. After studies at the Faculty of *Shari'a* of Riyadh, he became a judge in 1975 and then imam of al-Jawhara Mosque in the capital in 1981.[104] According to some accounts, it was his reading in mid-1990 of the book *The Manifest Evidence of the Impiety of the Saudi State,* in which Abu Muhammad al-Maqdisi supported his argument with numerous citations drawn from Wahhabi texts, that drew al-'Ubaykan into the opposition.[105] He thereafter became one of the most active *munasirun* in the early stages of the Sahwi protest movement. A third traditional sheikh, Abdallah al-Jilali, born in 'Unayza in the 1920s, also became one of the *munasirun,* but al-Jilali seems to have been involved with Sahwi circles since the time of Abd al-Rahman al-Dawsari, to whom he had close ties.[106]

Some sources claim the existence of broader support by the traditional Wahhabi ulema for the Sahwi opposition. They point to the fact that the September 1992 fatwa of the Council of the Committee of Senior Ulema condemning the *Memorandum of Advice (Mudhakkirat al-nasiha),* the main political manifesto of the Sahwi opposition, bore the signatures of only ten of its seventeen members.[107] According to these sources, the seven missing senior ulema had deliberately refused to denounce the protest movement by not signing the document.[108] The fact that two months later, on December 2, 1992, the seven nonsignatories were dismissed and replaced with ten new members (increasing the total number of council members from seventeen to twenty) is seen as a confirmation that they had challenged the regime.[109] However, interviews in Saudi Arabia of figures close to the ulema in question suggest that this supposition is without foundation.[110] As the text of the September 1992 fatwa indicates, the seven absent ulema were genuinely ill. Hence they were dismissed simply because they were unable to fulfill their duties. Most of them in fact died shortly after they were replaced, at a very advanced age: Abd al-Aziz bin Salih died in 1994 at the age of 83;[111] Abd al-Razzaq ʿAfifi in 1994 at 89; Abdallah al-Khayyat in 1995 at 87;[112] and Sulayman bin ʿUbayd in 1995 at 87.[113]

Ibn Baz and, to a lesser degree, Ibn ʿUthaymin are also often described as discreet but faithful supporters of the Sahwi opposition.[114] However, although they appear on various occasions to have sided with the Sahwa, a careful examination of their positions indicates that they provided as much support to the Sahwa's rivals in an attempt to retain their papal role, the essence of which was to stand above disputes. This policy sometimes applied even outside the religious field. This explains why both Ghazi al-Qusaybi, in *Until There Is No More Fitna*,[115] and his Sahwi adversary Walid al-Tuwayriqi, one of the authors of *Secularism Laid Bare: Al-Qusaybi, Poet Yesterday, Preacher Today*,[116] could claim in their writings to have received the support of Ibn Baz.

The third category of individuals who played an active role in the Sahwi protest movement was the Sahwi intellectuals who had come to the forefront through their struggle against the modernists in the 1980s. By the end of that decade the small group that Abd al-Aziz al-Wuhaybi, one of its mainstays, called the "enlightened Sahwi intellectuals" *(al-muthaqqafun al-sahawiyyun al-mustanirun)* stood out from the rest, and it soon imposed itself as the most vocal and active element among the Saudi Sahwi intellectuals.

In the early 1980s most of those who were to become the "enlight-ened" Sahwi intellectuals had, at a time when they had already been won over to Sahwi ideas, gone to study in the West, where they discov-ered a "more sophisticated form of Islamism" (as one member de-scribed it) than the variety current in the kingdom.[117] Socialized in student organizations close to the Muslim Brotherhood, like the Mus-lim Arab Youth Association in the United States, to which Muham-mad al-Hudayf, among others, belonged,[118] and Hizb al-Tahrir in Ger-many in the case of Muhammad al-Mas'ari,[119] they returned to Saudi Arabia with an unprecedentedly critical view of certain aspects of Wahhabism as it was embodied in the official religious institution, as well as in the Sahwa and its *jama'at*. More generally, their experience strengthened their distrust of both traditional and Sahwi ulema, whom they suspected of having a worldview that was too narrow and insufficiently politicized and of being fundamentally inclined to pre-serve their privileges by giving priority to the logic of the religious field over everything else.[120]

As several members of the group acknowledged, the ideas of the Sudanese Islamist ideologue Hasan al-Turabi and those of the Tuni-sian Rashid al-Ghannushi, whom they had had the opportunity to meet when he came to Riyadh for the 1989 Janadriyya festival, had the greatest influence on them.[121] These two ideologues had a particularly bad press both in official Saudi religious circles, because of their vehe-ment criticism of the Saudi position in the Gulf War, and among the Sahwi ulema, because they were seen as "rationalists" whose religious interpretations were considered much too audacious.[122] But it was this very boldness that attracted the "enlightened" Sahwi intellectuals. The model of the Islamic Republic of Khomeini, a figure who was gener-ally scorned in Saudi Arabia, was also a source of inspiration for these intellectuals, as some of them implicitly acknowledged.[123] In short, they saw change as indispensable, but they understood it as essentially political and aimed at the establishment of a "conservative Islamic democracy" that would not speak its name.

The first initiative that gave substance to this group was the estab-lishment in 1987 of a small weekly intellectual salon (*sabtiyya*, because it was held on Saturday) known as the "Islamic information meeting" (al-liqa' al-i'lami al-islami).[124] Among its principal organizers were Sa'd al-Faqih, born in 1957, professor of surgery at King Sa'ud University, and Abd al-Aziz al-Wuhaybi, also born in the late 1950s, a physics graduate from King Sa'ud University. It hosted lectures from Islamists from various Middle Eastern countries who were resident in the kingdom or simple visitors.[125] Contacts were also made with other Saudi intellectuals who shared the organizers' ideas, such as Ahmad al-Tuwayjiri, who had achieved local fame through a lecture in praise of Hasan al-Turabi delivered at the Riyadh literary club in 1989.[126] During the same period Muhammad al-Mas'ari, already noticed at the Janadriyya festival, gained a reputation through his articles in the official magazine *Al-Da'wa*, in which he subtly drew the first contours of a public critique of Wahhabism.[127] Thereafter he joined the Islamic information meeting.

In the wake of the Kuwait invasion, this small group of Sahwi intellectuals intensified its activities and increased its meetings, particularly at King Sa'ud University, where many of its members taught. In late 1991 Hamdan al-Hamdan, chairman of the department of Islamic culture and imam of the university mosque, was dismissed from his post for an inflammatory sermon denouncing Saudi participation in the Madrid conference.[128] This provoked the anger of these Sahwi intellectuals, who decided to demand that their colleague be rehired.[129] Fifteen of them, including Muhammad al-Mas'ari, Sa'd al-Faqih, Abd al-Aziz al-Wuhaybi, and Muhsin al-'Awaji, set up an informal organization called the University Committee for Reform and Advice (Lajnat al-jami'a li-l-islah wa-l-munasaha), known by its Arabic acronym Lijam.[130] Some Sahwi intellectuals outside the university joined the group, notably Hamad al-Sulayfih, founder of the eponymous Brotherhood *jama'a*. After meeting with Ibn Baz to plead the cause of al-Hamdan, they agreed to meet regularly with the elderly sheikh. Thereafter Lijam met every week alternatively at the university and at the home of Ibn Baz, who, by agreeing to sponsor these Islamist intellectuals, was continuing to play his papal role.[131]

Like the council of preachers, Lijam produced manifestos, which juridically did not count as fatwas because their signatories were laymen. For example, in January 1992 these intellectuals signed and distributed a document denouncing the suspension of the electoral process in Algeria and calling for support of the Islamic Salvation Front (FIS). This caused consternation in the Saudi regime, whose relations with the FIS were miserable. The document also explicitly attacked the treatment of the Algerian crisis in the Saudi media, the majority of which supported the government's repression of the Islamist opposition.[132] But these stands on regional questions were a minor aspect of Lijam's activism. The main focus of its activity was to promote domestic reform, and these intellectuals intended to be its driving force.

Struggling for Reform

The collaboration of these three groups, involved in separate but synchronized sectoral mobilizations, made it possible for the Sahwi protest movement to get organized and take hold. Indeed, it provided the movement with a sufficient quantity of the two kinds of resources indispensable for any successful mobilization: the legitimating resources possessed by the *munasirun* and, to a lesser extent, the Sahwi ulema; and militant resources, in the hands of the Sahwi intellectuals, particularly the "enlightened" Sahwi intellectuals.

The first attempt to organize the protest took place in October 1990 and was the result of collaboration between Sahwi ulema and *munasirun*. It originated with Abd al-Muhsin al-'Ubaykan, one of the *munasirun*, who, encouraged by the crowd of young Sahwis who attended his sermons, called from his pulpit at al-Jawhara Mosque for the establishment of a corps of volunteers to assist the Committee for Commanding Right and Forbidding Wrong.[133] The idea was primarily to enforce moral order in the shopping centers, the only places of entertainment frequented by individuals of both sexes, where the Sahwis were alarmed by the persistence of behavior they considered too liberal. In this initiative al-'Ubaykan was seconded by two other *munasirun*, Abd al-Rahman al-Barrak and Abdallah bin Jibrin. When Prince Salman heard of the plan, wishing to keep the situation under control, he summoned al-'Ubaykan and the other ulema involved to a meeting at the headquarters of the Committee of Senior Ulema, with Ibn Baz in attendance. The conclusion of the discussion, insistently pressed by Salman and finally ratified by Ibn Baz, was that the plan was contrary to *shariʿa*.[134]

The affair ended at that, but its importance lay elsewhere because it provided the occasion for the Sahwa's first major demonstration of strength. According to corroborating accounts, between ten thousand and thirty thousand Sahwis showed up to support the plan.[135] The number can also be explained by the fact that between al-ʿUbaykan's call in al-Jawhara Mosque and the meeting with Salman, the women's demonstration had taken place. Although most of the Sahwis who attended were unable to enter, their presence outside the building was an unprecedented challenge to the authorities.[136] In light of the nascent mobilization, this incident represented an authentic transformative event.[137] It has been noted that the Koranic principle of commanding right and forbidding wrong had been appropriated by the state from the time of the founding of the kingdom of Saudi Arabia, when the government had seized sole responsibility in the matter by creating the religious police. In the 1960s the JSM had been the first to try to challenge this monopoly. The same mechanism was at work here, but on a much larger scale. Al-ʿUbaykan's initiative was intended to restore the principle to the whole society by proclaiming that it was up to everyone to implement it. This would open Pandora's box: freed of its official complexion, the principle of commanding right and forbidding wrong could now be used to justify any form of individual or collective action in the name of Islam conducted outside the authorities' supervision.

At the same time, this notion remained vague enough that the various groups involved in the movement could attribute to it a significance that suited their worldview and objectives. For the *munasirun,* the aim was primarily to act against what they saw as the galloping liberalization of society. For the "enlightened" Sahwi intellectuals, the principle had very different implications, from the legitimacy of political opposition to the regime to the necessity for popular participation in managing the affairs of the state. The same ambiguity was found in another notion frequently used in the circles of the Sahwi opposition, *islah,* often translated as "reform" but actually meaning "making something conform more closely to Islam." Anyone could read this definition as he chose. For the *munasirun, islah* had an essentially social and moral meaning, whereas for the enlightened Sahwi intellectuals, its implications were primarily political. Under these circumstances the principles of commanding right and forbidding wrong and *islah* both became rallying cries for the incipient Sahwi protest movement.

In part because of this basic ambiguity, the mobilization sparked by al-ʿUbaykan aroused the interest of Sahwi intellectuals (particularly the "enlightened" ones), who until then, because of the sectorization of the social arena, had had only limited contacts with the religious field. These intellectuals were very impressed by the remarkable potential that had been demonstrated, and they hoped to profit from it for more political purposes.[138] This occurred in circumstances where the political crisis had made the junction of intellectuals and ulema structurally possible. The unthinkable was about to happen: the ulema, ordinarily so prompt to assert their preeminent role in society, would not only agree to collaborate but also, consciously or not, put their fate in the hands of individuals from the intellectual elite.

Because they belonged to both the world of the ulema and the world of the intellectuals, two figures played an essential role in the protest as powerful brokers between the two groups. The first was Abd al-Aziz al-Qasim, born in 1961, who had just been appointed a judge in the High Court of Justice in Riyadh. As a young, brilliant, and promising sheikh from a family that had produced major Wahhabi ulema,[139] al-Qasim was seen as a legitimate member of the religious field. At the same time, his ideas had brought him close to the "enlightened" Sahwi intellectuals and then to Lijam. Al-Qasim describes his role: "I went to see al-ʿUbaykan to tell him that what he was doing was wonderful, but why limit the reform to such small things? Why not think big?"[140] A few days later, in late October 1990, al-Qasim organized in his home the first secret meeting of al-ʿUbaykan with Sahwi ulema and Sahwi intellectuals, including Saʿd al-Faqih and Muhsin al-ʿAwaji, with the aim of putting together a common plan. The second bridging figure was Saʿid bin Zuʿayr, who had become known in Sahwi intellectual circles through his antimodernist stands at the Janadriyya festival.

Because the study of *shariʿa* had led him to choose communication and information sciences as his specialization, he also held the status of sheikh. Like al-Qasim, Ibn Zuʿayr belonged to both the religious and the intellectual fields and helped bring them together.[141]

In addition to individuals, certain salons *(salunat)* played a major role in the junction of the different groups. Like the political clubs in other contexts, Saudi salons, where everyone sat on the floor in a largely random arrangement, created an impression of "diffuse egalitarianism" that "tended to euphemize the status differences of their members. They created the possibility of bringing together individuals classifiable according to different principles, and from this ease of interaction could arise different forms of collaboration."[142] The salon held by the Sahwi sheikh Abdallah al-Tuwayjiri in the home of his father Hamud al-Tuwayjiri, one of the *munasirun,* played an especially influential role. At first a meeting place for Sahwi ulema and *munasirun,* it soon attracted the Sahwi intellectual elite and imposed itself as an essential intermediary among the three groups. According to Muhammad al-Masʿari, about forty people regularly attended, hence the name "group of forty" *(majmuʿat al-arbaʿayn)* given to its attendees.[143]

The structure of the *jamaʿat* also played a significant role in bringing the different groups together. Their leadership circles contained individuals with different specialties who belonged to distinct fields. In routine periods when sectorization was the rule, leadership meetings were infrequent, and interactions at the top were minimal; the *jamaʿat* at those times operated as very decentralized organizations. But in periods of crisis the multiplication of meetings of leaders of the *jamaʿa* revived the possibilities for interaction. This is exactly what happened around 1991. The *jamaʿat* thus started acting as transsectoral organizations, helping bring together the various components of the mobilization, beginning with the ulema and the intellectuals.

Once the various groups had agreed on the need to act, a crucial question arose: what repertoire of action should they adopt?[144] Each group had its own priorities. At stake for the Sahwi intellectuals was finding a means to communicate the demands of the movement to the population as a whole and then to the international community. For the Sahwi ulema and the *munasirun,* guarantors of the legitimacy of the repertoire, any action undertaken had to conform to the strict framework of Islamic practices.

After discussion, the petition seemed to be a mode of action acceptable to all. For the ulema, it corresponded to the Islamic tradition of advice to the prince *(nasiha).* For the intellectuals, it would enable the wide diffusion of the movement's demands, on the condition that the petition not be kept confidential. It appears that this last point was a bone of contention. Although some ulema agreed in principle that the document should be made public, others were strongly opposed, arguing that advice to the prince, by its very nature, had to be given in secret. To broaden their support, the drafters of the document were therefore forced to promise that it would be communicated only to the authorities. On this basis, the meetings initiated by al-Qasim at his home in late October 1990 led in January 1991 to the drafting of a one-page document titled "Letter of Demands" ("Khitab al-matalib").[145]

Letter of Demands [Khitab al-matalib]

To the servant of the two holy places, may God guide his steps.

Grace be on you, and the mercy of God and His blessings.

This state has distinguished itself by declaring its adhesion to Islamic *shari'a,* and the ulema and persons of good counsel have always fulfilled their duty to advise those who govern them. It therefore seems to us that the most pressing task in this critical period when everyone agrees on recognizing the need for change is to reform the situation in which we find ourselves, because it is responsible for the ordeals we are going through. For that reason, we draw the attention of the government to the necessity for undertaking the following reforms:

(1) Establish an advisory council ruling on domestic and foreign affairs, on the basis of Islamic *shari'a.* It will include among its members specialists in various areas, known for their moral uprightness and honesty. This council must be entirely independent and subject to no pressure preventing it from fully exercising its responsibilities.

(2) Examine and bring into conformity with Islamic *shari'a* the existing laws and political, economic, and administrative regulations, and abrogate anything that contravenes *shari'a.* This task will be entrusted to competent religious committees [*lijan shar'iyya*] that are deserving of trust.

(3) Ensure that in addition to being experienced, specialized, devoted, and honest, all officials and representatives of the state in the country and abroad have irreproachable moral conduct [*istiqamat al-suluk*]. Any breach of any of these conditions for whatever reason should be considered a betrayal of trust and a fundamental offense against the interests and the reputation of the country.

(4) Guarantee justice and the equality of rights and duties among all members of society, in a total way and with no indulgence for the privileged or condescension toward the deprived. When anyone uses his influence, whatever its source, to evade his duties or to violate the rights of others, that creates the risk of the disintegration of society, which could lead to the ruin against which the Prophet—peace be upon him—warned us.

(5) Ensure that all officials without exception are held accountable, particularly when they occupy positions of power. Any person, whoever he may be, who turns out to be corrupt or incompetent will be barred from state institutions.

(6) Guarantee a just distribution of the public wealth among all classes and groups in society, abolish income tax and lower other taxes that are a burden on people, while protecting the resources of the state from waste and exploitation for other purposes. Priority must be given to expenditure in the areas where the need is most pressing, whereas illegal monopolies must be ended and improperly acquired capital repaid. The prohibition on Islamic banks must be lifted, and all private and public financial institutions must be purged of usury [*riba*], which is a declaration of war against God and His prophet and deprives us of divine blessing.

(7) Build a strong and integrated army, armed with various kinds of weapons secured from different suppliers. Particular attention will be given to the construction and development of weaponry. The goal of the army will be to protect the country and its holy places.

(8) Reconstruct the media to bring them into conformity with the policies of the kingdom, so that they serve Islam, reflect the morality of society, and promote its culture. They must therefore be purified of everything that goes against those objectives. Their freedom to make individuals aware by broadcasting truthful news and constructive criticism in accord with the rules of *shari'a* must be protected.

(9) Build a foreign policy that preserves the interests of the *umma,* far removed from alliances contrary to God's law, and that joins in Muslim causes. The situation of embassies should be rectified so that they reflect the Islamic character of this country.

(10) Develop religious and *da'wa* institutions in the country, secure for them the material and human resources necessary for their operation, and remove all the obstacles preventing them from correctly fulfilling their mission.

(11) Unify the judicial system, grant it total and effective independence, and ensure that the authority of justice extends to everyone. An independent commission should be established to verify the application of judicial decisions.

(12) Protect the rights of the individual and of society, remove all existing restrictions against the will and the rights of the people, and guarantee human dignity, in accord with the norms of *shari'a*.

The document's twelve points reflected the preoccupations of the three groups involved. On the one hand, it intended to lay the groundwork for an "Islamic democracy" by calling for the creation of an advisory council *(majlis al-shura)* completely independent of the regime, made up of "specialists in various areas" (first point), and by urging the regime to "guarantee justice and the equality of rights and duties among all members of society" (fourth point), to make the accountability of the rulers an inviolable principle (fifth point), to work toward a fairer distribution of wealth (sixth point), and to "protect the rights of individuals and of society . . . in accordance with the norms of *shari'a*" (twelfth point). On the other hand, the document intended to strengthen the role of religion—and hence of the religious field—in society and in the political system by appointing religious committees *(lijan shar'iyya)* in charge of bringing laws in political, economic, and administrative areas into conformity with *shari'a* (second point); "[by developing] religious and *da'wa* institutions in the country, [by securing for them] the material and human resources necessary for their operation, and [by removing] all the obstacles preventing them from correctly fulfilling their mission" (tenth point); and by "unifying the judicial system" (which meant abolishing nonreligious courts where laymen officiated, retaining only religious courts, in which ulema served) and guaranteeing its "total and effective independence" (eleventh point). This last point most thoroughly reflects the ambiguities of the project because guaranteeing the independence of the judicial authority, which unquestionably contributes to the democratization of the system, also means strengthening the power of the ulema, who, in an Islamic system, are also the judges. These demands were supplemented by others that might be described as Islamic-nationalist, which were relatively consensual within the Sahwa, notably the construction of an army capable of defending the country (seventh point) and the definition of a "foreign policy that preserves the interests of the *umma*, far removed from alliances contrary to God's law" (ninth point).

A less literal reading of the document makes it possible to discern the outlines of a system in which the Sahwis—until then in a subordinate position in the various fields in which they were active—would have finally shifted the balance in their favor. This was true first of all for the administrative field. The document demanded that "in addition to being experienced, specialized, devoted, and honest, all officials and representatives of the state in the country and abroad have irreproachable moral conduct" (third point). In the Sahwis' view, the last condition definitively excluded their liberal rivals, while they saw themselves as perfect candidates for the offices in question. Similarly, the document demanded a complete reform of the media so that they would "serve Islam [and] reflect the morality of society" (eighth point), which would bar from them the modernists and other "secularists" while putting the Sahwi intellectuals at the heart of the intellectual field. The remedy proposed in the religious field was slightly different because it consisted not so much in excluding the traditional ulema who occupied the dominant position as in modifying the existing balance in the field of power so that the religious field as a whole would be in a position of strength. Rather than reflecting tensions between the different groups of ulema, the document thus aimed for their collective reempowerment.

Through this document the three groups involved in the reform project, all subordinate in their fields of activity, also hoped to establish an alliance, through what Pierre Bourdieu calls a mechanism of structural homology,[146] with the subordinate classes in society. For the economically subordinate, the document called for social justice. For the socially subordinate, who had been discriminated against because of their ancestry or region of origin, the document called for equality between "all members of society." Although these appeals were at first without effect, they may partially explain the belated rallying of rejectionists and jihadis starting in 1993.

The vagueness of the formulation "all members of society" also made it possible to skirt the Shiite question, a real bone of contention among the groups involved in the protest movement. Both the *muna-sirun* and most Sahwi ulema were known for their radically anti-Shiite tendencies, sometimes inspired by the most intransigent Wahhabism, as when Ibn Jibrin declared in October 1991 that the Shiites were guilty of apostasy and deserved death.[147] Although not going that far, in May 1993 Nasir al-ʿUmar published a report, *Situation of the Heretics in the Country of Tawhid*,[148] in which he called for banning the practice of Shiism in Saudi Arabia and the exclusion of all Saudi Shiites from any position of power or influence in the kingdom's administrative bodies.[149] Conversely, the majority of Sahwi intellectuals behind the reform project had a more moderate attitude on the sectarian question. An extreme example was Saʿd al-Ghamidi, an active member of Lijam and professor of medieval history at King Saʿud University, known as the author of an academic work in which he openly questioned Wahhabi historiography, which considers the Shiites, through the controversial figure of Ibn al-ʿAlqami, responsible for the fall of the Abbasid Empire.[150] Al-Ghamidi's work was subsequently described as "objective and balanced" by the historic Saudi Shiite leader Hasan al-Saffar.[151]

The process of collecting signatures for the "Letter of Demands" lasted from January to April 1991.[152] The drafters of the document saw the need to clothe the letter with unquestionable legitimacy by securing the broadest possible support in the religious field, beyond the Sahwi ulema and the *munasirun* who were already behind the cause and consequently signed in large numbers. The quasi-corporatist defense of the religious field the document contained, with no distinction between the dominant and the subordinate, would help them reach their goal, but it was not sufficient. To secure their ends, the initiators of the "Letter of Demands" had to use trickery, first by presenting the document to possible signatories as mere "advice to the prince," intended by nature to remain secret and addressed only to the king.[153] Their next step was to secure a letter of support *(tazkiya)* from Ibn Baz. Abdallah al-Tuwayjiri and his father, the highly respected Hamud al-Tuwayjiri, were sent to the elderly sheikh to persuade him.[154] After a discussion Ibn Baz, still playing his papal role, agreed to sign.[155] Upon reading the letter of support from his superior, Ibn ʿUthaymin, who had at first been hesitant, signed in turn.[156] All that then had to be done was to write in the margin of the "Letter of Demands" that it had received the support of Ibn Baz and Ibn 'Uthaymin for ulema to hasten to sign it, beginning with figures as official as Salih al-Fawzan, a member of the Committee of Senior Ulema, Abd al-Rahman al-Sudayyis and Salih bin Humayd, imams of the Great Mosque of Mecca, and, the height of irony, Rabi' al-Madkhali, a member of the loyalist Ahl al-Hadith and a sworn enemy of the Sahwa, who soon became prominent in the Jami movement.[157] In all, more than 400 signatures were collected, of which the 52 most prestigious were printed on the lower third of the page containing the document.

Despite the promises made when signatures were being collected, the drafters of the document intended from the very beginning to make it public and to distribute it with the aim of "creating political consciousness in the population and showing people what had to change."[158] Ease of distribution had even determined the decision to limit the document and the principal signatures to a single page. Exactly one week after Abdallah al-Tuwayjiri, Sa'id bin Zu'ayr, and Abd al-Muhsin al-'Ubaykan had submitted the document to the king early in May 1991, it was faxed to the four corners of the kingdom. Thereafter, "Thousands of copies of the document were distributed. Seeing the names of Ibn Baz and Ibn 'Uthaymin in the margin, people decided that there was no danger, and some of them photocopied it and naturally distributed it outside mosques or on street corners. There were sometimes shelves full of it in grocery stores."[159]

The phenomenon grew to such a large scale that the government called a special meeting of the Council of the Committee of Senior Ulema on June 1, 1991. The council issued a fatwa condemning the distribution of the "Letter of Demands" and pointing out that "advice should be given under certain conditions and in certain ways."[160] The reason that the condemnation was limited to the issue of distribution was not so much, as some have suggested,[161] that the ulema on the committee were in solidarity with the Sahwis as that the existence and wide distribution of Ibn Baz's and Ibn 'Uthaymin's letters of support made any condemnation of the content of the demands impossible because that would further undermine the legitimacy of the two principal religious figures in the kingdom by revealing their contradictions. In short, the regime had no choice but to acknowledge that the Sahwis had scored a point.

Galvanized by their success, the "enlightened" Sahwi intellectuals took on the role of driving force behind the reform project. Convinced that the summary content of the "Letter of Demands" required specifics, they considered what course to follow. The most eager first decided on the recording of a cassette by a disguised voice, copies of which were distributed starting in July 1991. The Sahwis called it the "supergun" *(al-midfaʿ al-ʿimlaq)* in reference to what they saw as its potential destructive force.[162] Its tone was distinctly more offensive than that of the "Letter of Demands." It forcibly attacked the official ulema and called on the police to side with the Sahwis or at least not to impede their plans.[163]

Nearly a year later, in mid-1992, the efforts of the intellectuals to provide specifics, carried out in the framework of Lijam, led to the drafting of the *Memorandum of Advice (Mudhakkirat al-nasiha)*, which mostly repeated in detail, with supporting examples, the requests set out in the "Letter of Demands." To produce this text, which filled a small-format book of 120 pages,[164] the members of the committee broke up into small working groups according to specialty, each one dealing with a particular question.[165] The ulema played no role in the conception of the document, merely signing it at the request of the intellectuals. According to Saʿd al-Faqih, who collected some of the signatures: "The ulema were in principle in full agreement with our efforts, in the name of the principle of commanding right and forbidding wrong and the duty of advising the prince. In practice, it was harder because they were not very pleased to have a doctor or an engineer try to influence them, the holders of *ʿilm*, and because some of them feared that our actions would eventually harm the *daʿwa*." Moreover, some ulema, including Abd al-Wahhab al-Turayri, disagreed with some aspects of the text (although al-Turayri eventually signed).[166] To get these signatures, in al-Faqih's words, "it was necessary to maneuver, which was not always easy."[167] But, according to Muhammad al-Masʿari, this was "what al-Faqih really knew how to do."[168]

As for the document itself,[169] its only significant difference from the "Letter of Demands" is found in the section titled "The Role of Ulema and Preachers," whose authors seemed inclined to favor Sahwi ulema against their official counterparts through the promotion of the alternative religious institution that the former were trying to establish by calling for "authorizing the creation of committees and associations of ulema and preachers independent from state organizations." By the same token, they implicitly challenged the competence of the members of the Committee of Senior Ulema by a call to strengthen the role of the committee "by appointing to it men of merit known for their ability to interpret the religious texts *(ijtihad),* which has earned them support from the people of the *umma,*" by which they meant the Sahwi ulema.[170] This change of tone is easily explained because the issue was no longer gaining support from the religious field as a whole, including the traditional ulema, as had been the case for the "Letter of Demands," but solely mobilizing the movement's core supporters.

Hence the list of signatories of the *Memorandum of Advice* reflects much more accurately than the list of signatories of the "Letter of Demands" the composition of the reformist coalition that took shape in the early 1990s. The comparative study of various sources makes it possible to determine the identity of 86 of the 110 signatories. Thirty-five of them were Sahwi intellectuals, 26 of whom taught at King Saʿud University and were members of or close to Lijam, and 45 were Sahwi ulema. Among the latter were most of the major figures in the council of preachers, including Salman al-ʿAwda, Abd al-Wahhab al-Turayri, ʿAʾid al-Qarni, ʿAwad al-Qarni, and Abdallah al-Tuwayjiri. The salon of Hamud al-Tuwayjiri made it possible to enlarge this group to include other Sahwi personalities.[171] In addition, at least 6 of the ulema who signed taught at the annex of Imam University in Burayda, where Salman al-ʿAwda was reportedly asked to circulate the document.[172]

Three of the *munasirun* also signed the *Memorandum:* Abdallah bin Jibrin, Hamud al-Shuʿaybi, and Abdallah al-Masʿari. A fourth, Abdallah al-Jilali, wrote one of the four letters of support *(tazkiyat)* that accompanied the document, along with Salman al-ʿAwda, Safar al-Hawali, and Abdallah bin Jibrin. A fifth, Abd al-Rahman al-Barrak, called on "to verify the conformity of the document with *shariʿa,*" approved it completely.[173] A sixth, Ibn Qu'ud, indicated his support for the project.[174] As for al-'Ubaykan, who had been dismissed from his position as a judge in retaliation for his oppositional activism, he had withdrawn his support from the movement and was now taking the side of the government. The last of the *munasirun,* Hamud al-Tuwayjiri, was seriously ill; he died a few months later, on December 30, 1992.[175]

But the contribution of the *munasirun* did not stop there. Two weeks after the *Memorandum* was submitted to King Fahd by a delegation including Muhammad al-Mas'ari and Abdallah al-Tuwayjiri, its publication in the newspaper published in Paris, *Al-Muharrir* (The Editor)—according to al-Faqih, without its authors' agreement; although they intended to make it public, they wanted more time to elapse[176]—provoked the royal family's anger. The government hastened to submit it to the Council of the Committee of Senior Ulema, which in mid-September issued a much more incisive fatwa than the one following the "Letter of Demands," denying any legitimacy to a document signed by "teachers and a few individuals who lay claim to religious science [*'ilm*]" and that "sows the seeds of dissension and hatred" and "denigrates the state by completely ignoring its qualities, which indicates the bad intentions of its authors or their ignorance of reality."[177]

Only the *munasirun* had the authority required to reply to such attacks. Urged by the intellectuals at the origin of the *Memorandum,* three of them—Abdallah bin Jibrin, Abdallah al-Mas'ari, and Hamud al-Shu'aybi—replied to the fatwa of the Council of the Committee of Senior Ulema with a counterfatwa known as the "Threefold Response" *(al-radd al-thulathi).* With a tone as vehement as that of their detractors, they denounced a text that "resembles a communiqué of the media or the security services, with no clear legal vision," and that included "a certain number of accusations with no real foundation." Adopting the terms of the committee's fatwa, they went on to say that "what sows the seeds of dissension and hatred is the lack of advice, or the fact of opposing it or casting doubt on it and on the intentions of its authors, while vices are permitted to multiply and spread." Explicitly setting their legitimacy against that of the committee, they made no bones about pointing out that among the signatories designated by the "se-nior ulema" as "teachers and a few individuals laying claim to reli-gious science," there were "eminent ulema ... whom the *umma* has agreed to recognize as such and in whom it has confidence, some of whom are the equals of the senior ulema, whereas others ... have taught some members of the committee."[178]

The *munasirun,* who had joined the opposition partially out of their hatred for—or jealousy of—the ulema of the official institution, thus gave free rein to their resentment, settling scores with their his-toric rivals. This "Threefold Response" was a manifest challenge to the authority of the "senior ulema" of the kingdom and contributed to the radicalization of the protest movement; its publication made the implicit rejection of the official religious institution, especially the Committee of Senior Ulema, explicit. According to Muhammad al-Mas'ari, "It was then that the nicknames 'committee of senior lackeys' [*hay'at kibar al-'umala'*] and 'committee of senior ignoramuses' [*hay'at kibar al-juhala'*] began to circulate in popular speech."[179]

Believing that they had won another victory, the members of Lijam thought that the time had come to break a taboo by organizing for-mally. For that purpose, they decided to emphasize the question of hu-man rights because that would guarantee wide media coverage out-side Saudi Arabia.[180] At the same time, to win the support of the Sahwi ulema and the *munasirun,* human rights were redefined as "rights guaranteed by *shari'a*" *(huquq shar'iyya),* whose defense fit into the framework of commanding right and forbidding wrong.

According to several accounts, the arrest of the Sahwi sheikh Ibra-him al-Dubayyan in Burayda in circumstances considered humiliat-ing impelled the reformists to step forward.[181] Following the arrest, in early January 1993, about forty people, the majority of whom were members of Lijam but including some Sahwi ulema, met at the home of Hamad al-Sulayfih to establish a "committee of assistance and for the defense of rights" *(lajnat al-nusra wa-l-huquq),* a name that was later changed to Committee for the Defense of Legitimate Rights (Lajnat al-difa' 'an al-huquq al-shar'iyya).[182] The release of al-Dubayyan shortly thereafter slowed the project.[183] A small group of Sahwi intel-lectuals led by Sa'd al-Faqih, Muhsin al-'Awaji, and Muhammad al-

Hudayf, later joined by Abd al-Aziz al-Qasim, Abd al-Aziz al-Wuhaybi, and Muhammad al-Mas'ari,[184] nonetheless continued to work in secret on setting up the committee. When al-Dubayyan was arrested again, a second large meeting was held in late April 1993, in the course of which al-Faqih, al-'Awaji, and al-Hudayf had their proposal adopted by all those present.[185]

It remained to determine who would be declared "founding members" of the committee. The *munasirun* seemed to be the best candidates. Abdallah al-Mas'ari and Abdallah bin Jibrin, who naturally were asked, agreed to accept the role, and al-Mas'ari was appointed secretary general of the committee. Hamud al-Shu'aybi was also considered, but because he was in the Qasim, the creators of the committee were unable to reach him in time.[186] Four other founding members were finally designated: two renowned Sahwi ulema, Abdallah al-Tuwayjiri and Sulayman al-Rashudi, said to have been the first lawyer to practice in the kingdom;[187] and two of the most respected Sahwi intellectuals, both active in Lijam, Hamad al-Sulayfih, father of the *jama'a* of the same name, and Abdallah al-Hamid, born in Buraydah in 1950, who taught literature at Imam University and had played a prominent role on the antimodernist front in the 1980s. Al-Hamid was also known for his talents as a poet, placed at the service of the opposition movement. Numerous Sahwis would soon know his "Armageddon of Reform" ("Malhamat al-islah")[188] by heart.[189] Whether deliberately or not, the committee symbolically represented the three groups involved in the reform project, each providing two of the six founding members.

On May 3, 1993, the six designated founding members, in a communiqué titled "Proclamation of the Foundation of the Committee for the Defense of Legitimate Rights (CDLR)"—"legitimate" *(shar'iyya)* meaning more precisely "guaranteed by *shari'a*"[190]—declared that they were "prepared to do everything necessary to bring an end to injustice, support the oppressed, and defend the rights guaranteed to human beings by *shari'a*."[191] During a trip to London a few months before,[192] Sa'd al-Faqih had been able to take advantage of the connections he had gained through his involvement with the Saudi Muslim Brotherhood to make contact with the Palestinian activist 'Azzam

Tamimi, who also had a Brotherhood background. Tamimi agreed to make Liberty, the pro-Islamist organization for the defense of human rights he headed in London, the intermediary in the West for the committee's activities.[193] Hence as soon as the communiqué was issued, it was sent to Liberty, which took charge of sending it to all the media and human rights organizations in Europe and the United States. By May 4 the Western media were reporting on what was seen as a notable development in the Saudi kingdom. The BBC even telephoned the home of Abdallah al-Mas'ari for an interview. Because he did not speak English, his son Muhammad, a good English speaker, answered the questions.[194] Following this fortuitous event, Muhammad al-Mas'ari was appointed, after the fact, official spokesman of the CDLR.

Unsurprisingly, one week after the CDLR was created, the Council of the Committee of Senior Ulema declared it illegitimate.[195] According to the supporters of the CDLR, this condemnation gave it unhoped-for publicity, and it won increased support.[196] But the repudiation by the official religious institution also gave the government a decisive weapon to legitimate repression against its founding members, who were dismissed from their jobs. More seriously, Ibn Jibrin announced his withdrawal from the committee and said that he had been deceived.[197] On May 26 the CDLR published its second communiqué, intended primarily to show that Ibn Jibrin's withdrawal and the attacks on the committee had not affected the determination of its founding members, who were now five. Confronted with this new provocation, the authorities arrested several members of the committee, including al-Hamid, as well as most of the Sahwi intellectuals involved behind the scenes, striking a fatal blow against the activities of the CDLR in Saudi Arabia.

The saga of the CDLR in Saudi Arabia can be looked at in various ways. According to some sympathetic media reports, it was the worthy representative of the protest movement, as demonstrated by the large mobilization in its support: Liberty spoke of four hundred letters of support,[198] while the opposition magazine *Al-Jazira al-'Arabiyya* (probably exaggerating) mentioned thousands of signatures and delegations flooding in from everywhere in the kingdom to meet the founders.[199] One of these delegations was allegedly made up of twenty ulema from the Qasim, led by Hamud al-Shuʿaybi, who, according to *Liberty*, expressed his support for the committee and asked to become an official member.[200]

But these exalted accounts masked the fact that the committee enjoyed far-from-unanimous support from the various elements of the Sahwi opposition. The CDLR was the result of the efforts of a small number of Sahwi intellectuals, and the ulema had been involved only at the point when the founding members had to be designated. To reach a consensus, these Sahwi intellectuals, aware of the differences in approach that separated them from the ulema and even more from the *munasirun*, sometimes were obliged to use subterfuge, as they had on several occasions before. Saʿd al-Faqih, for example, acknowledged that he had secured Ibn Jibrin's signature for the first communiqué before it was given the title "Proclamation of the Foundation of the CDLR."[201] Although he could not help but approve the principles expressed, Ibn Jibrin would probably have rejected the idea of an independent organization, something unthinkable according to his traditional way of thinking. Thus, although Ibn Jibrin's withdrawal undeniably occurred under royal pressure, it probably was also partly sincere.

The same hesitation was felt by some of the Sahwi ulema, for whom the question of the legitimacy of the existence of political parties, which is what they feared the CDLR would become, was still a subject of debate. The second communiqué of the CDLR was in part reacting to this dispute when it gave the assurance that "the committee does not consider itself a political party, contrary to what some media reports have said."[202] More generally, the Sahwi ulema feared that the intellectuals would draw them against their will into an escalation of conflict with the authorities that would threaten their position in the religious field. Yet the strengthening of this position through the establishment of a religious authority in competition with that of the traditional ulema remained one of the central goals of their participation in the protest movement. As a result, the only one of these ulema who publicly declared his support for the CDLR was Salman al-ʿAwda, who had been one of the most politicized from the outset. In a speech delivered on May 18, 1993, he even praised the committee's founders and urged young Sahwis to send letters of support.[203] Among the other ulema, some were privately pleased by the committee's creation, while others maintained an embarrassed silence.[204] Ironically, the repressive measures taken by the government against Salman al-ʿAwda and Safar al-Hawali, who were barred from preaching in September 1993, were what drove them to move openly closer to the committee.

By September 1993 Saʿd al-Faqih, Muhammad al-Hudayf, and Muhsin al-ʿAwaji, who had just been released from prison, were considering reestablishing the CDLR in London. For the plan to succeed, they had to secure the moral support of the major Sahwi ulema and the necessary sources of funding. The two requirements were linked because only the legitimating support of the ulema would enable the committee to collect donations. Therefore, Muhsin al-ʿAwaji went to see Safar al-Hawali to explain the plan. Al-Hawali, even though he had been silent when the CDLR was created in May 1993, assured him of his support.[205] Soon thereafter a meeting with al-ʿAwda was set up, and he made the same promise. But for reasons of security and because they were aware of the reluctance that had greeted the creation of the committee in May 1993, al-Faqih, al-Hudayf, and al-ʿAwaji did not inform other figures of their decision, and even al-Hamid and al-Sulayfih, who were founding members of the CDLR, were not informed of the details.[206]

Around the same time, Muhammad al-Hudayf went temporarily to London to prepare the ground with the help of ʿAzzam Tamimi and, more unexpectedly, Muhammad Surur Zayn al-ʿAbidin, the spiritual father of the Sururi *jamaʿa*. Surur agreed to put the infrastructure he had established in Great Britain at the service of the CDLR.[207] Saʿd al-Faqih and Muhammad al-Masʿari were chosen to represent the committee in London. In April 1994 both succeeded in eluding the surveillance of the Saudi authorities and traveling to London. On April 20 the CDLR published its third communiqué, in which it announced the resumption of its activities in London.[208]

Gradually, al-Faqih and al-Masʿari imposed their mark on the committee, which, without acknowledging the fact, took on more and more the appearance of an opposition political party, which is what most of the intellectuals active in the protest movement had envisaged from the start, despite the reluctance of the majority of ulema. In

March 1996 al-Faqih, excluded from the CDLR following disputes with al-Masʿari, officially took the leap by creating the Movement for Islamic Reform in Arabia (MIRA), which abandoned the rhetoric of legitimate rights and explicitly identified itself as an opposition party.[209] Whether al-Faqih wanted it or not, the break with the ulema was definitive.

The Golden Age of Saudi Islamism

In 1993 the rising tension between the government and the Sahwi opposition had led to an unexpected alliance between the Sahwi protesters and their historic opponents in the Saudi Islamist family. It was then that the rejectionists and the jihadis joined the protest, adding further complexity to the meaning and goals of the movement.

At first, however, the Sahwis were anything but certain of the support of their rejectionist rivals because of the historic antagonism between the Sahwis and the Ahl al-Hadith.[210] As the Sahwa asserted itself as a credible opposition force, the views of the rejectionists began to change. Although they continued to criticize the Sahwi activists for their doctrinal "errors," the rejectionists began to empathize with them.

This change affected the rejectionist community of Bayt Shubra in Riyadh. According to several former members of this community, before they were arrested in January 1992, they considered the Sahwi leaders religiously "misguided" and political "hypocrites," but after their release in August 1993, they discovered that the political situation had changed considerably and that the Sahwa was now in open conflict with the state.[211] They started getting interested in the opposition movement, and this led to an alliance with some of its representatives, including Muhammad al-Masʿari, whom they frequently went to see after his release from prison in late November 1993.[212]

For the Sahwis, this connection had the advantage of providing them with new bases and better defenses against the Jamis (heirs of the loyalist Ahl al-Hadith who gave unshakable support to the government in its fight against the opposition) because they could now rely on the support of individuals with the same intellectual background who were renowned for their *'ilm*. Salman al-'Awda played a pivotal role in this operation. Although he was a Sahwi, he was considered a specialist in hadith (he had a master's degree in sunna), through which he sought to gain the respect and support of some of the rejectionist sheikhs. In late 1993 he managed to establish a connection with Sulayman al-'Alwan, a former member of the Ikhwan of Burayda who was well respected in Ahl al-Hadith circles. This connection was particularly unexpected because al-'Alwan had a short time earlier expressed his contempt for al-'Awda.[213]

The jihadis, the other main Islamist group operating on the margins of the Sahwa, were initially concerned with the regional crisis (Bin Laden even offered the support of his mujahideen to the royal family to protect the kingdom against a possible Iraqi invasion)[214] but were remarkably indifferent to the Sahwi protest movement. Abd al-Aziz al-Qasim, for example, recalls having been met with a refusal from Osama bin Laden when he solicited his signature for the "Letter of Demands." According to al-Qasim, Bin Laden was preoccupied with financing the Yemeni jihadis who had returned from Afghanistan in their attempt to "reconquer" the formerly Marxist South Yemen, and he was afraid to attract the attention of the Saudi authorities.[215] As a traditional jihadi following in the footsteps of 'Azzam, Bin Laden continued to favor the defense of the borders of the *umma* against the "infidels" (in this case the Marxist regime of South Yemen and its traditional Soviet allies, with which it was identified) over the struggle against the regimes of Muslim countries. Like him, many jihadis who had come back from Afghanistan went in search of other fields of jihad, for example, in Bosnia or Tajikistan,[216] and took only a very superficial interest in the situation in Saudi Arabia. Their interaction with the Sahwis was minimal before 1993.

In mid-1991 Bin Laden left Saudi Arabia for Pakistan and, a few months later, Sudan.[217] There he met Islamist militants he had known in Peshawar in the late 1980s, particularly members of the Egyptian group al-Jihad, headed by Ayman al-Zawahiri. Although he was careful to make no public statements hostile to the Saudi government, his presence in the Sudan, the home country of Hasan al-Turabi (who was considered an enemy of the Saudi regime because of his stand on the Gulf War), his ties to radical militants, and the royal family's growing suspicion of jihadi veterans led the Saudi government to be seriously concerned about his activities. After he rejected offers from several emissaries to return home, his accounts were frozen in late 1992. On March 5, 1994, finally, King Fahd issued a decree stripping him of his Saudi citizenship.

A few days later Bin Laden published a long communiqué attacking the royal decision and announcing the creation of the Committee for Advice and the Defense of Legitimate Rights (CADLR) (Hay'at al-nasiha wa-l-difaʿ ʿan al-huquq al-sharʿiyya).[218] One might wonder why Bin Laden needed an organization of this kind when he had already headed al-Qaeda since 1988. The answer is indicated by the name of the committee: the jihadi leader was presenting himself as the guardian of the legacy of the *Memorandum of Advice* and of the CDLR. Bin Laden even explicitly laid claim to this connection in a second communiqué published on April 13, 1994, in which he outlined the history of the Sahwi protest movement from the "Letter of Demands" to the CADLR and declared that "on the occasion [of this communiqué] we confirm the demands formulated in the *Memorandum of Advice* and support what the CDLR called for and all other legitimate demands."[219] This reversal by Bin Laden, who after his initial indifference to the Sahwi protest movement had decided to become its spokesman, was a turning point in the alliance that had begun to form between jihadis and Sahwis thanks to the radicalization of Sahwi positions since 1993.

The Sahwi opposition could not help but be pleased with this support. The creation of the CADLR, which presented itself as the representative of the opposition abroad, was particularly welcome less than a year after the CDLR had been dismantled by the Saudi authorities. Following the unexpected resumption of activity by the CDLR in London a month and a half later, on April 20, 1994, Bin Laden's CADLR had to change its name to the Advice and Reform Committee (ARC) (Hay'at al-nasiha wa-l-islah).[220] On July 11, 1994, the ARC opened an office in London headed by the jihadi veteran of Afghanistan Khalid al-Fawwaz, assisted by two members of the Egyptian group al-Jihad.[221] It faxed to Saudi Arabia the eighteen communiqués that Osama bin

Laden issued in the name of the ARC up to late 1995. Through these communiqués he denounced the Saudi stand on the 1994 Yemen crisis,[222] the lack of independence of the Committee of Senior Ulema,[223] Ibn Baz's fatwa authorizing peace with Israel,[224] the insignificance of the political reforms implemented by the royal family, and the dramatic condition of the Saudi economy.[225] The language and themes chosen were clearly continuations of Sahwi concerns, but the tone was distinctly more offensive, with an increasingly marked tendency to proclaim the illegitimacy of the Saudi state.[226]

The alliance between Sahwis and jihadis was also visible on Saudi territory. It was noteworthy, for example, that Salman al-ʿAwda, known earlier for his opposition to sending young Saudi fighters to Afghanistan, now showed much less reluctance about fighting jihad abroad. While maintaining his opposition to ʿAzzam's opinion that jihad to free "occupied Muslim territory" was an individual duty for all Muslims and required no parental authorization for the participation of minors,[227] he played a significant role in equipping *(tajhiz)* young Saudi mujahideen sent to the Bosnian and Tajik battlefields.[228] Hence in 2002, when two former jihadis prepared a compilation titled *Stories of Arab Martyrs in Bosnia-Herzegovina,* al-ʿAwda wrote a preface for it in which he praised the pedagogical virtues of the stories of this "blessed group of valiant martyrs."[229]

On November 13, 1995, five Americans and two Indians were killed in a car-bomb explosion outside a United States–run training facility for the National Guard in Riyadh.[230] The four perpetrators accused by the authorities were three jihadis who had met in Afghanistan[231]— Khalid al-Saʿid, Riyad al-Hajiri, and Muslih al-Shamrani (who had also fought in Bosnia)—and a rejectionist, Abd al-Aziz al-Maʿtham, who had for a time frequented the Bayt Shubra community[232] and was in personal contact with al-Maqdisi, whom he had visited several times in Jordan.[233] The four young men were executed after staged confessions broadcast on Saudi television.[234] Although their guilt has not been independently established, different sources suggest that they were indeed responsible for the attack.[235]

The 1995 attack was thus the first joint action by jihadis and rejectionists. After they had begun to come together in Afghanistan in the late 1980s, their association continued in Saudi Arabia in the early 1990s. It was then that they discovered that they complemented each other—the jihadis were men of action and the rejectionists men of science ('ilm)—and established close ties, with the rejectionists acting as muftis for the jihadis.[236] The Bayt Shubra community in Riyadh frequently hosted visiting jihadis, some of whom became famous ten years later, like Abd al-Aziz al-Muqrin, future emir of al-Qaeda in the Arabian Peninsula.[237] In Jeddah rejectionist sheikhs were asked to give lectures in a house that was used as a base by local jihadis.[238] Jihadis and rejectionists were also mingling with a third group of individuals who were to have considerable influence on them, the dozens of mainly Libyan and Egyptian radical Islamist militants who had found shelter in Saudi Arabia because they were unable to return to their home countries.

The militarization of these groups had been going on for some time. When members of the Bayt Shubra community were arrested in January 1992, weapons were found. In Jeddah some militants had acquired handguns with the intention of robbing banks, which they saw as legitimate targets because they charged interest.[239] More broadly, the use of violence was widespread in the early 1990s in rejectionist groups, who claimed to be practicing "the changing of vice through action" (taghyir al-munkar bi-l-yad), an aggressive version of commanding right and forbidding wrong, by attacking videocassette stores or women's centers, accused of corrupting society.[240] There was therefore an undeniable predisposition to violent action among rejectionists and jihadis. However, this does not account for the timing of the 1995 bombing, which owes principally to the events taking place between the regime and the Sahwi opposition.

Although the Sahwa was not implicated in the 1995 attack, which most of its members condemned, the attack was in a way an epilogue to the alliance that had grown up since 1993 among the Sahwi opponents, the rejectionists, and the jihadis. Exasperated both by the determination of the domestic opposition and by the saber rattling of the CDLR in exile, the government had decided in September 1994 to launch a vast roundup in Islamist circles. At the head of the personalities arrested were Salman al-'Awda and Safar al-Hawali. Their imprisonment was seen by the entirety of the Saudi Islamist opposition as an unacceptable provocation by the regime. For the jihadis and rejectionists, who now identified with the combat of the two charismatic sheikhs, it was a declaration of war. In the wake of their arrest, the CDLR even transmitted communiqués issued by hitherto-unknown radical groups threatening the Saudi regime with an outbreak of violence.[241] The 1995 attack was a realization of that threat, because the United States, the target of the attack, had been denounced as the real organizer of the repressive policy of the Riyadh government. With that act, jihadis and rejectionists violently hijacked the Sahwi protest movement and diverted its meaning for their benefit.[242]

The entire saga of the Sahwi opposition was thus marked by the ambiguity of the relations among the groups involved, whose members had distinct views of the world and different goals and interests. As a result, their cooperation concealed a muted competition. This may have been conscious or unconscious, but it was in any event never openly expressed and was papered over by surface unanimity. What was at stake was the meaning and orientation to be given to the movement. For the Sahwi intellectuals, political reform with the aim of establishing a "conservative Islamic democracy" had to prevail, and that meant that the creation of modern political organizations had to be considered. The Sahwi ulema were divided between their desire for reform—which they understood as reform both of the political system, in a more conservative direction than the intellectuals, and of society against the ambient liberalism—and their desire to establish an independent religious authority. The permanent tension between these two goals, which corresponds to the natural tension between sectoral and transsectoral goals and mind-sets, explains the relative nervousness the Sahwi ulema manifested at certain stages vis-à-vis the reform project. As for the *munasirun*, their religious and political conceptions were directly inherited from the Wahhabi tradition, and they were particularly resistant to any form of modernity, even if it was clothed in Islam. The episode of the creation of the CDLR, marked by the enthusiasm of the Sahwi intellectuals, the caution of the Sahwi ulema, and the withdrawal of Ibn Jibrin, who announced that he had been deceived, was emblematic of these differences.

The years 1993 and 1994 appear in retrospect as a kind of golden age of Saudi Islamism, in the course of which representatives of all its currents—Sahwi, rejectionist, and jihadi—found themselves, after years, indeed decades, of rivalry and conflict, assembled under the banners of the major figures of the Sahwi protest movement, headed by Salman al-ʿAwda and Safar al-Hawali. But this circumstantial unity was to have further effects on the meaning of the movement. The "Sahwa insurrection" was no longer the symbolic property of the Sahwa alone but was incorporated into the "grand narrative" of all the Islamist groups involved. This explains why the authors of the 1995 attack saw their action as a response to the arrest of Sahwi leaders, whose legacy they were claiming to uphold.

On August 23, 1996, Osama bin Laden published his *Declaration of Jihad against the Americans Who Are Occupying the Land of the Two Holy Places*.[243] For the first time he made this declaration in his name alone, not on behalf of the ARC, which was neglected until the London office was officially closed on September 1998.[244] The tenor of this document contrasted radically with jihadi discourse in its classic form because it was not concerned with fighting on the borders of the *umma* anymore but spoke of conducting jihad against the American troops present in the heart of Saudi territory. This laid the foundations for the ideology of "global jihad." This ideology received its full expression less than two years later, on February 23, 1998, when, from Taliban-controlled Afghanistan, where they had found refuge, Bin Laden and his associates proclaimed that "killing the Americans and their allies—civilians and military—is an individual duty for every Muslim who can carry it out in any country where it proves possible."[245]

Similarly, the language used in the 1996 declaration was a definitive break with Sahwi discourse because the call for jihad was made against a backdrop of the explicit denunciation of the illegitimacy of the Saudi regime. But it is striking that even here Bin Laden presented himself as the natural heir of the Sahwa, and his decision to declare war as the logical conclusion of the efforts the protest movement had made since 1991. The reader was duly reminded of those efforts and of the dead end into which the Saudi regime had driven them. In the text, Bin Laden mentioned Salman al-'Awda and Safar al-Hawali several times, even explicitly basing his geopolitical views on the book *Leading the Ulema of the Umma out of Confusion*. In the process he explicitly traced back to the "Sahwa insurrection" the origin of the global jihad that al-Qaeda was about to embody. Because the major figures in that insurrection were behind bars, no one was there to contradict him.

6

Anatomy of a Failure

At the very moment when Osama bin Laden in Sudan was hijacking the Sahwi protest and its symbols, the movement itself was running out of steam in Saudi Arabia. In Riyadh, as elsewhere in the Saudi kingdom, all indications were that the Sahwa insurrection was coming to an end. Most observers attributed this decline in the protest primarily to state repression.[1] However, that explanation is insufficient because the repression was carried out in a more complex and less effective way than commonly believed, and it came belatedly, at a time when the movement had already been considerably weakened.

Although the rise of countermovements—supported and sometimes partially orchestrated by the authorities—contributed to this preliminary weakening, it was not its primary cause. Rather, the weakness was the result of an intrinsic flaw. Although the Sahwi protest in principle had the resources necessary for a successful mobilization, the movement's leaders needed the backing of reliable and solid grassroots networks in order for the protest to endure against the regime. That was precisely what was lacking.

The Limits of Repression

Contrary to widespread assumptions, the Saudi regime since the death of King Faysal has generally shown little inclination to use extreme coercion against its nonviolent critics.[2] When confronted with challenges, the regime preferred to impose pressures of graduated intensity, in a process akin to negotiation under constraint. As a Saudi observer argues, this process was characteristic of the "political paternalism of the Saudi state, which treats its subjects like children who have misbehaved."[3]

The regime's first reaction when confronting a Sahwi opponent was generally to have an individual connected to both the opponent and the authorities urge him to halt his activities and perhaps offer him advantages in return.[4] When this kind of informal mediation failed, the opponent might be summoned by the authorities to appear in person. If he was a second-rank Sahwi militant, the authorities would be represented by the secret police *(mabahith)*. However, in the early stages of protest, well-known preachers were met in person by a member of the royal family. Safar al-Hawali, for example, was summoned in May 1991 by Prince Ahmad, the deputy interior minister, who urged him to refrain from speaking about politics.[5] In November 1991 it was the turn of Abd al-Wahhab al-Turayri to be interrogated by Prince Salman, the governor of Riyadh.[6] A few months earlier Salman al-ʿAwda[7] and ʿAʾid al-Qarni[8] had received similar treatment. The usual procedure was to have these recalcitrant figures sign a promise *(taʿahhud)* not to cross any more red lines.

In the case of the ulema, this practice was revised in late 1991. The first summons of ulema had indeed been seen as a direct violation of the autonomy of the religious field by the political authorities and had provoked an uproar in religious circles, including among traditional sheikhs.[9] The government itself had reservations because it did not want to fall into the trap of desectorization by allowing the interactions between the agents of the political and religious fields to grow too visible. Therefore, convinced that a mechanism for the internal regulation of the religious field would help circumscribe the debate within it, the authorities set up in the winter of 1991 the Five-Party Commission (al-Lajna al-khumasiyya), composed of five members of the Council of the Committee of Senior Ulema: Abd al-Aziz bin Baz, Salih al-Luhaydan, Abd al-Aziz Al al-Shaykh, Salih al-Fawzan, and Abdallah al-Ghudayyan. This veritable police force of the religious field was charged with examining the "deviations" of the Sahwi preachers and taking the necessary measures.[10] Beginning in late 1991, the ulema would thus be interrogated only by their peers except in extraordinary circumstances.[11]

When the ulema did not comply with the orders they were given, they were usually temporarily banned from preaching, a step ratified by the Five-Party Commission after its creation. On April 2, 1991, Prince Abd al-Ilah, governor of the Qasim region, imposed this penalty on Salman al-ʿAwda "for getting involved in what was none of his business."[12] Six months later al-ʿAwda's suspension was removed after he had promised to stop talking about politics. He was again barred from preaching in early 1993 until May of that year.[13] In September 1993 another prohibition was imposed on both him and Safar al-Hawali, which lasted until they were arrested a year later. After that they no longer appeared in public but continued to teach and to give private lectures in their homes.[14] More generally, beginning in 1993, most of the rising stars of the Sahwi opposition had disappeared from pulpits and platforms, starting with ʿAʾid al-Qarni, who was barred from preaching in the summer of 1992.[15]

The cassettes of the recalcitrant ulema were also banned from sale. Until 1992 this measure was directed only against recordings whose content was considered subversive; cassettes by the same preachers containing no criticism of the government remained available in the specialized stores. But starting in early 1993, on orders of the Five-Party Commission, all cassettes by certain preachers, including al-ʿAwda and al-Hawali, were barred from sale, although they could continue to record their sermons and circulate them on their own.[16]

Prohibition on travel—passport confiscated and name placed on a blacklist—was another technique frequently used against ulema and intellectuals. In May 1991 all the signatories of the "Letter of Demands" were targeted with this sanction.[17] It was soon removed from most of them, but it was renewed in December 1991 against Salman al-ʿAwda, Safar al-Hawali, ʿAʾid al-Qarni, and Ahmad al-Tuwayjiri,[18] whom the authorities saw as those most implicated in the movement of protest. Everyone who had played a role in the creation of the CDLR later received the same treatment,[19] along with the sixty professors of King Saʿud University—many of whom were members of Lijam—who had signed a petition demanding the release of jailed CDLR members.[20] However, this prohibition did not prevent Saʿd al-Faqih and Muhammad al-Masʿari—through a series of tricks whose details are too numerous to be related here, but which show that the obstacles were not that difficult to evade—from leaving the country a year later to reestablish the CDLR in London.

When all the previous measures proved ineffectual, Sahwi activists were usually dismissed from their jobs. The first intellectual targeted was Muhammad al-Masʿari, who was suspended from King Saʿud University in the spring of 1991.[21] The first of the ulema similarly sanctioned was Abd al-Muhsin al-ʿUbaykan, dismissed from his positions as judge of the High Court in Riyadh and imam of al-Jawhara Mosque in the winter of 1991 because of his repeated vehement criticisms of the royal family in his sermons.[22] The publication of the *Memorandum of Advice* led to a large number of suspensions, most of which were rescinded after a few months.[23] Following the announcement of the creation of the CDLR, the six founding members of the committee were dismissed from their jobs. Sulayman al-Rashudi, a self-employed lawyer, even had his license suspended.[24] Soon thereafter, in July 1993, Salman al-ʿAwda and Safar al-Hawali were dismissed from their university posts.[25] Finally, beginning in late 1994, dozens of Sahwi ulema and intellectuals, almost all of whom were former members of Lijam who had not been imprisoned,[26] were dismissed from Saudi universities. In particular, an unprecedented wave of dismissals hit fifty Sahwi university professors in June 1996, among whom was Muhammad Qutb, who was even deported to Qatar.[27] When they were not dismissed, the Sahwis teaching at the university were sometimes transferred to other positions, generally administrative, where the government thought that they would have less influence. This was what happened to the ulema ʿAwad al-Qarni,[28] Saʿud al-Funaysan,[29] and Muhammad Saʿid al-Qahtani.[30]

As a last resort, the regime arrested its most recalcitrant opponents. The gradual approach adopted explains why the first arrests did not take place until 1992 and were then infrequent and isolated, like that of Sheikh Ibrahim al-Dubayyan, which was used as a pretext for the creation of the CDLR. The establishment of the committee provoked the first real wave of arrests in the ranks of the Sahwa since the beginning of the crisis: Muhammad al-Mas'ari,[31] the two founding members Abdallah al-Hamid and Sulayman al-Rashudi,[32] and fourteen members of Lijam were rounded up.[33] At the same time, Liberty reported the arrest of forty-four sympathizers of the committee in the Hejaz and the Eastern province.[34] All of them were released in early October after promising to end their activities,[35] except al-Mas'ari, who refused any compromise and was not released until the end of November.[36]

Beginning in April 1994, CDLR sympathizers found in possession of communiqués issued by the committee in London were arrested from time to time.[37] On September 9, 1994, in what appears to have been the first indication of the government's intent to put an end to the protest, Muhsin al-'Awaji and Abdallah al-Hamid were again jailed.[38] The arrests on September 13 and 16, 1994, of Salman al-'Awda and Safar al-Hawali, whom the authorities suspected of being the principal supporters of the CDLR, marked the beginning of the second great wave of arrests in the ranks of the Sahwa. It was much larger than the first, reaching most of the architects of the Sahwi protest, intellectuals[39] and ulema,[40] as well as hundreds of their supporters in the Sahwa generation.[41]

The protesters still at liberty in 1995 soon found themselves behind bars. In early March 1995 the Sahwi ulema Nasir al-'Umar and Muhammad Sa'id al-Qahtani and the Sahwi intellectual Sa'id bin Zu'ayr[42] were jailed after a visit to Ibn Baz in which they denounced the regime's purported inclination to join the Arab-Israeli peace initiative.[43] In June 1995 the regime crossed a red line by taking the unprecedented step of arresting one of the *munasirun,* Hamud al-Shu'aybi,[44] after he had been called in twice by the authorities[45] and dismissed from his position at Imam University.[46] According to one of his students, the reason was that he never missed an opportunity to praise the CDLR and even distributed its publications to his visitors.[47] Nonetheless, al-Shu'aybi was released a month and a half later.[48]

Before 1994 rejectionists and jihadis were only occasionally arrested, as in the case of the Bayt Shubra group, whose members were jailed in January 1992 for destruction of property and weapons possession. The great wave of arrests that hit the Sahwa starting in September 1994 did not spare those among the radical militants who were most openly associated with the Sahwi opposition, but it was the November 1995 attack that marked the beginning of a systematic policy of repression against them. Following the attack, dozens of rejectionists and jihadis, whether or not they were linked to it, were imprisoned.[49] Among them were most of the members of the Bayt Shubra community, except for Mishari al-Dhayidi and Abdallah bin Bijad al-'Utaybi, who had managed to escape through Yemen.[50] Similarly, beginning at this time, jihadis were systematically interrogated and detained when they returned to the kingdom.[51] The authorities also took advantage of the opportunity to round up some of the foreign radical Islamists on Saudi territory, among them Abu Layth al-Libi, then a member of the Libyan Armed Islamic Group and a future high-ranking member of al-Qaeda.[52]

The imprisoned Sahwis, particularly the ulema and the intellectuals, do not seem to have been subjected to physical torture on a large scale.[53] Psychological torture, on the other hand, was more common.[54] The rejectionists and jihadis, especially after November 1995, were treated in a much harsher way, as were the members of foreign radical Islamist groups arrested on Saudi territory. Accounts of their torture are abundant.[55]

Despite the increasing harshness of the government's response, the history of the Sahwi protest until 1996 contained only one "martyr" (shahid), Abdallah al-Hudayf, who, moreover, was not directly affiliated with the Sahwa but rather belonged to the jihadi-rejectionist milieu operating on its margins.[56] On November 11, 1994, he threw acid at the face of one of the investigators of the Saudi secret police. A rumor, which the CDLR had helped spread, accused this officer of bad treatment of jailed Sahwis, notably al-Hudayf's father and brother (the Sahwi intellectual Muhammad al-Hudayf), who were then behind bars. Although everything seemed to indicate that Abdallah al-Hudayf's gesture was an isolated action, the regime saw a plot behind it and tried him on that basis, along with several others, including his brother Muhammad and Muhsin al-ʿAwaji.[57] Abdallah al-Hudayf was sentenced to death and executed on August 12, 1995, while Muhammad al-Hudayf and Muhsin al-ʿAwaji were given fifteen-year prison terms.[58]

On May 31, 1996, the four presumed authors of the Riyadh attack were executed. In contrast to Abdallah al-Hudayf, their status as martyrs is disputed. Their rejectionist and jihadi friends believed that they should be celebrated as such, but the majority of Sahwis condemned the attack and refused to grant them that status. This affair once again raised the question of the meaning, methods, and objectives of the Sahwi protest.

In addition to these coercive measures, the Saudi authorities implemented a policy of institutional regulation directed against the Sahwa. Through it they intended to change the rules of the game and establish restrictions in the fields in which the Sahwa was active so as to strengthen government control. The goal was to reduce the quantity of material and symbolic resources flowing into the protest movement.

Government action in the universities, a bastion of the Sahwa, was emblematic of this policy. In November 1993 a new university code was adopted that established complete control by the authorities over all leadership posts,[59] previously filled by internal selection. The text indicated that the appointment of university presidents would depend exclusively on the king,[60] and that those presidents would submit to the minister of higher education a list of candidates for chairs of the various faculties.[61] Similarly, chairs of departments would be appointed by the university president on the nomination of faculty chairs.[62] The aim of these measures was to keep potential Sahwi opponents from reaching positions of power in the system.

Although similar decisions were taken in most fields in which the Sahwa had a presence, it was in the religious field, which the government saw as the main area of contention, that the most draconian measures were adopted. This led to a complete reorganization the field. Since 1971 the political field had exercised indirect control over the religious field through the appointment of the members of its two supreme bodies, the Council of the Committee of Senior Ulema and the General Office for the Management of Scientific Research, Fatwas, Preaching, and Guidance. Under this arrangement the religious field had however been able to maintain a large degree of autonomy, which had permitted the emergence within it of movements such as the JSM and the Sahwa and its *jama'at*. The regime was now calling into question that autonomy. This would eventually force it to rethink the mechanisms of religious legitimation in the kingdom.

On July 10, 1993, a royal decree announced the creation of the Ministry of Islamic Affairs, *Waqf*s, Preaching, and Guidance.[63] The two latter responsibilities were removed from the General Office for the Management of Scientific Research, Fatwas, Preaching, and Guidance, which was reduced to being the General Office for the Management of Scientific Research and Fatwas, whose only prerogative was the issuance of fatwas. In contrast, the new ministry was now in charge of everything to do with the institutions of *da'wa* inside and outside the kingdom, and of the management of the vast institutional and material resources allocated to them.[64] These resources had previously been in the hands of the head of the General Office, Sheikh Ibn Baz, who, the regime now thought, distributed them too carelessly, because some benefited the Sahwi opposition.[65]

The second responsibility of the new ministry, the supervision of the *waqf*s, had previously belonged to a relatively peripheral ministry,[66] the Ministry of Hajj and *Waqf*s (which would now be renamed the Ministry of Hajj). The question of *waqf*s (inalienable religious endowments) has crucial financial implications because some of them are estimated at hundreds of millions of riyals. These revenues were traditionally managed autonomously by the ulema, a source of concern for the regime, which was fearful that they might benefit groups hostile to it. The creation of the new ministry was thus aimed at putting the *waqf*s under tighter control. The subsequent adoption of a remodeled law of *waqf*s *(nidham al-awqaf)* was directed toward the same goal.[67] This transfer of responsibility had another implication that was no less crucial: traditionally in Saudi Arabia the management of mosques had been tied to that of *waqf*s. The mosques, particularly the private mosques *(ahliyya)* whose imam was named by the owner, had until then enjoyed a degree of independence.[68] Here again, much tighter control was expected from the new ministry.

At the same time, the new ministry was intended to be formally much more dependent on the government than the previous institutions in charge of religious affairs had been. As a ministry, it was an organ of the executive represented in the cabinet. Its head, Abdallah al-Turki, who had proved himself as the head of Imam University since 1974, was reputedly absolutely loyal to the royal family. His socialization in the Saudi Muslim Brotherhood, which he left at the turn of the 1970s to avoid hindrance to his rise in the circles of power, and from which he had thorough knowledge of Sahwi circles, was seen not as a risk but as an asset.

To complete the royal family's control over the ministry, the High Council of Islamic Affairs (al-Majlis al-aʿla li-l-shuʾun al-islamiyya) was created in October 1994.[69] It was presided over by Prince Sultan and included several high-ranking princes among its members. This was not the first time the royal family had created a high council of this kind. In 1981, shortly after the Mecca events, the High Council for Information, presided over by Prince Nayif, had been established. On each occasion the strategy was the same: to guarantee control by the political field over a given portion of the social arena while trying to maintain the appearance of the autonomy of that portion. It is noteworthy, for example, that the Ministry of Islamic Affairs and the Ministry of Information were traditionally headed by commoners.

In the first months of its existence, the new ministry multiplied the tools for its control over the religious field by establishing various institutions, notably, the High Council for *Waqf*s (al-Majlis al-aʿla li-l-awqaf),[70] the High Council for Charitable Associations for the Memorization of the Koran (al-Majlis al-aʿla li-l-jamaʿat al-khayriyya li-tahfidh al-qurʾan al-karim),[71] and the Council of Preaching and Guidance (Majlis al-daʿwa wa-l-irshad),[72] all presided over by the minister of Islamic affairs, Abdallah al-Turki. Similarly, it organized a series of programs intended to reeducate the agents of the religious field. For example, it held the "First Forum of Imams and Mosque Orators" ("Al-multaqa al-awwal li-l-aʾimma wa-l-khutabaʾ") in early April 1994 in Riyadh,[73] which consisted of several days of lectures and debates involving members of the Committee of Senior Ulema and addressed to the hundreds of imams and orators invited for the occasion.[74] The "First Meeting of Heads of Charitable Associations for the Memorization of the Koran" ("Al-liqa' al-awwal li-ru'us al-jamaʿat al-khayriyya li-tahfidh al-qur'an al-karim")[75] and the "First Forum of Preachers" ("Al-multaqa al-awwal li-l-duʿat"),[76] organized in June and November 1994, followed the same pattern. Finally, in various parts of the kingdom the ministry organized training programs led by representatives of the official religious institution and intended for imams and orators.[77]

The authorities also strove to combat all the independent initiatives that had been launched in the religious field thanks to the autonomy it had enjoyed, many of which were suspected of providing the opposition with bases or sources of funding. Various informal neighborhood NGOs were dissolved.[78] Similarly, the collection of donations for Islamic causes outside official channels was prohibited in mid-1993[79] because some of the money collected was suspected of going to Sahwi protesters. Particularly targeted was the al-Haramayn Foundation,[80] created in 1992 at the initiative of Sururis who were concerned about the control of the Muslim Brotherhood over humanitarian organizations, which was now considered to have too much autonomy. Pressures on the foundation had begun as soon as it was created when the festivities organized to make it known to the public were canceled a few hours before they were scheduled to be held.[81] To be tolerated, al-Haramayn had to cut all ties with the Sahwi opposition. For example, although Abdallah al-Jilali, one of the *munasirun,* was a founding member of al-Haramayn, he was excluded from the foundation's board of directors by his peers.[82]

The announcement on July 10, 1993, the very day the Ministry of Islamic Affairs was established, of the appointment of Ibn Baz to the position of general mufti of the kingdom *(mufti ʿamm li-l-mamlaka),*[83] which the regime had deliberately left vacant since the death of Muhammad bin Ibrahim, completed the new arrangement. More than a promotion, as it has often been interpreted,[84] this decision seems to have been a consolation prize for the old sheikh, who had been deprived of a large part of his real powers.

All this shows that it was only starting in mid-1993, and especially after the end of 1994, that consequential coercive measures were taken and institutional regulations were established against the Sahwi opposition. Both arrived relatively late in the course of the protest. Earlier there had been diverse kinds of pressure, but perhaps because the country lacked any genuine repressive culture with respect to nonviolent Islamic actors, fear of sanctions did not play the role it did elsewhere in the Middle East. Hence state measures had only limited effect on the major figures of the movement, who, with rare exceptions, persevered in their activism. Coercion and institutional regulation alone therefore cannot explain the failure of the Sahwi protest, especially because the movement was crushed with relative ease in September 1994, revealing its fragile status even before the great wave of arrests later in the year.

The Rise of Countermovements

A preliminary explanation for the weakening of the Sahwi opposition might be found in the rise of countermovements that, with the active support of the government, reduced the appeal of the protest and eroded the bases for its support.

The Jamis: Between Purism and Loyalty

The first and most effective of these countermovements is known as the Jami movement. In the aftermath of the Iraqi invasion of Kuwait, it asserted itself as both an implacable opponent of the Sahwi opposition and an ardent defender of the royal family. It soon gave rise to a relatively organized network that extended its reach to most cities in the kingdom. The term "Jami," which has become widespread, was first used by the Sahwis. It refers to Sheikh Muhammad Aman al-Jami, born in 1930, head of the Faculty of Hadith at the Islamic University of Medina and one of most vocal opponents of the Sahwi protest. As had been the case with "Sururi," the use of "Jami" was intended to delegitimate the adversary by stigmatizing his foreign origin because al-Jami was from Ethiopia and immigrated to Saudi Arabia only when he was twenty.[85] For lack of a more neutral term, however, the label "Jami" will be used here because the Jamis have refused to identify themselves other than by such unspecific qualifiers as "the *salafis*" or sometimes "the ulema of Medina," because the most eminent among them were based there, mainly at the Islamic University. They were also recognizable because they sometimes added to their names the suffixes *al-salafi* or *al-athari* (from *athar,* tradition, that is, that of the Prophet and the pious ancestors), which the Sahwis deplored, arguing that only God could decide who was a proper *salafi* and who was not.[86]

Although al-Jami, despite himself, gave his name to the movement, its most emblematic figure was Sheikh Rabiʿ bin Hadi al-Madkhali. Born in 1931, he taught until the late 1990s in the Faculty of Hadith at the Islamic University of Medina,[87] which was chaired by al-Jami until his death in 1995.[88] Although he was a student of al-Albani and had briefly been close to the JSM in the mid-1970s,[89] al-Madkhali had managed not to go to prison and thereafter had demonstrated exemplary loyalty to the regime. In the late 1980s he made a name in the Saudi religious field with a very controversial book, *The Method Followed by the Prophets in Religious Preaching Contains Wisdom and Reason.*[90] Faithful to his Ahl al-Hadith beliefs, he explained that the priority in matters of *daʿwa* should be the purification of the creed.[91] He thus fiercely attacked the Pakistani ideologue Abu al-Aʿla Mawdudi, the founder of Jamaat-e Islami and a source of inspiration for Sayyid Qutb, for his concern with politics and his efforts to build an Islamic state in India "although the Indian people are ignorant of Islam and their religious practice is tainted with innovation and deviance."[92] In al-Madkhali's view, Mawdudi's priority should have been to correct the creed of the Indians instead.

As tension between the Sahwa and the government was increasing, al-Madkhali was one of the first ulema openly to criticize the Sahwi sheikhs in August 1990. He was soon joined in what became the Jami movement by other religious figures from the loyalist wing of the Ahl al-Hadith, in particular, Falih al-Harbi,[93] a former member of the JSM who, unlike al-Madkhali, had spent time in Saudi jails,[94] Farid al-

Maliki, Mahmud al-Haddad, and Ali Rida bin Ali Rida.[95] For those sheikhs whose worldview had developed in explicit opposition to the Sahwa, this was a perfectly natural position to adopt. After the loyalist Ahl al-Hadith had started being looked at favorably by the regime because of their stance during the Afghan jihad, it was also a way for them to complete their return to favor with the authorities.

In return, the Saudi government provided abundant support to the Jami movement, notably through the minister of the interior, Prince Nayef.[96] The significant material and institutional resources it soon had at its disposal made it attractive to those who felt marginalized in the social arena or in the religious field. To many, Jamism became a strategy for social or religious ascent. A large number of those who joined the movement were non-Saudi residents. The example of Usama ʿAtaya al-Filastani is instructive in this regard: born in a Palestinian refugee camp in Jordan, he was raised in Saudi Arabia, where his father worked.[97] By the conclusion of his secondary education in 1990, he was passionately interested in religion and wanted to enroll in the Islamic University of Medina, but he was refused admission because non-Saudis living in the kingdom were barred from Saudi universities.[98] At the same time, he achieved a certain reputation among the ulema of his city, Rabigh. When he joined the Jamis, he finally secured the connections *(wasita)* he needed to enroll in the Islamic University in 1993.[99] Ten years later he became one of the major figures in the Jami movement, where he demonstrated remarkable zeal, to judge from the titles of some of his works: *The Strong Proofs of the Necessity to Defend the Saudi State* and *To Repel the Zionist Aggression against the Al Saʿud, the Family of Jihad and Mujahideen.*[100] In the interim he had adopted the name Abu ʿUmar al-ʿUtaybi, hoping by attaching himself to one of the major tribes on the peninsula, ʿUtayba, to conceal the signs of his social marginality.[101]

Along with non-Saudi residents, the ranks of the Jamis contained many people from peripheral and socially marginalized regions of the kingdom. The Jazan region on the Yemeni border was particularly well represented, including, among the leading figures of the movement, ulema such as Rabiʿ al-Madkhali, Muhammad al-Madkhali, Zayd al-Madkhali (these three belonged to the same tribe), Ali al-Fuqaihi, and Ahmad al-Najmi. Coming from a region that traditionally did not produce major Wahhabi ulema, these figures were thereby claiming a place in the religious field. This strong presence in the Jami movement of figures from the Jazan region, inhabited by the Bani Yam tribe, earned it the nickname in some Sahwi circles of Bani Jam.[102] The term was intended to be particularly injurious because the name Bani Yam had strong associations with the Ismaili branch of Shiism, which was still practiced by a significant number of its members.

Although individuals lacking in social capital initially dominated the Jami movement, over time growing numbers of peripheral ulema in search of increased status joined, regardless of their social origins. Classic examples are Abd al-Aziz al-'Askar and Sulayman Aba al-Khayl, two ulema from Najd described as thoroughly marginal in the religious field before the Gulf War,[103] who became hard-core Jamis in the early 1990s. For instance, Abd al-Aziz al-'Askar is known for having called in one of his sermons for the execution of Salman al-'Awda and Safar al-Hawali and for having openly rejoiced at the execution of Abdallah al-Hudayf.[104] As a result of their zeal, they were appointed to high positions: al-'Askar became the chairman of the department of *da'wa* at Imam University,[105] while Aba al-Khayl was first given the strategic position of dean of student affairs at the university annex in the Qasim and then that of vice president.[106] The Jami movement became so attractive that soon ulema active in the Sahwi opposition left the protest to join it, including Abd al-Muhsin al-'Ubaykan and 'Isam al-Sinani, even though the latter had previously signed the *Memorandum of Advice*.[107]

Starting in 1993, positions opened up by the dismissal of Sahwis were almost systematically offered to the new Jami converts. At the Islamic University of Medina, for example, the Sahwis Musa al-Qarni, Abd al-Aziz Qari', and Jubran al-Jubran were replaced by the Jamis Tarahib al-Dawsari (author under the pseudonym Abu Ibrahim al-'Adnani of one of the most emblematic books of Jamism, *Qutbism Is Fitna, So Learn How to Recognize It*),[108] Sulayman al-Ruhayli, and Abd al-Salam al-Suhaymi.[109] In Ha'il the Jami Abdallah al-'Ubaylan replaced a Sahwi at the head of the office of religious affairs.[110] Many more such anecdotes were duly recorded in the publications of the CDLR and MIRA.

The discourse of the Jamis had two main foci: vehemently opposing the Sahwa and demonstrating intense loyalty to the Saudi royal family. In their radical critique of the Sahwa, the Jamis relied heavily on the Ahl al-Hadith who made up the core of their movement and had the best-tried oppositional discourse to the Sahwa. As a result, their favorite target was the Sahwis' creed. Identifying them with the Muslim Brotherhood, they reiterated al-Albani's attacks on Sayyid Qutb, accused of adhering to the "heterodox" doctrine of the oneness of being, and they quoted over and over the remarks of leading Brothers who had shown indulgence or support toward the cult of saints.[111] Acknowledging implicitly that the orthodoxy of the creed of some Sahwis—who, like Safar al-Hawali, had dedicated entire books to denouncing the "deviations" of Sufis and Ash'arites[112]—could not easily be questioned, the Jamis introduced a new distinction: these Sahwis might be *salafis* in terms of creed *('aqida)*, they explained, but their methodology *(manhaj)* was not orthodox. In other words, what they believed might conform to what the pious ancestors believed, but the methods they used were blameworthy innovations *(bida'),* so they were not true *salafis.*

Inspired by the Ahl al-Hadith, the Jami attacks on the Sahwis' methodology targeted their interest in politics, which allegedly turned them away from *'ilm.*[113] The Jamis added to that a relatively new accusation, formulated for the first time by the former JSM member Muqbil al-Wadi'i in *The Way out of Fitna.*[114] The Sahwis, as always identified with the Muslim Brotherhood, were guilty of *hizbiyya,* which might be translated as "factionalism," designating organization in parties (singular *hizb*), which goes against the principle of unity inherent in *salafi* Islam.[115] Jami critiques also aimed at Sahwi methods in the most technical sense: the whole infrastructure of the Sahwa, from the circles for the memorization of the Koran to the summer camps,[116] as well as Islamic chants[117] and the use of theater,[118] were denounced as reprehensible innovations.

At the same time, the Jamis constantly denounced the Sahwa's alleged hostility to existing regimes. For these ulema, obedience to the government was an absolute obligation. This insistence led Muhammad Surur, mocking their eagerness to defend the Saudi royal family, to call them the "party of the rulers" *(hizb al-wula)*.[119] The Jamis added to this unfailing loyalty an unconditional respect for the ulema of the official religious institution, particularly for the Committee of Senior Ulema, whose fatwas, in their view, could not be subject to the slightest criticism.

The Jamis' principal form of action was to produce dozens of refutations *(rudud)* of the writings and declarations of their Sahwi adversaries. They described this practice as an extension of the science of critique and fair evaluation *('ilm al-jarh wa-l-ta'dil)*, which the Ahl al-Hadith had made the essence of their study of the hadith. For the Jamis, not only the transmitters of hadith but anyone who spoke in the name of Islam had to be subjected to this process.[120] Because of the very large number of refutations of Sayyid Qutb,[121] Salman al-'Awda,[122] Safar al-Hawali,[123] and other members of the Muslim Brotherhood and the Sahwa that he had written, Rabi' al-Madkhali was given by his disciples the prestigious title of "bearer of the flag of critique and fair evaluation in our time" *(hamil liwa' al-jarh wa-l-ta'dil fi hadha al-'asr)*.[124]

The Jamis even broadened the reach of their refutations by stepping into the Sahwis' favorite field: the Islamic cassette. Jami stores for Islamic recordings sprang up in Saudi cities in 1990 and 1991, often not far from those run by Sururis or Muslim Brothers, hoping to compete with them.[125] These stores sold cassettes exclusively from ulema such as Rabi' al-Madkhali, Muhammad Aman al-Jami, and Falih al-Harbi. The Jamis also multiplied their public lectures with the support of the authorities, who hastened to find venues for them. They even went so far as to impose themselves in places considered Sahwi bastions. Hence in the Prince Mit'ab Mosque in Jeddah, where Safar al-Hawali taught on Sundays, al-Jami was given the right to give a lesson on Thursdays.[126]

This sometimes led to physical confrontations between Sahwis and Jamis. In the early 1990s Muhammad Aman al-Jami was attacked in the middle of a sermon in al-Jawhara Mosque in Riyadh (where al-'Ubaykan had launched the movement of protest in October 1990) by a group of young Sahwis, "one of whom tried to hit him with his microphone."[127] Shortly thereafter Salih al-Suhaymi and Abd al-Razzaq

al-ʿAbbad, sent to Burayda by the Ministry of Islamic Affairs to uphold the Jami line, were interrupted while preaching when young
Sahwis cut the electricity, disabling the loudspeakers, and started
chanting, "Burayda rejects you, you Jami!"[128] According to some accounts, al-Suhaymi was struck in the face, and his glasses were broken.[129] Similar confrontations led to a major incident, the violent aggression in Haʾil against the Jami sheikh Abdallah al-ʿUbaylan, who
had to be taken to a hospital emergency ward. Dozens of young Sahwis were subsequently arrested.[130]

The Jamis also made it a practice to write reports on their Sahwi
colleagues, which they transmitted to the secret police—with which
their fatwas urged cooperation—with the aim of encouraging them to
act against their rivals. Sahwi literature mentions these reports frequently,[131] but one was an object of special attention, for good reason,
because, according to Saʿd al-Faqih, it was largely responsible for convincing the government that the Sahwa represented a danger that had
to be suppressed.[132] Its title is eloquent: *The Secret World Organization,
between Planning and Application in Saudi Arabia—Documents and
Facts.* Long excerpts were printed in an article by the radical Palestinian Islamist ideologue Abu Qatada, who had obtained a copy.[133] Its
authors, who identify themselves as "the loyal *salafis*" *(salafiyyu ahl
al-walaʾ),* denounce the existence of a secret Islamist organization inspired by the ideology of Sayyid Qutb, with the goal of overthrowing
the regime. In describing it, they mix genuine facts tied to the activities of the Sahwi *jamaʿat* (for example, their use of the summer camps,
scouts, and mosque "libraries") with contrived elements, such as the
existence of organic ties between the Sahwa and foreign Islamist
groups and personalities, notably Hasan al-Turabi.[134] They conclude
by calling on authorities to end the activities of this organization.[135]

The Jami attacks intensified starting in 1991 and 1992 and forced
the Sahwa to develop defenses by redefining its discourse and action.
To counter the accusation that they paid too little attention to ʿilm, the
Sahwis multiplied courses and lectures in which they turned away
from contemporary politics to concentrate on the classics of the Wahhabi corpus. For example, Salman al-ʿAwda taught a series of 146
classes in Burayda on *The Attainment of the Objective,*[136] a collection

of hadiths by the medieval traditionist Ibn Hajar al-ʿAsqalani (1372–1448). Around the same time, Safar al-Hawali intensified his classes in Jeddah on *The Profession of Faith of al-Tahawi*. The organization of a great competition for the memorization of the sunna in Burayda by Salman al-ʿAwda in October 1992 followed the same logic. More generally, reacting to the Jamis' identification of the Sahwa with the Muslim Brotherhood, the Sahwis tried "to shed their Muslim Brotherhood skin."[137] The change was particularly visible in the *jamaʿat*'s study circles. Works by Muslim Brothers were now taught less frequently, while intensive courses on the writings of Ibn al-Wahhab were added to the curricula.[138] Starting in 1993, this practice became systematic with the establishment of a new kind of extracurricular activity, "scientific training sessions" *(al-dawrat al-ʿilmiyya),* intended to give young Sahwis a solid knowledge of the Wahhabi corpus.[139]

At the same time, the Sahwis denied any lack of respect for the senior ulema, particularly Ibn Baz and Ibn ʿUthaymin. They even engaged in a veritable bidding war with their Jami rivals in showing esteem and consideration for the two sheikhs.[140] Nasir al-ʿUmar published a pamphlet, *The Flesh of the Ulema Is Poisoned,*[141] in which he denounced everyone who attacked the ulema, while Salman al-ʿAwda delivered a sermon titled "The Breeze of Hejaz on the Biography of Ibn Baz,"[142] in which he presented the life of the venerable sheikh as a model for all Muslims. At the same time, the Sahwis encouraged their followers to attend lectures by Ibn Baz and Ibn ʿUthaymin so as not to abandon the field to the Jamis.[143]

The real issue soon became whether the Jamis or the Sahwis enjoyed the support of Ibn Baz, but he, retaining his papal role, refused to choose, sometimes supporting one group, sometimes the other. The ambiguity of this position was at the source of the so-called war of *tazkiyat* (recommendations) that the Jamis and Sahwis began to wage against each other in 1992. It began with a long communiqué from Ibn Baz published in the Saudi press on January 2, 1992, in which the old sheikh declared: "A rumor has been circulating recently that some of those who claim to represent *ʿilm* and *daʿwa* have questioned the reputations of well-known preachers. . . . They do this secretly in their meetings, and it is even said that they make their remarks in public lectures in mosques and that they have recorded them on cassettes that are circulating among the people. This attitude is contrary to what God and His prophet have commanded."[144]

The Sahwa was quick to see in these words a disavowal of its Jami adversaries. Safar al-Hawali and ʿAʾid al-Qarni each devoted an entire sermon to justifying this interpretation.[145] The Jamis, on the defensive, categorically rejected this interpretation of the communiqué. A month later, on February 6, 1992, a delegation led by al-Jami and al-Madkhali went to Ibn Baz to seek from him a declaration enabling them to counter the Sahwa's attacks. Still intent on staying above disputes, Ibn Baz assured them of his support: "We have not the slightest doubt about our brothers, the noted sheikhs of Medina," he said. "We know them for their uprightness, their ʿilm, and the correctness of their creed."[146] Thousands of copies of pamphlets and cassettes containing these remarks by Ibn Baz were distributed by the Jamis and their supporters in competition with the wide distribution of Ibn Baz's previous communiqué by the Sahwis.[147]

The war of tazkiyat did not stop there and even grew in magnitude. In late 1992 the condemnation of the Memorandum of Advice by the Council of the Committee of Senior Ulema, which accused the signatories of "intellectual deviance and defending the principles of foreign movements and parties," was distributed by the Jamis, who saw it as full and open adherence to their line. In response, the Sahwis circulated copies of a recording of Ibn Baz defending al-ʿAwda and al-Hawali in a 1992 meeting at the home of Nasir al-ʿUmar,[148] along with the laudatory preface that the old sheikh had written for the book Separation and Mixture,[149] published around the same time by Salman al-ʿAwda.[150] Sahwis also put together a compilation titled The Senior Ulema Speak about the Preachers,[151] which contained older and newer recorded passages in which Ibn Baz, Ibn ʿUthaymin, Ibn Quʿud, Ibn Jibrin, and even al-Albani (who, because he was in the process of becoming "papal," was now looking for a modus vivendi with his former adversaries) praised al-ʿAwda and al-Hawali. This cassette, too, was distributed in large quantities.

These various Sahwi attempts, however, did not succeed in stopping the Jami momentum. By 1993 Jamis had established a significant presence in Saudi religious circles. It was only then that the Jami movement started to be weakened, principally by a series of splits that largely resulted from the contradictions inherent in its discourse and the composition of its membership. The first split saw the emergence of a "Haddadist" submovement that, following the line of the Egyptian Mahmud al-Haddad,[152] advocated total *ijtihad* and the rejection of some collections of hadiths traditionally used by Wahhabi ulema, such as *The Victory of the Creator* by Ibn Hajar al-ʿAsqalani and *The Forty* by Imam Muhyi al-Din al-Nawawi (1234–1278),[153] because their authors adhered to the Ashʿarite conception of creed, considered heterodox by the Wahhabis. Despite this, the Saudi ulema had accepted these works because they were classics of Sunnism and did not deal with questions of creed. As Yusuf al-Dayni explains, "Al-Haddad was bringing out a fundamental contradiction of the Jamis. He was telling them: you are not coherent; how can you criticize Safar al-Hawali while saying not a word about Ibn Hajar and al-Nawawi, who are not even *salafis*?"[154] This redefinition of the contours of the Wahhabi corpus had problematic implications because it called into question the authority of the senior ulema who were its official guardians. In this sense it was incompatible with the loyalty advocated by the Jamis. This explains why refuting al-Haddad[155] and those who joined him, like Farid al-Maliki,[156] became for al-Madkhali and his associates a full-time occupation, to some extent diverting their attention from the Sahwis.[157]

A second schism arose out of the contradiction between adherence to the Ahl al-Hadith line and the proclaimed intent to follow the Wahhabi ulema of the kingdom. As was shown earlier, al-Albani and his disciples had been remarkably critical of the unspoken Hanbalism of the Wahhabis. The loyalist Ahl al-Hadith had attempted to downplay this aspect of their discourse, but some Jamis who supported the official ulema and were unhappy with the predominance of the Ahl al-Hadith line in the movement used it to challenge the authority of Rabiʿ al-Madkhali and Falih al-Harbi. Led by Abd al-Latif Bashumayyil, a former engineer who had become the owner of the principal Jami Islamic recordings store in Jeddah,[158] and Musa al-Duwaysh, who taught at the Islamic University of Medina, they dug up from the writings and recordings of al-Albani all his stands hostile to Wah-habism for the sole purpose of embarrassing the major Jami sheikhs.[159] Following that, there were more exchanges of refutations, further re-ducing the focus on the conflict with the Sahwa and, eventually, the impact of the Jami movement.

The Revival of Hejazi Sufism

The second group to enjoy a degree of support from the authorities for the purpose of obstructing the Sahwa were the Sufis of Hejaz. The term "Sufis" was first applied as an anathema by the Wahhabis to the adher-ents of traditional Hejazi Islam who had refused to accept the "attenu-ated Wahhabism" of the Muslim reformists. They maintained their attachment to the framework of the four canonical legal schools of *fiqh,* as well as to the Ash'arite creed and to certain mystical practices such as *dhikr,*[160] frequent at celebrations of the Prophet's birthday *(mawlid)* and during the cult of saints. Although those Sufis initially rejected the label and insisted on being called "the original school" *(al-madrasa al-asliyya),*[161] some of them have now cautiously started to identify with it.

During the first decades following the conquest of Hejaz, the Sufis had been persecuted by the Wahhabis, but partly because of the inclu-sivist turn of the Wahhabi institution and partly thanks to the seg-mented nature of the social arena, the conflict had been gradually pacified. It returned with renewed force in the late 1970s. This was due, first of all, to a revival of Hejazi Sufism, linked to a reawakening of Hejazi identity in reaction to the increasing marginalization of the Hejazi elite in the political and economic spheres.[162] Their resentment was all the stronger because the Hejazis had been among the major beneficiaries of the system until the end of the Faysal era. Sufi circles at the time included several thousand active members,[163] gathered under the authority of the man who had imposed himself as the leader of the revival, Sheikh Muhammad 'Alawi al-Maliki, a descendant of the Malekite muftis of Mecca before the Saudi conquest. But this was just at the time when the Sahwa was rising in power, spreading its con-trol throughout the social arena. The Sahwis had inherited from the

Wahhabi ulema their hostility to Sufism,[164] which they intended to pursue much more zealously than their elders. Under Sahwi pressure, in 1980 one of the members of the Committee of Senior Ulema, Abdallah al-Munayʿ, published *Dialogue with al-Maliki to Respond to His Erring Ways and His Aberrations*,[165] in which he declared impious the positions on the legitimacy of the cult of the saints held by al-Maliki. In September 1981 the Council of the Committee of Senior Ulema demanded that al-Maliki be barred from participating in any public activity and that his passport be confiscated.[166] This decision was especially unexpected because until then he had enjoyed a degree of tolerance from the political and religious authorities. He had been able to inherit the teaching position that his father had held at the Great Mosque of Mecca until his death in 1971 and had even been put in charge of giving a course at the Faculty of *Shariʿa* at Umm al-Qura University.[167] Following the 1981 statement of the council, he was removed from both positions.

Starting in 1994, however, Hejazi Sufism entered a period of more tranquil relations with the authorities, signaled by the authorization given to al-Maliki to resume teaching.[168] Some of the restrictions weighing on the activities of the Sufis, notably with respect to the organization of private gatherings for the celebration of the Prophet's birthday, were partially lifted.[169] Although these developments remained limited and the Sufis continued to face major obstacles to their religious practice, they nonetheless enabled Hejazi Sufism to continue its renaissance and to compete for influence with the Sahwa, with the regime's blessings, in Hejaz.

The Shirazi Shiite Opposition in Exile: Unlikely Allies

To weaken the Sahwi movement of protest, the Saudi authorities also played the card of the Shirazi Shiite opposition. Historically, Shiite Islamism in Saudi Arabia had two principal strands: the Khomeinis, whose source of emulation *(marjaʿ al-taqlid)* was Ayatollah Khomeini; and the Shirazis, who placed themselves under the spiritual authority of Sayyid Muhammad al-Shirazi, a controversial Iraqi sheikh who had proclaimed himself a source of emulation in the 1960s.[170] As opposed to the Khomeinis, who were politically aligned with Iran, the Shirazis were intent on cultivating their difference with the Iranians. Enjoying a majority over the Khomeinis, the Shirazis were behind the establishment in 1975 of the Organization of the Islamic Revolution in the Arabian Peninsula (OIRAP) (Munazzamat al-thawra al-islamiyya fi-l-jazira al-ʿarabiyya), led by Hasan al-Saffar and largely responsible for the uprising in the Eastern Province, known as the Intifada of Muharram, in November 1979.[171] In the wake of the ensuing repression, the organization shifted the center of its activities outside the country, first for a few years to Iran, then to Syria, Great Britain, and the United States. In their exile the Shirazi Islamists turned out to be accomplished propagandists, able to successfully promote the cause of their coreligionists, who were discriminated against in Saudi Arabia, with human rights organizations and Western governments. At the same time, they gradually abandoned the revolutionary rhetoric of their beginnings and adopted a more polished and universalist political discourse centered on the values of pluralism and civil society.[172] To signal this transformation, in early 1991 they even gave up the name OIRAP and now called themselves the Reformist Movement (al-Haraka al-islahiyya).[173] This was a period when, hoping to take advantage of a weakening of the regime, they became increasingly vocal in their calls for reform.

In its relations with the Shirazi Shiite opposition in exile, the regime's objectives were somewhat different from what they had been with the Jamis and the Sufis. In this case there was no question of supporting a movement able to oppose the Sahwa by tapping into Sahwi bases, because Sahwi Sunnis and Shirazi Shiites operated in distinct spheres. Rather, the goal was to reduce pressure on the royal family so that it could concentrate its efforts on its most formidable opponent, the Sahwa, while cutting off the Sahwi opposition from potential allies. Indeed, despite the radical anti-Shiism of most Sahwi ulema, sustained contacts had been established between the Shirazi opposition and some "enlightened" Sahwi intellectuals, notably, according to Hamza al-Hasan, then one of the Shirazi representatives in London, Ahmad al-Tuwayjiri and Tawfiq al-Qusayyir.[174] Another sign of a rapprochement was that the magazine *Al-Jazira al-ʿArabiyya* (The Arabian Peninsula), the central organ of the Shirazis in exile, which was launched in January 1991, provided extraordinarily detailed and remarkably empathetic treatment of the Sahwi opposition movement.[175] In October 1992, for instance, the magazine published an article by Tawfiq al-Sayf, then secretary general of the Reformist Movement, in which he stated: "The *Memorandum of Advice* expresses the opinion of all the people. . . . In that sense, it represents our point of view regarding the necessary reforms in the country."[176]

Whatever the real status and the eventual viability of an alliance between Sahwis and Shirazis, the possibility persuaded the royal family to open negotiations with the Shirazi opposition.[177] The discussions began in mid-1993 and ended with the activist exiles' return to the country after the regime promised to release the Shiite political prisoners in its jails and to take steps against the discrimination affecting Shiites in the kingdom.[178] The Reformist Movement then put an end to its activities, and *Al-Jazira al-'Arabiyya* ceased publication, depriving the Sahwi opposition of an indirect but influential voice.

The effective impact of these various countermovements on the Sahwi protest remains to be examined. In the case of the Shirazi Shiites, that impact was probably minimal. Outside the personal relations noted earlier, there was no operational partnership between Sahwis and Shirazis that the co-optation of the latter by the regime could have compromised. Their return to favor therefore did not directly affect the resources available to the protest on the ground. In addition, the Sahwi bases were not affected, because Sahwis and Shiites did not recruit from the same populations. With the Sufis of Hejaz, the impact was a little more significant because Sahwis and Sufis addressed the same Sunni youth. There were even examples of young Hejazis who were drawn away from the influence of the summer camps by the revived attraction of Sufi circles,[179] but they appear to have been isolated cases, particularly because the Sahwa continued to enjoy much greater resources than its new Sufi competitors. Moreover, in the case of the Sufis, as well as that of the Shirazis, the regime's support came relatively late, in 1994 and late 1993, respectively.

The rise of Jamism had a much more significant impact on the protest. Not only was the Jami movement, thanks to the abundant resources at its disposal, able to secure some success in the Saudi religious field, but also, through its claim inherited from the Ahl al-Hadith to represent an original and purified *salafi* Islam, it was able to construct a genuine popular base. Consequently, whereas in 1991 "only a few dozen people attended the courses of Muhammad Aman al-Jami at Prince Mit'ab Mosque in Jeddah, while there were thousands listening to Safar al-Hawali,"[180] things began to change in 1992 and 1993, even in the Sahwi bastion of the Qasim, as Mansur al-Nuqaydan confirmed: "When I was imprisoned in January 1992, the Jamis in Burayda were virtually nonexistent. Imagine my surprise when I left prison in the summer of 1993 to discover that they were now numerous and well established, and that many young people I knew had joined them!"[181] Other Islamists have spoken of the same phenomenon, including Yusuf al-Dayni and Sa'ud al-Sarhan, who were for a while close to the Jamis,[182] as well as Sulayman al-Dahayyan and Ibrahim al-Sikran, who were then active in Sururi circles.[183]

Contrary to common assumptions, the Jami countermovement seems to have had a definite effect on the religious field and on the youth. It thereby appreciably helped weaken the Sahwa and the movement of protest it was spearheading. At the same time, there is every indication that this impact came relatively late: although the rise of the Jamis had begun by the end of 1990, they did not, according to most accounts, become truly competitive with the Sahwa until 1993, at the very moment when the Jamis' internal disputes were emerging, thereby reducing the pressure on the Sahwis. Consequently, the rise of Jamism is certainly not sufficient to explain the failure of the Sahwi protest.

A Lack of Reliable Mobilizing Structures

A closer look at the internal dynamics of the movement shows that by 1993 the future of the Sahwi movement had already been compromised. This is all the more surprising since, because it was in possession of a powerful mobilizing discourse that resonated with the interpretive frameworks and aspirations of an entire generation of young Saudis, because it had the militant and legitimating resources necessary for the movement to get organized and for the mobilization to gain momentum, and because it occurred in extremely favorable political circumstances, the Sahwi protest had at first seemed to be in a position to reach its objectives. This perception was strengthened by the fact that it had demonstrated a remarkable mobilizing capacity, as illustrated by the gathering of ten thousand to thirty thousand people outside the headquarters of the Committee of Senior Ulema after the demonstration by liberal women in November 1990. But the Sahwis soon encountered growing difficulties in finding a reliable infrastructure for mobilization. Such an infrastructure was particularly important because in case of a test of strength with the regime, it would be needed to display the magnitude of the support the movement enjoyed.

Although intellectuals and ulema involved in the Sahwi protest, by relying on their respective resources, were initially able to create the informal embryo of a mobilizing organization, they soon had to recognize the limitations of that strategy. As has been demonstrated in other contexts, the absence of an open public sphere in an authoritarian regime means that a social movement has great difficulty organizing itself in action and must generally rely on preexisting mobilizing structures or organizations.[184] This is the point at which the *jama'at*, the most organized element of the Sahwa, entered the picture. By using both persuasion and subversion, the architects of the protest would try to put the infrastructure they represented at the service of their goals.

This was all the more difficult because the birth of the protest movement was completely independent of the *jama'at*. Many of its early promoters, including a significant portion of the "enlightened" Sahwi intellectuals, products of an Islamist socialization that had taken place partly outside Saudi Arabia, had only distant connections with the *jama'at*. Some who were members of *jama'at*, such as Sa'd al-Faqih, who held a relatively senior position in the Brothers of Zubayr, "first concealed the plan from [their] own *jama'a*, out of fear that the *jama'at*'s leaders would cause it to fail, because they had the power to do that."[185] Some, like Salman al-ʿAwda[186] and Safar al-Hawali,[187] both Sururis, decided to distance themselves from their *jamaʿa* so they could act freely without having to account for their actions. This was also true of Hamad al-Sulayfih, who surrendered command of his *jamaʿa*.[188] Others, disappointed by the inertia of their *jamaʿa*, decided to leave it for good.[189]

The Gulf War, the call on American troops, and the emergence of the protest movement provoked among these *jamaʿat* as a whole a vigorous debate on the position to adopt. This was chiefly between the grassroots members, many of whom supported the movement of protest because its discourse resonated with their own convictions, and the leaders, who believed that the *jamaʿat* had nothing to gain by getting involved in a battle that would risk diverting them from their top priority, the formation of a Sahwi identity through the education of the youth. The controversy was so intense that the Kuwaiti Brother Ismaʿil al-Shatti remembers coming expressly to Saudi Arabia to persuade his Saudi counterparts, who were confronted with a revolt of their rank and file, to stand with the Brothers of Kuwait who supported the liberation of their country by the American army.[190] The crisis even led to the unprecedented creation of a "council of the *jamaʿat*" that brought together representatives of the five existing groups (the four affiliated with the Muslim Brotherhood and the Sururis). But these meetings were unproductive, and, in the words of Saʿd al-Faqih, "The leaders of the *jamaʿat* showed themselves to be unable to adopt the slightest official position on the question, demonstrating their incompetence."[191]

The question of mobilizing organizations was initially not as pressing for the Sahwi opposition leaders. The "Letter of Demands" was even explicitly conceived to sidestep the problem. Because it was contained on one page and mentioned the support of Ibn Baz and Ibn ʿUthaymin, the letter could be, and was, distributed by everyone, far beyond Sahwi circles or even politicized Saudis. But when the reformists recorded the tape known as the supergun, whose content was far more subversive, the question became who would take the risk of copying and distributing it. For some Sahwi intellectuals, foremost among them al-Faqih, it seemed clear that the movement of protest needed an effective infrastructure for mobilization on which it could rely.[192]

It would have been ideal if the *jama'at* had rallied to the cause be-cause the reformists saw them as a ready-to-use infrastructure,[193] but the position their leaders had adopted made that unlikely. The reform-ists then sought to take advantage of the vertical dissensions within the *jama'at*. Thus began an intense campaign of lobbying the midlevel members of the *jama'at*—and the rank and file so they would pressure their supervisors—to persuade them to join the movement.

In these circumstances the Sururis adopted the most ambivalent position. Although most of the mid-ranking members of the *jama'a* refused to associate themselves formally with protest activities, they agreed at first to support them behind the scenes by putting the infra-structure they controlled at their service. As Muhammad al-Mas'ari explained, "The purpose of this ambivalence was simple: to make sure they would share the potential gains of the protest without risking any losses."[194] This two-sided position appeared as well in the editorial lines of the two journals most read in the *jama'a*, *Al-Bayan*, very politically correct, and *Al-Sunna*, much more offensive.

Attitudes in the Muslim Brotherhood were less homogeneous. According to some accounts, the debates among the Brothers of al-Funaysan were so vehement that they produced a virtual disintegration of the *jama'a*.[195] The case of the Brothers of Zubayr is particularly inter-esting. Sa'd al-Faqih, one of its senior members, tried at first to bring his *jama'a* along with him. When he lost hope of succeeding, he orga-nized a split in mid-1992. A large part of the student division, over which he had held major responsibilities for some time, left the *jama'a* to follow him. The few hundred young men behind him were known thereafter in Sahwi circles as "the dissidents" *(al-munshaqqun).*[196]

Despite these few successes, which made possible a relatively wide distribution of the supergun and the *Memorandum of Advice*, the re-sult of the operation turned out to be disappointing. The reformists had been able at first to divert a portion of the infrastructure of the *jama'at* to their benefit, but as the conflict with the regime widened, the leaders of the *jama'at* resumed control over their troops. All of the *jama'at* associated with the Brotherhood were the first to definitively abandon the reformist ship, probably in late 1992. By early 1993 the Sururis had unequivocally lined up behind the regime. They even tried to pressure Salman al-ʿAwda and Safar al-Hawali into giving up the protest. In 1994 they prohibited their members, on pain of exclusion, from distributing the leaflets of the CDLR or from complying with calls to demonstrate, notably during the episode of the Intifada of Burayda, discussed later.[197] Thus, from a potential reservoir and vector for mobilization, the *jamaʿat* became the primary obstacle in its way, revealing their nature as "double-edged networks."[198]

This decision by the *jamaʿat* deeply affected the mobilizing capacities of the movement of protest, which had now been deprived of the greater part of its grassroots infrastructure. It has already been pointed out that the *jamaʿat* were very cohesive, able to hold their members in the name of what they considered the group interest, even when such pragmatism contradicted certain aspects of their ideological discourse. In this instance they demonstrated once again their power over their members, as they had done during the episode of the Afghan jihad, when they had been able to discourage many of their followers from going to fight against the Soviets. The *jamaʿat* also had a more general influence over all "committed" *(multazimun)* young men, even when they were not directly affiliated with one of the groups and merely participated in the public activities that any particular *jamaʿa* organized. The decision by the *jamaʿat* to boycott the Sahwi protest therefore had some effect, beyond the first circle of affiliates *(muntamun)*, on the second circle of the Sahwa. Beyond that, the status as opinion leaders that, in the absence of contradictory frames of reference, the figures of the *jamaʿat* enjoyed among the youth of the Sahwa generation meant that all Saudi young men were to some extent influenced by the decision.

A last potential resort for mobilization was the non-Sahwi Islamists—jihadis and rejectionists—who had started supporting the protest after 1993. At the sociological level this rapprochement could have prefigured an alliance between the pious middle classes, embodied by the Sahwa, and the poor urban youth (and more broadly the youth from subordinate social groups), from whom rejectionists and jihadis sprang in part.[199] This kind of alliance might, as in the case of the Khomeini revolution in Iran, have enabled the Islamist protest to win out.[200] In Saudi Arabia, however, it came much too late, at a time when the most powerful and best-organized elements of the Sahwa, represented by the *jama'at*, had already turned their backs on the movement. Further, this belated rapprochement was not enough to weaken the popularity of the Jamis, which is what the Sahwis hoped for from the support of the rejectionists. Most important, it could not remedy the problems with mobilization that the Sahwis were encountering, because the rejectionist and jihadi networks contained at most a few hundred individuals, often under surveillance by the authorities, whose methods continued to differ from those favored by the Sahwis.

The question arises whether the reversal by the *jama'at* was prompted by the repressive measures adopted by the regime in response to the protest. However, it seems that the mechanisms at work were more structural than conjunctural. The fact is that until late 1993 repression was concentrated on public opposition figures (primarily those whose names appeared on the petitions or who were at the origin of the CDLR). At no point had the more underground world of the *jama'at* been targeted. In addition, repression did not become severe before mid-1993, with the first systematic arrests. Yet, the equivocations of the *jama'at* went back to the early days of the protest, and their decision to distance themselves from the movement dates from late 1992 and early 1993, well before the repression widened.

Ironically, it was well after the last holdouts among *jama'at* members had rallied to the regime's line that the *jama'at* were affected by repression. From mid-1993 the measures of institutional regulation aimed at restoring order to the various fields in which the Sahwa was active limited their freedom of action. Starting in late 1994, some figures known for being linked to the *jama'at*, but who had taken no active part in the protest, were transferred or fired. This purge culminated with the deportation of Muhammad Qutb in 1996, even though he had never been involved in Saudi politics.[201] It was thus well after the fact that the regime decided to punish the *jama'at* for their initial hesitations. The Jamis, delighted finally to be able to get rid of their historic rivals, played a role in persuading the regime to take action.

Thus to understand the attitude of the *jama'at* toward the opposition, it is necessary to consider the place they occupy and have historically occupied in the Saudi system, of which they are, in the final analysis, an integral part. Given the magnitude of the resources and privileges from which they had benefited since the late 1960s, how could they challenge a state that had treated them so well, thereby risking the loss of everything they had constructed and their special position? It appears that full awareness of these facts explains the first hesitations of the *jama'at* as early as 1990, followed by their irrevocable rallying to the regime in late 1992 and early 1993.

Taking note of the "betrayal" of the *jama'at,* some opposition leaders took the gamble that it was possible to do without grassroots organizational support as long as the protest could be turned into a vast popular movement, independent of the Sahwa and its networks and able spontaneously to mobilize the entire society. From the early days of the protest, the idea of generating a popular movement, beyond the Sahwa and its *jama'at,* had been present in the minds of its architects. The "Letter of Demands," through its requests for equality and social justice, already contained a call for the mobilization of the subordinate groups in the social sphere. As time passed, and as the *jama'at* obstructed their members' participation in the protest, it became a vital necessity to produce a popular mobilization. The great popularity the movement enjoyed in Saudi Arabia, even beyond Islamist circles, suggested to its promoters that mobilizing society would be an easy matter.

To get around the organizational problem, Sa'd al-Faqih and Muhammad al-Mas'ari, starting with the resumption of the activities of the CDLR in London in April 1994, made intensive use of the fax machine, which enabled them to reach large segments of Saudi society beyond already-established networks. In their view, the goal was to create a Saudi "public opinion" ready to be mobilized against the "culpable negligence" of the royal family, duly denounced in the committee's publications. For this purpose, four themes they believed would appeal to the entire Saudi population became the leitmotifs of the CDLR's writings. First was the demand for security in the face of crime described as increasing at an astronomical rate and to which the government was depicted to be powerless to react.[202] The second pointed to the deterioration in public services (electricity, water, telephones, hospitals, universities, and so on), also presented as drastic, even though the costs of these services were constantly rising.[203] The third referred to the land expropriations that members of the royal family were accused of carrying out with impunity.[204] The fourth concerned the conduct of the hajj, with each mass death of pilgrims presented as further evidence of the authorities' inability to fulfill their role as guardians of the holy places.[205]

To measure the success of the transformation of the movement of protest into a popular mobilization, the demonstration of September 13, 1994, which the CDLR called the "Intifada of Burayda" *(intifadat Burayda)* for propaganda purposes, provides a test case because, according to most accounts, it marked the apogee of the protest, and because its results were not distorted by repression, which did not interrupt it but only struck after the fact. The following account is based on the testimony of two of its initiators, Sulayman al-Dahayyan and Sulayman al-Rashudi, and of several young participants, notably Kassab al-ʿUtaybi, as well as on communiqués published by the CDLR as events unfolded.

On September 10, 1994, the CDLR published a communiqué reporting the arrest of Safar al-Hawali (he was immediately released and was not re-arrested until the sixteenth) and the imminent arrest of Salman al-ʿAwda, who was sought by the authorities.[206] On September 11 the CDLR announced that al-ʿAwda had just gone to Burayda surrounded by a host of his supporters determined to prevent his capture, and it launched a general appeal "to go to the home of Sheikh Salman from all corners of the Arabian Peninsula, to show him the highest degree of support, and to execute the sheikh's orders as to what should be done in the face of this challenge launched by the forces of evil."[207] This appeal, faxed to thousands of people, signaled the start of the mobilization.

When al-ʿAwda reached "his" mosque (the one he usually frequented), he galvanized his supporters with a sermon.[208] He explained that the promoters of change should be prepared to suffer because "this total corruption requires a total reform, and it is a mistake to imagine that the reform will be carried out simply by words, or simply because our hearts are pure and our intentions peaceful, without our having to endure some suffering and pain for the words we have spoken or for our convictions."[209] The sermon was recorded and widely distributed after his arrest under the title "Letter from behind Bars."

On September 12 an imposing force of police went to the mosque, where al-ʿAwda was entrenched, to persuade him to surrender to the authorities. After negotiations the sheikh agreed to go to the governorate of the Qasim, which he did, surrounded by a large number of supporters. There al-ʿAwda refused to sign the promise to cease all activities that was presented to him, but the governor was forced to allow the sheikh to leave under pressure from his supporters.[210] On his return his supporters, including the sheikhs Ibrahim al-Dubayyan, Ali al-Khudayr, and Sulayman al-Rashudi and the intellectual Sulayman al-Dahayyan, announced that they were launching a "festival of solidarity with the oppressed" *(mahrajan al-tadamun maʿ al-madhlumin)* in the mosque.[211] Each of them then spoke in turn to denounce the negligence of the Saudi leaders and their repression of the opposition. Some attacked the Committee of Senior Ulema, which was accused of sharing responsibility for the situation.[212]

At dawn on September 13 Saudi police took advantage of the fact that al-ʿAwda was surrounded by only a handful of supporters—the others were resting—to arrest him.[213] His principal followers immediately assembled and decided to organize a march that afternoon from al-ʿAwda's house to the governorate of the Qasim, about four kilometers away, to demand his release.[214] The news was immediately transmitted to the CDLR, which early that day faxed thousands of copies of a communiqué in which it "relayed the extremely urgent appeal of the ulema and religious leaders concerning the necessity of a total mobilization of the entire *umma* to go immediately to the home of Sheikh Salman al-ʿAwda in Burayda."[215] With this communiqué the CDLR forcefully reiterated the appeals for mobilization that had been launched since September 11. The march did take place on the afternoon of September 13 and led to an encounter between its principal initiators and the vice governor, to whom they handed a document demanding al-ʿAwda's release. To gain time and calm them down, the vice governor promised that their wishes would be granted promptly.[216] The march then ended peacefully, and most of the demonstrators returned home. The rest of the story is well known: al-ʿAwda remained in prison, and most organizers of the march were arrested in the ensuing days.[217]

The CDLR had some of its supporters film the march and widely distributed cassettes of it. Although the committee used this to propagandize the event as a great achievement of the Sahwi protest, it was rather manifest evidence of the movement's inability to mobilize effectively. According to various accounts, the marchers numbered only five hundred to one thousand people[218] (far from the fifteen thousand proclaimed by the CDLR).[219] This figure did not represent only people from Burayda, because supporters of the movement had streamed in from around the kingdom in response to the CDLR's appeals. Kassab al-ʿUtaybi, for instance, came expressly from Jawf, accompanied by fifteen cars. According to him, there were also participants from Riyadh, Jeddah, and other cities of the Hejaz.[220]

Moreover, most demonstrators—more than 80 percent according to Sulayman al-Dahayyan[221]—were *multazimun* (this was easy to determine because they had a number of identifying external signs of religiosity), the vast majority of whom were younger than thirty.[222] They were probably the small number of young Sahwis of the first and second circles who had defied the prohibitions of the *jamaʿat* or escaped from their control. The remaining 20 percent may have been Sahwis of the third circle (who did not have specific signs of religiosity) or "average Saudis." In any event, the number of the latter among the demonstrators appears to have been minimal. The Sahwi protest had not succeeded in engendering a popular movement.

The day after the Intifada of Burayda, on September 14, 1994, a demonstration organized in Riyadh was a complete fiasco because of both poor coordination[223] and the same difficulty in mobilizing people. Thus the police had no trouble blocking access and arresting the fifty demonstrators who had managed to reach the site.[224] Although "reactions following the Intifada did not match the committee's hopes,"[225] as Muhammad al-Masʿari acknowledged, other demonstrations were organized by the CDLR nearly six months later to try to relaunch the movement. On Friday, March 17, 1995, the CDLR called on its supporters in Riyadh, Jeddah, and Haʾil to conduct their midday prayer in a designated mosque and then to stay in the mosque for one hour after the prayer in sign of protest.[226] On March 31 the CDLR called for a similar demonstration in Burayda,[227] and on May 5, like demonstrations were organized in eight cities of the kingdom.[228] The impact of these three days was even more minimal than that of the Intifada of Burayda. On the first day the CDLR spoke of two thousand people who stayed after prayers in Riyadh and six hundred who waited for an hour before leaving—probably exaggerated figures—and did not even mention the outcome in Jeddah and Ha'il.[229] On the second day the CDLR counted four thousand to five thousand people—a very inflated figure according to various observers on the scene[230]—without distinguishing between those who simply came to pray and those who made the effort to stay for an hour as requested.[231] The result of the third day was so bad that the CDLR gave it only a few lines in the bulletin of May 10, 1995,[232] in terms that amounted to an implicit acknowledgment of failure. The CDLR organized no further days of demonstrations. Moreover, at the same time, the committee, which had spent the bulk of its funds inundating Saudi Arabia with fax messages, was approaching bankruptcy.[233] Recognizing the failure of the strategy followed by the CDLR, Muhammad al-Mas'ari declared: "To achieve this result, we had to ruin ourselves by sending thousands of fax messages. If there had been a structure or an organization on the ground, four faxes would have been enough!"[234] The CDLR's financial difficulties were further aggravated by the September 1994 arrests, which affected some of the major collectors of funds for the committee, starting with al-'Awda and al-Hawali.[235]

Moreover, since the movement had shifted its location to London and even more after September 1994, it suffered from a glaring deficit of legitimating resources because its leadership now only consisted of intellectuals, starting with al-Faqih and al-Mas'ari. To remedy this failing, they systematically mentioned the "religious leaders" (qiyadat shar'iyya) who were allegedly leading the movement from Saudi Arabia, but who had to remain anonymous for security reasons.[236] However, this argument does not seem to have convinced their readership.[237] The coup de grâce to the hopes of al-Mas'ari and al-Faqih came from a relative improvement in the economic situation starting in 1994,[238] which made possible an increase in state expenditure, particularly for public services. As a result, the new rhetoric of the CDLR became seriously outdated. It is reasonable to assume that starting in late 1995, the impact of the CDLR in Saudi Arabia, and after that of Saʿd al-Faqih's MIRA, was limited, and that they had no significant mobilizing power.

A hasty consideration of the effects of the Sahwa insurrection at the overall level would seem to indicate that it was a patent failure. Despite their efforts, the spearheads of the Sahwi protest had not made the regime give way on any point. The government did adopt three reforms in March 1992—the establishment of the Advisory Council (Majlis al-shura) and the adoption of a basic law *(al-nidham al-asasi)* and of a law of regions *(nidham al-manatiq)*—but they were in no way an adequate response to the opposition's demands.[239] The basic law and the law of regions were primarily "ornaments" that changed nothing in the nature of the political system or the balance of power.[240] The Advisory Council, which had been the first demand in the "Letter of Demands," finally began operating in August 1993 but was given only marginal powers and was totally subservient to the royal family, who appointed its members.[241] Worse, many of them were liberal technocrats, the very people whose influence the Sahwis had sought to limit. The Sahwi opposition was represented on the council by a single individual, Ahmad al-Tuwayjiri, one of the originators of the "Letter of Demands" who had thereafter distanced himself from the protest, and whose membership in one of the families closest to the royal family had won the regime's trust.

However, an exclusive focus on the big picture errs by considering only the changes the Sahwi protest would have brought about in the existing political system. This amounts to assuming that the objectives of the movement were homogeneous, and that those objectives were targeted primarily at political reform, which would amount to identifying the sole rationale of the Sahwi intellectuals as the meaning of the protest. However, two other levels of success can be examined and are a better expression of the objectives of some of the other components of the movement, especially of the ulema: the middle level (that of the movement itself and its component groups), and the micro level (that of individuals). There the evaluation is much more positive. At the micro level the major Sahwi sheikhs, starting with Salman al-'Awda and Safar al-Hawali, considerably reinforced their aura both in the religious field and in the social arena. This would become a key asset for them once released from prison. In this sense the protest enriched them. At the middle level the result was also significant. The Sahwa had managed to impose itself as representing a legitimate religious authority, which was one of the main reasons for the involvement of Sahwi religious figures in the protest. Those who were only preachers *(du'at)* in the late 1980s were now considered by everyone as ulema *('ulama')*. Most important, the protest episode enabled the Sahwa to impose itself in the field of social movements in Saudi Arabia as an unavoidable framework into which even its historic rivals, the rejectionists and jihadis, had fitted themselves by joining the protest in 1993 and 1994. That would have essential consequences for the future because any new attempt at mobilization would have to claim the legacy of the Sahwa insurrection.

7

The Islamists after the Insurrection

The year 1995 marked the end of the Sahwa insurrection. Unable to create a viable mobilization, fiercely opposed by some of the Sahwa's historic rivals, and finally crushed by repression, the movement had fizzled out. Almost all the Sahwi leaders involved in the protest were behind bars, as were the hundreds of rejectionists and jihadis arrested during the same period or after the November 1995 attack. Most of them were released in slow stages starting in 1997.

At the end of the 1990s the Islamist scene started reconstituting itself and quickly recovered its former central place in the Saudi social arena. However, the environment in which Islamists operated had been considerably modified as a result of a series of important changes that marked the second half of the 1990s. Externally, there were significant developments with the rise to power of the global jihad embodied by Osama bin Laden, culminating in the September 11 attacks, and with the affirmation of pro-democratic Islamist movements in various Middle Eastern countries.[1] These developments influenced Saudi Islamism by providing its agents with sources of inspiration and possible allies. Domestically, decisive changes were also taking place, primarily in the political field. In November 1995 King Fahd suffered a major stroke that made him unable to govern and led to his de facto replacement by Crown Prince Abdallah. Abdallah's promotion to the rank of uncrowned monarch subtly but perceptibly modified the balance of power in the Saudi political field, which had until then been under the control of the Sudayris. Now at the head of a union of princes who had previously occupied subordinate positions in the field—including Mish'al and Mit'ab, along with the sons of the late King Faysal, notably Sa'ud and Turki—Abdallah inexorably increased his influence. The year 1999 may be seen as the first since the period of rivalry between Faysal and his predecessor Sa'ud at the turn of the 1960s when there was relative bipolarity in the political field. Although the Sudayris remained well established, their dominance was threatened. To reinforce their positions, both the Sudayris and Abdallah's newfound clan went in search of allies in the social arena, in what some Saudis compared to a veritable "election campaign."[2] Thus the struggles in the political field now directly affected Saudi society.

Important changes were also occurring within the religious field. On May 13, 1999, Abd al-Aziz bin Baz, mufti of the kingdom and unchallenged "pope" of Wahhabism, died. This was followed by the death on January 11, 2001, of Muhammad bin 'Uthaymin, unofficially considered the number two of the official religious institution, who also enjoyed wide popularity. The death of these two figures left a huge void at the top of the religious field, which the appointment of Abd al-Aziz Al al-Shaykh to the post of mufti simply could not fill.[3] Al al-Shaykh was unknown to the general public and had only a limited aura in religious circles. By choosing him, the regime was openly transgressing the tacit rule that only individuals who had accumulated sufficient religious capital could be appointed to leadership positions in the official religious institution. The appointment of Al al-Shaykh thus represented the logical outcome of the policy of institutional regulation that had been implemented in the religious field since 1993.

The autonomy (or apparent autonomy) of the religious field nonetheless remained a major imperative for the Saudi regime because it is a condition for the religious legitimacy of the state to be effective. Yet, Al al-Shaykh was too weak to play the legitimating role that he in principle ought to have been able to play. The regime was therefore obliged to seek the support of religious actors whose independence could not so readily be doubted. There was only one possible candidate for this role, the group of Sahwi ulema, whose aura had been reinforced by their participation in the protest movement and their subsequent imprisonment.

In exchange for their support of the regime, the Sahwi ulema would be allowed to use their material and symbolic resources freely to conquer, de facto rather than de jure, the supreme religious authority that Al al-Shaykh could hardly claim. For these dissident ulema, whose religious ambitions had been a major motivation even at the height of the protest movement, the offer was particularly tempting. Hence the appointment of Al al-Shaykh inaugurated a succession crisis at the head of a religious field that had become, like the political field, de facto headless.

The regime began by pardoning the past offenses of the Sahwi ulema. On June 25, 1999, Salman al-ʿAwda, Safar al-Hawali, and Nasir al-ʿUmar were released from prison.[4] Their release was ordered by Prince Nayef, who received them in person and started cultivating a special relationship with them.[5] The distribution of roles in the political field was now established: Nayef would be the "conservative," the ally of the religious field, whereas Abdallah, pursuing the line he had established when he supported the creation of the Janadriyya festival in 1985, would be the "liberal," the friend of the intellectual field. With the fragmentation of the royal family came the splitting up of the system of collusive transactions that until then had bound the political field to the fields of cultural production, with each clan in the royal family instead diverting some of these transactions to its own purposes.

In the field of the media, Abdallah's increased power was expressed by a relative opening (infitah). Foreign satellite channels, starting with the controversial al-Jazeera of Qatar, established in November 1996, were officially authorized. Domestically, the regime allowed the Saudi press to broach more daring questions than had previously been the case and to express a greater variety of opinions. At the forefront of this opening was the newspaper Al-Watan, founded in May 1998 under the auspices of Prince Khalid Al Faysal, an ally of Abdallah, with the aim of rejuvenating the Saudi media landscape.[6] The introduction of the Internet for public use in late January 1999, despite the persistence of certain forms of censorship that Saudi net surfers would learn to evade, further strengthened the tendency. Large numbers of discussion forums *(muntadayat)* soon sprang up, constituting a veritable "Saudi parliament" whose members on the Web had only to choose a pseudonym to debate freely the country's political, religious, and economic affairs. The proliferation of these forums on the Web was accompanied by the revival of the traditional weekly salons *(salunat)*, for which they were a sort of extension in the virtual world.

One consequence of this opening was the emergence of an authentic public sphere, even though it remained severely restricted. Hence established networks, including the *jama'at*, no longer held a monopoly on influence or information. One of the primary reasons for the failure of the Sahwa insurrection had apparently been removed. This perception helped convince some activists that a new mobilization might be possible. Another consequence of the proliferation of sites for debate was to restore life to an intellectual field that the regime had essentially stifled after the excesses of the late 1980s and the protest of the early 1990s. These new spaces offered new opportunities for intellectual recognition, breaking the monopoly of the literary clubs and other official channels. In these very favorable circumstances the Saudi *muthaqqaf* (intellectual) flourished and diversified.

In this new context the Sahwa split into three fiercely competitive entities: the "new Sahwa," in favor of abandoning political activism for an exclusive return to social activism; the "Islamo-liberals," who called for a radical reform of the political system coupled with a revision of the dominant religious discourse; and the neojihadis, who, while continuing to criticize the Saudi regime openly, made total war against the United States and support for al-Qaeda their absolute priority. The emergence of these groups and the conflicts between them preceded the events of September 11, 2001, whose effects in Saudi Arabia merely accelerated processes already under way.

Struggling for a Legacy

The episode of the Sahwi protest deeply affected the Sahwa by complexifying the rationale of the movement. Although some considered that the Sahwa in the mid-1990s remained defined primarily by the social activism that it had demonstrated from the early days of its existence, for others it had become inseparable from the political activism it had engendered beginning in the late 1980s. The debate between these two orientations became more acute in 1993 when the *jama'at* decided definitively to turn their backs on the protest and to limit their field of action to society. In that same year the meaning, methods, and goals of Sahwi political activism, always a subject of latent contention between the ulema and the intellectuals in the movement, started being contested by the rejectionists and the jihadis, who were now openly supporting the protest.

Nonetheless, at the peak of the insurrection, the differences between the ways in which the movement's various groups of supporters interpreted the Sahwi protest—and the Sahwa itself—were barely perceptible because the immediacy of the struggle against the common enemy engendered shared frames of reference that masked dissonances. But with the end of protest euphoria, the divergences came to light, and the Sahwa became a field of conflict in which determination of the movement's legitimate nature and thereby of its natural representatives and heirs was at stake. The outcome was significant because of the strong symbolic capital the Sahwa now enjoyed in the Saudi social arena. These legacy disputes were especially fierce because the conflict was a zero-sum game. The share of symbolic capital that each heir would bear away would depend on his capacity to delegitimate his competitors by presenting them as traitors to the "true" Sahwi spirit.

Disputes first broke out in 1995 in al-Ha'ir prison in Riyadh and to a lesser extent in al-Ruways prison in Jeddah, where Saudi political prisoners were traditionally detained. After several months of solitary confinement, the jailed Islamists were placed in shared cells where they could communicate with each other. They spent a significant part of their time debating their experiences and the reasons for the failure of their "insurrection." Several groups took shape in the course of these debates, each of which identified with one of the different meanings that the Sahwi protest had acquired.

The New Sahwa, or the Quietist Temptation

The first group was made up of the major Sahwi ulema, including Salman al-ʿAwda and Safar al-Hawali, whose primary purpose was now to pursue their program of establishing themselves as an alternative religious authority. To accomplish this, they decided to return to the social activism of the Sahwa's early days based on grassroots moral education *(tarbiya)*, and they adopted a quietist attitude toward the regime, refraining from any criticism of domestic affairs. In major crises they would even stand by the royal family, as when they issued a joint fatwa to condemn the Riyadh attacks of May 12, 2003. They thereby played the legitimating role that de jure fell to the official religious institution, one that the mufti Abd al-Aziz Al al-Shaykh was having great difficulty performing.[7] Through the adoption of these stances, these Sahwi ulema established what one of their foes, Sheikh Ali al-Khudayr, called "the new Sahwa" *(al-sahwa al-jadida)*.[8]

On the few occasions when the neo-Sahwi sheikhs took stands on social questions, they did so to denounce what they thought contributed to the relaxation of moral standards in the kingdom. Their chief themes in this area were the battle against any reform in the status of women (notably concerning the right to drive)[9] or of the educational system,[10] which they knew was vital for the survival of the Sahwi networks. However, even in these cases they never explicitly challenged the regime, although they knew that the princes were the ultimate decision makers on these subjects.

Wasatiyya, which, following moderate Egyptian Islamists,[11] they defined as a principle of "golden mean" or "moderation," particularly in relations with the non-Muslim Other, became a central theme in their writings.[12] In the name of this principle, combined with more pragmatic considerations (which were connected in legal terms to notions such as the "common good," *al-maslaha al-ʿamma*), the sheikhs of the new Sahwa condemned the attacks of September 11, 2001.[13] Also relying on *wasatiyya,* in April 2002 these sheikhs signed a manifesto titled "How We Can Coexist," an initiative of other heirs of the Sahwa, the Islamo-liberals. This document was published in response to the open letter "What We Are Fighting For" signed by 60 American intellectuals, including Samuel Huntington and Francis Fukuyama, intended to justify the American policy of "war on terror." Its 153 Saudi signatories called for peaceful coexistence with the West while reaffirming their attachment to their Saudi and Islamic identity.[14]

But this episode also revealed the limits of neo-Sahwi *wasatiyya*. Subject to intense pressure from their base and unprecedentedly violent attacks from the neojihadis, who accused them of having betrayed their principles, the sheikhs ended up signing a humiliating "explanatory manifesto" in which they called into question, point by point, the arguments presented in the earlier document.[15] While continuing to emphasize their *wasatiyya*, the sheikhs of the new Sahwa were thereafter careful not to be seen as making overly conspicuous concessions to the regime and to the West. They reasserted their support for "Islamic causes," starting with Palestine, and in November 2004 they signed a document legitimizing jihad in Iraq and calling on the Saudi population to support the insurgents by any means possible.[16]

Beyond its shared positions, the new Sahwa was torn after 2002 by battles for influence of growing intensity among its various figures, who, in their struggle to take control of the religious field, developed distinct strategies. Salman al-ʿAwda, for example, continued his efforts to appear as a "moderate" and increasingly presented himself as the promoter of "Saudi national unity" regardless of sectarian considerations. In an unprecedented gesture he even agreed to sit together with Saudi Sufi and Shiite clerics at a "conference for national dialogue" organized by Crown Prince Abdallah in June 2003. Conversely, Safar al-Hawali refused any rapprochement with non-Wahhabi groups in Saudi Arabia while emphasizing his support for "Islamic causes" (meaning Sunni causes) throughout the world, notably by establishing the so-called Global Antiaggression Campaign (al-Hamla al-ʿalamiyya li-muqawamat al-ʿudwan) in May 2003.[17] By doing so, al-Hawali maintained great popularity in Sahwi circles, which al-ʿAwda increasingly lacked because many of his former disciples saw him as too conciliatory. Since his stroke in June 2005, however, al-Hawali has been much less present in the Saudi debate. It is now Nasir al-ʿUmar, another major figure of the Sahwi protest movement of the early 1990s, who seems to have taken up the torch of intransigent neo-Sahwism, continuing the competition with al-ʿAwda in the same terms.

The Islamo-Liberals in Search of a Constitutional Monarchy

Countering the neo-Sahwis, two very different groups emerged that shared several characteristics. Ideologically, these groups thought it necessary (and because of the nascent public sphere, they now considered it possible) to continue down the path of political activism, although in new ways. Sociologically, their members had generally occupied a subordinate position in the original Sahwi protest movement: most of them were second-rank Sahwis (in the sense that they did not appear to be leading figures in the movement, although they sometimes played important roles behind the scenes) and rejectionists.

The first of these groups, the "Islamo-liberals," identified with the ideas of the "enlightened" Sahwi intellectuals, which they hoped to push one step further. The "enlightened" Sahwi intellectuals had been the first, in the late 1980s, to call for the establishment of a "conservative Islamic democracy" while at the same time cautiously criticizing Wahhabi discourse. Emphasizing the nature of the Sahwi protest as a movement for political reform, these self-declared heirs of the Sahwa now called for a radical reshaping of the Saudi political system, leaving room for a constitutional monarchy. In their view, this change had to be coupled with, and in the end made possible by, a thoroughgoing reform of the dominant religious discourse. To reach their objective, these activists called for an unprecedented union of all Saudi political and religious segments, Islamists and liberals, Sunnis and Shiites. It is to signal the specificity of this stance that they are designated here as "Islamo-liberals."[18]

The first outlines of this Islamo-liberal movement took shape inside Saudi prisons during debates among imprisoned Islamists. It was built around figures like the Sahwi intellectuals Abd al-Aziz al-Qasim and Abdallah al-Hamid and, at the outset, the former rejectionist militant Mansur al-Nuqaydan.[19] Because these three, largely unknown to the public, were considered activists of the second rank, the regime released them in late 1997.[20] On their release from prison, they took advantage of the void left by the absence of al-ʿAwda and al-Hawali to try to impose their own interpretation of the Sahwi protest[21] while at the same time profiting from the changes stimulated by Prince Abdallah in the media and intellectual fields to organize and achieve a degree of visibility.

Islamo-liberal salons made their appearance in Riyadh, under the impulse of Abdallah al-Hamid and Abd al-Aziz al-Qasim, among others, and in Burayda thanks to the activism of Sulayman al-Dahayyan. The press, which was now allowed greater diversity of opinion, was also opened to the Islamo-liberals. As early as 1998 Mansur al-Nuqaydan and Abdallah bin Bijad al-ʿUtaybi made a name for themselves by publishing vitriolic articles exposing the artificial character of Wahhabi orthodoxy, while al-Hamid and al-Qasim set out the first elements of a *salafi* theory of civil society and democracy.[22] But it was the Internet and some of its forums, particularly the *"wasatiyya* forum" *(muntada al-wasatiyya)*,[23] established in 2000 by the Sahwi intellectual Muhsin al-ʿAwaji, and "Tuwaa" *(tuwa)*,[24] which described itself as a "site for free thought," that became the preferred platform for the Islamo-liberals. Because they assembled a broad spectrum of Web users from all regions of the kingdom and from all backgrounds, these virtual spaces made it possible to establish the first contacts between the Islamo-liberals and their future allies in their reformist adventure: in particular, liberals, Shirazi Shiite Islamists, and Hejazi reformists.

The al-Qaeda attacks on New York and Washington on September 11, 2001, made local circumstances particularly propitious for the reception of the Islamo-liberal discourse. In the aftermath of the attacks, Saudi Arabia, which was heavily implicated (fifteen of the suicide attackers on the airplanes and the originator of the attacks, Osama bin Laden, were of Saudi origin), was singled out by media and governments around the world.[25] This prompted a national crisis of conscience in the kingdom. In response, many in Saudi intellectual and religious circles felt the need to show some openness and moderation, but they also wanted to reaffirm their attachment to their cultural and religious specificities in the face of the criticism to which they were subjected. Reconciling these two imperatives was precisely what the Islamo-liberals offered to do.

Understanding that circumstances were particularly favorable, some of the Islamo-liberals launched a large-scale public initiative: the manifesto "How We Can Coexist," published in April 2002, which called for peaceful coexistence with the West and mutual respect for each other's values. The document, drafted primarily by Abd al-Aziz al-Qasim and the Sahwi intellectual Abdallah al-Subayh,[26] secured the support of a significant number of former figures of the Sahwi opposition, starting with the three sheikhs Salman al-ʿAwda, Safar al-Hawali, and Nasir al-ʿUmar, who saw it as a unique opportunity to display the *wasatiyya* that they had recently decided to endorse. For the Islamo-liberals, this support consecrated their efforts to present themselves as the legitimate heirs of the Sahwa, but the consecration was short lived because of the withdrawal of the three sheikhs a few days later, under the two-fold pressure of their followers and their neojihadi adversaries. To the Islamo-liberals, the conclusion seemed inescapable that the ulema, too dependent on their base and in the end too "corporatist" to be prepared to take real political risks, were not reliable. The Islamo-liberal movement would be a movement of intellectuals.

Although the Islamo-liberals had lost a significant source of support, they had maintained another, in principle more important: that of Crown Prince Abdallah, who, in the conflict with his brothers in the political field, had chosen to support behind the scenes reformists of every variety, including the Islamo-liberals. Because of their desire to change a political status quo that had been favorable to the Sudayris for decades, the crown prince considered them his objective allies. Hence the publication on January 30, 2003, of the first Islamo-liberal petition calling for an "Islamic" democratization of the Saudi system, titled "Vision for the Present and the Future of the Homeland,"[27] was preceded by informal contacts between associates of Abdallah and the principal drafters of the document.[28] In early February the crown prince received in person 40 of the 104 signatories and told them in plain language, "Your vision is my program."[29]

On December 20, 2003, a second Islamo-liberal petition, "Patriotic Appeal to the People and the Government—Constitutional Reform

First,"[30] whose principal author was Abdallah al-Hamid (the preceding petition had had multiple authors, including liberals),[31] adopted a tone that was both more overtly Islamic and more pressing. It demanded that an Islamic constitutional monarchy guaranteeing equal rights and the participation of all be established within three years. The list of its 116 signatories presented the image of an unprecedented political consensus around Islamo-liberal ideas. It contained former liberals like Muhammad Saʿid Tayyib, former Shirazi Shiite Islamists like Jaʿfar al-Shayib, Hejazi reformists like Muhammad Salahuddin, Islamic regionalists from the Ahsaʾ region like Muhanna al-Hubayyil, and a significant number of Sahwi intellectuals, including the most influential of the "enlightened" Sahwi intellectuals of the early 1990s who had remained in the kingdom, notably Abdallah al-Hamid, Abd al-Aziz al-Qasim, Hamad al-Sulayfih, Muhsin al-ʿAwaji, Muhammad al-Hudayf, and Abd al-Aziz al-Wuhaybi. Following an intensive lobbying campaign, a handful of relatively minor ulema finally joined them, including Abdallah al-Zayid, Musa al-Qarni, and Hamza Hafiz, all three of whom were professors at the Islamic University of Medina, and Sulayman al-Rashudi, who had been a founding member of the CDLR along with al-Hamid and al-Sulayfih.

Aware that the movement remained confined to a certain elite and had little impact in the wider society, some of the Islamo-liberals thought that the time had come to establish the organizations necessary for a popular mobilization in favor of reform. This was the Sadad program, the reverse acronym of Daʿwat al-islah al-dusturi al-saʿudiyya (Call for Constitutional Reform in Saudi Arabia), which also means "rightness." The idea was to create secretariats linked to the program in all the provinces of the kingdom and to establish reformist *diwaniyyat* (salons) in every city to bring people into the debate.[32] On February 26, 2004, an Islamo-liberal meeting that brought together several dozen activists was organized in a Riyadh hotel to discuss it. Three weeks later the major reformist leaders were arrested, bringing the Islamo-liberal movement to a halt. Though ordered by Nayef, these arrests were made possible by Abdallah's change of direction because of his exasperation at the radicalization of Islamo-liberal demands. Significantly, these arrests provoked no major reaction in

Saudi society, which, except for relatively minor moves such as a petition signed by 105 sympathizers of the Islamo-liberals,[33] remained mostly indifferent. Abdallah al-Hamid, Matruk al-Falih, and the liberal Ali al-Dumayni were kept in prison until the accession of Abdallah to the throne on August 1, 2005. Perhaps remembering his past alliances, he then decided to pardon them. Since then al-Hamid and al-Falih have tried to relaunch the mobilization, but with no greater success.

The Neojihadis in the Service of Global Jihad

The neojihadis, a third group of self-proclaimed heirs of the Sahwa made up exclusively of ulema, agreed with the Islamo-liberals that it was necessary to continue on the path of political activism, although they had a radically different view of what it meant. The ideological heart of their worldview was the principle of allegiance and rupture (al-wala' wa-l-bara'), which they interpreted in a totalizing way, beyond the mere rejection of non-Wahhabi Muslims. To do so, they took cues from both rejectionist and Sahwi interpretations of the principle. Like Abu Muhammad al-Maqdisi, they made it into an imperative to reject existing states, going as far as takfir; and like Muhammad Saʿid al-Qahtani, they considered it a call for a break with the West, which for them meant total war. Jihad was therefore at the core of their ideology, but their background and some of their interpretations set them apart from the other "jihadi" groups. For this reason, they are referred to here as "neojihadis."

As in the case of the Islamo-liberals, the embryo of what would become the neojihadi strain developed in Saudi prisons, principally in al-Haʾir.[34] It sprang from the encounter between two colorful figures who, because they came from distinct Islamist circles, had not previously had the occasion to get acquainted: the Sahwi sheikh Ali al-Khudayr, born in 1954 in Burayda, a graduate of the Qasim branch of Imam University and a signatory of the Memorandum of Advice, who until 1994 had operated in the shadow of Salman al-ʿAwda and had even been one of the instigators of the "Intifada of Burayda"; [35] and the young sheikh Nasir al-Fahd, born in Riyadh in 1968, for a time a lecturer in the department of creed of Imam University and historically close to rejectionist circles, who had been arrested in August 1994 for a poem taunting the conduct of Maha al-Sudayri, the wife of Prince Nayef.[36]

Like their Islamo-liberal adversaries, al-Khudayr and al-Fahd, because the authorities considered them Islamists of the second rank, were released in 1997,[37] at a time when the major Sahwi sheikhs remained behind bars. With no restrictions on their movements, they made connections with other ulema who shared their convictions, notably the rejectionist and former messianic sheikh Ahmad al-Khalidi, who had also been imprisoned in al-Ha'ir in 1995 and 1996,[38] as well as Abdallah al-Sa'd and the former member of the Ikhwan of Burayda, Sulayman al-'Alwan, two well-known Ahl al-Hadith sheikhs who had had close relations with rejectionist circles, notably the Bayt Shubra community, in the early 1990s.[39]

Perhaps aware of their relatively peripheral position in the Saudi religious field, these ulema placed themselves under the authority of an old and respected sheikh, Hamud al-Shu'aybi, the only former member of the *munasirun* to join the neojihadi current. The adhesion of al-Shu'aybi was no surprise. Among the *munasirun* of the 1990s, al-Shu'aybi already had the reputation of being the most intransigent. For that reason, starting in 1995, while most opposition sheikhs remained in prison, he had attracted in his teaching circles the most radical elements of Saudi Islamism: some radicalized Sahwis, many rejectionists, and a significant number of jihadis.[40] These were the circumstances under which he met Ali al-Khudayr, who subsequently became his closest student and introduced him to al-'Alwan, al-Khalidi, and the other future leading figures of the neojihadi current.

In the late 1990s a connection began to be established between these neojihadi sheikhs and the Saudi global jihadi militants, members of Osama bin Laden's network. Although these militants, following Bin Laden's symbolic hijacking of the Sahwi protest in 1994, also traced their mobilization to the Sahwa insurrection, they were, as Thomas Hegghammer has shown, an exogenous entity that came out of a process of radicalization taking place outside Saudi Arabia and based on ideological transformations largely disconnected from the Saudi context.[41] Despite this, their doctrine had strong ideological affinities with that of the neojihadis, who shared their radical hostility to the West and to the Saudi regime. Disagreements remained, however, because the neojihadi sheikhs attributed much more importance to questions of creed and were stricter on social questions, for example, the prohibition of photographs of living beings, which the global jihadis used intensively for strategic and propaganda purposes.[42] Similarly, while the neojihadi sheikhs were radically hostile to Shiites, global jihadi militants, not wishing to alienate any potential supporter, had traditionally—at least until 2005—avoided raising the sectarian question in their public statements.[43]

Yusuf al-'Ayiri acted as a broker between the global jihadi militants and the neojihadi ulema. Born in 1974, he had at an early age joined jihad in Afghanistan, where he had served as Osama bin Laden's bodyguard. Following the lead of his mentor, he had converted to global jihad at the end of the 1990s. Although most of Bin Laden's associates came from the Hejaz or the Eastern Province, al-'Ayiri had the distinction of coming from Burayda and could use his family networks to gain access to the religious circles of the Qasim.[44] He soon established contact with most of the rising stars of neojihadism and won their esteem. This was revealed by his marriage to a sister of one of the wives of Sheikh Sulayman al-'Alwan, through which he became his 'adil (something akin to a brother-in-law).[45] Al-'Ayiri was so well connected, both to neojihadi ulema and to militants in Afghanistan, that in March 2001 he set up a telephone call between Mullah Omar and Sheikh Hamud al-Shu'aybi. It fell through for an incongruous reason: al-'Ayiri ran into a camel when he was driving on the road to Burayda and ended up behind bars until August 2001.[46]

The activism of the neojihadi ulema, which began manifesting itself in 1999, had two goals: to strengthen their position in the religious field by asserting themselves as the legitimate heirs of the Sahwa against their rivals, and to provide support and legitimacy to their global jihadi allies. The neojihadis directed their first attacks against the Islamo-liberals, who were enjoying a growing media presence at the turn of 2000. In a sign of the times, the arena for the first blows was the Internet, where disputes flew between Islamo-liberals and neojihadis. According to the Islamo-liberal intellectual Sulayman al-Dahayyan, his debate on the forums with Nasir al-Fahd extended over several hundred pages.[47] The violence of the controversy culminated on January 24, 2003, when four radical sheikhs led by Ali al-Khudayr accused Mansur al-Nuqaydan of apostasy and called for "him to receive the punishment reserved for apostates [death], if *shari'a* is really the law of the land."[48]

But for the neojihadis, the conflict with the Islamo-liberals, outsiders as they were in the field of the Sahwa, very soon became secondary. In their struggle to appropriate the Sahwi legacy, they had to attack a more formidable adversary, the former leaders of the Sahwi protest movement, Salman al-'Awda and Safar al-Hawali, whom they accused of having "capitulated" *(inhizam)* and having "changed their methodology" *(taghyir al-manhaj)*. Against them, in the words of Ali al-Khudayr, "the original Sahwa has remained—thanks be to God— faithful to principles of Sunnism concerning creed, *tawhid, takfir, fiqh,* jihad, politics, the attitude toward the infidels, the deviant, and the innovators, and the rejection of coexistence and other secularist theories." This "original Sahwa"—in al-Khudayr's view obviously embodied by the neojihadi ulema—"now makes up the majority of the Sahwa from which only those few individuals fomenting discord and dissension have drawn apart."[49]

Before September 11, 2001, the debate between neojihadis and neo-Sahwis remained private. In 2000, for example, al-'Ayiri sent Salman al-'Awda, to whom, he wrote, "belong—after God—the merits of what the Sahwa accomplished . . . more than to any other sheikh," two confidential letters in which he told al-'Awda of the growing criticism of him "in the salons" and urged him to join the neojihadi line.[50] But with the events of September 11, the disagreement between neo-Sahwis and neojihadis broke out into the open for the first time. While the former condemned the attacks, Hamud al-Shu'aybi (who died a few months later, in January 2002), followed by several other sheikhs in the movement, declared them perfectly legitimate because, since America was a democracy, all its citizens were responsible for its "oppression of Muslims" and could therefore be targeted.[51]

But the conflict really grew bitter with the publication of "How We Can Coexist." There were dozens of refutations of the manifesto from almost all major neojihadi figures, who saw it as a unique opportunity to discredit the historic leaders of the Sahwa once and for all.[52] Summing up the general thinking of his peers in the movement, Nasir al-Fahd wrote: "This manifesto is a danger for *tawhid,* it denigrates the dogma of allegiance and rupture, it invalidates the commandments of jihad, it goes against the Koran, the Sunna, and the consensus of Muslims, it denatures the sacred texts, it strays from *shari'a* and follows the path of the unbelievers."[53] The sheikhs were soon not alone in conducting the offensive. Saudi Islamist forums became full of attacks against the manifesto and its signatories, particularly al-'Awda, al-Hawali, and al-'Umar. Under this pressure, the three sheikhs had no choice but to publish their humiliating "explanatory manifesto," the outcome of a mediation conducted by Abd al-Rahman al-Barrak, one of the *munasirun,* which consecrated the victory of the neojihadis.[54] In the ensuing months the leaders of the neojihadi movement published fatwa after fatwa, reaffirming their principles with increasing assurance and popularity.

The other favorite theme of the neojihadis was support for global jihad and their allies in al-Qaeda. This explains the alacrity with which al-Shu'aybi and his students supported the cause of the Taliban as early as 2000. Global jihadis had made Afghanistan their refuge, to which they encouraged their sympathizers to emigrate for training in the camps they had established. By proclaiming the legitimacy of the Taliban regime, the neojihadis intended to counter the Jami fatwas that considered it un-Islamic because the Taliban tolerated the worship of saints.[55] When the Buddhas of Bamyan were destroyed in March 2001, the neojihadis were also the first to respond to the evasions of the neo-Sahwi sheikhs who questioned the usefulness of the act.[56] More significantly, when the Americans attacked the Taliban in the wake of September 11, the neojihadis, with al-Shu'aybi and al-Khudayr in the lead, spearheaded the calls for jihad, encouraging young Saudis to go to the defense of the "Islamic Emirate of Afghanistan."[57]

The approach of the American invasion of Iraq, not surprisingly, unleashed the same sort of reactions from the neojihadis, who called for all-out jihad. On this occasion the neojihadis crossed a red line: by proclaiming the "impiety of those who support America against the

Muslims in Iraq,"[58] al-Fahd, al-Khudayr, al-Saʿd, and al-Khalidi were directly challenging the Saudi regime because it was an open secret that Saudi territory was being used as a rear base for military attacks against its Iraqi neighbor. This provocation led to the first repressive measures against the neojihadis, which drove al-Fahd, al-Khalidi, and Al-Khudayr to go underground and seek the protection of their global jihadi allies in the kingdom. After having received orders early in 2002 from Bin Laden and his associates to prepare for jihad in Saudi Arabia, the Saudi global jihadis had started organizing themselves in what would soon be known as Al-Qaeda in the Arabian Peninsula (AQAP).[59]

The explicit signs of support from the three sheikhs for Saudi global jihadis proliferated thereafter, taking the form of a series of communiqués encouraging the "mujahideen" to continue on "the path followed by the prophets and the just who went before them" and threatening the agents of the security forces with excommunication if they intervened.[60] Not surprisingly, given these declarations, al-Khudayr, al-Fahd, and al-Khalidi became major suspects following the first AQAP attacks on May 12, 2003, which targeted three residential compounds for Westerners in Riyadh and caused thirty-nine deaths. Actively pursued, they were arrested in Medina on May 28. This success by the authorities was soon supplemented by a symbolic victory. In November and December 2003 the three sheikhs appeared successively on Saudi television to express their "retraction" *(tarajuʿ)* and condemn the actions of AQAP.[61] The global jihadi militants had lost their principal supporters among ulema enjoying a minimum of centrality in the religious field. Soon after, the remainder of the neojihadi ulema of the first circle distanced themselves from AQAP out of fear of reprisals, as in the case of Sulayman al-ʿAlwan, who fell completely silent. This did not prevent his arrest in 2004.

Other AQAP operations followed the May 2003 attacks: an attack on the al-Muhayya compound on November 8, 2003, killed seventeen; an intrusion into a petrochemical factory in Yanbuʿ on May 1, 2004, killed six; an assault on a compound and two oil sites in al-Khobar on May 29, 2004, killed twenty-two; and the siege of the American consulate in Jeddah on December 6, 2004, killed five. In addition, there was a relatively large number of assassinations of Westerners between May and

September 2004. But starting in 2005, AQAP's campaign considerably declined in intensity, and subsequent attacks were rare and isolated.[62]

Studies of those who were active members of AQAP during this period have shown that most of them had been to Afghanistan and had belonged to global jihadi circles for several years.[63] In contrast, AQAP seems to have had a good deal of difficulty recruiting among young Saudis who had not gone through that radicalization abroad. Security reasons may have played a role: it is not easy to join an underground movement engaged in open warfare with the state. But this difficulty in recruiting can also be generally explained by the absence of sympathy for AQAP in Saudi Arabia, even in Islamist circles, and even among those who approved of global jihad when it struck at a distance from the Land of the Two Holy Places.[64] Hence it was in large part because of lack of troops that global jihadi activism experienced a sharp decline in 2005.

Aborted Attempts at Remobilization

The Islamo-liberal mobilization and the AQAP campaign were obviously different in nature, but they also had significant points in common. Both involved small-scale mobilizations, bringing together at most a few hundred people, far below the expectations of their supporters. In addition, starting in late 2003, both seemed to provoke primarily indifference or aversion in Saudi society.[65] They therefore cannot be compared with the Sahwi mobilization of the early 1990s.

The immediate causes of the loss of steam by these mobilizations were numerous: repression, internal divisions, withdrawal of Prince Abdallah's support of the Islamo-liberals, and organizational unpreparedness, to name a few.[66] But even before one considers their ultimate failure, a preliminary question arises: why did these mobilizations never really gain momentum or even "resonate" beyond a small core of the persuaded? This might seem especially surprising because the global situation was arguably quite favorable to both movements: the September 11 attacks and the powerful media presence of al-Qaeda created a propitious environment for AQAP; and the momentum gained by the rhetoric of "democratization" in global discourse made the Islamo-liberal initiative particularly timely. Moreover, the Saudi regime, in accordance with its habitual behavior, used repression against the neojihadis and the Islamo-liberals only several years after they had initiated their activism, allowing them the time to "prove themselves."

To understand this failure, it is necessary to consider the time sequence of the Saudi Islamist cycle. The period after 1995 was a time of demobilization for the Sahwi protest movement. As soon as the political crisis had ended, the political, religious, and intellectual fields had reconstituted their boundaries, and the logic of sectorization had taken over again. Only a new multisectoral mobilization could have challenged it, but the conditions, particularly at the economic level, were obviously not ripe.[67] As the following pages will show, each of the two new movements was thus the prisoner of the field to which its initiators belonged: the Islamo-liberals to the intellectual field and the neojihadis to the religious field. As a consequence, each movement in theory had only some of the resources indispensable for a successful mobilization: the Islamo-liberals were rich in militant resources but lacked legitimating resources, and vice versa for the neojihadis. Each tried to compensate for the lack in different ways, but these eventually proved not to be enough to escape from the trap of sectorization.

The core of the Islamo-liberal movement was made up of Sahwi intellectuals, joined by a handful of rejectionists who were militants rather than religious scholars. These Islamo-liberals, in short, were agents of the intellectual field who by definition could not boast of belonging to the caste of ulema. The sole exception was Abd al-Aziz al-Qasim, who had acted as a broker between the two groups in the early 1990s, but whose relentless involvement with the group of "enlightened" Sahwi intellectuals had eventually marginalized him in the religious field. Although the Islamo-liberals did try, they were never able to cross the borders of the intellectual field to secure lasting support from the ulema. Thus the Sahwi sheikhs who signed "How We Can Coexist" did so with the sole purpose of completing their rehabilitation in the eyes of the royal family by appearing to be champions of *wasatiyya* before issuing a retraction when the pressure grew too great, convincing the Islamo-liberals that they were not reliable partners. In any case the manifesto "How We Can Coexist" was not, strictly speaking, an act of mobilization, because the document was directed against no particular enemy, and especially not against the regime. During the real episodes of mobilization constituted by the two petitions of January and December 2003, the ulema, with very few exceptions, were nowhere to be seen.

Aware that the intellectual field was the limit of their range, the Islamo-liberals tried to make belonging to that field a principle for mobilization in itself. For that purpose, the Islamo-liberals had to redefine the raison d'être of the intellectual (muthaqqaf) through what amounted to a veritable symbolic hijacking. In their rhetoric they made pains to present the muthaqqaf as possessing, in addition to his "natural" intellectual competence, a fundamental political competence. He ought to be deeply concerned with the affairs of the country while maintaining complete independence from the regime.[68] Therefore, it was not surprising that in November 2003 the Islamo-liberals were the first signatories of a manifesto of support for the Egyptian writer Sunʿ Allah Ibrahim, who, in the name of the "independence of the intellectual" and "his refusal to be used to enhance the prestige of the ruling powers," had just refused to accept the "Arab novel award" presented by President Mubarak of Egypt.[69] By his gesture Sunʿ Allah Ibrahim had embodied the model of the intellectual the Islamo-liberals hoped to bring into being in Saudi Arabia.

The new intellectual depicted by the Islamo-liberals also possessed religious competence. He was therefore, as al-Hamid proclaimed, able to go beyond the existing dichotomy between the religious sheikh "who knows nothing of the things of the world" and the secular intellectual "who knows those things but does not know how to draw from religion human rights or the idea of civil society." To do so, he had to combine ijtihad and what al-Hamid called civil jihad (jihad madani).[70] Relying on this model, al-Hamid allowed himself to offer new interpretations of Islam in his books in order to provide religious justifications for the Islamo-liberal project. Such a move would not be surprising if it came from an Egyptian or Syrian Islamist intellectual. However, in Saudi Arabia, where the ulema had preserved their historic monopoly of the interpretation of the Islamic corpus, what al-Hamid and, through him, the Islamo-liberals as a whole were doing was practically unprecedented.[71]

The new intellectual of the Islamo-liberals was thus presented as a "total intellectual," endowed with every competence and located above the sectoral divisions splitting the social arena. The intellectual field thereby transfigured would fulfill a socially and culturally legitimating function, to some extent supplanting the religious field. In other words, it would become a superfield producing both militant and legitimating resources. Through this discursive device, by trying to redefine the category to which they belonged, the Islamo-liberals hoped to free themselves from the rules imposed by the resectorization of the social arena.

This appropriation of the *muthaqqaf* by the Islamo-liberals came at a moment that was propitious in another way. It was a period when, thanks to the media *infitah,* the proliferation of arenas in which it was possible to gain recognition as an intellectual had ended the official—and liberal—monopoly over the intellectual field, which was now flourishing and fostering true diversity. That made it possible to make the intellectual field the basis for the integration into the national debate of groups and individuals who until then had been excluded from it. This was true in particular for all those who, because they did not recognize themselves in the Wahhabi tradition, had been barred from access to the religious field. To them, the intellectual field offered an alternative legitimacy. Presenting themselves as the voice of the *muthaqqafs,* the Islamo-liberals thus succeeded in bringing together on a single platform representatives of many of the subordinate groups of the social arena in the name of the unity of the Saudi intellectual field. On this basis liberals, Shiites, and regionalists from the Hejaz and the Ahsa' joined the movement.

As seductive as this Islamo-liberal construction might have been on paper, however, it remained an abstraction. Although a segment of the elite may have been attracted by al-Hamid's arguments, those arguments clearly carried no weight with ordinary Saudis. What al-Hamid was advocating was an authentic transformation of the existing political culture. It was not theoretically impossible to conduct such an operation, but it could not be accomplished in a few years, and it required considerable resources, which the Islamo-liberals did not have. Consequently, for the bulk of Saudi society, the legitimacy of the Islamo-liberals, who had been abandoned by the ulema, remained subject to doubt. Divisions within the social arena, the result of long-term historical processes, could not give way so easily before the ad hoc rhetorical developments of a group of activists.

The logic presiding over the failure of the AQAP campaign was fairly similar. The neojihadis, who were all agents of the religious field lacking militant resources, had at first been unable to relaunch the Sahwi mobilization on the ground. To get around the obstacle, they had looked for allies among a group that had been radicalized outside the kingdom but was symbolically associated with the Sahwi protest: the global jihadis led by Osama bin Laden. The latter contributed militant resources of a new kind in the form of a repertoire of action that had been infrequent in Saudi Arabia: violence.

AQAP's mobilization seemed to gain momentum at first. An analysis of reactions on forums shows that the May 2003 attacks, aimed purely at Westerners and sanctioned by ulema who had earned some religious capital in the course of their battles with the new Sahwa, enjoyed appreciable support in the population, particularly among Islamists.[72] But the illusion of a remobilization was short lived. In the months after AQAP's first operations, most of the ulema who supported the organization were neutralized, and Yusuf al-ʿAyiri, the go-between who had established contact with religious circles, was killed by the police in June 2003. As a result, the global jihadis realized that their search for legitimating resources was fundamentally compromised. The situation was all the more desperate because there was nothing to indicate the possibility of a new mobilization in their favor in the religious field.

The global jihadis did try to circulate a document allegedly written by al-Fahd in prison, in which he "retracted his alleged retraction" and reaffirmed his commitment to their cause,[73] but the maneuver had little effect. During 2004 they attempted to present some AQAP activists, all aged about thirty, who had studied at Imam University (of which they were usually dropouts), as the movement's new religious authorities. They were, with one relative exception,[74] completely unknown, without established legitimacy in religious circles, and then they were killed or captured within a few months, leaving the movement without even that recourse.[75]

Simultaneously with these desperate efforts to produce the impression of support from the religious field for AQAP, the global jihadis imitated the Islamo-liberals by redefining their raison d'être and the purpose of their action. In their writings jihad became a crystalline principle whose implications, notably the obligation for everyone to engage in armed combat against the infidels, were so clear that no interpreters were needed. According to their rhetoric, any exegesis even seemed dangerous because it risked sullying the purity of the jihad by introducing elements of political pragmatism. As a result, action by ulema was unnecessary and might even turn out to be harmful.

Jihad was thus presented as a totalizing category that encompassed and went beyond ʿilm. According to the Saudi global jihadi Luwis ʿAtiyyat ʿAllah, known for his strong presence on the Web, "True tawhid consists [of conducting jihad,] not repeating texts like parrots or transmitting them like donkeys. . . . That is why the best evidence of tawhid is the gift of one's soul to God on the fields of jihad or in the struggle against the tyrant."[76] The "mujahideen," who had made jihad a praxis, were therefore presented as "total individuals" whose degree of awareness was greatly superior to that of those partial individuals (because they were prisoners of the religious field), the ulema.[77] Jihad, in that sense, was to be a principle for the unification of the social arena. As with the Islamo-liberals, however, these rhetorical efforts remained without real effects and did not make possible any significant remobilization.

The dominance of the logic of the field recurred in the third group of heirs of the Sahwa, the neo-Sahwi ulema. Their main objective was now to profit from the aura they had gained through their activism in the early 1990s in order to compete for authority within the religious field. Acting as purely religious figures, they refrained from taking any stands on questions that touched on the political field. Because of the intense field corporatism that once again characterized them after the fiasco of "How We Can Coexist," which had earned them the supreme insult of being called "intellectuals" by the neojihadis,[78] they also avoided collaborating with actors outside their world. This, among other things, explains the absence of any support from the neo-Sahwi sheikhs for the Islamo-liberals' or the global jihadis' attempts at remobilization. It must be noted here that the interventions of a divided royal family certainly contributed to the resectorization that followed the end of the Sahwi protest. Indeed, Nayef supported the new Sahwa and more broadly tried to maintain a privileged relationship with the religious field, while his brother Abdallah, until late 2003, supported the Islamo-liberals, playing the card of the intellectual field. The brothers' rivalry, then, reinforced the separation between the fields.

In these circumstances the municipal elections of 2005, the first in the recent history of the kingdom,[79] marked the culmination of the process of "normalization" under way. They were reserved for adult males and involved half the seats on the 178 municipal councils in the kingdom. They took place in three stages: in February in the central region, in March in the eastern and northern provinces, and in April in the western and southern provinces. This staggered schedule was intended to guarantee the local character of the elections by blocking in advance any national dynamic. This went along with one of the conditions imposed on the candidates: their programs could deal only with purely local questions, and no adoption of an ideological position would be tolerated. In most Saudis' view, these were elections with nothing at stake: the elected councilors would not have a majority in the councils, and although their prerogatives remained undefined, everyone expected them to be fairly limited. At the same time, these elections offered the unique opportunity of an electoral campaign and could easily be diverted for political purposes. This is what some liberals attempted to do by proclaiming, in defiance of the electoral commission, the demand that women be allowed to drive.[80] No comparable attempt was made by the Islamists.

The Islamo-liberals were completely absent from the candidates, as, less surprisingly, were the neojihadis. In contrast, the traditional Islamists—those active in the *jama'at*—were strongly represented. In most Sunni urban districts,[81] a Sururi candidate confronted a candidate from the Brotherhood, in the face of a host of liberal and independent Islamist candidates.[82] None of this, of course, was ever said explicitly. Moreover, all the programs were remarkably similar (with the isolated exception of the liberal candidates' programs mentioned earlier) and did not indicate the ideological position of the candidate, which was intelligible only for someone who mastered the grammar of the religious field. In these circumstances where ideas did not count, the result depended only on the mobilizing structures on which each candidate could rely. The Sururis and the Brothers were the only groups with a solid infrastructure, and it was therefore not surprising that their affiliates won the majority of the votes. In this competition the neo-Sahwi sheikhs were also present by proxy, so to speak: the ulema close to Sururi circles issued fatwas supporting Sururi candidates, while ulema sympathetic to the Brotherhood did the same for candidates it supported.[83] The result was inevitable. To take only two examples, in Riyadh, the Brotherhood won very broadly, winning five of the seven seats at stake (the two others went to independents close to them), while in Dammam, seven Sururis were elected.[84]

For the *jama'at*, then, everything seemed to indicate that these municipal elections were only the latest episode of the sterile competition between them, conducted for decades with essentially the same methods. The ulema, for their part, had hastened to transform the elections into a continuation of the struggles among them in the religious field. Never in the electoral activism of any of these groups was there the slightest desire to politicize the event, much less to generate a broader social dynamic.

A Post-Islamist Scenario?

Since the 1990s the Saudi Islamist movement has split into three currents, each claiming to represent the Sahwa and the "insurrection" it spearheaded at the turn of the 1990s. The new Sahwa, grouping the major ulema who dominated the protest, now preaches the abandonment of all political activism and is primarily concerned with constructing its religious authority. In contrast, the Islamo-liberals and neojihadis (and their global jihadi allies), in very different registers, call for continuing the struggle and deplore the "betrayal" of the neo-Sahwi sheikhs. However, the efforts of this hard core have come up against the resectorization of the social arena, which has doomed them to failure.

The breakup of the Islamist movements into three orientations of this kind is not specific to Saudi Arabia. Similar developments have been observed in other places. To designate this phenomenon, which is described as a consequence of the "failure" or the "decline" of Islamism, several writers—notably Asef Bayat, Gilles Kepel, and Olivier Roy—have spoken of "post-Islamism."[85] Although most works on the subject have been primarily concerned with describing the evolution of the discourse and strategies of Islamist actors, it seems possible in the Saudi case to decode what this transformation reveals about the dynamics at work in the social arena.

The Sahwa insurrection represented a mobilization in which several central sectors of society took part, particularly the ulema and the intellectuals. In the course of the episode it was precisely the collapse of sectoral barriers and the transformation of the social arena into a unified space that momentarily gave life to what Islamist discourse had long proclaimed: the utopia of a fusion of politics and religion. But the crisis was short lived and inevitably ended with a return to the logic of sectorization. This is what paved the way for post-Islamism. In an attempt to escape from sectoral confines, "Islamism [became] compelled . . . to reinvent itself."[86] Because Islamo-liberals and global jihadis had become prisoners of the fields to which they belonged and, under these circumstances, were unable to secure the legitimating resources they needed to re-create a viable mobilization, they were brought to redefine their discourse and their identity in a "total" sense that generated new forms of legitimacy. Hence the Islamo-liberals proclaimed the advent of a "new intellectual" who was both the bearer of a democratic Islamic discourse able to forge alliances with the other components of the intellectual field and endowed with all the resources of the social arena, which meant that he was no longer dependent on the ulema for legitimacy. This "new intellectual" corresponds precisely to the "post-Islamist" intellectual described in the literature. Similarly, the global jihadis have redefined jihad as a totalizing principle, a metacategory encompassing the entire social arena and thereby invalidating its divisions. The resulting "jihad for the sake of jihad," which requires no justification or clearly defined political objective, also echoes the description of post-Islamism in the literature.[87]

It remains to determine whether post-Islamism outside Saudi Arabia is the expression of the same structural inability of social actors to get hold of the legitimating resources traditionally held by the religious field, and whether post-Islamist discourse, as in Saudi Arabia, consists of those actors' strategies for reformulating their identity in order to transcend that inability. If that is the case, the success of the post-Islamists will depend essentially on their capacity to transform the dominant political culture and the conceptions of legitimacy that inform it, which is conceivable only in the presence of a largely open public sphere. This is perhaps why movements categorized as "post-Islamist" (or, in this sense, "Islamo-democratic") have had significant success in Morocco and most of all in Turkey. This augurs badly, on the other hand, for the future of post-Islamism in more rigid authoritarian systems, where the public sphere remains severely constrained. The Saudi case seems to confirm this.

Conclusion

The Lessons of the Insurrection

After having long acted as a pivotal element within a highly fragmented Saudi Islamist sphere, the Sahwa movement ended up imposing itself as an unavoidable frame of reference for all Islamists. Although the extraordinary diversity underlying Saudi Islamism has not disappeared, it is now broadly expressed in terms derived from the Sahwa's language and legacy.

Historically, the Sahwa represented a highly distinctive form of Islamism, particularly compared with its Middle Eastern counterparts. To begin with, it emerged as an imported Islamism. That is not to say that there is nothing Saudi in the Sahwa's discourse. On the contrary, it has been shown that its ideology is not a simple transposition of the ideology of the Muslim Brotherhood but a hybrid of that and the Wahhabi tradition, designed in part to make it acceptable in Saudi Arabia. But this Islamism did not arise from local causes; it was grafted onto a situation foreign to the one that had produced its frames of interpretation. For its first supporters, the "enemy" was not an entity immediately identifiable in society but a pure abstraction that had to be experienced through representations, in theatrical performances, for example. As a result, the young Islamists of the Sahwa were at first "rebels without a cause."

This is linked to a second characteristic that made for the originality of this form of Islamism. In almost all countries in the Muslim world, Islamism arose and developed outside the state. The converse was true of Saudi Arabia: from the beginning, Islamism was integrated into the official institutions. Foreign members of the Muslim Brotherhood, for example, were in charge in the 1960s of various state sectors, chiefly the educational system. That system became the bastion of the Sahwa, the illegitimate offspring of the Brotherhood, from which it extended its networks and propagated its interpretive frameworks. With no obstacles from the government, the Sahwa thereby operated within the system, taking control of whole segments of the state machinery. Above all, it had access to considerable resources. For these reasons, the Sahwa initially represented what could be called a state Islamism.

The third noteworthy attribute of the Sahwa contradicts decades of studies of a country from which it had been thought that all nonstate forms of organization had been banished. Saudi Islamism is an organized Islamism whose origins go back to the late 1960s, with structured entities, the *jamaʿat*, at its core. Like the Sahwa, the *jamaʿat* were at first not a source of opposition to the government. Indeed, historically they even performed a stabilizing role in the Saudi system, first by playing the regime's game by entering into competition with rival *jamaʿat* to obtain resources, thereby maintaining sectoral logic, and second by challenging the government's enemies on the ground on several occasions: leftists and nationalists in the 1970s, rejectionists and jihadis (although the latter were not yet seen as a threat) in the 1980s.

There was thus nothing to indicate that starting in the late 1980s, the Sahwa would find itself at the head of an "insurrection" against the government. This was all the more surprising because the government had succeeded in establishing a system of control that was theoretically extremely effective, based on the sectorization of the social arena. The field of power, in particular, had been divided into a set of apparently very autonomous fields, in which the force of sectoral logic should have prevented any politicization. But this system had a major flaw: to perpetuate itself, it needed a constant stream of resources. When those resources started declining in the mid-1980s because of the recession engendered by the decline in oil revenues, the carefully calibrated machine began to malfunction. In the various fields the particularly large new generation saw its expectations frustrated. This was the Sahwa generation, the first to have been socialized in the educational system re-created by the Brotherhood, and it had a strong sense of shared identity. Suddenly, ideas that had remained abstract and organizations that had served the stability of the system were transformed into weapons against the government. Instantaneously, mobilizations sprang up in various central fields, such as the intellectual and the religious fields. Catalyzed by the political circumstances of the Gulf War and the American military presence in Saudi Arabia, grievances soon converged, and sectoral logic collapsed. The "Sahwa insurrection" broke out. It lasted until 1994.

This was a period of extraordinary ferment for the Sahwa, which established unity and gathered around its leadership the whole of the Saudi Islamist family. The meaning of the movement it embodied became more complex, divided between social and political activism, reformist demands and opposition to the United States, and violence and nonviolence. In the late 1990s, a few years after the collapse of the protest, the Sahwa had split into three components laying claim to this ambiguous legacy. One was a "new Sahwa" made up of ulema who had once again become committed to the exclusive logic of the religious field and refrained from any politicization. The others were the Islamo-liberals and the neojihadis, who tried for a few years to relaunch the mobilization until they were crushed by repression without having achieved the success they had hoped for.

With the fading of its two competitors, the new Sahwa now seems to have won the battle of the heirs. This apparent victory marks the end of a cycle: in 2011 there is no major political mobilization in the name of the Sahwa taking place in Saudi Arabia. It would be tempting to think that Saudi Islamism has returned to a situation comparable to that of the Sahwa before the mid-1980s, when no one considered it a threat to the government. But there are reasons to doubt that conclusion.

First, the physical victory of the new Sahwa is not yet a symbolic victory. The interpretations of the Sahwa and its "insurrection" on which the neojihadis and the Islamo-liberals relied have admittedly been put on hold, but they remain present in memories and could provide the intellectual justifications necessary for a remobilization if conditions permitted. Moreover, the Sahwi corpus of writings still contains an obvious subversive potential despite increased efforts by Saudi authorities to water it down (they have, for example, on several occasions removed books by Sayyid Qutb from school libraries).[1] This is also one of the central issues in the attempts to reform the school curricula, which have for the moment led to only very partial results.[2]

In addition, despite the growth of competing influences made possible by the emergence of a public sphere since the late 1990s, Sahwi organizations remain well in control on the ground, as was shown in the landslide of the 2005 municipal elections, in which mostly candidates supported by the *jama'at* won in the large cities. So far the *jama'at* have acted as allies of the government except, and partly despite themselves, in the aftermath of the Gulf War until late 1992. At the same time, structurally they remain double-edged networks and are always, in principle, liable to play a destabilizing role.

Direct government control over the religious field starting in 1993 and 1994, coupled with the death of the historic figures of the field, Sheikhs Abd al-Aziz bin Baz and Muhammad bin 'Uthaymin, also had significant consequences. The royal family now had to seek support from its past adversaries, the sheikhs of the new Sahwa, to restore the illusion of autonomy without which no religious legitimation is effective. But the alliance of neo-Sahwi sheikhs with the regime had the effect of eroding their reputation insofar as they were seen as having been co-opted. This tendency is a danger both for the new Sahwa and for the regime. Indeed, if the neo-Sahwi sheikhs were to lose all credibility, the regime would lose what has become an indispensable source of legitimation. At the same time, a loss of credibility by the neo-Sahwi ulema might encourage a bidding war in the religious field, a possible source of remobilization leading to the rise of more radical actors.

In addition, the study of the Sahwa insurrection demonstrates that in a system based on redistribution, a sudden diminution in the resources of the state can have serious consequences. Because those resources continue to depend to a very large extent on the price of oil, nothing can be excluded for the future. Saudi Arabia does possess substantial financial reserves that would enable it to cushion the shock in the short or medium term, but several years of slashed prices would certainly create the conditions for a new political crisis from which the Islamists, who alone still have the necessary ideas and organizations, would be the first to profit.

Another variable might enter into play. Some of King Abdallah's liberal advisers seem intent on encouraging him to accelerate the process of social liberalization timidly under way in the kingdom. On several occasions minor royal decisions (on the question of reforming school curricula, for example, but also on the rights of women) have provoked the anger of the Islamists. In current conditions of economic prosperity, that anger had no consequences, but if conditions were to deteriorate, such measures could have dramatic effects, as the women's demonstration did in November 1990. This is Abdallah's dilemma: if he wants to neutralize in the long term the counterpower represented by the Sahwa, he has to fundamentally reform Saudi society; but if such a reform is undertaken clumsily or in unfavorable circumstances, it could provoke a backlash.

Any analysis of the potentialities of Saudi Islamism must take into account a final factor: the global context. The fact that the neojihadis were able to relaunch the mobilization by entering an alliance with exogenous actors, the global jihadis, shows its importance. But there is more to this intertwining of the local and the global because the Islamist currents described in this book have long ceased to be exclusively Saudi, since the Islamic sphere in Saudi Arabia has the notable particularity of exporting itself. Some central institutions of the Saudi religious field—for example, the Islamic University of Medina, which admits students from around the world, the World Assembly of Muslim Youth, and the Muslim World League—even have foreign proselytism as their primary function. The result has been the emergence of a constantly expanding transnational *salafi* movement with disciples in the four corners of the earth, from Orange, New Jersey, to Amsterdam, Paris, Kuwait, and Jakarta. These disciples transport the debates described here into social and political situations radically different from those of Saudi Arabia, and they therefore tend to provide different responses. Until the late 1990s the various groups of *salafi*s distributed around the planet communicated relatively little, but in the age of the new media, the *salafi* discussion has become global. Developments that affect *salafi*s in one country are liable to influence other *salafi*s, and Saudi *salafi*s are certainly not immune to these influences. The meaning of the debates running through Saudi Islamism is thus being enriched, and potential mobilizations find new resources at their disposal.

In short, although it is legitimate to speak of "post-Islamism" to describe developments under way in Saudi Arabia, the implications of that concept need to be qualified. Unless one believes in historical necessity, there is no reason to think that the current changes signal the end of Islamism in Saudi Arabia. Rather, they indicate the end of a particular Islamist mobilization that had its own logic and its own expression. This is confirmed by a structural approach to post-Islamism. If the reinventions that characterize it are a response to a blocked situation in which actors wishing to pursue the protest are unable to mobilize outside their own field, those reinventions become obsolete when the conditions for a new multisectoral mobilization come into being. To be sure, the next Islamist mobilization, if it occurs, will not necessarily resemble the first one, because the actors will have accumulated new resources of meaning. But there is nothing to indicate that it will be different in nature.

In this sense, if the prospect of a new "Islamist insurrection" seems improbable in the short term, it cannot be excluded in the medium term. For that reason, as well as for the others previously outlined, the Saudi Islamists—and the Sahwa—will remain central actors on the kingdom's political stage for years, and possibly decades, to come.

Glossary

ahl al-hadith: literally, "supporters of the hadith"; medieval school opposed, in accordance with the teachings of Ahmad Ibn Hanbal (780–855), to the use of reason in religious interpretation. The opponents of the *ahl al-hadith* are the *ahl al-ra'y* (supporters of opinion).

'alim (pl. 'ulama', ulema): religious scholar.

al-amr bi-l-ma'ruf wa-l-nahi 'an al-munkar: the principle of commanding right and forbidding wrong.

anashid: unaccompanied Islamic chants.

'aqida: the creed, or the conception of creed. The dominant conception in the Muslim world is the Ash'arite conception, derived from Abu al-Hasan al-Ash'ari (874–936), who gave a limited role to reason in theological speculation. This conception was fiercely opposed by Muhammad bin Abd al-Wahhab.

badawi (pl. badu'): literally, "Bedouin"; tribesman who remains a nomad or has become sedentary in the recent past.

bid'a (pl. bida'): blameworthy innovation.

da'iya (pl. du'at): literally, "preacher"; name adopted by Sahwi ulema before the turn of the 1990s.

da'wa: literally, "the preaching of Islam." The term designates the action of preaching, the message that is preached, and sometimes the movement that preaches it. Islamist movements usually describe their activism as *da'wa*.

fard 'ayn: individual duty incumbent on every Muslim.

fard kifaya: collective duty that a group of Muslims must fulfill in the name of the community.

fiqh: law or jurisprudence.

fiqh al-waqi': *fiqh* of reality, or understanding of reality.

fitna: sedition, division, chaos

ghutra: white cloth worn on the head.

hadathi: modernist, supporter of *hadatha* (modernism).

hadith: narrative reporting a deed or a word of the Prophet Muhammad. A *hadith* is made up of a text *(matn)* introduced by a chain of transmitters *(isnad)*.

hajj: pilgrimage to Mecca.

hakimiyya: divine sovereignty (particularly in the exercise of power).

halqa (pl. halaqat): study circle.

hijra: exile, separation. This was also the name given to the camps where the Bedouins were sedentarized during the first decades of the twentieth century.

hizbiyya: factionalism.

ijtihad: independent interpretation of the sacred texts.

Ikhwan: literally, "brothers"; the same term designates the Muslim Brotherhood (Al-ikhwan al-muslimun), the Bedouin auxiliaries attached to the army of Abd al-Aziz bin Sa'ud (Ikhwan), a small group of exclusivists in Burayda (the Ikhwan of Burayda), and the members of al-Jama'a al-Salafiyya al-Muhtasiba (also sometimes called Juhayman's Ikhwan).

'ilm: religious science.

'ilm al-hadith: the science of hadith, which studies the authenticity of hadiths. A hadith can be called *sahih* (authentic), *hasan* (good), *da'if* (weak), or *mawdu'* (forged).

'ilmani (pl. 'ilmaniyyun): secularist.

infitah: opening.

'iqal: cord holding the *shmagh* or the *ghutra*.

irja': during the great *fitna* of 657, attitude consisting of postponing one's judgment and not taking sides; political quietism.

islah: action of bringing into conformity with Islam; reform.

jahiliyya: period of "ignorance" before the coming of Islam; pre-Islam.

jama'a (pl. *jama'at*): literally, "group"; organized network within the Sahwa.

jihad: effort to propagate Islam, often understood to be military.

khadiri (pl. khadiriyyun): sedentary without tribal ancestry.

Kharijite: a sect that came out of the great *fitna* of 657; deprecatory term designating anyone opposed to a legitimate Islamic authority.

kufr: unbelief. A *kafir* is an unbeliever.

mabahith: secret police.

madhhab (pl. madhahib): school of law in which the principle of jurisprudence is applied. There are four canonical *madhahib* in Islam, which differ according to the respective importance they attribute to the use of reason in the interpretation of texts: Hanbali (the most antirationalist school), Maliki, Shafi'i, and Hanafi (the most open to reason).

Mahdi: the messiah of Islam, expected to come at the end of time *(al-sa'a)*.

manhaj: methodology.

Al-maslaha al-'amma: in Islamic law, public interest.

mufti: any person who issues fatwas; in Saudi Arabia, the mufti is the leader of the Wahhabi religious institution.

multazim: literally, "committed"; young man who has adopted the practices, notably in dress, of the Sahwa.

munafiq: literally, "hypocrite"; in the sacred texts, someone who claims to be a Muslim and conceals his unbelief.

munasir (pl. munasirun): literally, "sympathizer"; traditional Wahhabi sheikh who supported the "Sahwa insurrection."

muntami (pl. muntamun): literally, "affiliated"; young man who belongs to a *jama'a*.

murji'a (Murjites): those who practice *irja'*.

muthaqqaf (pl. *muthaqqafun*): intellectual, in the modern sense of the term.

nasab: genealogy.

nasiha: advice to the prince.

riba: usury, which Islamists identify as any charging of interest.

salafi: faithful to the practice of the first generations of Muslims, the "pious ancestors" *(al-salaf al-salih).*

shari'a: Islamic law.

sharif: descendant of the Prophet.

sharit islami: literally, "Islamic cassette"; designates recorded cassettes containing political-religious sermons.

shirk: literally, "associationism"; action of associating God with other entities.

shmagh: checkered cloth worn on the head.

sunna: the Prophetic tradition, essentially accessible through the hadiths.

tafsir: exegesis of the Koran.

takfir: excommunication.

taqlid: literally, "imitation"; reproduction of previous legal opinions instead of a new interpretation.

al-tasfiya wa-l-tarbiya: literally, "purification and education"; method of *da'wa* advocated by Nasir al-Din al-Albani.

tasjilat islamiyya: literally, "Islamic recordings"; designates the stores where recorded sermons are sold.

tawhid: divine oneness, unity, and transcendence.

tawhid al-hakimiyya: literally, "unity of sovereignty"; Sahwi principle according to which the complete application of *shari'a* is an integral part of *tawhid.*

tazkiya: recommendation from a religious authority.

thawb: tunic worn in Saudi Arabia.

umma: the community of believers in Islam.

usra (pl. usar): literally, "family"; study group in the *jama'at*.

wahdat al-wujud: Sufi dogma of the "oneness of being."

al-wala' wal-bara': dogma of allegiance and rupture.

waqf: inalienable religious endowment, whose revenue in most cases
serves for charitable purposes.

wasatiyya: principle of the "golden mean" in Islam; now often understood
as "moderation."

Note on Sources and Transliterations

This book is based primarily on fieldwork carried out between June 2003 and May 2007, chiefly in Saudi Arabia, but also in Kuwait, Bahrain, the United Arab Emirates, Egypt, Jordan, and Great Britain. In the course of my visits, I was able to conduct fifty long interviews with participants involved at various levels of the Saudi Sunni Islamist movement. Many of these meetings required long preparatory work. It is not easy for a Western researcher to establish direct contact for an interview with a Saudi Islamist activist unused to this exercise. The activist is likely to dismiss the would-be interviewer or, worse, grant a formal and empty interview. As a result, in most cases it was necessary to put together a social network that could be relied on to meet the activist in question. This process turned out to be extremely fruitful. Wishing to meet the major figures of Saudi Sunni Islamism, I made the acquaintance of many "foot soldiers" of the cause, simple members (or former members) of the *jama'at,* the organized Islamist networks that constitute the backbone of the movement. More than intermediaries with the leadership (which they were), they turned out to be extremely rich sources of information. Thanks to their help, I was able to grasp the various levels of the movement and get a view of the whole. I also managed to meet numerous non-Saudi Islamists with ties to the Saudi Islamist movement, who offered a different perspective on what I was observing in Saudi Arabia and provided information on the regional spread of the networks. Finally, wishing to place the Islamist movement in its broader environment, I spoke with a large number of individuals belonging to other intellectual and sectarian groups active in the Saudi kingdom. Some of my interlocutors agreed to be quoted by name, while the majority chose to remain anonymous. This explains the heterogeneity of the notes referring to interviews, some with an individual's name, others with a more or less thorough description of the person.

To these primary sources I added a substantial number of secondary sources in Arabic. This required going through public and private libraries, bookstores, and stores selling Islamic recordings in numerous countries, including Saudi Arabia, Kuwait, Egypt, the United Arab Emirates, and the United Kingdom, to assemble the largest possible sample of Saudi Islamist materials, beginning with the works of the movement's principal ideologues, the pamphlets and recorded sermons of its ulema, the biographies of its various figures, and the most influential journals read by its members. I have also consulted the archives of the principal Saudi newspapers and magazines published over the last fifty years. Finally, the Internet was of invaluable help: first, because some Islamist sites have very well-stocked online libraries in which it is possible to find works hard to access elsewhere; and second, because Islamist forums are a very rich source of information for the most recent events.

ON TRANSLITERATIONS

Arabic words are transliterated following a simplified version of the standard adopted by the *Encyclopedia of Islam* and appear in italics in the text, except when they are found in English-language dictionaries (for example, Koran, hadith, sunna). For ease of reading, the ʿayn is not included at the beginning of common Arabic names in the body of the text (for example, Abdallah, Umar). When some proper names or place names have a commonly accepted form in English, that form is used (for example, Osama bin Laden, Riyadh).

Notes

1. ISLAMISM IN A FRAGMENTED SOCIETY

1. The term "Islamist" is used in a relatively broad sense to designate any formally or informally organized agent acting or wishing to act on his social and/or political environment with the purpose of bringing it into conformity with an ideal based on a particular interpretation of the dictates of Islam.

2. See, for example, R. Hrair Dekmejian, *Islam in Revolution: Fundamentalism in the Arab World*, 2nd ed. (Syracuse, N.Y.: Syracuse University Press, 1995), 130. For a characteristic formulation, see "Islam in Saudi Arabia: A Double-Edged Sword," *Economist*, September 27, 2001.

3. See, for example, Emmanuel Sivan, *Medieval Theology and Modern Politics* (New Haven, Conn.: Yale University Press, 1985).

4. A rentier state is a state that derives a substantial portion of its revenues from a rent (in this case, oil). Several authors have argued that, in such a state, society tends to be depoliticized through the redistribution of rent money. See for instance Afsaneh Najmabadi, "Depoliticisation of a Rentier State: The Case of Pahlavi Iran," in *The Rentier State*, ed. Hazem Beblawi and Giacomo Luciani (London: Croom Helm, 1987), 211–227.

5. See Joshua Teitelbaum, *Holier than Thou* (Washington, D.C.: Washington Institute for Near East Policy, 2000), 5–7; R. Hrair Dekmejian, "The Rise of Political Islamism in Saudi Arabia," *Middle East Journal* 48, 4 (Autumn 1994): 629.

6. This is what Mamoun Fandy suggested in his portraits of al-ʿAwda and al-Hawali. Mamoun Fandy, *Saudi Arabia and the Politics of Dissent* (Basingstoke: Macmillan, 1999), 61–114.

7. Gwenn Okruhlik, for instance, has shown how imbalances in the distribution of rent have affected distinct groups in different ways. Gwenn Okruhlik, "Rentier Wealth, Unruly Law, and the Rise of Opposition: The Political Economy of Oil States," *Comparative Politics* 31, 3 (April 1999): 295–315.

8. Pierre Bourdieu, "Genèse et structure du champ religieux," *Revue Française de Sociologie* 12, 3 (1971): 332 (English translation: "Genesis and Structure of the Religious Field," trans. Jenny B. Burnside, Craig Calhoun, and Leah Florence, *Comparative Social Research* 13 (1991): 1–44).

9. For the broad outlines of this theory, see Donatella della Porta and Mario Diani, *Social Movements: An Introduction,* 2nd ed. (Malden, Mass.: Blackwell, 2006). After having been ignored for a long time by Middle East specialists, this theory has recently attracted the attention of several scholars who have bolstered their analyses with elements taken from that body of work, while others have undertaken a consideration of the ways in which the theory could be adapted to contexts, such as Middle Eastern authoritarianism, that differ widely from those in which the theory arose, namely, Western democracies. See Mounia Bennani-Chraïbi and Olivier Fillieule, eds., *Résistances et protestations dans les sociétés musulmanes* (Paris: Presses de la Fondation Nationale des Sciences Politiques, 2003); Quintan Wiktorowicz, ed., *Islamic Activism: A Social Movement Theory Approach* (Bloomington: Indiana University Press, 2004).

10. Ted Gurr, *Why Men Rebel* (Princeton, N.J.: Princeton University Press, 1970).

11. Pierre Bourdieu, *Réponses* (Paris: Seuil, 1992), 74, emphasis in original.

12. Pierre Bourdieu, *Questions de sociologie* (Paris: Minuit, 2002), 115.

13. These relations between the political and the religious fields derive from the rules of "legitimate politics" *(al-siyasa al-shariyya)* set forth notably by Ibn Taymiyya. On this aspect, see Frank E. Vogel, *Islamic Law and Legal System: Studies of Saudi Arabia* (Leiden: Brill, 2000), 169ff.

14. Michel Dobry, *Risques collectifs et situations de crise: Réflexions à partir d'une analyse sociologique des crises politiques* (Paris: CNRS, 1995), 24.

15. Although this title is no longer used by the princes, it is still used to designate tribal chiefs.

16. David Long, *The Kingdom of Saudi Arabia* (Gainesville: University of Florida Press, 1997), 51.

17. Michael Herb, *All in the Family: Absolutism, Revolution, and Democracy in the Middle Eastern Monarchies* (Albany: State University of New York Press, 1999), 104.

18. Mordechai Abir, *Saudi Arabia in the Oil Era: Regime and Elites; Conflict and Collaboration* (London: Croom Helm, 1988), 135.

19. On this use of the word "tradition," see Muhammad Qasim Zaman, *The Ulama in Contemporary Islam: Custodians of Change* (Princeton, N.J.: Princeton University Press, 2002), 4.

20. Muhammad bin ʿAbd al-Wahhab, *Kitab al-tawhid* (Beirut: al-Maktab al-Islami, 1988); ʿAbd al-Wahhab, *Kashf al-shubuhat*, in *Muʾallafat al-shaykh al-imam Muhammad bin ʿAbd al-Wahhab* (Riyadh: Jamiʿat al-Imam Muhammad bin Saʾud al-Islamiyya, 1976), vol. 1, 153–181.

21. On the doctrine of Ibn Abd al-Wahhab, see David Commins, *The Wahhabi Mission and Saudi Arabia* (London: I. B. Tauris, 2006); and Abdulaziz al-Fahad, "From Exclusivism to Accommodation: Doctrinal and Legal Evolution of Wahhabism," *New York University Law Review* 79 (2004): 485–879.

22. Commins, *Wahhabi Mission and Saudi Arabia*, 12.

23. Article "Wahhabiya," *Encyclopédie de l'Islam* (Leiden: Brill, 1954–2004), vol. 11, 39–42.

24. Vogel, *Islamic Law and Legal System*, 74–76.

25. Michael Cook, *Commanding Right and Forbidding Wrong in Islamic Thought* (Cambridge: Cambridge University Press, 2001), 169ff.

26. Ibid., 182ff.

27. Al-Fahad, "From Exclusivism to Accommodation," 512.

28. Reinhard Schulze, *Islamischer Internationalismus im 20. Jahrhundert: Untersuchungen zur Geschichte der Islamischen Weltliga* (Leiden: Brill, 1990), 123.

29. Henri Laoust, *Pluralismes dans l'Islam* (Paris: Geuthner, 1983), 182.

30. Schulze, *Islamischer Internationalismus im 20. Jahrhundert*, 132; Guido Steinberg, *Religion und Staat in Saudi-Arabien: Die wahhabitischen Gelehrten, 1902–1953* (Berlin: Ergon, 2002), 30.

31. This aspect is particularly emphasized by Toby Jones, "The Dogma of Development: Technopolitics and the Making of Saudi Arabia, 1950–1980" (Ph.D. diss., Stanford University, 2006), 98ff.

32. Interview with former activists of the Saudi left.

33. Interview with Abdallah al-Husayn.

34. Ghassane Salameh, "Political Power and the Saudi State," *MERIP Reports,* October 1980, 8.

35. In 1962, 1,200 young Saudis were studying abroad; the number had grown to 5,000 in the mid-1970s. Abir, *Saudi Arabia in the Oil Era,* 92, 122.

36. William A. Rugh, "Emergence of a New Middle Class in Saudi Arabia," *Middle East Journal* 27, 1 (1973): 13; Ayman Al-Yassini, *Religion and State in the Kingdom of Saudi Arabia* (Boulder, Colo.: Westview, 1985), 98.

37. The past association of these figures (and many others) with nationalist or leftist circles is widely known in Saudi Arabia. For some evidence, see Abir, *Saudi Arabia in the Oil Era,* 109.

38. See Madawi Al-Rasheed, *A History of Saudi Arabia* (New York: Cambridge University Press, 2002), 135ff.

39. Giacomo Luciani, "Allocation vs. Production State: A Theoretical Framework," in *The Rentier State,* ed. Hazem Beblawi and Giacomo Luciani (London: Croom Helm, 1987), 76.

40. Mordechai Abir, *Saudi Arabia: Government, Society, and the Gulf Crisis* (London: Routledge, 1993), 74.

41. Interview with Abdallah al-Majid.

42. Shakir al-Nablusi, *Nabat al-samt: Dirasa fi-l-shiʿr al-saʿudi al-muʿasir* [The Buds of Silence: A Study of Contemporary Saudi Poetry] (Beirut: Al-ʿasr al-hadith li-l-nashr wa-l-tawziʿ, 1992), 37.

43. Ali al-Dumayni, *Al-hadatha al-shiʿriyya fi-l-mamlaka al-ʿarabiyya al-saʿudiyya—Tajruba shakhsiyya* [Poetic Modernism in the Kingdom of Saudi Arabia—A Personal Experience], www.arabrenewal.com.

44. Faysal's ability to rely on religious circles came from the fact that he had a notable particularity in the royal family: his mother was an Al al-Shaykh, a descendant of Muhammad bin Abd al-Wahhab, which symbolically connected him to the religious field. This indirect violation of the principle of autonomy of fields remained an isolated case.

45. Saddeka Arebi writes that "in contemporary Arabia, in the absence of other forms of political participation, literature is transformed into a political forum in which expression—however limited and constrained—gives the illusion of political participation." Saddeka Arebi, *Women and Words in Saudi Arabia: The Politics of Literary Discourse* (New York: Columbia University Press, 1994), 5.

46. Ibid.

47. Al-Dumayni, *Al-hadatha al shiʿriyya.*

48. ʿAbdallah al-Ghadhdhami, *Hikayat al-hadatha fi-l-mamlaka al-ʿarabiyya al-saʿudiyya* [The History of Modernism in the Kingdom of Saudi Arabia] (Beirut: Al-markaz al-thaqafi al-ʿarabi, 2004), 133.

49. As Saddeka Arebi shows in *Women and Words in Saudi Arabia.*

50. This is the thesis of the book by Shakir al-Nablusi, *Nabat al-samt.*

51. Interview with Saʿid al-Surayhi.

52. Jill Crystal, *Oil and Politics in the Gulf: Rulers and Merchants in Kuwait and Qatar* (Cambridge: Cambridge University Press, 1990), 75.

53. F. Gregory Gause III, *Oil Monarchies: Domestic and Security Challenges in the Arab Gulf States* (New York: Council on Foreign Relations Press, 1994), 57. The members of the royal family who have been present in the economic field have traditionally acted through intermediaries, never in their own name or in the name of their family. However, this has recently begun to change with the advent of a new generation of princes, among whom the billionaire businessman al-Walid bin Talal is one of the most emblematic.

54. Salameh, "Political Power and the Saudi State," 9–10.

55. Amélie Le Renard, "Le rose et le noir: Le développement d'une sphère féminine en Arabie Saoudite," mémoire de DEA en Science Politique (Paris: Sciences Po, 2005), 44ff.

56. According to Joseph Kostiner, in the 1980s only 35 percent of Saudis still lived at subsistence level, while the others "now enjoyed comfort, if not luxury." Joseph Kostiner, "Transforming Dualities: Tribe and State Formation in Saudi Arabia," in *Tribes and State Formation in the Middle East,* ed. Philip S. Khoury and Joseph Kostiner (Berkeley: University of California Press, 1990), 242.

57. Abdulaziz H. Al-Fahad, "The ʿImama vs. the ʿIqal: Hadari Bedouin Conflict and the Formation of the Saudi State," in *Counter-narratives: History, Contemporary Society, and Politics in Saudi Arabia and Yemen,* ed. Madawi Al-Rasheed and Robert Vitalis (New York: Palgrave Macmillan, 2004), 58 n. 7.

58. See in particular Steve Coll, *The Bin Ladens: An Arabian Family in the American Century* (New York: Penguin, 2008), 58; e-mail exchange with Steve Coll.

59. The social and economic situation of the "Bedouins" was particularly fraught until the 1980s. It has improved slightly since then.

60. Al-Fahad, "ʿImama vs. the ʿIqal," 36.

61. Philippe Schmitter defines corporatism as "a system of interest representation in which the constituent units are organized into a limited number of singular, compulsory, non-competitive, hierarchically ordered and functionally differentiated categories, recognized or licensed (if not created) by the state and granted a deliberate representational monopoly within their respective categories in exchange for observing certain controls on their selection of leaders and articulation of demands and supports." Philippe Schmitter, "Still the Century of Corporatism?" *Review of Politics* 36, 1 (January 1974): 93–94.

62. Nazih Ayubi, *Over-stating the Arab State: Politics and Society in the Middle East* (London: I. B. Tauris, 1995), 183ff. See also Michel Camau, *Remarques sur la consolidation autoritaire et ses limites* (Cairo: CEDEJ, 2004).

63. Steffen Hertog, "Building the Body-Politic: Emerging Corporatism in Saudi Arabia," *Chroniques Yéménites* 12 (2004): 103–18.

64. Steffen Hertog, "Segmented Clientelism: The Political Economy of Saudi Economic Reform Efforts," in *Saudi Arabia in the Balance: Political Economy, Society, Foreign Affairs,* ed. Paul Aarts and Gerd Nonneman (New York: New York University Press, 2005), 112.

65. Steffen Hertog, *Princes, Brokers, Bureaucrats: Oil and the State in Saudi Arabia* (Ithaca, N.Y.: Cornell University Press, 2010), chap. 1.

66. Amin Rihani, *Ibn Sa'oud of Arabia* (London: Kegan Paul, 2002), 135.

67. For a study of the history of al-Dikhna, see *Al-Riyad,* March 3, 2008.

68. Al-Ghadhdhami, *Hikayat al-hadatha,* 119–123.

69. Michael Hudson, *Arab Politics: The Search for Legitimacy* (New Haven, Conn.: Yale University Press, 1977), 180; emphasis added.

70. Ibid., 176.

71. Al-Yassini, *Religion and State in the Kingdom of Saudi Arabia,* 134–136.

72. Joseph A. Kechichian, "The Role of the Ulama in the Politics of an Islamic State: The Case of Saudi Arabia," *International Journal of Middle East Studies,* 18, 1 (February 1986): 66.

73. Abd al-Rahman al-Qasim, *Al-durar al-saniyya fi-l-ajwiba al-najdiyya* [The Glittering Pearls of the Najdi Answers] (Beirut, 1978), 15:364; *Fatawa wa rasa'il samahat al-shaykh Muhammad bin Ibrahim Al al-shaykh* [Fatwas and Letters from His Excellency Sheikh Muhammad bin Ibrahim Al al-Shaykh] (Mecca: Matba'at al-hukuma, n.d.), 4:76, 6:231.

74. *Fatawa wa rasa'il,* vol. 13, nos. 4038, 4040, 4107, 4042, and 4045.

75. For others, see Muhammad al-Mas'ari, *Al-adilla al-qat'iyya 'ala 'adam shar'iyyat al-dawla al-sa'udiyya* [The Irrefutable Proofs of the Illegitimacy of the Saudi State], www.tajdeed.org.uk, 424–49.

76. Muhammad bin Ibrahim Al al-Shaykh, *Risala fi tahkim al-qawanin al-wad'iyya* [Letter on Governing through Man-Made Laws], www.tawhed.ws.

77. Emphasis added. This nuance is essential because it is all that separates the position of Muhammad bin Ibrahim from *takfir* (because the Saudi government is accused of committing isolated, not systematic, errors).

78. Al al-Shaykh, *Risala fi tahkim.*

79. Jill Crystal, "Civil Society in the Arabian Gulf," in *Civil Society in the Middle East,* ed. Augustus Richard Norton (New York: Brill, 1996), 2:273–274.

80. Philippe Droz-Vincent, "Quel avenir pour l'autoritarisme dans le monde arabe?" *Revue Française de Science Politique* 54, 6 (December 2004): 950.

81. On the concept of legitimating apparatus, see Michel Dobry, "Légitimité et calcul rationnel: Remarques sur quelques 'complications' de la soci-

ologie de Max Weber," in *Être gouverné: Hommages à Jean Leca,* ed. Pierre Favre, Jack Hayward, and Yves Schemeil (Paris: Presses de Sciences Po, 2003), 134–135.

82. Dobry, *Risques collectifs et situations de crise,* 87–88.

83. Mohammed Nabil Mouline, "'Ulama al-Sultan: Parcours et évolution dans le champ politico-religieux des membres du comité des grands oulémas (1971–2005)," mémoire de DEA en Science Politique (Paris: Sciences Po, 2005), especially 96.

84. Aldon Morris and Suzanne Staggenborg, "Leadership in Social Movements," in *The Blackwell Companion to Social Movements,* ed. David Snow, Sarah Soule, and Hanspeter Kriesi (Malden, Mass.: Blackwell, 2004), 178.

85. On this point, see especially Lilian Mathieu, *Comment lutter? Sociologie et mouvements sociaux* (Paris: Textuel, 2004), 75–83.

86. Ron Aminzade, Jack A. Goldstone, and Elizabeth J. Perry, "Leadership Dynamics and Dynamics of Contention," in *Silence and Voice in the Study of Contentious Politics,* ed. Ronald R. Aminzade et al. (Cambridge: Cambridge University Press, 2001), 129–130.

87. Gilles Kepel, *Jihad: The Trail of Political Islam,* trans. Anthony F. Roberts (Cambridge, Mass.: Harvard University Press, 2003), 175.

88. Séverine Labat, *Les islamistes algériens: Entre les urnes et le maquis* (Paris: Seuil, 1995), 129, 151.

89. Gilles Kepel, *Muslim Extremism in Egypt: The Prophet and Pharaoh,* trans. Jon Rothschild (Berkeley: University of California Press, 2003), 241.

90. Ibid., 15.

91. Michel Dobry, *Sociologie des crises politiques: La dynamique des mobilisations multisectorielles* (Paris: Presses de la FNSP, 1986), 141–154.

92. Labat, *Islamistes algériens,* 79–80.

93. Ibid., 83–90.

94. Ibid., 146.

95. On the tense relations and rivalries between "Islamist theocrats" and "Islamist technocrats" in the Algerian movement, see ibid., 171.

96. Evrand Abrahamian, "Ali Shari'ati: Ideologue of the Iranian Revolution," in *Islam, Politics, and Social Movements,* ed. Edmund Burke III and Ira M. Lapidus (Berkeley: University of California Press, 1988), 295.

97. This is shown in Malika Zeghal, *Gardiens de l'Islam: Les oulémas d'al-Azhar dans l'Égypte contemporaine* (Paris: Presses de Sciences Po, 1996).

98. On this point (at a more general level), see Aminzade, Goldstone, and Perry, "Leadership Dynamics and Dynamics of Contention," 132.

99. Michel Dobry, "Calcul, concurrence et gestion du sens: Quelques réflexions à propos des manifestations étudiantes de novembre–décembre 1986," in *La manifestation,* ed. Pierre Favre (Paris: Presses de la FNSP, 1990), 357.

100. Labat, *Islamistes algériens,* 227ff.

2. THE DEVELOPMENT OF THE SAHWA

1. In this regard, despite the crucial role played by the Brotherhood, Madawi al-Rasheed is right to say the Sahwis cannot be considered "blind disciples of the Islamist exiles from Egypt and Syria." Madawi al-Rasheed, *Contesting the Saudi State: Islamic Voices from a New Generation* (Cambridge: Cambridge University Press, 2007), 73.

2. Sayyid Qutb, *Fi dhilal al-Qur'an;* Sayyid Qutb, *Ma'alim fi-l-tariq.* (Cairo: Dar al-Shuruq, 1998).

3. Gilles Kepel, *Muslim Extremism in Egypt: The Prophet and Pharaoh,* trans. Jon Rothschild (Berkeley: University of California Press, 2003), 29–59.

4. Muhammad Abu al-As'ad, *Al-sa'udiyya wa-l-ikhwan al-muslimun* [Saudi Arabia and the Muslim Brotherhood] (Cairo: Markaz al-dirasat wa-l-ma'lumat al-qanuniyya li-huquq al-insan, 1995), 106–107.

5. Husam Tammam, "Al-ikhwan wa-l-sa'udiyya—Hal daqqat sa'at al-firaq?" [The Brotherhood and Saudi Arabia—Has the Time for Separation Come?], *Jaridat al-qahira* (Egypt), December 3, 2002.

6. Reinhard Schulze, *Islamischer Internationalismus im 20. Jahrhundert: Untersuchungen zur Geschichte der Islamischen Weltliga* (Leiden: Brill, 1990), 106.

7. 'Umar Muhammad al-'Izzi, "Al-ikhwan al-sa'udiyyun . . . Al-tayyar al-ladhi lam yaqul kalimatahu ba'd!" [The Saudi Brotherhood . . . The Movement Whose Voice Has Not Yet Been Heard!], www.alasr.ws, July 25, 2004.

8. Tammam, "Al-ikhwan wa-l-sa'udiyya."

9. Schulze, *Islamischer Internationalismus im 20. Jahrhundert,* 163–164.

10. Ibid., 182.

11. Ibid., 162.

12. Malika Zeghal, *Gardiens de l'Islam: Les oulémas d'al-Azhar dans l'Égypte contemporaine* (Paris: Presses de Sciences Po, 1996), 25–26.

13. Schulze, *Islamischer Internationalismus im 20. Jahrhundert,* 156.

14. On Faysal's vision, see Joseph A. Kechichian, *Faysal: Saudi Arabia's King for All Seasons* (Gainesville: University Press of Florida, 2008), 172ff.

15. Interviews with 'Abdallah al-Ghadhdhami and Muhammad al-Ahmari.

16. "Tatawwur al-jami'a wa numuwwuha" [The Development of the University and its Growth], www.ksu.edu.sa.

17. Schulze, *Islamischer Internationalismus im 20. Jahrhundert,* 158.

18. *Dalil al-jami'a al-islamiyya, 1396–1397* [Guide to the Islamic University, 1396–1397], in the author's possession.

19. Muhammad al-Majdhub, *'Ulama' wa mufakkirun 'araftuhum* [Ulema and Thinkers I Have Known] (Cairo: Dar al-i'tisam, 1986), 1:229–263.

20. See Ali al-Tantawi's biography at www.makkawi.com.

21. Sayyid Sabiq, *Fiqh al-sunna* (Cairo: Dar al-bayan li-l-turath, 1987).

22. See Sayyid Sabiq's biographies at www.islamway.com and www.islamonline.net.

23. See Muhammad al-Ghazzali's biography at www.daawa-info.net. Al-Ghazzali and Sabiq were not formally members of the Brotherhood anymore, although they remained closely associated with it.

24. According to Thomas Hegghammer, who is working on a book on 'Azzam.

25. Al-Majdhub, *'Ulama' wa mufakkirun 'araftuhum,* 1:451.

26. See Muhammad al-Rawi's biography at www.bab.com.

27. See Abd al-Fattah Abu Ghudda's biography at www.daawa-info.net.

28. *Dalil al-jami'a al-islamiyya, 1396–1397.*

29. Interview with an associate of Abdallah al-Turki who chose to remain anonymous.

30. Husam Tammam, "Al-tandhim al-duwali li-l-ikhwan … Al-wa'd wa-l-masira wa-l-mal" [The International Organization of the Brotherhood … Promise, Trajectory, and Outcome], *Al-Manar al-Jadid* (Summer 2004).

31. Bakri Shaykh Amin, *Al-haraka al-adabiyya fi-l-mamlaka al-arabiyya al-sa'udiyya* [The Literary Movement in Saudi Arabia], 14th ed. (Beirut: Dar al-'ilm li-l-malayin, 2005), 167.

32. 'Abdallah al-'Aqil, *Min a'lam al-haraka wa-l-da'wa al-islamiyya al-mu'asira* [Some Figures of the Contemporary Islamic Movement and Preaching] (Kuwait: Maktabat al-manar al-islamiyya, 2001), 445, 449.

33. Sa'id Hawwa, *Jundullah. Thaqafa wa akhlaq* [Soldiers of God: Culture and Morals] (Beirut: Dar al-Kutub al-'ilmiyya, 1979).

34. Itzchak Weismann, "Sa'id Hawwa: The Making of a Radical Muslim Thinker in Modern Syria," *Middle Eastern Studies* 29, 4 (1993): 617.

35. Zeghal, *Gardiens de l'Islam,* 339.

36. Schulze, *Islamischer Internationalismus im 20. Jahrhundert,* 157.

37. Ibid., 158.

38. Al-Majdhub, *'Ulama' wa mufakkirun 'araftuhum,* 2:331.

39. ʿAbdallah al-Zayidi, "Al-ʿawlama wa dawr al-thaqafa al-islamiyya wa risalat al-mamlaka [Globalization, the Role of Islamic Culture, and the Kingdom's Message], *Al-Jazira*, August 16, 2002.

40. Al-Majdhub, *ʿUlamaʾ wa mufakkirun ʿaraftuhum*, 1:248–254.

41. Ibid., 1:452.

42. *Siyasat al-taʿlim fi-l-mamlaka al-ʿarabiyya al-saʿudiyya* [Educational Policy in the Kingdom of Saudi Arabia], art. 28.

43. Ibid., art. 1.

44. Ibid., art. 39.

45. On this point, see also Eleanor Abdella Doumato, "Saudi Arabia: From 'Wahhabi Roots' to Contemporary Revisionism," in *Teaching Islam: Textbooks and Religion in the Middle East*, ed. Eleanor Abdella Doumato and Gregory Starrett (Boulder, Colo.: Lynne Rienner, 2007), 167.

46. Religious sciences were taught 8 hours per week to all students in secular primary and intermediate schools (out of a total of from 28 to 33 hours). Students in secular secondary schools took 3 to 4 hours of religious sciences and, in addition, up to 11 hours of social sciences, which were "Islamic social sciences," a preserve of the Muslim Brotherhood. Religious schools had 13 to 20 hours of religious sciences per week. William A. Rugh, "Education in Saudi Arabia: Choices and Constraints," *Middle East Policy* 9, 2 (June 2002): 51.

47. *Siyasat al-taʿlim fi-l-mamlaka al-ʿarabiyya al-saʿudiyya*, art. 11.

48. An analysis of two university textbooks of "Islamic culture" from 1976 leaves no doubt: the first, for first-year students, was written by Muhammad al-Ghazzali and Abd al-Rahman al-Habannaka. The second, for fourth-year students, was a collaborative work in which Muhammad Qutb and Muhammad al-Mubarak participated. The bibliography of the first textbook sets the tone: it is largely made up of works by the Brothers (or former Brothers) al-Habannaka, al-Ghazzali, Sayyid Sabiq, Ali al-Tantawi, al-Mubarak, Saʿid Hawwa, and Yusuf al-Qaradawi.

49. Faris al-Zahrani [also known as Abu Jandal al-Azdi], *Usama bin Ladin—Mujaddid al-zaman wa qahir al-amrikan* [Osama bin Laden—Reformer of Our Age and Conqueror of the Americans], www.tawhed.ws. For Muhammad Qutb, see also Steve Coll, "Young Osama," *New Yorker*, December 12, 2005; for Abdallah ʿAzzam, see Jonathan Randal, *Osama: The Making of a Terrorist* (New York: Vintage, 2005), 63. Randal calls it a conjecture that ʿAzzam taught Bin Laden, but says that it is "entirely plausible."

50. See, for example, Muhammad Qutb, Hawla al-taʾsil al-islami li-l-ʿulum al-ijtimaʿiyya [*On the Islamization of the Social Sciences*] (Cairo: Dar al-shuruq).

51. *Siyasat al-taʿlim fi-l-mamlaka al-ʿarabiyya al-saʿudiyya*, art. 12.

52. Interview with Khalid al-ʿUjaymi.

53. *Dalil kulliyat usul al-din bi jamiʿat al-imam Muhammad bin Saʿud, 1397–1398* [Guide to the Faculty of the Fundamentals of Religion at Imam Muhammad bin Saʿud University, 1397–1398], document in the author's possession.

54. Safar al-Hawali, *Al-ʿilmaniyya: Nashʾatuha was tatawwuruha wa atharuha fi-l-haya al-islamiyya al-muʿasira* [Secularism: Its Creation, Development, and Influence on Contemporary Islamic Life], www.alhawali.com, 4–5.

55. *Siyasat al-taʿlim fi-l-mamlaka al-ʿarabiyya al-saʿudiyya,* art. 31.

56. Ibid., art. 35.

57. Interview with Tariq al-Mubarak, in charge of the program in the school where he teaches.

58. Interview with officials from the Ministry of Islamic Affairs, Riyadh.

59. "Idarat al-tawʿiya al-islamiyya" [The administration of the raising of Islamic consciousness], www.tawayah.com.

60. Interview with Hamad al-Sulayfih.

61. *Jamaʿat tahfidh al-qurʾan al-karim bi-makka al-mukarrama—Al-taqrir al-sanawi, 1382–1387* [Association for the Memorization of the Holy Koran in Mecca—Annual Report, 1382–1387] (n.p.: n.p., 1967).

62. *Jamaʿat tahfiz al-qurʾan al-karim bi-l-riyad—Al-taqrir al-sanawi, 1391* [Association for the Memorization of the Holy Koran in Riyadh—Annual Report, 1391] (n.p.: n.p., 1971).

63. Interview with an official in the Ministry of Islamic Affairs.

64. *Al-Riyad,* August 30, 2003.

65. "Al-nashat al-tullabi fi-l-mamlaka al-ʿarabiyya al-saʿudiyya" [Student Activities in the Kingdom of Saudi Arabia], www.northedu.gov.sa.

66. "Dalil al-nashat al-tullabi" [Guide to Student Activities], www.moe.gov.sa.

67. "Al-haraka al-kashfiyya fi-l-mamlaka al-ʿarabiyya al-saʿudiyya" [The Scouting Movement in the Kingdom of Saudi Arabia], www.moe.gov.sa.

68. On the Brotherhood scouts, see Brynjar Lia, *The Society of the Muslim Brothers in Egypt: The Rise of an Islamic Mass Movement, 1928–1942* (Reading, England: Ithaca Press, 1998), 166–172.

69. ʿAbdallah al-ʿUmari, "Al-kashshafa fi khidmat duyuf al-rahman" [Scouts at the Service of Pilgrims], *Al-Jazira,* January 3, 2006.

70. "Al-marakiz al-sayfiyya wa masirat 15 ʿaman" [Summer Camps, a 15-Year Journey], *Al-Daʿwa,* September 13, 1991.

71. Lia, *Society of the Muslim Brothers in Egypt,* 169.

72. Interview with Saʿd al-Faqih.

73. "Al-marakiz al-sayfiyya wa masirat 15 ʿaman."

74. Ibid.

75. The term *umma* designates the community of Muslims.

76. Interview with a young Sahwi.

77. Interviews with young Sahwis.

78. Muhammad Sulayman, "Muhammad Qutb namudhajan" [Muhammad Qutb as Example], *Al-ʿAsr,* May 17, 2002.

79. "ʿAbd al-Rahman al-Dawsari . . . al-ʿAllama alladhi sabaqa zamanahu" [ʿAbd al-Rahman al-Dawsari, the precursor *ʿalim*], www.tawhed.ws.

80. Al-Majdhub, *ʿUlamaʾ wa mufakkirun ʿaraftuhum,* 2:277.

81. Ibid., 2:280

82. Zaynab al-Ghazzali, *Ayyam min hayati* [Days of My Life], 1977, www .daawa-info.net, 81.

83. Al-Majdhub, *ʿUlamaʾ wa mufakkirun ʿaraftuhum,* 2:275.

84. Muhammad Qutb, *Jahiliyyat al-qarn al-ʿishrin* [The Jahiliyya of the Twentieth Century] (Cairo: Dar al-shuruq, 1995), 45–46.

85. Muhammad Qutb, *Mafahim yanbaghi an tusahhah* [Notions That Must Be Corrected], www.tawhed.ws, 103.

86. ʿAli al-ʿUmaym, "Awraq asqataha al-ikhwan al-muslimum min taʾrikh Sayyid Qutb" [Pages in the History of Sayyid Qutb that the Muslim Brothers Left Out], *Al-Majalla,* May 1, 2005.

87. Sayyid Qutb, *Al-taswir al-fanni fi-l-qurʾan.* (Cairo: Dar al-shuruq, 2004).

88. Sayyid Qutb, *Al-ʿadala al-ijtimaʿiyya fi-l-islam* (Cairo: Dar al-shuruq, 1995).

89. Mustafa al-Sibaʿi, *Ishtirakiyyat al-Islam* (Cairo: Matabiʿ dar al-shaʿb, 1977).

90. Passages from various editions are quoted in ʿAbdallah al-Zafiri, *Mal-hudhat wa tanbihat ʿala fatwa fadilat al-shaykh ʿAbdallah bin ʿAbd al-Rahman bin Jibrin fi difaʿihi ʿan Hasan al-Banna wa Sayyid Qutb wa ʿAbd al-Rahman ʿAbd al-Khaliq* [Remarks and Warnings Regarding the Fatwa of the Noble Sheikh ʿAbdallah bin ʿAbd al-Rahman bin Jibrin in Which He Defends Hasan al-Banna, Sayyid Qutb, and ʿAbd al-Rahman ʿAbd al-Khaliq], www.albeed .com.

91. Quoted by Rabiʿ al-Madkhali, *Al-tawdih li-ma fi khitab Muhammad Qutb ʿan kutub akhihi min al-tasrih* [Clarification on the Statements of Muhammad Qutb about His Brother's Books], www.al-barq.net.

92. Muhammad Qutb, *Kayfa nadʿu al-nas?* [How Do We Preach to People?], www.tawheed.ws, 99.

93. Abu Qatada al-Filastini, "Al-jarh wa-l-taʿdil: Muhammad Qutb" [Critique and Fair Evaluation: Muhammad Qutb], www.altaefa.com.

94. Muhammad Saʿid al-Qahtani, *Al-walaʾ wa-l-baraʾ fi-l-islam* [Allegiance and Rupture in Islam], www.saaid.net.

95. Sulayman al-Tayyar, *Hayat al-daʿiya al-shaykh ʿAbd al-Rahman bin Muhammad al-Dawsari* [The Life of the Preacher Sheikh ʿAbd al-Rahman bin Muhammad al-Dawsari] (n.p.: n.p., 2003), 23.

96. Ibid., 52–55.

97. Al-ʿAqil, *Min aʿlam al-haraka wa-l-daʿwa al-islamiyya al-muʿasira*, 437.

98. Al-Tayyar, *Hayat al-daʿiya al-shaykh ʿAbd al-Rahman bin Muhammad al-Dawsari*, 67.

99. ʿAbd al-Rahman al-Dawsari, *Al-Ajwiba al-mufida li-muhimmat al-ʿaqida* [Useful Answers to Questions of Creed], www.saaid.net, 83.

100. Ibid., 106.

101. Ibid.

102. Ibid., 134.

103. Interview with Mansur al-Nuqaydan.

104. Al-Tayyar, *Hayat al-daʿiya al-shaykh ʿAbd al-Rahman bin Muhammad al-Dawsari*, 76.

105. Ibid., 175ff.

106. Ibid., 81, 83, 99, 111.

107. "Mawaqif li-l-shaykh" [Some of the Sheikh's Stances], http://dosa.netfirms.com.

108. Al-Tayyar, *Hayat al-daʿiya al-shaykh ʿAbd al-Rahman bin Muhammad al-Dawsari*, 125, 200.

109. It should be noted that he had strong ties to those who would become the major figures of the Sahwa. In the 1970s he taught the young Salman al-ʿAwda (interview with Abdallah bin Salman al-ʿAwda). He was also very close to Muhammad Surur Zayn al-ʿAbidin (al-Tayyar, *Hayat al-daʿiya al-shaykh ʿAbd al-Rahman bin Muhammad al-Dawsari*, 71). The publishing house founded by the latter in Kuwait, Dar al-arqam, even published some of al-Dawsari's books, notably *Useful Answers to Questions of Creed*.

110. See Muhammad Ahmad al-Rashid's biography at www.daawa-info.net.

111. Interview with Ismaʿil al-Shatti.

112. Muhammad Ahmad al-Rashid, *Al-muntalaq* [The Point of Departure], www.daawa-info.net.

113. Muhammad Ahmad al-Rashid, *Al-masir* [The Journey] (Tanta: Dar al-bashir, 2004), 5.

114. Interview with Isma'il al-Shatti.

115. Interview with a former member of the Saudi Muslim Brotherhood.

116. Interview with Isma'il al-Shatti.

117. 'Ali al-'Umaym, "'Abdallah al-Nafisi, sira ghayr tabjiliyya" [Abdallah al-Nafisi: An Irreverent Biography], *Al-Majalla,* October 2, 2004.

118. Verta Taylor and Nancy Whittier, "Analytical Approaches to Social Movement Culture: The Culture of the Women's Movement," in *Social Movements and Culture,* ed. Hank Johnston and Bert Klandermans (Minneapolis: University of Minnesota Press, 1995), 173.

119. 'Ali al-'Umaym, "Mashayikhuna wa mashayikh al-sahwa—Nadharat fi-l-islam al-sa'udi al-haraki" [Our Sheikhs and the Sheikhs of the Sahwa—Perspectives on Saudi Islamism], *Elaph,* June 12, 2003.

120. Observation of Sahwi circles in Riyadh and Jeddah.

121. Interviews with Sahwis.

122. Ibid.

123. Ibid.

124. In a meeting I attended, a celebrated sheikh, wanting to know the organizational affiliation of the young Islamist who had introduced me, asked him, "From whom did you receive your *tarbiya?*" (*'Ala yad man tarabbayta?*).

125. Interview with Sa'd al-Faqih.

126. Interview with a Saudi Brother whose wife was active in the female section of the movement.

127. Richard Dekmejian mentions the existence before the Gulf War of *jama'at al-da'wah* but gives no details about these groups. Dekmejian, "Rise of Political Islamism in Saudi Arabia," 628. In a 1987 article Ghassan Salamé notes the existence of a "local Saudi section of the Muslim Brotherhood." Ghassan Salamé, "Islam and Politics in Saudi Arabia," *Arab Studies Quarterly* 9, 3 (Summer 1987): 317. More recently, Lawrence Wright devoted a few lines to the Saudi Muslim Brotherhood, noting that Osama bin Laden had belonged to it. Lawrence Wright, *The Looming Tower: Al-Qaeda and the Road to 9/11* (New York, Knopf, 2006), 78.

128. The television program *Ida'at* [Highlights] presented by Turki al-Dakhil, with Salman al-'Awda, *Qanat al-'arabiyya* [Al-Arabiya TV], March 10, 2006.

129. 'Ali 'Ashmawi, *Al-ta'rikh al-sirri li-jama'at al-ikhwan al-muslimin—Mudhakkarat 'Ali 'Ashmawi Akhar qadat al-tandhim al-khass* [The Secret History of the Muslim Brotherhood—Memoirs of 'Ali Ashmawi, the Last Leader of the Special Organization] (Cairo: Dar al-hilal, 1993), 58.

130. Interview with Isma'il al-Shatti.

131. 'Ashmawi, *Al-ta'rikh al-sirri*, 62.

132. Interview with Isma'il al-Shatti.

133. On Hamad al-Sulayfih's life, see some articles published after his death in 2005: *Al-Riyad*, July 13, 2005; *Al-Madina*, May 6, 2005; www.ennahada.net, May 1, 2005; www.ala7rar.net, April 29, 2005.

134. Interview with a Saudi Islamist close to al-Sulayfih.

135. Ibid.

136. Interview with Sa'd al-Faqih.

137. Interview with former members of the al-Funaysan network.

138. Interview with Sa'd al-Faqih.

139. Muhammad al-Raqraq, *Lamahat min madi al-Zubayr* [Sketches of the Past of Zubayr] (Riyadh: Al-'Ubaykan, 1994), 11, 34–36.

140. Abdulaziz al-Fahad, "From Exclusivism to Accommodation: Doctrinal and Legal Evolution of Wahhabism," *New York University Law Review* 79 (2004): 500, n.45.

141. Al-Raqraq, *Lamahat min madi al-Zubayr*, 19–20.

142. Interview with Sa'd al-Faqih.

143. Interviews with Tawfiq al-Qusayyir. See also Al-Raqraq, *Lamahat min madi al-Zubayr*, 39.

144. Interview with Isma'il al-Shatti.

145. Interview with Sa'd al-Faqih.

146. Interview with a former member of the network.

147. Interview with Sa'd al-Faqih.

148. Interview with an anonymous member of the Saudi Brotherhood.

149. Interviews with 'Abd al-'Aziz al-Wuhaybi, Sa'd al-Faqih, and Isma'il al-Shatti.

150. Interview with Muhanna al-Hubayyil.

151. Interview with Sahwis and former Sahwis.

152. Interview with an anonymous member of the Saudi Brotherhood.

153. Mustafa Mashhur, *Wahdat al-'amal al-islami fi-l-qutr al-wahid*, www.daawa-info.net; interviews with Saudi Brothers.

154. Interview with Sa'd al-Faqih.

155. Interviews with various *jama'at* members.

156. 'Abdallah al-Nafisi, *Al-haraka al-islamiyya: Ru'ya mustaqbaliyya— Awraq fi-l-naqd al-dhati* [The Islamist Movement: A Prospective View— Articles of Self-Criticism] (Cairo: Maktabat madbuli, 1989), 243–251.

157. Interview with Isma'il al-Shatti.

158. *Al-Sharq al-awsat*, July 18, 2009.

159. Tammam, "Al-ikhwan wa-l-sa'udiyya."

160. Interviews with Sa'd al-Faqih and anonymous former Sururis.

161. Gilles Kepel, *The War for Muslim Minds: Islam and the West,* trans. Pascale Ghazaleh (Cambridge, Mass.: Belknap Press of Harvard University Press, 2004), 176.

162. Muhammad Surur Zayn al-'Abidin, "Al-wahda al-islamiyya 7" [Islamic Unity 7], *Al-Sunna* 26, Jumadi al-Awwal 1413 [November 1992].

163. Al-'Umaym, "Mashayikhuna wa mashayikh al-sahwa."

164. Muhammad Surur Zayn al-'Abidin, "Al-wahda al-islamiyya 8" [Islamic Unity 8], *Al-Sunna* 27, Jumadi al-Ukhra 1413 [December 1992].

165. Ibid.

166. Surur told Gilles Kepel that he did not recall al-'Awda. Kepel, *War for Muslim Minds,* 176. However, interviews with Sahwi activists suggest al-'Awda was indeed his student.

167. Kepel, *War for Muslim Minds,* 176.

168. Zayn al-'Abidin, "Al-wahda al-islamiyya 8."

169. Ibid.

170. Interviews with Sa'd al-Faqih and Ibrahim al-Sikran.

171. Zayn al-'Abidin, "Al-wahda al-islamiyya 8." Muhammad Surur addressed the question in his first-ever television interview. He acknowledged his instrumental role in the emergence of a Sururi *jama'a* (whose existence he implicitly recognized) while emphasizing that he had "never been the leader of any organization." This seven-part interview was broadcast on the al-Hiwar network as part of the program called *Muraja'at* [Revisions], beginning in March 2008.

172. Interview with Sa'd al-Faqih.

173. Interview with Isma'il al-Shatti.

174. Zayn al-'Abidin, "Al-wahda al-islamiyya 8."

175. Interview with a young member of the Saudi Brotherhood.

176. Interview with 'Abd al-'Aziz al-Wuhaybi.

177. Interviews with Walid al-Tabtaba'i and Isma'il al-Shatti.

178. Zayn al-'Abidin, "Al-wahda al-islamiyya 7."

179. Interview with Sulayman al-Dahayyan.

180. Interviews with various Saudi Islamists.

181. Interview with Sa'd al-Faqih.

182. Interview with a young Sahwi.

183. Muhammad al-Muzayni, *Mafariq al-'atama* [Paths in the Darkness] (Beirut: Al-mu'assasa al-'arabiyya li-l-dirasat wa-l-nashr, 2004), 92–93, for example.

184. Ibid., 89.

185. Ibid., 136.

186. ʿAbdallah Thabit, *Al-irhabi 20* [The Twentieth Terrorist] (Damascus: Dar al-mada, 2006), 73.

187. Interview with a Brother from the Eastern Province.

188. Mohammed Nabil Mouline, "ʿUlama al-Sultan: Parcours et évolution dans le champ politico-religieux des membres du comité des grands oulémas (1971–2005)," mémoire de DEA en Science Politique (Paris: Sciences Po, 2005), 23.

189. Ibid., 28.

190. Ibid., 24.

191. Ibid., 25.

192. Ibid., 42–44.

193. Guido Steinberg, "The Wahhabi Ulama and the Saudi State: 1745 to the Present," in *Saudi Arabia in the Balance: Political Economy, Society, Foreign Affairs,* ed. Gerd Nonneman and Paul Aarts (New York: New York University Press, 2005), 25–26.

194. Mouline, "ʿUlama al-Sultan," 25.

195. See, for example, *Al-Daʿwa,* October 31, 1984.

196. *Al-Furqan* 28 (August 1992): 12.

197. Revenues increased from $1,214 billion to $84,466 billion. Richard Nyrop, ed., *Saudi Arabia: A Country Study,* 4th ed. (Washington, D.C.: Foreign Area Studies, American University, 1984), 312.

198. Interview with Nasir al-Huzaymi.

199. Interview with Sulayman al-Dahayyan.

200. Interview with Mazin al-Mutabaqqani.

201. Mazin S. Motabagani, *Islamic Resurgence in the Hijaz Region (1975–1990)* (n.p., n.d.), 12.

202. Interview with Ismaʿil al-Shatti.

203. This group will be introduced in Chapter 3.

204. The Saudi Tablighis differed from their Indian and Pakistani counterparts in their stronger adherence to the fundamentals of the Wahhabi doctrine, a necessary condition for their acceptance in the Saudi religious field. On the Tabligh in Saudi Arabia, see Mufid al-Zaydi, *Taʾrikh al-mamlaka al-ʿarabiyya al-saʿudiyya: Al-hadith wa-l-muʿasir* [History of the Kingdom of Saudi Arabia: Contemporary and Present Day] (Amman: Dar usama li-l-nashr wa-l-tawziʿ, 2004), 293.

205. See, for example, the fatwa in which Ibn Baz supports the Tabligh, "Al-khuruj maʿ jamaʿat al-tabligh" [Participation in the Activities of the Tabligh], www.binbaz.org.sa; and the one where he declares it lawful to belong to

Islamist movements, "Al-intima' ila-l-jama'at al-islamiyya" [Membership in Islamist Movements], www.binbaz.org.sa.

206. Interviews with the British journalist James Buchan (then based in Saudi Arabia), Jamil Farsi, Muhammad Al Zulfa, and Hamza al-Muzayni. On the importance of entertainment programs on Saudi television in the 1970s, see William A. Rugh, "Saudi Mass Media and Society in the Faysal Era," in *King Faisal and the Modernisation of Saudi Arabia,* ed. Willard A. Beling (London: Croom Helm, 1980), 136. It should be pointed out, however, that the singers in question were always foreigners, never Saudis.

207. Olivier Roy, "Les nouveaux intellectuels islamistes: Essai d'approche philosophique," in *Intellectuels et militants de l'Islam contemporain,* ed. Gilles Kepel and Yann Richard (Paris: Seuil, 1990), 267.

208. Gilles Kepel, "Intellectuels et militants de l'islam contemporain," in Kepel and Richard, *Intellectuels et militants de l'Islam contemporain,* 19.

209. Pierre Bourdieu, *Questions de sociologie* (Paris: Minuit, 2002), 114.

210. Ahmad S. Moussalli, *Moderate and Radical Islamic Fundamentalism: The Quest for Modernity, Legitimacy, and the Islamic State* (Gainesville: University Press of Florida, 1999), 32.

211. For a paradigmatic example, see Nasir bin Sulayman al-'Umar, *Luhum al-'ulama' masmuma* [The Flesh of the Ulema Is Poisoned] (Riyadh: Dar al-watan li-l-nashr, 1991).

3. RESISTANCE TO SAHWA ASCENDANCY

1. Some of the material concerning al-Albani was previously published in Stéphane Lacroix, "Between Revolution and Apoliticism: Nasir al-Din al-Albani and His Impact on the Shaping of Contemporary Salafism," in *Global Salafism: Islam's New Religious Movement,* ed. Roel Meijer (London: Hurst/ Columbia University Press, 2009), 58–80.

2. David Commins, *Islamic Reform: Politics and Social Change in Late Ottoman Syria* (New York: Oxford University Press, 1990), 42.

3. 'Abdallah al-Shamrani, *Thabatu mu'allafat al-muhaddith al-kabir al-imam Muhammad Nasir al-Din al-Albani* [Index of the Writings of the Great Traditionalist Imam Muhammad Nasir al-Din al-Albani], www.dorar.net, 17.

4. Ibrahim al-'Ali, *Muhammad Nasir al-Din al-Albani—Muhaddith al-'asr wa nasir al-sunna* [Muhammad Nasir al-Din al-Albani—The Traditionist of the Century and the Defender of the Sunna] (Damascus: Dar al-qal'a, 2001), 11–17.

5. Al-Shamrani, *Thabatu mu'allafat,* 40.

6. Muhammad Nasiral-Din al-Albani, *Tahdhir al-sajid min ittikhadh al-qubur masajid* (Beirut: al-Maktab al-islami, 1983). Muhammad al-Majdhub, *'Ulama' wa mufakkirun 'araftuhum* [Ulema and Thinkers I Have Known] (Cairo: Dar al-i'tisam, 1986), 1:290.

7. Daniel Brown, *Rethinking Tradition in Modern Islamic Thought* (Cambridge: Cambridge University Press, 2003), 40–41.

8. Ibid., 113–117.

9. Al-Shamrani, *Thabatu mu'allafat,* 109–110.

10. Brown, *Rethinking Tradition in Modern Islamic Thought,* 41.

11. A hadith is declared weak if the scholar who examines it determines there are strong presumptions that it is not authentic.

12. Al-'Ali, *Muhammad Nasir al-Din al-Albani,* 30.

13. See the biography of al-Albani at www.islamway.com.

14. On the Ahl-e Hadith, see Barbara Metcalf, *Islamic Revival in British India: Deoband, 1860–1900* (Princeton, N.J.: Princeton University Press, 1982), 268–296.

15. Sound recording available at www.albrhan.org.

16. Al-Ansari's first refutation was titled *Authorization for Women to Wear Gold in the Form of Rings or Bracelets and Refutation of al-Albani's Prohibition of Them* [*Ibahat al-tahalli bi-l-dhahab al-muhallaq li-l-nisa' wa-l-radd 'ala-l-Albani fi tahrimihi*]. The second, which answered al-Albani's accusations that Ibn Abd al-Wahhab was ignorant in matters of hadith, was titled *Defense of the Sheikh of Islam Muhammad bin 'Abd al-Wahhab through Refutation of al-Albani's Deviation from the Truth* [*Al-intisar li-shaykh al-Islam Muhammad bin 'Abd al-Wahhab bi-l-radd 'ala mujanabat al-Albani li-l-sawab*].

17. Muhammad Nasir al-Din al-Albani, *Hijab al-mar'a al-muslima,* 8th ed. (Beirut: Al-maktab al-islami, 1987).

18. Interview with a former disciple of al-Albani.

19. Al-'Ali, *Muhammad Nasir al-Din al-Albani,* 31.

20. Muhammad Surur Zayn al-Abidin, "Shaykh muhaddithi al-'asr fi dhimmat allah" [The Sheikh of the Traditionists of the Era by the Grace of God, *Al-Sunna* 90 (October 1999) [rajab 1420].

21. Biography of al-Albani at www.islamway.com.

22. Quintan Wiktorowicz, *The Management of Islamic Activism: Salafis, the Muslim Brotherhood, and State Power in Jordan* (Albany: State University of New York Press, 2001), 120.

23. Al-'Ali, *Muhammad Nasir al-Din al-Albani,* 31.

24. However, he was often invited to conferences and did make frequent pilgrimages.

25. Interview with Yusuf al-Dayni.

26. The doctrine of the oneness of being is based on the belief that God and his creation are one.

27. Muhammad Nasir al-Din al-Albani, "Mafahim yajib an tusahhah" [Conceptions That Need to Be Corrected], audiocassette.

28. Recording available at www.albrhan.org.

29. *Min al-siyasa tark al-siyasa;* interviews with disciples of al-Albani.

30. Al-Majdhub, *'Ulama' wa mufakkirun 'araftuhum,* 1:302.

31. On this fatwa, see, for example, Wiktorowicz, *Management of Islamic Activism,* 169 n. 76.

32. Al-Albani, *Mafahim yajib an tusahhah.*

33. Sound recording available at www.islamgold.com.

34. Muhammad Nasir al-Din al-Albani, *Sifat salat al-nabi min al-takbir ila-l-taslim ka'annaka taraha* [The Characteristics of the Prophet's Prayer from Beginning to End as Though You Were There], 14th ed. (Beirut: Al-maktab al-islami, 1987).

35. Interview with Nasir al-Huzaymi.

36. The Dar al-Hadith institute was founded in 1931 by Ahmad bin Muhammad al-Dahlawi, a sheikh from the Indian Ahl-e Hadith who had settled in Medina and was eager to encourage the study of the hadith in the Hejaz and, by doing so, to spread the ideas of his movement. Again, this illustrates how the early influence of the Indian Ahl e-Hadith facilitated the subsequent spread of al-Albani's ideas.

37. "Ru'usa' al-jama'a mundhu insha'i'ha" [The Heads of the Association since Its Creation], www.elsonna.com.

38. Interviews with Nasir al-Huzaymi and an anonymous sheikh from Burayda.

39. Interview with Nasir al-Huzaymi.

40. Much of what follows is drawn from Thomas Hegghammer and Stéphane Lacroix, "Rejectionist Islamism in Saudi Arabia: The Story of Juhayman al-'Utaybi Revisited," *International Journal of Middle East Studies* 39, 1 (February 2007): 103–122.

41. Interview with Nasir al-Huzaymi.

42. Ibid.

43. Ibid.

44. Fahd al-Qahtani, *Zalzal Juhayman fi Makka* [The Earthquake of Juhayman in Mecca], 1987, www.alhramain.net, 25. Fahd al-Qahtani is a pseudonym of Hamza al-Hasan, a Shiite activist exiled in London who was a member of the Organization of the Islamic Revolution in the Arabian Peninsula. Al-Hasan

claims that his book is based on accounts from two close associates of Juhayman al-'Utaybi whom he was able to meet. Interview with Hamza al-Hasan.

45. Interview with an anonymous Islamist.

46. Interview with Nasir al-Huzaymi.

47. Al-Qahtani, *Zalzal Juhayman fi Makka*, 24.

48. Interviews with the Kuwaiti *salafi* leaders Khalid Sultan and Walid al-Tabtaba'i. For more details, see Hegghammer and Lacroix, "Rejectionist Islamism in Saudi Arabia," 111, 113.

49. Interview with Nasir al-Huzaymi.

50. Muqbil al-Wadi'i, *Al-makhraj min al-fitna* [The Way Out of Fitna] (Cairo: Dar al-haramayn, n.d.), 140.

51. Ibid., 140–141; interview with Nasir al-Huzaymi.

52. Interview with Nasir al-Huzaymi.

53. Rifa'at Sayyid Ahmad, *Rasa'il Juhayman al-'Utaybi, Qa'id al-muqtahimin li-l-masjid al-haram bi-Makka* [The Letters of Juhayman al-'Utaybi, Leader of the Attackers of the Grand Mosque of Mecca] (Cairo: Maktabat madbuli, 2004), 84.

54. Al-Qahtani, *Zalzal Juhayman fi Makka*, 25.

55. Muqbil al-Wadi'i, *Tarjamat Abi 'Abd al-Rahman Muqbil bin Hadi al-Wadi'i* [Biography of Abu 'Abd al-Rahman Muqbil bin Hadi al-Wadi'i] (Sana'a: Dar al-athar, 2002), 26.

56. Interview with Nasir al-Huzaymi.

57. Al-Wadi'i, *Tarjamat*, 27.

58. Interview with Nasir al-Huzaymi.

59. Nasir al-Huzaymi, "Al-shabab min al-tamarrud ila-l-ta'a al-'umya'" [Young Men, from Revolt to Blind Obedience], *Al-Riyad*, June 18, 2003.

60. Interview with Nasir al-Huzaymi.

61. Al-Huzaymi, "Ayyam ma' Juhayman," unpublished document, 20.

62. On these letters, see Joseph A. Kechichian, "Islamic Revivalism and Change in Saudi Arabia: Juhayman al-Utaybi's 'Letters' to the Saudi People," *The Muslim World* 80, 1 (January 1990): 1–16.

63. Interview with Nasir al-Huzaymi.

64. Ibid.

65. *Raf' al-iltibas 'an millat man ja'alahu Allah imaman li-l-nas.*

66. This set of letters is titled *Group of Letters on the State, Tawhid, the Preaching of the Ikhwan, and the Criterion for the Life of Man* [*Majmu'at rasa'il al-imara wa-l-tawhid wa-da'wat al-ikhwan wa-l-mizan li-hayat al-insan*] (S. al-'Utaybi, *Thawra fi rihab Makka* [Revolution in Mecca] [n.p., n.d.], 247). The work reprinted under the pseudonym of S. al-'Utaybi was attributed to Abu

Dharr, its real author, in its first version. Although Abu Dharr's exact identity is unknown, it seems that he was a member of the Saudi branch of the Baath party because an early version of the same text appeared in 1980 in the magazine *Sawt al-Tali'a*, published in Baghdad. See Abu Dharr, "Ahdath al-haram bayna al-haqa'iq wa-l-abatil" [The Events of the Grand Mosque, between Truth and Lies], *Sawt al-Tali'a* 21 (April 1980). According to Hamza al-Hasan, Abu Dharr's information came from Iraqi intelligence sources in Saudi Arabia. Interview with Hamza al-Hasan.

67. Juhayman al-'Utaybi, *Da'wat al-ikhwan* [The Preaching of the Ikhwan], quoted by al-Qahtani, *Zalzal Juhayman fi Makka*, 28.

68. Interview with Nasir al-Huzaymi.

69. Al-Wadi'i, *Tarjamat*, 27.

70. François Burgat and Muhammad Sbitli, "Les salafis au Yémen ou . . . la modernisation malgré tout," *Chroniques Yéménites* 10 (2002), available online at http://cy.rerues.org/index137.html.

71. Juhayman al-'Utaybi, *Raf' al-iltibas 'an millat man ja'alahu Allah imaman li-l-nas* [Clarification Concerning the Community of the One God Designated as Guide of the People], www.tawhed.ws, 7.

72. See, for example, Juhayman al-'Utaybi, "Awthaq 'ura al-iman: Al-hubb fi-llah wa-l-bughd fi-llah" [The Indissoluble Bonds of Faith: Love in God and Hatred in God], in Ahmad, *Rasa'il Juhayman al-'Utaybi*, 269–290.

73. Ahmad, *Rasa'il Juhayman al-'Utaybi*, 17.

74. Juhayman goes surprisingly far in his rejection of *takfir*, for instance criticizing the Wahhabi religious institution, headed by Ibn Baz, for having excommunicated Tunisian president Habib Bourguiba. Juhayman al-'Utaybi, "Bayan al-shirk wa khatarihi" [Exposing Idolatry and the Danger It Represents], in Ahmad, *Rasa'il Juhayman al-'Utaybi*, 237.

75. The view that the caliph of the Muslims must be from the Quraysh (the tribe of the Prophet Muhammad) was commonplace in medieval juridical literature. It was held by, among others, Abu-l-Hasan al-Mawardi, author of the canonical *The Rules of Government (Al-ahkam al-sultaniyya)* (Beirut: Dar al-Kutub al-'ilmiyya, 1985).

76. Juhayman al-'Utaybi, "Al-imara wa-l-bay'a wa-l-ta'a" [The State, Allegiance, and Obedience], in Ahmad, *Rasa'il Juhayman al-'Utaybi*, 65.

77. The letter *Da'wat al-ikhwan* (also called "the counsel of the Ikhwan," *nasihat al-ikhwan*) is almost entirely devoted to these two questions. See S. al-'Utaybi, *Thawra fi rihab Makka*, 269–271.

78. Juhayman al-'Utaybi, "Al-imara wa-l-bay'a wa-l-ta'a," 87.

79. Interview with Nasir al-Huzaymi.

80. Juhayman al-ʿUtaybi, "Al-fitan wa akhbar al-mahdi wa nuzul ʿisa alayhi al-salam wa ashrat al-saʿa" [*Fitnas*, Traditions of the Mahdi, the Coming of Jesus—Peace Be upon Him—and the Signs of the End of the World], in Ahmad, *Rasaʾil Juhayman al-ʿUtaybi*, 183–225.

81. According to al-Qahtani, his ancestors were Egyptian *ashraf* (plural of *sharif*, descendant of the Prophet) who had come with the army of Muhammad ʿAli in the early nineteenth century and had settled in one of the villages inhabited by the tribe of Qahtan. They had thus become "Qahtanis by alliance," adopting the patronymic of their hosts.

82. Interview with Nasir al-Huzaymi, who learned this from discussions with al-Qahtani.

83. Interview with Nasir al-Huzaymi.

84. The British journalist James Buchan, who was in Saudi Arabia at the time, interviewed a farmer living near Mecca in December 1979. The farmer told him that he "had seen strange-looking young men doing firing practice in his field." Interview with James Buchan.

85. Interview with Nasir al-Huzaymi, who was able to talk in prison to some members of the JSM who had participated in the attack.

86. Interview with Nasir al-Huzaymi.

87. For an excellent account of the siege, see Yaroslav Trofimov, *The Siege of Mecca* (New York: Doubleday, 2007).

88. Interview with Nasir al-Huzaymi.

89. Interviews with Saudi disciples of al-Albani.

90. Interview with Yusuf al-Dayni.

91. On the term "rejectionist," see Stéphane Lacroix and Thomas Hegghammer, "Saudi Arabia Backgrounder: Who Are the Islamists?" International Crisis Group, *Middle East Report* 31 (September 21, 2004).

92. Interview with Yusuf al-Dayni.

93. Interviews with Mishari al-Dhayidi, ʿAbdallah bin Bijad al-ʿUtaybi, and Fahd al-Shafi.

94. Interview with Yusuf al-Dayni.

95. Interviews with Khalid Sultan and Walid al-Tabtabaʾi.

96. Interview with Mishari al-Dhayidi, who went to Pakistan in 1991 for this purpose.

97. Interview with Fahd al-Shafi, a former rejectionist who went to study with Muqbil al-Wadiʿi in 1989.

98. "Nidaʾ al-islam tuhawir al-shaykh al-asir Abu Muhammad al-Maqdisi" [Web Site Nidaʾ al-islam Interviews the Imprisoned Sheikh Abu Muhammad al-Maqdisi], 1997, www.tawhed.ws.

99. Abu Muhammad al-Maqdisi, *Millat Ibrahim wa daʿwat al-anbiyaʾ wa-l-mursalin* [The Community of Abraham and the Preaching of Prophets and Messengers], www.tawhed.ws.

100. Mansur Al-Nuqaydan, "Kharitat al-islamiyyin fi-l-saʿudiyya wa qissat al-takfir" [The Map of Islamist Movements in Saudi Arabia and the History of *Takfir*], *Elaph*, February 27, 2003.

101. Al-Maqdisi praised Juhayman in his books while criticizing him for refusing to excommunicate the rulers. He writes, for example: "Unfortunately, Juhayman thought that rebelling against the rulers no matter what they did . . . was contrary to the sunna. . . . A thousand times unfortunately, he thought that this [Saudi] government was Muslim." Abu Muhammad al-Maqdisi, *Al-kawashif al-jaliyya fi kufr al-dawla al-saʿudiyya* [The Manifest Evidence of the Impiety of the Saudi State], www.tawhed.ws, 198.

102. The book was first published in Peshawar under the pseudonym Abu al-Baraʾ al-ʿUtaybi al-Najdi. By adopting an assumed name connecting himself to the tribe of ʿUtayba and to Najd, al-Maqdisi hoped to make his writings more acceptable to a Saudi public.

103. Interview with a member of Bayt Shubra.

104. Al-Wadiʿi, *Al-makhraj min al-fitna*, 141.

105. Interview with Saʿud al-Sarhan.

106. Interview with Yusuf al-Dayni.

107. Munazzamat al-Madda 19 [Organization of Article 19], *Mamlakat al-samt: Hurriyyat al-taʿbir fi-l-ʿarabiyya al-saʿudiyya* [The Kingdom of Silence: Freedom of Expression in Saudi Arabia], October 1, 1991, www.cdhrap .net.

108. They relied particularly on the book by Hamud al-Tuwayjiri, *Al-qawl al-baligh fi-l-tahdhir min jamaʿat al-tabligh* [*Eloquent Words to Warn against the Tabligh Movement*], 2nd ed. (Riyadh: Dar-al-sumayʿi, 1997). Interview with Saudi Tablighis.

109. Interview with Sulayman al-Dahayyan.

110. Guido Steinberg, *Religion und Staat in Saudi-Arabien: Die wahhabitischen Gelehrten, 1902–1953* (Berlin: Ergon, 2002), 168–185.

111. Ibid., 184.

112. Interview with Mansur al-Nuqaydan, who belonged to the Ikhwan of Burayda from 1985 to 1990.

113. Ibid.

114. Ibid.

115. Ibid.

116. ʿAbdallah al-Duwaysh, *Al-mawrad al-ʿadhb al-zulal fi-l-tanbih ʿala akhtaʾ al-zilal* [The Fountain of Sweet Water to Guard against the Errors of "The Shade"] (Burayda: Dar al-ʿulayan, 1991).

117. Unlike al-Hawali, who earned a doctorate in 1986, al-ʿAwda did not get his until 2005. Despite this, his popularity in Sahwi circles in the late 1980s was considerable.

118. Salman al-ʿAwda, *Al-muslimun bayna al-tashdid wa-l-taysir* (n.p.: n.p., 1985).

119. Interview with a sheikh from Burayda.

120. ʿAbdallah al-Duwaysh, *Al-naqd al-rashid fi-l-radd ʿala muddiʿi al-tashdid*, www.ahlalhdeeth.com.

121. Interview with Sulayman al-Dahayyan.

122. Interview with Mansur al-Nuqaydan.

123. Interview with Sulayman al-Dahayyan.

124. Interview with Mansur al-Nuqaydan.

125. ʿAbdallah bin ʿAbd al-Rahman, *Sirat al-ʿAllama Hamud al-Tuwayjiri* [Biography of the Great Sheikh Hamud al-Tuwayjiri], www.sahab.org.

126. Hamud al-Tuwayjiri, *Tuhfat al-ikhwan bi-ma jaʾ fi-l-muwala wa-l-hubb wa-l-bughd wa-l-hijran*, www.tawhed.ws, 2.

127. Interview with Yusuf al-Dayni.

128. Interview with Fahd al-Shafi.

129. Cited in ʿAbd al-ʿAziz al-Rayyis, *Al-adilla al-sharʿiyya fi hukm al-anashid al-islamiyya* [The Legal Evidence Regarding the Judgment Related to Islamic *Anashid*], http://mypage.ayna.com.

130. Interview with Mansur al-Nuqaydan.

131. Hamud al-Tuwayjiri, *Ithaf al-jamaʿa bi-ma jaʾ fi-l-fitan wa-l-malahim wa ashrat al-saʿa*, www.saaid.net.

132. Interview with Nasir al-Huzaymi.

133. Ahmad, *Rasaʾil Juhayman al-ʿUtaybi*, 39.

134. Interview with Sahwis who were active at the time.

135. Thomas Hegghammer, "Abdallah Azzam: The Imam of Jihad," in *Al-Qaeda in Its Own Words*, ed. Gilles Kepel and Jean-Pierre Milelli (Cambridge, Mass.: Belknap Press of Harvard University Press, 2008), 91–92.

136. Basil Muhammad, *Safahat min sijill al-ansar al-ʿarab fi Afghanistan* [Pages from the Saga of the Arab *Ansar* in Afghanistan] (Riyadh: Sharikat dar al-ʿilm li-l-tibaʿa wa-l-nashr, 1991), 65. *Join the Caravan!* [*Ilhaq bi-l-qafila!*] is the title of a later work by ʿAbdallah ʿAzzam. See Kepel and Milelli, *Al-Qaeda in Its Own Words*, 110–125.

137. For an English translation of this work, see Kepel and Milelli, *Al-Qaeda in Its Own Words*, 102–109.

138. Muhammad, *Safahat min sijill*, 88.

139. Kepel and Milelli, *Al-Qaeda in Its Own Words*, 102

140. See, for example, *Al-Mujahid* 10 (September 1989 [safar 1410]).

141. Safar al-Hawali, "Mafhum al-jihad" [The Notion of Jihad], recorded speech.

142. Bernard Rougier, *Everyday Jihad*, trans. Pascale Ghazaleh (Cambridge, Mass.: Harvard University Press, 2007), 84.

143. Mansoor Alshamsi, "The Discourse and Performance of the Saudi Sunni Islamic Reformist Leadership (1981–2003)" (Ph.D. diss., University of Exeter, 2003), 137.

144. Al-Hawali, "Mafhum al-jihad."

145. ʿAbd al-Qadir bin ʿAbd al-ʿAziz, *Radd kalam al-Hawali fi kitab al-difaʿ ʿan aradi al-muslimin* [Refutation of What al-Hawali Has Said on the Book *The Defense of Muslim Territories*], www.tawhed.ws.

146. Muhammad al-ʿAwadi, "Safar al-Hawali—Namudhaj li-l-waʿi al-mubakkir" [Safar al-Hawali, Model of Precocious Awareness], *Al-Raʾy al-ʿAmm* (Kuwait), June 14, 2005.

147. Mamoun Fandy, "Safar al-Hawali: Saudi Islamist or Saudi Nationalist?" *Islam and Christian-Muslim Relations* 9, 1 (1998): 5–21.

148. He was probably thinking primarily of Communist South Yemen, but the term is obviously ambiguous.

149. Al-Hawali, "Mafhum al-jihad."

150. Interview with Sulayman al-Dahayyan.

151. Muhammad, *Safahat min sijill*, 99.

152. Ibid., 63; interview with Jamal Khashogji; Lawrence Wright, *The Looming Tower: Al-Qaeda and the Road to 9/11* (New York, Knopf, 2006), 78. Steve Coll suggests that he became a member of the *jamaʿa* in 1971 or 1972 and did not leave it until the mid-1980s, when he joined up with ʿAzzam. Steve Coll, "Young Osama," *New Yorker*, December 12, 2005.

153. Muhammad, *Safahat min sijill*, 111.

154. Ibid., 88.

155. Ibid., 200.

156. On the dominance of natives of the Hejaz among the first jihadis, see Thomas Hegghammer, *Jihad in Saudi Arabia* (Cambridge: Cambridge University Press, 2010), chap. 3.

157. "Musa al-Qarni: Harradtu al-afghan al-ʿarab" [Musa al-Qarni: I Incited the Afghan Arabs], *Al-Hayat*, March 8, 9, and 10, 2006.

158. ʿAbd al-Rahman al-Surayhi, who joined the jihadis in 1984, was in charge of recruitment in Jeddah ("Tawbat ahad al-afghan al-ʿarab" [The Repentance of One of the Afghan Arabs], www.sahab.net). Tamim al-ʿAdnani was sent to the east (Al-Jihad 50 [December 1988–January 1989]: 33). Bin Laden recruited in Medina. A man named Abu Hanifa was in charge of recruitment in Taif (Al-Jihad 53 [March–April 1989]: 36).

159. "Dhikrayat mujahid wa iʿtirafat insan, al-haqiqa min al-alif ila-l-ya'" [Memories of a Mujahid, and Confessions of a Man, the Truth from A to Z], www.wasatyah.com.

160. Osama bin Laden, "Ahwal al-jihad" [The Situation of the Jihad], recorded speech, www.al-hesbah.org.

161. "Dhikrayat mujahid wa iʿtirafat insan, al-haqiqa min al-alif ila-l-ya'."

162. Ibid.

163. Interview with Saʿd al-Faqih, who at that time occupied a senior position in the Brothers of Zubayr.

164. Interviews with Saudi Brothers.

165. "Musa al-Qarni: Harradtu al-afghan al-ʿarab." Al-Qarni was appointed to this position in 1980.

166. This conclusion is derived from the analysis of a sample of forty-five jihadi "martyrs" who fought in Afghanistan in the 1980s. For details, see Stéphane Lacroix, "Les Champs de la discorde: Une sociologie politique de l'islamisme en Arabie Saoudite" (Ph.D. diss., Sciences Po, 2007), 301–302. For a much more exhaustive study, see also Thomas Hegghammer, "The Power and Perils of Pan-Islamic Nationalism: Violent Islamism in Saudi Arabia (1971–2006)" (Ph.D. diss., Sciences Po, 2007), 183–184.

167. Peter L. Bergen, The Osama bin Laden I Know (New York: Free Press, 2006), 80–81.

168. A relatively reliable estimate of the number of individuals meeting these criteria, and by extension the size of the jihadi network, is ten thousand. Jamal Khashogji, quoted ibid., 41. Another observer of the Afghan jihad, ʿAli al-Namla, estimates their number at twenty thousand. ʿAli al-Namla, Al-jihad wa-l-mujahidun fi Afghanistan [The Jihad and the Mujahideen in Afghanistan] (Riyadh: Maktabat ʿUbaykan, 1994), 118.

169. Gilles Kepel, Jihad: The Trail of Political Islam, trans. Anthony F. Roberts (Cambridge, Mass.: Harvard University Press, 2003), 147.

170. Ibid., 137.

171. This is suggested, among other sources, by Wright, Looming Tower, 144.

172. Mishari al-Dhayidi, "Falastini nasha' fi-l-kuwait . . ." [A Palestinian Raised in Kuwait . . .], Al-Sharq al-Awsat, July 7, 2005.

173. Al-Maqdisi, *Al-kawashif al-jaliyya.*

174. Mishari al-Dhayidi, "Matbakh bishawar wa tabkhat gharnata" [The Kitchen of Peshawar and the Dish of Gharnata], *Al-Sharq al-Awsat,* May 14, 2003.

175. See, for example, "Abu al-Lujari: Al-mukhabarat al-saʿudiyya qatalat ʿAzzam wa-l-mujahidun thabbatu al-dawla wa aqamu nal-nidham" [Abu al-Lujari: The Saudi Secret Services Killed ʿAzzam, and the Mujahideen Strengthened the State and Imposed Order], *Al-Wasat* (Yemen), March 15, 2006.

176. "Fadilat al-shaykh Jamil al-Rahman fi liqaʾ maʿ al-mujahid" [The Noble Sheikh Jamil al-Rahman in an Interview with *Al-Mujahid*], *Al-Mujahid* 5–6 (April–May 1989), 18.

177. "Jamaʿat ahl al-hadith" [The Ahl-e Hadith Movement], www.saaid.net.

178. "Fadilat al-shaykh Jamil al-Rahman fi liqaʾ maʿ al-mujahid."

179. Musa al-Qarni, "Haqaʾiq ʿan al-jihad" [Facts about the Jihad], recorded lecture.

180. Muqbil al-Wadiʿi, *Al-suyuf al-batira li-ilhad al-shuyuʿiyya al-kafira* [The Sharp Swords for the Atheism of Impious Communism] (n.p: n.d.), 71.

181. Al-Albani even recorded a cassette devoted to Jamil al-Rahman titled "A Word of Truth about Sheikh Jamil al-Rahman" ["Kalimat haqq fi-l-shaykh Jamil al-Rahman"].

182. Al-Madkhali published several articles in Jamil al-Rahman's magazine *Al-Mujahid.* See Rabiʿ al-Madkhali, "Al-difaʿ ʿan al-sunna wa ahliha" [Defense of the Sunna and the Sunnis], *Al-Mujahid* 9, 10, and 11 (August, September, and October 1989).

183. Muqbil al-Wadiʿi devoted a whole section of his book *The Sharp Swords for the Atheism of Impious Communism* to Jamil al-Rahman's organization. He described it as the only legitimate representative of jihad in Afghanistan. Al-Wadiʿi, *Al-suyuf al-batira,* 71–82.

184. Rougier, *Everyday Jihad,* 79.

185. Al-Dhayidi, "Matbakh bishawar wa tabkhat gharnata."

186. Interview with Mishari al-Zaydi, who went to join Jamil al-Rahman in 1991.

187. *Al-Mujahid* 22 (September 1990): 30.

188. Five thousand copies (out of a total of between ten thousand and fifty thousand) were sent to Saudi Arabia every month. Ahmad Muaffaq Zaydan, *The Afghan Arabs: Media at Jihad* (Islamabad: PFI, 1999), 85.

189. Muqbil al-Wadiʿi, *Maqtal al-shaykh Jamil al-Rahman al-Afghani rahamahu Allah* [The Assassination of the Afghan Sheikh Jamil al-Rahman—May God Be Merciful to Him], www.muqbel.net.

190. Interview with Mansur al-Nuqaydan.

191. As Mordechai Abir has shown, development, particularly with regard to education, in the 1970s benefited primarily city residents. The third five-year plan (1980–1985) had as its principal goal remedying these inequalities, but Abir points out that the recession of the 1980s meant that this goal could not be reached. Mordechai Abir, *Saudi Arabia: Government, Society, and the Gulf Crisis* (London: Routledge, 1993), 95. On this point, see also Ali a. al-Sultan, "Social Class and University Enrollment in Saudi Arabia" (M.A. thesis, Michigan State University, 1979), 52.

192. Interview with Sulayman al-Dahayyan.

193. To mention only a few examples, Salman al-ʿAwda and Nasir al-ʿUmar are from Banu Khalid; ʿAʾid al-Qarni and ʿAwad al-Qarni are from Balqarn; Safar al-Hawali is from Ghamid; and Abd al-Wahhab al-Turayri is from ʿAnaza.

194. The kingdom had more than 2 million students in its primary and secondary schools in 1986. There had been only a little more than 400,000 in 1970. In universities, 15,301 Saudis received degrees in 1986, whereas only 808 had in 1970. Fouad al-Farsy, *Modernity and Tradition: The Saudi Equation* (London: Kegan Paul International, 1990), 256.

4. A SACRIFICED GENERATION

1. An example was Hamad al-Sulayfih, who was even for a time an attaché at the Saudi embassy in Teheran.

2. The remaining minor differences between the two *jamaʿat* concerned neither personal appearance nor ideology but certain aspects of behavior. According to ʿAli, a member of the Saudi Muslim Brotherhood in the 1980s: "Some of us smoked in secret. When our supervisor [*mushrif*] learned of this, he made a remark, but nothing more. The *salafiyyun* [Sururis] were much harsher; for them smoking meant immediate exclusion!"

3. Muhammad al-Ghazzali, *Al-sunna al-nabawiyya bayna ahl al-fiqh wa ahl al-hadith* (Cairo: Dar al-shuruq, 2005).

4. Salman al-ʿAwda, *Hiwar hadiʾ maʿ al-shaykh al-Ghazzali,* 1989, www.islamway.com.

5. Saʿid Hawwa, *Tarbiyatuna al-ruhiyya* (Beirut: Dar al-kutub al-ʿarabiyya, 1979).

6. Interview with Muhanna al-Hubayyil.

7. Interview with Usama al-Ghamidi.

8. Interview with a former Sururi.

9. "Gamal Sultan ʿarrab fikr al-sahwa al-saʿudiyya li-l-sharq al-awsat" [Gamal Sultan, the Godfather of Saudi Sahwi Thought, in an interview with *Al-Sharq al-Awsat*], *Al-Sharq al-Awsat*, May 5, 2004.

10. A young Brother who chose to remain anonymous told an anecdote illustrating this: "In the technical faculty [*kulliyat al-taqniyya*] of Riyadh, there was a group of people belonging to the Brothers of al-Funaysan who organized the faculty's summer camp every year. One day a Sururi was appointed head of student activities at the Institution of Technical Education [*Muʾassasat al-taʿlim al-fanni*, which supervised the technical faculties in the kingdom]. He dismissed the group that had until then organized the summer camp and replaced it with people from his *jamaʿa*."

11. "Mishari al-Dhayidi . . . wa rihlat al-tahawwulat al-fikriyya (hiwar maʿ jasad al-thaqafa)" [Mishari al-Dhayidi . . . and the Journey of Intellectual Changes (Dialogue with the Jasad al-thaqafa Forum)], August 2003, www .jsad.net.

12. Interview with Sulayman al-Dahayyan.

13. Interviews with ʿAli, a former Brother, and Muhammad, a former Sururi.

14. Interview with Yusuf al-Dayni.

15. Interview with Sulayman al-Dahayyan.

16. Interview with a former Sururi. An embryonic form of what became al-Haramayn saw the light of day in Pakistan in 1988, but it was not until 1992 that the organization took on its final form and established its headquarters in Riyadh.

17. *Al-Hayat*, July 10, 2004.

18. Mordechai Abir, *Saudi Arabia in the Oil Era: Regime and Elites; Conflict and Collaboration* (London: Croom Helm, 1988), 179.

19. Mordechai Abir, *Saudi Arabia: Government, Society, and the Gulf Crisis* (London: Routledge, 1993), 99.

20. Ibid., 100; Madawi Al-Rasheed, *A History of Saudi Arabia* (New York: Cambridge University Press, 2002), 149.

21. Starting in 1981, more than two thousand Saudis annually returned with degrees from foreign universities, the majority of them American. Fouad al-Farsy, *Modernity and Tradition: The Saudi Equation* (London: Kegan Paul International, 1990), 257.

22. Al-Rasheed, *History of Saudi Arabia*, 153.

23. Abir, *Saudi Arabia in the Oil Era*, 181–182.

24. The annual increase in the number of public employees declined in the course of the 1980s until in 1988, for the first time, their number stag-

nated. See Alexei Vassiliev, *The History of Saudi Arabia* (London: Saqi, 2000), 455.

25. Steffen Hertog, "Segmented Clientelism: The Politics of Economic Reform in Saudi Arabia" (Ph.D. diss., Oxford University, 2006), 150.

26. Ibid., 152.

27. Ibid., 149.

28. Walid al-Tuwayriqi, Muhammad Saʿid al-Qahtani, and Saʿid bin Zuʿayr, *Al-ʿilmaniyya fi-l-ʿira'—Al-Qusaybi shaʿir al-ams wa waʿiz al-yawm* [Secularism Exposed: Al-Qusaybi, Poet Yesterday and Preacher Today] (Chicago: Dar al-kitab, 1991), quoted in *Al-Jazira al-ʿArabiyya* 6 (July 1991): 41.

29. Interview with an anonymous Sahwi.

30. See, for example, Muhammad Qutb, *Al-ʿilmaniyyun wa-l-islam* [The Secularists and Islam], new ed. (Cairo: Dar al-shuruq, 1995).

31. Safar al-Hawali, *Al-ʿilmaniyya: Nash'atuha was tatawwuruha wa atharuha fi-l-haya al-islamiyya al-muʿasira* [Secularism: Its Creation, Development, and Influence on Contemporary Islamic Life], www.alhawali.com.

32. Interviews with Sahwi intellectuals.

33. Interview with Sahwi activists.

34. Document reprinted as an appendix to Ghazi al-Qusaybi, *Hatta la takun fitna* [Until There Is No More *Fitna*] (n.p.: n.p., 1991), 174.

35. "Laysat hayat al-muslimin al-mutamassikin bi-sharʿ Allah haya la insaniyya" [The Life of Muslims Attached to the Law of God Is Not an Inhuman Life], *Al-Mujtamaʿ* 456 (October 23, 1979).

36. *Newsweek*, April 17, 1978.

37. Interview with Sahwis active during this period.

38. Interview with a Sahwi university professor, who taught at the Institute of Public Administration.

39. "Saʿudi wajah al-sahawiyyin wa uttuhim bi-idarat maʿhad masuni" [A Saudi Who Confronted the Sahwis and Was Accused of Heading a Masonic Institute], *Elaph*, December 28, 2005.

40. ʿAbdallah al-Ghadhdhami, *ʿUkadh*, October 15, 1986.

41. ʿAli al-Dumayni, *Al-hadatha al-shiʿriyya fi-l-mamlaka al-ʿarabiyya al-saʿudiyya—tajruba shakhsiyya* [Poetic Modernism in the Kingdom of Saudi Arabia—A Personal Experience], www.arabrenewal.com.

42. ʿAbdallah al-Ghadhdhami, *Al-khati'a wa-l-takfir*, 1985, photocopy in the author's possession.

43. Interview with ʿAbdallah al-Ghadhdhami.

44. Interview with Husayn Bafaqih.

45. Interview with Saʿid al-Surayhi.

46. Saʿid al-Surayhi, *Shiʿr Abi Tammam bayna al-naqd al-qadim wa-ruʾyat al-naqd al-jadid.* (Jeddah: Al-nadi al-adabi al-thaqafi, 1983). Abu Tammam was a poet of the first half of the ninth century known for the innovative quality of his work in both form and content.

47. Husayn Bafaqih, *Itlala ʿala-l-mashhad al-thaqafi fi-l-mamlaka al-ʿarabiyya al-saʿudiyya* [Sketch of the Intellectual Scene in the Kingdom of Saudi Arabia] (Riyadh: Al-majalla al-ʿarabiyya, 2005), 26.

48. "Asmaʾ wa maʿlumat" [Names and News], www.adabislami.org.

49. Interview with ʿAbdallah al-Ghadhdhami.

50. Interview with a Sahwi intellectual.

51. Najm ʿAbd al-Karim, "Al-Tuwayjiri shabab fi-l-thamanin" [Al-Tuwayjiri, a Young Octogenarian], *Elaph,* December 20, 2004.

52. *Mawsuʿat al-adab al-ʿarabi al-saʿudi al-hadith: Nusus mukhtara wa dirasat* [Encyclopedia of Modern Saudi Literature: Selected Works and Studies] (Riyadh: Dar al-mufradat, 2001), 1:182.

53. Interview with ʿAli al-ʿUmaym, who covered the festival as a reporter.

54. Ibid.

55. Interview with Muhammad al-Masʿari.

56. Interview with Saʿid al-Surayhi.

57. Interview with Husayn Bafaqih.

58. ʿAbdallah al-Ghadhdhami, *Hikayat al-hadatha fi-l-mamlaka al-ʿarabiyya al-saʿudiyya* [The History of Modernism in the Kingdom of Saudi Arabia] (Beirut: Al-markaz al-thaqafi al-ʿarabi, 2004), 213.

59. Ibid., 210. Al-Milibari died in August 1991.

60. Ibid., 207.

61. *Al-Nadwa,* April 29, 1987.

62. Al-Ghadhdhami, *Hikayat al-hadatha,* 207.

63. Ibid., 213.

64. Ibid., 237–278.

65. Interview with ʿAbdallah al-Ghadhdhami. ʿAbd al-Shaytan means "worshipper of the devil" and is a pun on the name ʿAbdallah, literally "worshipper of God."

66. Ibid.

67. Interview with Saʿd al-Faqih.

68. According to al-Ghadhdhami, every young Sahwi bought dozens of copies to distribute. Al-Ghadhdhami, *Hikayat al-hadatha,* 242. According to the modernist literary critic Uthman al-Sini, the first printing of thirty

thousand copies was sold out in a few days. Interview with ʿUthman al-Sini.

69. ʿAwad al-Qarni, *Al-hadatha fi mizan al-islam*, new ed. (Jeddah: Dar al-andalus al-khudraʿ, 2002), 137–155.

70. Ibid., 20.

71. Interview with ʿAwad al-Qarni.

72. Al-Qarni, *Al-hadatha fi mizan al-islam*, 15.

73. Interview with ʿAbdallah al-Ghadhdhami, who devotes the first chapter of his *History of Modernism* to demonstrating the connection.

74. Interview with Saʿd al-Faqih.

75. ʿAli-al-ʿUmaym, "Mashayikhuna wa mashayikh al-sahwa—Nadharat fi-l-islam al-saʿudi al-haraki" [Our Sheikhs and the Sheikhs of the Sahwa—Perspectives on Saudi Islamism], *Elaph*, June 12, 2003.

76. Ibid.

77. Interview with Fahd al-Shafi.

78. For these terms, see Malika Zeghal, *Gardiens de l'Islam: Les oulémas d'al-Azhar dans l'Égypte contemporaine* (Paris: Presses de Sciences Po, 1996), 31.

79. Salman al-ʿAwda, "Al-sharit al-islami—Ma lahu wa ma ʿalayhi" [The Islamic Cassette—Its Advantages and Disadvantages], recorded lecture, December 19, 1990.

80. Interview with Mansur al-Nuqaydan.

81. Gilles Kepel, *Muslim Extremism in Egypt: The Prophet and Pharaoh*, trans. Jon Rothschild (Berkeley: University of California Press, 2003), 173.

82. On the radio program *Safahat min hayati* ["Pages from My Life"], *Qanat al-majd* [Al-Majd TV] July 9 and 16, 2004.

83. ʿAli al-ʿUmaym, "Kishk al-Khalij," *Al-Majalla*, October 28, 2000.

84. *Qanat al-majd*, July 9 and 16, 2004.

85. Ibn Qayyim al-Jawziyya, *Iʿlam al-muwaqqiʿin* [Informing the Signatories], quoted in Nasir al-ʿUmar, "Fiqh al-waqiʿ," www.almoslim.net, 20.

86. Al-ʿUmar, "Fiqh al-waqiʿ," 6.

87. Ibid., 16.

88. Ibid., 36.

89. Miles Copeland, *The Game of Nations* (New York: Simon and Schuster, 1969). In this book Copeland, a former Central Intelligence Agency (CIA) agent, analyzes American policy toward Egypt in the 1950s and 1960s and the role played by the CIA.

90. Al-ʿUmar, "Fiqh al-waqiʿ," 37.

91. Muhammad Qutb, *Waqiʿuna al-muʿasir,* www.tawhed.ws.

92. In this book al-ʿAbda compares the contemporary period with various stages in the history of Islam to determine the strategy Islamists should follow. Considering Saladin's victories, he concludes that they were the result of the decades of education in jihad that preceded them, and he argues that the same method should be applied today. Muhammad al-ʿAbda, *Ayuʿid al-taʾrikh nafsahu?—Dirasa li-ahwal al-ʿalam al-islami qabla Salah al-Din—Muqarana maʿ taʾrikhina al-muʿasir* [Does History Repeat Itself? A Study of the State of the Islamic World before Saladin, in Comparison with Our Current History], 2nd ed. (London and Riyadh: Al-muntada al-islami, 1999).

93. Al-ʿUmar, "Fiqh al-waqiʿ," 38.

94. ʿAbdallah al-Gharib [pseudonym of Muhammad Surur Zayn al-ʿAbidin], *Wa jaʾ dawr al-majus,* www.almeshkat.net.

95. Al-ʿUmar, "Fiqh al-waqiʿ," 16.

96. Ibid., 20.

97. Ibid., 24.

98. Salman al-ʿAwda, "Maʾkhadh ʿala talabat al-ʿilm" [A Reproach to Students of Religion], recorded lecture.

99. Interview with Yusuf al-Dayni.

100. Salman al-ʿAwda, *Al-ighraq fi-l-juzʾiyyat* (Riyadh: Maktabat al-rushd, 2003).

101. "Murdjiʾa," in *Encyclopédie de l'Islam* (Leiden: Brill, 1954–2004): 605–607.

102. Gilles Kepel, *The War for Muslim Minds: Islam and the West,* trans. Pascale Ghazaleh (Cambridge, Mass.: Belknap Press of Harvard University Press, 2004), 182–183.

103. Safar al-Hawali, *Dhahirat al-irjaʾ fi-l-fikr al-islami,* www.alhawali. com, 1:3–4.

104. Interviews with Yusuf al-Dayni, Tariq al-Mubarak, and Ibrahim al-Sikran.

105. Huwaydi is mentioned in a footnote. Al-Hawali, *Dhahirat al-irjaʾ fi-l-fikr al-islami,* 1:30 n. 7.

106. Ibid., 2:146–148.

107. Ahmad al-Tahawi (853–935) is one of the few ulema before Ibn Abd al-Wahhab and Ibn Tamiyya whose conception of creed is recognized as orthodox by the Wahhabis.

108. Muhammad bin Ibrahim Al al-Shaykh, *Risala fi tahkim al-qawanin al-wadʿiyya,* www.tawhed.ws.

109. Interview with Yusuf al-Dayni, who attended all the lectures.

110. Mansoor Alshamsi, "The Discourse and Performance of the Saudi Sunni Islamic Reformist Leadership (1981–2003)" (Ph.D. diss., University of Exeter, 2003), 61.

111. Interview with Yusuf al-Dayni.

5. THE LOGIC OF THE INSURRECTION

1. On the ambiguity of the Saudi position, see Sonoko Sunayama, *Syria and Saudi Arabia: Collaboration and Conflicts in the Oil Era* (London: I. B. Tauris, 2007), 92–94.

2. ʿAli-al-ʿUmaym, "Mashayikhuna wa mashayikh al-sahwa—Nadharat fi-l-islam al-saʿudi al-haraki" [Our Sheikhs and the Sheikhs of the Sahwa—Perspectives on Saudi Islamism], *Elaph*, June 12, 2003.

3. Jonathan Randal, *Osama: The Making of a Terrorist* (New York: Vintage, 2005), 65–66.

4. Interview with Muhammad al-Masʿari.

5. From the long autobiography of Muhammad al-Masʿari on his Web site, www.tajdeed.net.

6. Interview with an anonymous Brother.

7. Nasir al-ʿUmar, "Fiqh al-waqiʿ," www.almoslim.net, 9.

8. As Muhammad Surur explained in the preface to *The Situation of the Sunnis in Iran* [*Ahwal ahl al-sunna fi Iran*], available on his recently created Web site, www.surour.net.

9. Interview with ʿAbd al-ʿAziz al-Wuhaybi.

10. Interview with Ibrahim al-Sikran.

11. Interview with Muhammad al-Masʿari.

12. This pseudonym is derived from the name of his first son, Muʿadh, and the name of his tribe, Banu Khalid.

13. Interview with Muhammad al-Hudayf. Articles by him were published in issues 3, 5, 9, 11, 12, 13, and 14 of *Al-Sunna*.

14. Interview with Kassab al-ʿUtaybi.

15. Mentioned in Abu Muhammad al-Maqdisi, *Al-kawashif al-jaliyya fi kufr al-dawla al-saʿudiyya* [The Manifest Evidence of the Impiety of the Saudi State], www.tawhed.ws, 163.

16. Munazzamat al-Madda 19 [Organization of Article 19], *Mamlakat al-samt: Hurriyyat al-taʿbir fi-l-ʿarabiyya al-saʿudiyya* [The Kingdom of Silence: Freedom of Expression in Saudi Arabia], October 1, 1991, www.cdhrap.net.

17. Al-Maqdisi, *Al-kawashif al-jaliyya*, 157 n. 94.

18. Munazzamat al-Madda 19, *Mamlakat al-samt.*

19. Interview with Saʿid al-Surayhi.

20. ʿAwad al-Qarni, *Al-hadatha fi mizan al-islam,* new ed. (Jeddah: Dar al-andalus al-khudraʾ, 2002), 6–7.

21. Interview with ʿUthman al-Sini.

22. Munazzamat al-Madda 19, *Mamlakat al-samt.*

23. Shakir al-Nablusi, *Nabat al-samt: Dirasa fi-l-shiʿr al-saʿudi al-muʿasir* [The Buds of Silence: A Study of Contemporary Saudi Poetry] (Beirut: Al-ʿasr al-hadith li-l-nashr wa-l-tawziʿ, 1992), 58 n. 14.

24. For example, ʿAbdallah al-Sikhan and Muhammad al-Harbi were forced to resign from *Al-Yamama.* Interview with ʿUthman al-Sini.

25. See, for example, *Iqraʾ* 691 (November 11, 1988), 699 (January 6, 1989), 702 (January 27, 1989), and 726 (July 13, 1989).

26. *Iqraʾ* 710 (March 24, 1989), 711 (March 31, 1989), 712 (April 16, 1989), 713 (April 13, 1989), and 714 (April 20, 1989).

27. Interviews with ʿAbdallah al-Ghadhdhami and Saʿid al-Surayhi.

28. "Al-nadi al-adabi bi-l-Riyad—al-nashatat" [The Literary Club of Riyadh—Activities], www.adabi.org.sa.

29. See, for example, *Iqraʾ* 712 (June 6, 1989).

30. Najm ʿAbd al-Karim, "Al-Tuwayjiri shabab fi-l-thamanin" [Al-Tuwayjiri, a Young Octogenarian], *Elaph,* December 20, 2004.

31. Daud al-Shiryan, "Al-hiwar sa-yanjah . . ." [Dialogue Will Succeed . . .], *Al-Hayat,* March 8, 2006.

32. Interviews with ʿAli al-ʿUmaym and Muhammad al-Masʿari.

33. *Iqraʾ* 711 (March 31, 1989).

34. Interview with ʿAli al-ʿUmaym.

35. "Qiraʾa thaqafiyya fi taʾrikh dawrat al-janadriyya" [A Cultural Perspective on the History of the Sessions of Janadriyya], *Al-Taqwa* 131 (December 2003).

36. Mordechai Abir, *Saudi Arabia: Government, Society, and the Gulf Crisis* (London: Routledge, 1993), 174.

37. The United States did not withdraw its armed forces from Saudi Arabia until after the overthrow of Saddam Hussein in the spring of 2003.

38. Notably R. Hrair Dekmejian, *Islam in Revolution: Fundamentalism in the Arab World,* 2nd ed. (Syracuse, N.Y.: Syracuse University Press, 1995), 142.

39. Michel Dobry, *Sociologie des crises politiques: La dynamique des mobilisations multisectorielles* (Paris: Presses de la FNSP, 1986), 279.

40. *Umm al-Qura* 3319 (August 18, 1990).

41. *Arab News* 15; 261 (August 15, 1990).

42. Ghazi al-Qusaybi, *Hatta la takun fitna* [Until There Is No More *Fitna*] (n.p.: n.p., 1991), 119.

43. Mishari al-Dhayidi, "Ma bayn al-Qusaybi wa-l-Turabi: Al-ʿasifa tuhibb marratayn" [Between al-Qusaybi and al-Turabi: The Storm Breaks Out Twice], *Al-Sharq al-Awsat,* March 28, 2006.

44. Safar al-Hawali, "Fasatatadhakkarun ma aqul lakum" [You Will Remember What I Tell You], recorded speech, August 19, 1990.

45. Safar al-Hawali, *Kashf al-ghumma ʿan ʿulamaʾ al-umma* [Leading the Ulema of the *Umma* out of Confusion] (London: Dar al-hikma, 1991), 138.

46. Ibn Baz had written: "If there was a higher interest in making an alliance with infidels, Arab or not, or in calling on their help, then God would have authorized it and allowed his creatures to do so. But since God knows the considerable evils and the disastrous consequences that would bring about, he has forbidden it and condemned anyone who indulges in it." ʿAbd al-ʿAziz bin Baz, *Naqd al-qawmiyya al-ʿarabiyya ʿala dawʾ al-islam wa-l-waqiʿ* [Critique of Arab Nationalism in the Light of Islam and Reality] (Beirut: Al-maktab al-islami, 1988), 43.

47. Interviews with former Sahwis.

48. Nasir al-ʿUmar, "Al-sakina . . . al-sakina" [Tranquility . . . Tranquility], recorded lecture.

49. Ghazi al-Qusaybi, "Taghayyur al-fatwa" [The Evolution of Fatwas], *Al-Sharq al-Awsat,* January 18, 1991.

50. Al-ʿUmar, "Al-sakina . . . al-sakina."

51. ʿAʾid al-Qarni, "Siham fi ʿayn al-ʿasifa," recorded speech.

52. Salman al-ʿAwda, "Al-sharit al-islami—Ma lahu wa ma ʿalayhi" [The Islamic Cassette—Its Advantages and Disadvantages], recorded lecture, December 19, 1990; al-ʿUmar, "Al-sakina . . . al-sakina."

53. "Fight them until there is no more dissension [*fitna*] and religion is all for Allah. But if they cease, then lo! Allah is Seer of what they do" (Koran, 8:39).

54. Al-Qusaybi, *Hatta la takun fitna,* 151, 159, 193.

55. See *Al-Sharq al-Awsat,* February 18, 1991.

56. Al-Qusaybi, *Hatta la takun fitna,* especially 125.

57. Walid al-Tuwayriqi, Muhammad Saʿid al-Qahtani, and Saʿid bin Zuʿayr, *Al-ʿilmaniyya fi-l-ʿiraʾ—Al-Qusaybi shaʿir al-ams wa waʿiz al-yawm* (Chicago: Dar al-kitab, 1991).

58. Safar al-Hawali, "Al-mumtaz fi sharh bayan Ibn Baz" [The Excellent in the Explanation of the Communiqué from Ibn Baz], recorded sermon.

59. The first edition was published in Bahrain in early 1991, the second in London in mid-1991.

60. Salman al-ʿAwda, "Hasad al-ghayba" [The Fruit of Absence], recorded speech, October 10, 1992.

61. ʿAbd al-Amir Musa, "Hawla kitab hatta la takun fitna" [Concerning the Book *Until There Is No More Fitna*], *Al-Jazira al-ʿArabiyya* 5 (June 1991): 16–20.

62. Interview with Fawziyya al-Bakr, one of the organizers of the demonstration.

63. Indeed, several of those women were married to prominent liberal figures, as their Sahwi opponents were quick to point out. A leaflet distributed shortly after the incident by young Sahwi militants contained the names of the husbands of some of the participants. Leaflet in the author's possession.

64. Interview with the liberal Ahmad al-Hanaki.

65. Interview with Saʿd al-Faqih.

66. Al-ʿUmar, "Al-sakina . . . al-sakina."

67. Interview with Fawziyya al-Bakr.

68. According to a Sahwi leaflet distributed the day after the incident and presented as the "report of a member of the Committee for Commanding Right and Forbidding Wrong," published in *Al-Jazira al-Arabiyya* 2 (February 1991): 32.

69. "Hal kan al-amir Salman waraʾ al-mudhahara al-nisaʾiyya?" [Was Prince Salman behind the Women's Demonstration?], *Al-Jazira al-ʿArabiyya* 1 (January 1991): 17.

70. Interview with Saʿd al-Faqih.

71. *Al-Daʿwa*, November 23, 1990.

72. Salman al-ʿAwda, "Asbab suqut al-duwal," recorded lecture, August 28, 1990.

73. Al-Hawali, *Kashf al-ghumma ʿan ʿulamaʾ al-umma*, 138.

74. Al-Hawali, "Fasatatadhakkarun ma aqul lakum."

75. Mamoun Fandy, *Saudi Arabia and the Politics of Dissent* (Basingstoke: Macmillan, 1999), 68, 72. Muhammad Qasim Zaman makes a similar point. See Zaman, *The Ulama in Contemporary Islam,* 158.

76. Interview with Salman al-ʿAwda.

77. Interview with ʿAbd al-ʿAziz al-Qasim.

78. Mansoor Alshamsi, "The Discourse and Performance of the Saudi Sunni Islamic Reformist Leadership (1981–2003)" (Ph.D. diss., University of Exeter, 2003), 157.

79. Quoted in Nasir al-ʿUmar, "Al-dars al-akhir min durus fiqh al-daʿwa" [The Last Lecture of the Courses on the *Fiqh* of Daʿwa], recorded lecture, 1992.

80. Quoted in Salman al-ʿAwda, "Adab al-hiwar" [The Rules of Dialogue], recorded lecture, 1991.

81. Reprinted in *Al-Sunna* 45 (February 1995).

82. *Al-Jazira al-ʿArabiyya* 31 (August 1993): 9.

83. Alshamsi, "Discourse and Performance of the Saudi Sunni Islamic Reformist Leadership," 217.

84. *Al-Daʿwa,* June 30, 1994.

85. Interview with a Sahwi sheikh.

86. "Hifl musabaqat al-sunna" [The Celebration of the Sunna Competition], recorded lecture.

87. Al-ʿAwda, "Hasad al-ghayba."

88. Ibid.

89. Mohammed Nabil Mouline, "ʿUlama al-Sultan: Parcours et évolution dans le champ politico-religieux des membres du comité des grands oulémas (1971–2005)," mémoire de DEA en Science Politique (Paris: Sciences Po, 2005), 42.

90. ʿAbd al-Rahman al-Harfi, *Al-sira al-dhatiyya li-samahat al-shaykh Hamud al-ʿUqla al-Shuʿaybi* [The Biography of His Eminence Sheikh Hamud al-ʿUqla al-Shuʿaybi], www.saaid.net; ʿAbd al-Rahman al-Jafan, *Inas al-nubalaʾ fi sirat shaykhina al-ʿUqla* [The Company of Nobles in the Biography of Our Sheikh Hamud al-ʿUqla], www.saaid.net.

91. Interview with Saʿud al-Sarhan.

92. See the biography of Abdallah bin Jibrin at www.ibn-jebreen.com.

93. Mouline, "ʿUlama al-Sultan," 24 n. 49.

94. Fandy, *Saudi Arabia and the Politics of Dissent,* 118.

95. Fouad Ibrahim, "The Shiite Movement in Saudi Arabia" (Ph.D. diss., King's College, London, 2006), chap. 1.

96. Interview with a specialist in genealogy in Riyadh.

97. According to the biography of Abd al-Rahman al-Barrak published in ʿAbd al-Rahman al-Barrak, *Sharh al-ʿaqida al-tadmuriyya* [Commentary on the *ʿAqida Tadmuriyya*], www.saaid.net.

98. Ahmad al-Furayh, *Al-shaykh Ibn Baz wa mawaqifuhu al-thabita* [Sheikh Ibn Baz and the Constancy of His Positions] (Kuwait: Maktabat al-rushd, 2000), 12.

99. See the biography of Abd al-Rahman al-Barrak at www.saaid.net.

100. Interview with Muhammad al-Masʿari.

101. See the biography of Abdallah bin Quʿud at www.saaid.net.

102. Mouline, "ʿUlama al-Sultan," 65.

103. Ibid., 89.

104. Interviews with ʿAbd al-ʿAziz al-Qasim and Saʿd al-Faqih. See also Mishari al-Dhayidi, "Al-ʿUbaykan . . . shaykh wa faqih fi wajh al-nawazil" [Al-ʿUbaykan . . . a Sheikh and a Jurist in the Face of the Accidents of Life], *Al-Sharq al-Awsat,* April 15, 2005; *Al-Riyad,* November 3, 2004.

105. Interview with an anonymous Sahwi sheikh.

106. Interview with Mansur al-Nuqaydan; on ʿAbdallah al-Jilali, see also *Al-Sunna* 43 (November 1995).

107. *Al-Daʿwa,* September 25, 1992.

108. See, for example, R. Hrair Dekmejian, "The Rise of Political Islamism in Saudi Arabia," *Middle East Journal* 48, 4 (Autumn 1994): 634; Joshua Teitelbaum, *Holier than Thou* (Washington, D.C.: Washington Institute for Near East Policy, 2000), 39–40.

109. *Al-Daʿwa,* December 5, 1992.

110. Interviews with ʿAbd al-ʿAziz al-Fahd and ʿAbd al-ʿAziz al-Qasim.

111. Mouline, "ʿUlama al-Sultan," appendix.

112. *Al-Sharq al-Awsat,* October 22, 2004.

113. Mouline, "ʿUlama al-Sultan," appendix. Of the three remaining Sheikhs, Salih bin Ghusun and Abd al-Majid Hasan died in 1999, and Ibrahim bin Muhammad Al al-Shaykh died in 2007.

114. For example, Teitelbaum, *Holier Than Thou,* 41.

115. Al-Qusaybi, *Hatta la takun fitna,* 128–129.

116. Al-Tuwayriqi, al-Qahtani, and Ibn Zuʿayr, *Al-ʿilmaniyya fi-l-ʿiraʾ,* 1–20.

117. Interview with Saʿd al-Faqih.

118. Interview with Muhammad al-Hudayf. Al-Hudayf studied in the United States and later in Great Britain (where he contributed to *Al-Sunna*) while maintaining contact with the "enlightened" Sahwi intellectuals.

119. Interview with Muhammad al-Masʿari.

120. Interviews with Saʿd al-Faqih and Sahwi intellectuals.

121. Interviews with Hamad al-Sulayfih and ʿAbd al-ʿAziz al-Wuhaybi.

122. Safar al-Hawali's doctoral dissertation, for example, contains attacks against Hasan al-Turabi. See Safar al-Hawali, "Dhahirat al-irjaʾ fi-l-fikr al-islami," www.alhawali.com, 1:31 n. 6.

123. Interviews with Sahwi intellectuals.

124. Interview with ʿAbd al-ʿAziz al-Wuhaybi.

125. Interview with Saʿd al-Faqih.

126. Broadcast *Idaʾat* [Highlights] presented by Turki al-Dakhil, with Ahmad al-Tuwayjiri, *Qanat al-ʿarabiyya* [Al-Arabiya TV], February 23, 2006.

127. One of his boldest articles, published in December 1990, was titled "The Environment, Conduct, and Thought." In it al-Mas'ari discusses the influence of the environment in which human societies develop on their conduct and thought, in a veiled reference to the artificiality of Saudi Wahhabism, a product of its environment rather than of an inviolable Islamic essence. Muhammad al-Mas'ari, "Al-bi'a wa-l-suluk wa-l-fikr," Al-Da'wa, December 14, 1990.

128. Al-Jazira al-'Arabiyya 12 (January 1992): 27.

129. Interview with 'Abd al-'Aziz al-Wuhaybi.

130. Lijam also means a horse's "bit"—in this case the bit of reform.

131. Interview with 'Abd al-'Aziz al-Wuhaybi.

132. Al-Jazira al-'Arabiyya 14 (March 1992): 13.

133. Interview with 'Abd al-'Aziz al-Qasim.

134. Interview with Sa'd al-Faqih.

135. Ibid. See also Wasim al-Dandashi, "Al-'Ubaykan . . . bayna fatratay khusuba kan fihima al-najm" [Al-'Ubaykan . . . Between Two Periods of Abundance of Which He Was the Star], July 3, 2005, www.alarabiya.net.

136. Interview with Sa'd al-Faqih.

137. "Transformative events" are defined as events that "come to be interpreted as significantly disrupting, altering, or violating the taken-for-granted assumptions governing routine political and social relations," precipitating the opening of a political crisis. Doug McAdam and William H. Sewell Jr., "It's about Time: Temporality in the Study of Social Movements and Revolutions," in Silence and Voice in the Study of Contentious Politics, ed. Ronald R. Aminzade et al. (Cambridge: Cambridge University Press, 2001), 110.

138. Interview with Sa'd al-Faqih.

139. His grandfather, Abd al-Rahman al-Qasim, had compiled the fatwas of the major Wahhabi ulema since the time of Ibn Abd al-Wahhab in a book considered an essential work of reference in the Saudi religious field: Al-durar al-saniyya fi-l-ajwiba al-najdiyya [The Glittering Pearls of the Najdi Responses], www.islamspirit.com.

140. Interview with 'Abd al-'Aziz al-Qasim.

141. Interview with Muhammad al-Mas'ari.

142. Loïc Blondiaux, "Les clubs: Sociétés de pensée, agencement de réseaux ou instances de sociabilité politique?" Politix 1, 2 (1988): 39–40.

143. Interview with Muhammad al-Mas'ari.

144. Charles Tilly, The Contentious French (Cambridge, Mass.: Belknap Press of Harvard University Press, 1986), 391ff.

145. Interview with ʿAbd al-ʿAziz al-Qasim. For the text of the document, see *Al-Jazira al-ʿArabiyya* 5 (June 1991): 4–6.

146. On structural homology and the use made of it in mobilizations, see Pierre Bourdieu, *Homo Academicus,* trans. Peter Collier (Stanford: Stanford University Press, 1988), 173ff.

147. *Al-Jazira al-ʿArabiyya* 11 (December 1991): 15.

148. Nasir al-ʿUmar, *Waqiʿ al-rafida fi bilad al-tawhid,* www.almeskat.net.

149. "Al-tawsiyat al-naziyya li-Nasir al-ʿUmar" [The Nazi Recommendations of Nasir al-ʿUmar], December 22, 2004, www.arabianews.org.

150. Saʿd al-Ghamidi, *Suqut al-dawla al-abbasiyya* [The Fall of the Abbasid Empire] (Beirut: Muʾassasat al-risala, 1981).

151. *Al-Madina—Mulhaq al-Risala,* October 1, 2004.

152. Interview with ʿAbd al-ʿAziz al-Qasim.

153. Interviews with Saʿd al-Faqih and ʿAbd al-ʿAziz al-Qasim.

154. Interview with ʿAbd al-ʿAziz al-Qasim.

155. Ibn Baz's letter of support was reprinted in *Al-Jazira al-ʿArabiyya* 8 (September 1991): 12.

156. Interview with Saʿd al-Faqih.

157. *Al-Jazira al-ʿArabiyya* 5 (June 1991): 4–6.

158. Interview with ʿAbd al-ʿAziz al-Qasim.

159. Interview with Saʿd al-Faqih.

160. *Al-Daʿwa,* June 6, 1991.

161. Notably Teitelbaum, *Holier than Thou,* 35.

162. Interview with Saʿd al-Faqih.

163. The transcript of the text of this cassette can be found in *Al-Jazira al-ʿArabiyya* 9 (October 1991): 15–21.

164. *Mudhakkirat al-nasiha* (n.p.: n.p., 1992).

165. Interview with Muhammad al-Masʿari.

166. Interview with ʿAbd al-Wahhab al-Turayri.

167. Interview with Saʿd al-Faqih.

168. Interview with Muhammad al-Masʿari.

169. For a relatively exhaustive presentation of the document, see Fandy, *Saudi Arabia and the Politics of Dissent,* 50–59.

170. *Mudhakkirat al-nasiha,* 18–19.

171. Interview with ʿAbd al-ʿAziz al-Wuhaybi.

172. Interview with an anonymous Sahwi sheikh.

173. Interview with Muhammad al-Masʿari.

174. Interview with an anonymous Sahwi sheikh.

175. *Al-Daʿwa,* January 8, 1993.

176. Interview with Saʿd al-Faqih.

177. *Al-Daʿwa*, September 25, 1992.

178. "Al-radd al-thulathi," *Al-Jazira al-ʿArabiyya* 22 (November 1992): 4.

179. Muhammad al-Masʿari, *Markaz al-tijara al-ʿalami* [The World Trade Center], www.tajdeed.org.uk.

180. Interview with Saʿd al-Faqih. See also Muhsin al-ʿAwaji, "Lajnat al-difaʿ mashruʿ jamaʿi la ʿawajiyya wa la masʿariyya wa la faqihiyya [The Defense Committee Is a Collective Project, It Is Neither ʿAwajist, nor Masʿarist, nor Faqihist], March 13, 2004, www.wasatyah.com.

181. Interview with Saʿd al-Faqih; al-ʿAwaji, "Lajnat al-difaʿ mashruʿ jamaʿi."

182. Al-ʿAwaji, "Lajnat al-difaʿ mashruʿ jamaʿi."

183. Interview with Saʿd al-Faqih.

184. Interview with Muhammad al-Hudayf.

185. Interview with Saʿd al-Faqih; al-ʿAwaji, "Lajnat al-difaʿ mashruʿ jamaʿi."

186. Interview with Muhammad al-Masʿari.

187. Interview with Sulayman al-Rashudi.

188. Lajnat al-Difaʿ ʿan al-Huquq al-Sharʿiyya [Committee for the Defense of Legitimate Rights], *Diwan al-islah: Ibdaʿ shuʿaraʾ al-jazira fi masirat al-taghyir* [Collection of Poetry of Reform: The Creation of the Poets of the Peninsula on the Road to Change] (n.p., n.d.), 77–116.

189. Interviews with ʿAbdallah al-Hamid and ʿAbd al-ʿAziz al-Qasim.

190. I have kept the term "legitimate" because it is found in the English name its founders gave the committee, Committee for the Defense of Legitimate Rights (CDLR), but it should be kept in mind, as Mamoun Fandy points out, that this translation is deceptive and is intended for a Western audience. Fandy, *Saudi Arabia and the Politics of Dissent*, 116.

191. Lajnat al-Difaʿ ʿan al-Huquq al-Sharʿiyya, "Iʿlan taʾsis lajnat al-difaʿ ʿan al-huquq al-sharʿiyya—Bayan raqm 1" [Announcement of the Creation of the Committee for the Defense of Legitimate Rights—Communiqué no. 1], May 3, 1993.

192. Interview with ʿAzzam Tamimi.

193. Ibid.

194. Fandy, *Saudi Arabia and the Politics of Dissent*, 121.

195. *Al-Daʿwa*, May 21, 1993.

196. Interview with Saʿd al-Faqih.

197. The CDLR had gotten wind of Ibn Jibrin's decision and tried to save appearances by announcing suspension of his membership on May 23, 1993.

Liberty, "Tajmid ʿadawiyyat Ibn Jibrin" [Suspension of Ibn Jibrin's Membership], May 23, 1993.

198. Liberty, "Lajnat al-difaʿ ʿan al-huquq al-sharʿiyya—Mutabaʿa 3" [The Committee for the Defense of Legitimate Rights—Cover 3], May 14, 1993.

199. *Al-Jazira al-ʿArabiyya* 29 (June 1993): 13.

200. Liberty, "Lajnat al-difaʿ ʿan al-huquq al-sharʿiyya—Mutabaʿa 2" [The Committee for the Defense of Legitimate Rights—Cover 2], May 12, 1993.

201. Interview with Saʿd al-Faqih.

202. Lajnat al-Difaʿ ʿan al-Huquq al-Sharʿiyya, "Bayan raqm 2" [Communiqué 2], May 25, 1993.

203. Salman al-ʿAwda, "Akhi rajul al-amn" [My Brother, in the Security Forces], taped speech, May 18, 1993.

204. Interviews with Sahwi officials active at the time.

205. Muhsin al-ʿAwaji, "Karam al-Hawali wa luʾm al-Faqih—Sirr akshifuhu li-awwal marra" [The Generosity of al-Hawali and the Petty-Mindedness of al-Faqih—A Secret I Am Revealing for the First Time], June 13, 2005, www.wasatyah.com.

206. Interview with Saʿd al-Faqih.

207. Interviews with Muhammad al-Hudayf and Saʿd al-Faqih.

208. Lajnat al-Difaʿ ʿan al-Huquq al-Sharʿiyya, "Bayan raqm 3" [Communiqué 3], April 20, 1994.

209. *Al-Islah* [Reform] (a publication of MIRA) 1 (March 16, 1996).

210. Interview with Mishari al-Dhayidi.

211. Interviews with ʿAbdallah bin Bijad al-ʿUtaybi, Mishari al-Dhayidi, and Fahd al-Shafi.

212. Interview with Fahd al-Shafi.

213. Interview with Saʿud al-Sarhan, at that time a student of al-ʿAlwan.

214. Randal, *Osama*, 105.

215. Interview with ʿAbd al-ʿAziz al-Qasim. Despite his efforts, Bin Laden eventually attracted the attention of the authorities, and he was barred from traveling until mid-1991. Randal, *Osama*, 99–103.

216. For many examples of such stories, see Hamad al-Qatari and Majid al-Madani, *Min qisas al-shuhadaʾ al-ʿarab fi-l-busna wa-l-hirsik* [Stories of Arab Martyrs in Bosnia-Herzegovina], 2002, www.saaid.net.

217. Randal, *Osama*, 112–113.

218. Hayʾat al-Nasiha wa-l-Islah [Advice and Reform Committee], "Bayan raqm 1" [Communiqué 1].

219. Hayʾat al-Nasiha wa-l-Islah, "Bayan raqm 2" [Communiqué 2], April 13, 1994.

220. Hay'at al-Nasiha wa-l-Islah, "Bayan raqm 3" [Communiqué 3], June 7, 1994.

221. Lawrence Wright, *The Looming Tower: Al-Qaeda and the Road to 9/11* (New York, Knopf, 2006), 195.

222. Hay'at al-Nasiha wa-l-Islah, "Bayan raqm 3"; "Bayan raqm 4" [Communiqué 4], July 12, 1994.

223. Hay'at al-Nasiha wa-l-Islah, "Bayan raqm 5" [Communiqué 5], July 19, 1994.

224. Hay'at al-Nasiha wa-l-Islah, "Bayan raqm 11" [Communiqué 11], December 29, 1994.

225. Hay'at al-Nasiha wa-l-Islah, "Bayan raqm 17" [Communiqué 17], August 3, 1995.

226. This tendency, however, also appeared in communiqués from the CDLR in exile, which, perhaps in a bidding contest, from then on did not hesitate to declare that the Saudi regime was illegitimate.

227. Salman al-ʿAwda, "Akhta' sha'iʿa fi-l-siyam" [On Common Errors in the Fast], recorded speech.

228. "Tandhim al-Qaʿida min al-dakhil kama yarwi Abu Jandal (Nasir al-Bahri) . . . al-haris al-shakhsi li-Ibn Ladin" [The al-Qaeda Organization From the Inside as Told by Abu Jandal (Nasir al-Bahri) . . . Bin Laden's Personal Bodyguard], part 1, *Al-Quds al-ʿArabi*, March 17, 2005.

229. Hamad al-Qatari and Majid al-Madani, *Min qisas al-shuhada' al-ʿarab fi-l-busna wa-l-hirsik.*

230. *Al-Majalla*, April 28, 1996.

231. "Al-iʿtirafat: Mufaja'at al-dakhiliyya al-saʿudiyya" [Confessions: The Surprise of the Saudi Interior Ministry], www.alhramain.com.

232. Interview with a former resident of Bayt Shubra.

233. Mishari al-Dhayidi, "Abu Muhammad al-Maqdisi . . . rihat fikr yabdhur al-taʿassub wa yahsud al-dama'" [Abu Muhammad al-Maqdisi . . . The Peregrinations of a Thought That Sows Intransigence and Harvests Blood], *Al-Sharq al-Awsat*, July 7, 2005. Al-Maqdisi confirmed these visits from al-Maʿtham in an interview on the al-Jazeera channel on July 10, 2005.

234. "Al-iʿtirafat: Mufaja'at al-dakhiliyya al-saʿudiyya."

235. Interviews with former residents of Bayt Shubra. See also Thomas Hegghammer, *Jihad in Saudi Arabia* (Cambridge: Cambridge University Press, 2010), 73.

236. Interview with Yusuf al-Dayni.

237. Interview with ʿAbdallah bin Bijad al-ʿUtaybi.

238. Interview with Yusuf al-Dayni, one of those sheikhs at that time.

239. Interview with Yusuf al-Dayni.

240. Interview with Mansur al-Nuqaydan.

241. *Al-Huquq* [Rights] (a CDLR publication), September 15, 1994, *Nashra istithna'iyya* [Special Issue] 3.

242. The al-Khobar attack that killed nineteen American soldiers on June 25, 1996, is not considered here because responsibility for it has not been determined, although it seems very likely that it was carried out by Shiites of Saudi Hezbollah, not by Sunni jihadi militants. See Thomas Hegghammer, "Deconstructing the Myth about al-Qa'ida and Khobar," *CTC Sentinel* 1, 3 (February 2008): 20–22.

243. Excerpts translated in *Al-Qaeda in Its Own Words*, ed. Gilles Kepel and Jean-Pierre Milelli (Cambridge, Mass.: Belknap Press of Harvard University Press, 2008), 47–52.

244. After August 1995 the ARC published only three communiqués in three years (one in August 1997, one not dated, and one in August 1998.)

245. Translated in Kepel and Milelli, *Al-Qaeda in Its Own Words*, 53–56, quotation on page 55.

6. Anatomy of a Failure

1. Moreover, repression is often understood as simply coercion, whereas, as we shall see, "soft" techniques also play a considerable role.

2. Faysal, however, had been merciless toward nationalist and leftist opposition groups, jailing and sometimes executing many of their members.

3. Interview with a Saudi intellectual.

4. Interviews with various Saudi activists.

5. *Al-Jazira al-'Arabiyya* 5 (June 1991): 12.

6. *Al-Jazira al-'Arabiyya* 11 (December 1991): 10.

7. *Al-Jazira al-'Arabiyya* 5 (June 1991): 20.

8. Munazzamat al-Madda 19 [Organization of Article 19], *Mamlakat al-samt: Hurriyyat al-ta'bir fi-l-'arabiyya al-sa'udiyya* [The Kingdom of Silence: Freedom of Expression in Saudi Arabia], October 1, 1991, www.cdhrap .net.

9. Salman al-'Awda, "Wa lakin fi-l-tahrish baynahum" [But about Setting Them against One Another], recorded speech.

10. *Al-Islah* [Reform] (a publication of MIRA) 33 (October 28, 1996).

11. This principle was breached when, in the wake of the creation of the CDLR, Prince Salman summoned all the founding members, including ulema.

12. *Al-Jazira al-'Arabiyya* 5 (June 1991): 19.

13. Salman al-ʿAwda, "Akhi rajul al-amn" [My Brother, in the Security Forces], taped speech, May 18, 1993.

14. Mansoor Alshamsi, "The Discourse and Performance of the Saudi Sunni Islamic Reformist Leadership (1981–2003)" (Ph.D. diss., University of Exeter, 2003), 210, 216.

15. Salman al-ʿAwda, "Durus wa waqafat tarbawiyya min al-sunna an-nabawiyya" [Lessons and Reflections Drawn from the Sunna of the Prophet], recorded speech, August 10, 1992.

16. Salman al-ʿAwda, "Ulaʾika hum al-sabirun" [Those Are the Patient Ones], recorded lecture, August 31, 1993.

17. Interviews with ʿAbd al-ʿAziz al-Qasim and Saʿd al-Faqih.

18. Al-Jazira al-ʿArabiyya 13 (February 1992): 25.

19. Interviews with Saʿd al-Faqih, ʿAbd al-ʿAziz al-Qasim, and Muhammad al-Hudayf.

20. Liberty, "Al-sulutat al-saʿudiyya tamnaʿ 60 ustadhan jamiʿan min al-safar" [The Saudi Authorities Bar 60 University Professors from Traveling], August 8, 1993.

21. Munazzamat al-Madda 19, Mamlakat al-samt.

22. A copy of his letter of dismissal can be found in Al-Jazira al-ʿArabiyya 14 (March 1992): 26.

23. Human Rights Watch, Saudi Arabia 1993 Report, www.hrw.org.

24. Interview with Sulayman al-Rashudi.

25. Interview with Salman al-ʿAwda.

26. Al-Huquq (publication of the CDLR) 58 (July 26, 1995); Al-Huquq 64 (September 6, 1995); interviews with Sahwi activists.

27. Al-Islah 14 (June 17, 1996).

28. Interview with ʿAwad al-Qarni.

29. Al-Huquq 58 (July 26, 1995).

30. Al-Huquq 64 (September 6, 1995); Al-Huquq 86 (February 6, 1996).

31. Liberty, "Al-sulutat al-saʿudiyya taʿtaqil Muhammad al-Masʿari" [The Saudi Authorities Arrest Muhammad al-Masʿari], May 15, 1993.

32. Liberty, "Al-sulutat al-saʿudiyya taʿtaqil Sulayman al-Rashudi" [The Saudi Authorities Arrest Sulayman al-Rashudi], August 9, 1993.

33. Human Rights Watch, Saudi Arabia 1993 Report.

34. Liberty, "Liberty tunashid al-ʿalam al-daght ʿala-l-hukuma al-saʿudiyya" [Liberty Appeals to the World to Put Pressure on the Saudi Government], May 18, 1993.

35. Liberty, "Itlaq al-muʿtaqalin fi-l-saʿudiyya" [Release of Detainees Held in Saudi Arabia], October 10, 1993.

36. Liberty, "Liberty tuʿarrib ʿan qalaqiha li-ikhtifaʾ al-Masʿari fi dhuruf ghamida" [Liberty Expresses Its Concern after the Disappearance of al-Masʿari in Mysterious Circumstances], April 3, 1994.

37. Interviews with Kassab al-ʿUtaybi and Sulayman al-Dahayyan, both active sympathizers of the CDLR during this period.

38. Lajnat al-Difaʿ ʿan al-Huquq al-Sharʿiyya, "Bayan raqm 16" [Communiqué 16], September 9, 1994.

39. Notably Muhammad al-Hudayf, Sulayman al-Dahayyan, Abd al-Aziz al-Wuhaybi, Abd al-Aziz al-Qasim, and Hamad al-Sulayfih. *Al-Huquq* 16 (October 5, 1994); *Al-Huquq,* 22 (November 16, 1994); interviews with Sahwi activists.

40. Notably ʿAʾid al-Qarni, Nasir al-ʿUmar, Sulayman al-Rashudi, and Ali al-Khudayr.

41. At the end of September 1994 the Ministry of the Interior had already announced 110 arrests, while the CDLR counted thousands, which is probably exaggerated. *Al-Daʿwa,* September 29, 1994; *Al-Huquq—Nashra istithnaʿiyya* [Special Bulletin] 4 (September 18, 1994).

42. Lajnat al-Difaʿ ʿan al-Huquq al-Sharʿiyya, "Bayan raqm 25" [Communiqué 25], March 6, 1995.

43. *Al-Huquq* 39 (March 15, 1995); interview with Muhammad al-Hudayf.

44. Lajnat al-Difaʿ ʿan al-Huquq al-Sharʿiyya, "Bayan raqm 36" [Communiqué 36], June 4, 1995.

45. *Al-Huquq* 20 (November 2, 1994).

46. *Al-Huquq* 32 (January 25, 1995).

47. Interview with Saʿud al-Sarhan.

48. *Al-Huquq* 57 (July 19, 1995).

49. *Al-Huquq* 76 (November 29, 1995).

50. Interviews with Mishari al-Dhayidi and ʿAbdallah bin Bijad al-ʿUtaybi.

51. See, for example, *Al-Huquq* 81 (January 6, 1996).

52. Al-Libi managed to escape a few years later from al-Ruways prison and to tell his story. See "Qissat hurub al-shaykh Abu Layth al-Libi min sijn al-Ruways" [Story of the Flight of Sheikh Abu Layth al-Libi from al-Ruways Prison], *Majallat al-Fajr* 40 (July, 1998).

53. Interview with Saʿd al-Faqih.

54. See Liberty, "Al-Tuwayjiri yataʿarrad li-l-taʿdhib al-nafsi" [Al-Tuwayjiri Is Subjected to Psychological Torture], September 15, 1993.

55. Anonymous interviews; see also "Qissat hurub al-shaykh Abu Layth al-Libi min sijn al-Ruways"; Thomas Hegghammer, *Jihad in Saudi Arabia* (Cambridge: Cambridge University Press, 2010), 74.

56. Abdallah al-Hudayf was designated by the CDLR as "the first martyr on the road to reform" *(awwal shahid fi masirat al-islah).* Lajnat al-Difaʿ ʿan al-Huquq al-Sharʿiyya, "Bayan raqm 38" [Communiqué 38], August 12, 1995.

57. An indication that there was no plot was that al-ʿAwaji and al-Hudayf had both been behind bars for several weeks at the time of the offense.

58. Lajnat al-Difaʿ ʿan al-Huquq al-Sharʿiyya, "Bayan raqm 38" [Communiqué 38], August 12, 1995.

59. Sulayman al-Nahdi, *Li-madha khafu min al-lajna al-sharʿiyya?* [Why Were They Afraid of the Committee of Legitimate [Rights]] (n.p.: n.p., 1993), 97.

60. *Nidham majlis al-taʿlim al-ʿali wa-l-jamiʿat* [Higher Education and University Council Code], art. 23.

61. Ibid., art. 36.

62. Ibid., art. 44.

63. *Al-Daʿwa,* July 15, 1993.

64. Interview with officials of the Ministry of Islamic Affairs, Riyadh.

65. *Al-Jazira al-ʿArabiyya* 31 (August 1993): 16.

66. Ibid., 17.

67. *Al-Daʿwa,* April 24, 1994.

68. Interview with Mansur al-Mutayri, official in the Ministry of Islamic Affairs.

69. *Al-Daʿwa,* October 13, 1994.

70. *Al-Daʿwa,* April 28, 1994.

71. *Al-Daʿwa,* September 15, 1994.

72. *Al-Daʿwa,* October 20, 1994.

73. *Al-Daʿwa,* March 25, 1994.

74. For a detailed account, see *Al-Daʿwa,* April 8, 1994.

75. *Al-Daʿwa,* June 10, 1994.

76. *Al-Daʿwa,* August 18, 1994.

77. *Al-Daʿwa,* April 14, 1994.

78. *Al-Huquq* 7 (July 9, 1994).

79. *Al-Jazira al-ʿArabiyya* 29 (June 1993): 13.

80. *Al-Huquq* 30 (January 11, 1995).

81. Al-Nahdi, *Li-madha khafu min al-lajna al-sharʿiyya?* 96.

82. *Al-Islah* 52 (March 31, 1997).

83. *Al-Daʿwa,* July 15, 1993.

84. See, for example, Joshua Teitelbaum, *Holier than Thou* (Washington, D.C.: Washington Institute for Near East Policy, 2000), 101–102.

85. "Tarjama li-l-shaykh Muhammad Aman al-Jami rahamahu Allah" [A Biography of Sheikh Muhammad Aman al-Jami], www.sahab.org.

86. Interview with Yusuf al-Dayni. See, for instance, Abu Abdallah al-Athari, quoted in note 111.

87. "Tarjama mujaza li-l-shaykh Rabiʿ bin Hadi al-Madkhali" [Succinct Biography of Sheikh Rabiʿ bin Hadi al-Madkhali], www.rabee.net.

88. "Tarjama li-l-shaykh Muhammad Aman al-Jami rahamahu Allah."

89. Interview with Saʿud al-Sarhan.

90. Rabiʿ al-Madkhali, *Manhaj al-anbiyaʾ fi-l-daʿwa ila-llah fihi al-hikma wa-l-ʿaql* (Ajman, UAE: Maktabat al-furqan, 2001).

91. Ibid., 138–196.

92. Ibid., 144.

93. "Tarjama mujaza li-fadilat al-shaykh Falih al-Harbi" [Succinct Biography of the Noble Sheikh Falih al-Harbi], www.sahab.net.

94. Fata al-Adghal, "Al-kashf ʿan al-taʾrikh al-mudhlim li-firqat al-jamiyya" [Revelation of the Dark History of the Gang of Jamis], www.alhesbah .org.

95. Interview with Saʿud al-Sarhan.

96. *Al-Islah* 47 (February 24, 1997). These links were confirmed by interviews with former Jamis in Saudi Arabia.

97. "Tarjamat al-shaykh Abu ʿUmar al-ʿUtaybi" [Biography of Sheikh Abu ʿUmar al-ʿUtaybi], www.aldaawah.ws.

98. Al-Khanjar [pseudonym meaning "dagger"], "Abu ʿUmar al-ʿUtaybi alladhi ʿaraftuhu—Haqaʾiq tunshar li-awwal marra" [Abu ʿUmar al-ʿUtaybi as I Knew Him—Facts Published for the First Time], www.muslm.org.

99. "Tarjamat al-shaykh Abu ʿUmar al-ʿUtaybi."

100. Abu ʿUmar al-ʿUtaybi, *Al-hujaj al-qanuniyya li-wujub al-difaʿ ʿan al-dawla al-saʿudiyya,* www.otiby.net; Abu ʿUmar al-ʿUtaybi, *Sadd ʿudwan al-sahayina al-muʿtadin ʿala Al Saʿud usrat al-jihad wa-l-mujahidin,* www.otiby .net.

101. In addition to his case, there are many anecdotes about foreign residents converting to Jamism to obtain Saudi nationality, providing grist for Sahwi publications.

102. Interview with ʿAbd al-Razzaq al-Shayji, a Kuwaiti *Salafi* known for his refutations of Jamism.

103. Interviews with Sahwis.

104. *Al-Huquq* 65 (September 13, 1995).

105. *Al-Huquq* 19 (October 26, 1994).

106. *Al-Islah* 32 (October 21, 1996). Aba al-Khayl was finally appointed president of Imam University in May 2006.

107. Al-Sinani won fame in the late 1990s with an anti-Qutbist pamphlet in which he adopted the exact opposite of the positions he had held in 1992. 'Isam al-Sinani, *Bara'at 'ulama' al-umma min tazkiyat ahl al-bid'a wa-l-madhamma* [The Ulema of the *Umma* Free Themselves from Any Recommendation to Those Who Preach Innovation and Denigration], www.fatwa1 .com.

108. Abu Ibrahim bin Sultan al-'Adnani, *Al-qutbiyya hiya al-fitna fa-i'rifuha* (Algiers: Dar-al-athar, 2004).

109. *Al-Huquq* 69 (October 11, 1995).

110. *Al-Huquq* 59 (August 2, 1995).

111. See, for example, Abu 'Abdallah al-Athari, *Ta'liq al-fawa'id 'ala-l-fatwa al-baziyya fi jama'at al-ikhwan al-muslimin* [The Benefits Attached to Ibn Baz's Fatwa on the Movement of the Muslim Brotherhood], www.sahab .net.

112. See Safar al-Hawali, *Manhaj al-asha'ira fi-l-'aqida* [The Methodology of the Ash'arites in creed], www.alhawali.com; al-Hawali, *Al-radd 'ala-l-khurafiyyin* [Refutation of the Superstitious], www.saaid.net.

113. Interview with Yusuf al-Dayni.

114. Muqbil al-Wadi'i, *Al-makhraj min al-fitna* (Cairo: Dar al-haramayn, n.d.).

115. See, for example, Rabi' al-Madkhali, *Jama'a wahida la jama'at . . . wa sirat wahid la 'asharat* [A Single *Jama'a*, Not Several *Jama'at* . . . Just as There Is Only One Path, Not Ten], www.rabee.net.

116. See, for example, Ahmad al-Zahrani and Ahmad Bazamul, *Al-intiqadat al-'alaniyya li-manhaj al-kharajat wa-l-tala'at wa-l-maktabat wa-l-mukhayyamat wa-l-marakiz al-sayfiyya* [Public Criticisms of the Methodology of Trips, Excursions, Libraries, Camps, and Summer Centers], www .sahab.org.

117. See, for example, 'Isam 'Abd al-Mun'im al-Murri, *Al-qawl al-mufid fi hukm al-anashid* [Helpful Words on the Legal Opinion on the *Anashid*] (Ajman, UAE: Maktabat al-furqan, 2000).

118. Interview with Ibrahim al-Sikran.

119. Muhammad Surur Zayn al-'Abidin, *Al-salafiyya bayna al-wula wa-l-ghula* [Salafism between the Rulers and the Extremists], http://209.1.224,15/ sa3wah/12.zip.

120. Rabiʿ al-Madkhali, *Manhaj ahl al-sunna wa-l-jamaʿa fi naqd al-rijal wa-l-kutub wa-l-tawaʾif* [The Sunni Method for Criticizing People, Books, and Groups], www.sahab.org.

121. See, for example, Rabiʿ al-Madkhali, *Al-ʿawasim mimma fi kutub Sayyid Qutb min al-qawasim* [Protection against the Destruction Contained in the Works of Sayyid Qutb], or *Mataʿin Sayyid Qutb fi ashab rasul Allah* [The Calumnies of Sayyid Qutb about the Companions of the Prophet], www.sahab.org.

122. See, for example, Rabiʿ al-Madkhali, *Ahl al-hadith hum al-taʾifa al-mansura al-najiyya—Hiwar maʿ Salman al-ʿAwda* [The Ahl al-Hadith Are the Victorious Group That Will Be Saved—Dialogue with Salman al-ʿAwda], www.rabee.net.

123. See Rabiʿ al-Madkhali, *Makhidh manhajiyya ʿala-l-shaykh Safar al-Hawali* [Methodological Criticisms Addressed to Sheikh Safar al-Hawali], www.rabee.net.

124. ʿAbd al-Malik Ramadani al-Jazaʾiri, *Madarik al-nadhar fi-l-siyasa* [The Fruits of Reflection on Politics], www.sahab.org.

125. For instance, in the heart of the al-Suwaydi neighborhood of Riyadh, an Islamist bastion, a few steps from the Sururi bookstore the Pious (al-Tayyiba) of Sheikh Abd al-Aziz al-Julayyil, the Jamis opened a cassette shop called the Methodology of the Sunna (Manhaj al-sunna). Interview with a Sahwi from al-Suwaydi.

126. Interview with Yusuf al-Dayni.

127. "The Neo-Khawaarij of Saudi Arabia and Their Violent Behavior towards the Scholars," www.salafipublications.com.

128. *Burayda tanfik ayyuha al-jami!* See *Al-Huquq* 42 (April 5, 1995).

129. "Madha hadath li-l-mashayikh al-salafiyyin fi Burayda?" [What Happened to the *Salafi* Sheikhs in Burayda?], www.sahab.net.

130. *Al-Huquq* 42 (April 5, 1995).

131. See, for example, al-Adghal, "Al-kashf ʿan al-taʾrikh al-mudhlim li-firqat al-jamiyya"; *Al-Huquq* 6 (June 2, 1994); *Al-Huquq* 21 (November 9, 1994).

132. Interview with Saʿd al-Faqih.

133. Salafiyyu ahl al-walaʾ, *Al-tanzim al-sirri al-ʿalami bayna al-takhtit wa-l-tatbiq fi-l-mamlaka al-ʿarabiyya al-saʿudiyya—Haqaʾiq wa wathaʾiq*, quoted in Abu Qatada al-Filastini, *Bayna manhajayn—Halaqa raqm 76* [Between Two Methodologies—Part 76], www.altaefa.com.

134. Interview with Saʿd al-Faqih.

135. Al-Filastini, *Bayna manhajayn—Halaqa raqm 76*.

136. Ibn Hajar al-ʿAsqalani, *Bulugh al-maram* (Cairo: Matbaʿat Mustafa al-Babi al-Halabi, 1998).

137. Interview with Ibrahim al-Sikran.

138. Interview with Sulayman al-Dahayyan.

139. "Saʿud al-Funaysan: Al-dawrat al-ʿilmiyya dhahira sawtiyya" [Saʿud al-Funaysan: Scientific Training Sessions Are Only an Acoustic Phenomenon], September 8, 2005, www.islamtoday.net.

140. Interview with Ibrahim al-Sikran.

141. Nasir al-ʿUmar, *Luhum al-ʿulamaʾ masmuma* (Riyadh: Dar al-watan li-l-nashr, 1991).

142. Salman al-ʿAwda, "Nasim al-hijaz fi sirat Ibn Baz," recorded sermon.

143. Interview with Ibrahim al-Sikran.

144. *Al-Daʿwa,* January 2, 1992.

145. Safar al-Hawali, "Al-mumtaz fi sharh bayan Ibn Baz" [The Perfect in the Explanation of the Communiqué of Ibn Baz], recorded sermon; ʿAʾid al-Qarni, "Khitab ʿalim al-umma" [The Letter of the Sheikh of the *Umma*], recorded sermon.

146. Quoted in Khalid al-Zafiri, *Al-thinaʾ al-badiʿ min al-ʿulamaʾ ʿala-l-shaykh Rabiʿ* [The Marvelous Praise of the Ulema for Sheikh Rabiʿ], www.sahab.org.

147. Interview with Ibrahim al-Sikran.

148. "Ibn Baz fi diyafat al-shaykh Nasir al-ʿUmar" [Ibn Baz Invited by Sheikh Nasir al-ʿUmar], cassette recording.

149. Salman al-ʿAwda, *Al-ʿuzla wa-l-khulta,* 2nd ed. (Dammam: Dar Ibn al-Jawzi, 2005).

150. Interviews with Sahwi militants who were active at the time.

151. "Kibar al-ʿulamaʾ yatakallamun ʿan al-duʿat," cassette recording.

152. Interview with Saʿud al-Sarhan.

153. Ibn Hajar al-ʿAsqalani, *Fath al-bari* (Beirut: Dar al-fikr, 1993); Imam al-Nawawi, *Al-arbaʿun al-nawawiyya.* (Jeddah: Dar al-minhaj, 2008).

154. Interview with Yusuf al-Dayni.

155. Al-Haddad was deported from Saudi Arabia to his native country under pressure from the Jamis. See "Al-kawashif al-nuraniyya fi bayan madhhab al-haddadiyya" [Luminous Evidence to Expose the Haddadist School], www.alsaha.fares.net.

156. Interview with Yusuf al-Dayni.

157. See Rabiʿ al-Madkhali, *Mujazafat al-Haddad wa mukhalafatuhu li-manhaj al-salaf* [The Carelessness of al-Haddad and His Distortion of the Method of the Ancestors], www.rabee.net.

158. Al-Adghal, "Al-kashf ʿan al-taʾrikh al-mudhlim li-firqat al-jamiyya."

159. See, for example, Musa al-Duwaysh, *Al-tawajjuh al-siyasi al-haraki ʿinda al-shaykh Muhammad Nasir al-Din al-Albani* [The Activist Political Orientation of Sheikh Nasir al-Din al-Albani], www.alsaha.fares.net.

160. *Dhikr* consists of repeating many times the names of God, the Muslim declaration of faith, or even a verse of the Koran.

161. Interview with the sheikh of the *baʿalawiyya* Sufi brotherhood al-Habib ʿAli al-Jifri, who grew up in the Hejaz.

162. Mai Yamani, *Cradle of Islam: The Hijaz and the Quest for an Arabian Identity* (London: I. B. Tauris, 2004), 56–58.

163. Interview with al-Habib ʿAli al-Jifri.

164. For an example of the Sahwa's attacks against Muhammad ʿAlawi al-Maliki, see Safar al-Hawali, *Al-radd ʿala-l-khurafiyyin* [Refutation of the Superstitious], www.saaid.net.

165. ʿAbdallah al-Munayʿ, *Hiwar maʿ al-Maliki fi radd dalalatihi wa munkaratihi*, www.saaid.net.

166. "Bayan hayʾat kibar al-ʿulama bi-l-dall Muhammad ʿAlawi al-Maliki" [Communiqué of the Committee of Senior Ulema Regarding the Deviant Muhammad ʿAlawi al-Maliki], September 10, 1981, www.metransparent.com.

167. Interview with Samir Barga, Muhammad ʿAlawi al-Maliki's son-in-law.

168. R. Hrair Dekmejian, "The Rise of Political Islamism in Saudi Arabia," *Middle East Journal* 48, 4 (Autumn 1994): 642.

169. Interview with Samir Barga.

170. On Sayyid Muhammad al-Shirazi, see Laurence Louër, *Transnational Shia Politics: Religious and Political Networks in the Gulf* (New York: Columbia University Press, 2008), 90ff.

171. Muharram is the first month of the Hijri calendar. On these events, see Toby Jones, "Rebellion on the Saudi Periphery: Modernity, Marginalization, and the Shiʿa Uprising of 1979," *International Journal of Middle East Studies* 38, 2 (May 2006): 213–233.

172. Mamoun Fandy, *Saudi Arabia and the Politics of Dissent* (Basingstoke: Macmillan, 1999), 211–212.

173. Fouad Ibrahim, "The Shiite Movement in Saudi Arabia" (Ph.D. diss., King's College, London, 2006), chap. 5.

174. Interview with Hamza al-Hasan.

175. *Al-Jazira al-ʿArabiyya* is thus an essential primary source for the study of the Sahwi protest. Questioned about the magazine's sources of information, Hamza al-Hasan, then editor in chief, said: "We were an organized

movement [he was speaking of the Shirazi movement]. We had people every-where who wrote reports for us. We had ways of finding out everything that was happening in the kingdom, down to the tiniest detail." Interview with Hamza al-Hasan.

176. *Al-Jazira al-ʿArabiyya* 21 (October 1992): 2–4.

177. Interviews with Hamza al-Hasan and Fouad Ibrahim.

178. Ibrahim, "Shiite Movement in Saudi Arabia," chap. 6.

179. Interviews with Sufis in Jeddah.

180. Interview with Yusuf al-Dayni.

181. Interview with Mansur al-Nuqaydan.

182. Interviews with Yusuf al-Dayni and Saʿud al-Sarhan.

183. Interviews with Sulayman al-Dahayyan and Ibrahim al-Sikran.

184. Maryjane Osa, *Solidarity and Contention: Networks of Polish Opposition* (Minneapolis: University of Minnesota Press, 2003), 21.

185. Interview with Saʿd al-Faqih.

186. Interview with Sulayman al-Dahayyan, at that time close to al-ʿAwda.

187. Interview with a former Sururi midranking figure

188. Interviews with former Brothers.

189. This was the case, among others, of Abd al-Aziz al-Wuhaybi, who left the Sururi jamaʿa.

190. Interview with Ismaʿil al-Shatti.

191. Interview with Saʿd al-Faqih.

192. Ibid.

193. Interview with ʿAbd al-ʿAziz al-Qasim.

194. Interview with Muhammad al-Masʿari.

195. Interviews with former Brothers.

196. Interview with a young Muslim Brother who was one of the dissidents.

197. Interview with Sulayman al-Dahayyan.

198. Guilain Denoeux, *Urban Unrest in the Middle East: A Comparative Study of Informal Networks in Egypt, Iran, and Lebanon* (Albany: State University of New York Press, 1993), 21ff.

199. Only in part, because, as noted earlier, recruitment into the jihadi movement had become more diversified after 1987.

200. Gilles Kepel, *Jihad: The Trail of Political Islam,* trans. Anthony F. Roberts (Cambridge, Mass.: Harvard University Press, 2003), 23–25.

201. He was later authorized to return and appears to be still living in Mecca.

202. See, for example, *Al-Huquq* 19 (October 26, 1994); 22 (November 23, 1994); 29 (January 4, 1995).

203. See, for example, *Al-Huquq* 18 (October 19, 1994); 19 (October 26, 1994); 30 (January 11, 1995); 31 (January 18, 1995).

204. See, for example, *Al-Huquq* 14 (August 31, 1994); 27 (December 21, 1994).

205. James Piscatori, "Managing God's Guests: The Pilgrimage, Saudi Arabia, and the Politics of Legitimacy," in *Monarchies and Nations: Globalisation and Identity in the Arab States of the Gulf,* ed. Paul Dresch and James Piscatori (London: I. B. Tauris, 2005), 232.

206. Lajnat al-Difaʿ ʿan al-Huquq al-Sharʿiyya, "Bayan raqm 17: Iʿtiqal Safar wa Salman" [Communiqué 17: Arrest of Safar and Salman], September 10, 1994.

207. Lajnat al-Difaʿ ʿan al-Huquq al-Sharʿiyya, "Bayn raqm 18" [Communiqué 18], September 11, 1994.

208. Interview with Sulayman al-Rashudi.

209. Salman al-ʿAwda, "Risala min waraʾ al-qudban" [Letter from behind Bars], September 11, 1994.

210. *Al-Huquq—Nashra istithnaʾiyya* [Special Bulletin] 1 (September 12, 1994).

211. Interviews with Sulayman al-Dahayyan and Sulayman al-Rashudi; *Al-Huquq—Nashra istithnaʾiyya* [Special Bulletin] 2 (September 14, 1994).

212. These speeches were recorded on a cassette titled "Mashruʿ al-tadamun maʿ al-madhlumin" [Project of Solidarity with the Oppressed].

213. *Al-Huquq—Nashra istithnaʾiyya* [Special Bulletin] 2.

214. Interviews with Sulayman al-Rashudi and Sulayman al-Dahayyan.

215. Lajnat al-Difaʿ ʿan al-Huquq al-Sharʿiyya, "Bayan raqm 19" [Communiqué 19], September 13, 1994.

216. Interview with Sulayman al-Rashudi.

217. Ibid.

218. Sulayman al-Dahayyan spoke of five hundred participants, while Sulayman al-Rashudi estimated them at one thousand. Other anonymous participants confirmed these figures.

219. *Al-Huquq—Nashra istithnaʾiyya* [Special Bulletin] 3 (September 12, 1994).

220. Interview with Kassab al-ʿUtaybi.

221. Interview with Sulayman al-Dahayyan.

222. Interviews with Sulayman al-Dahayyan and Kassab al-ʿUtaybi.

223. Interview with ʿAbd al-ʿAziz al-Wuhaybi.

224. *Al-Huquq—Nashra istithnaʾiyya* [Special Bulletin] 3 (September 12, 1994).

225. Muhammad al-Mas'ari, "Ahdath Burayda" [The Events of Burayda], recorded speech, www.22lajnah22.co.uk.

226. Lajnat al-Difa' 'an al-Huquq al-Shar'iyya, "Bayn raqm 24" [Communiqué 24], February 8, 1995.

227. Lajnat al-Difa' 'an al-Huquq al-Shar'iyya, "Bayn raqm 28" [Communiqué 28], March 22, 1995.

228. Lajnat al-Difa' 'an al-Huquq al-Shar'iyya, "Bayan raqm 33" [Communiqué 33], April 12, 1995; "Bayan raqm 34" [Communiqué 34], May 3, 1995.

229. Lajnat al-Difa' 'an al-Huquq al-Shar'iyya, "Bayan raqm 27" [Communiqué 27], March 18, 1995.

230. Interviews in Burayda with anonymous young men who participated in the demonstration.

231. Lajnat al-Difa' 'an al-Huquq al-Shar'iyya, "Bayan raqm 31" [Communiqué 31], March 31, 1995; "Bayn raqm 32" [Communiqué 32], March 31, 1995.

232. Al-Huquq 47 (May 10, 1995).

233. Interview with Muhammad al-Mas'ari. However, al-Mas'ari did not declare bankruptcy officially until May 1998. Fandy, Saudi Arabia and the Politics of Dissent, 142.

234. Interview with Muhammad al-Mas'ari. See also al-Mas'ari, "Ahdath Burayda."

235. Muhsin al-'Awaji, "Karam al-Hawali wa lu'm al-Faqih—Sirr akshifuhu li-awwal marra" [The Generosity of al-Hawali and the Petty-Mindedness of al-Faqih—A Secret I Am Revealing for the First Time], www.wasatyah.com.

236. See, for example, Lajnat al-Difa' 'an al-Huquq al-Shar'iyya, "Bayan raqm 18" [Communiqué 18], September 11, 1994; "Bayan raqm 28" [Communiqué 28], March 22, 1995.

237. Interviews with Saudi Sahwis.

238. Steffen Hertog, "Segmented Clientelism: The Political Economy of Saudi Economic Reform Efforts," in Saudi Arabia in the Balance: Political Economy, Society, Foreign Affairs (New York: New York University Press, 2005), 148.

239. On these reforms, see Al-Rasheed, History of Saudi Arabia, 172–173.

240. Abdulaziz H. Al-Fahad, "Ornamental Constitutionalism: The Saudi Basic Law of Governance" (paper presented at the Sixth Mediterranean Social and Political Research Meeting, Montecatini Terme, Italy, March 16–20, 2005).

241. R. Hrair Dekmejian, "Saudi Arabia's Consultative Council," Middle East Journal 52, 2 (Spring 1998): 204–218.

7. THE ISLAMISTS AFTER THE INSURRECTION

1. For a detailed analysis of these developments, see Gilles Kepel, *Jihad: The Trail of Political Islam*, trans. Anthony F. Roberts (Cambridge, Mass.: Harvard University Press, 2003).

2. Interview with a Saudi intellectual.

3. See the biography of Abd al-Aziz Al al-Shaykh at www.saaid.net.

4. Agence France Press, June 6, 1995.

5. *Al-Islah* 167 (June 28, 1999); 168 (July 5, 1999).

6. Stéphane Lacroix, "Between Islamists and Liberals: Saudi Arabia's New Islamo-Liberal Reformists," *Middle East Journal* 58, 3 (Summer 2004): 358.

7. "Bayan hawla hawadith al-tafjirat" [Manifesto on the Attacks], May 16, 2003, www.islamtoday.net.

8. ʿAli al-Khudayr, *Usul al-sahwa al-jadida* [The Principles of the New Sahwa], www.tawhed.net.

9. For example, "Bayan hawla huquq al-marʾa wa manzilatiha fi-l-islam" [Statement on the Rights of Women and Their Place in Islam], June 13, 2003, www.almoslim.net; "Bayan al-ʿulamaʾ hawla qiyadat al-marʾa li-l-sayyara" [Statement of the Ulema on Women Driving Cars], July 13, 2005, www.islam-light.net. On the question of women driving, starting in 2004, the positions of some Sahwis started shifting, notably those of ʿAʾid al-Qarni (*Al-Hayat*, January 10, 2004) and Salman al-ʿAwda (personal interview).

10. See "Bayan hawla taghyir al-manahij fi-l-saʿudiyya" [Statement on Changes in Curricula in Saudi Arabia], January 4, 2004, www.islamtoday.net.

11. Raymond William Baker, *Islam without Fear: Egypt and the New Islamists* (Cambridge, Mass.: Harvard University Press, 2003).

12. Salman al-ʿAwda, "Fi Mafhum al-wasatiyya" [On the Concept of *Wasatiyya*], May 15, 2001, www.islamtoday.net.

13. Salman al-ʿAwda, "Ruʾya hawla ahdath amrika" [A Vision about the Events in America], September 17, 2001, www.islamtoday.net; Safar al-Hawali, "Bayan li-l-umma ʿan al-ahdath" [Statement to the *Umma* on the Events], October 15, 2001, www.alhawali.com.

14. "ʿAla ayy asas nataʿayash" [How We Can Coexist], April 29, 2002, www.islamtoday.net.

15. "Al-bayan al-tawdihi," May 19, 2002, www.wasatyah.com.

16. "Khitab maftuh ila-l-shaʿb al-ʿiraqi al-mujahid" [Open Letter to the *Mujahid* Iraqi People], November 5, 2004, www.islamtoday.net.

17. See the campaign's Web site, www.qawim.org.

18. This term was first used by a key figure of the movement, Abd al-Aziz al-Qasim.

19. Al-Nuqaydan ultimately distanced himself from the Islamo-liberals and embraced an uncompromising liberalism. So did Abdallah bin Bijad al-ʿUtaybi and Mishari al-Dhayidi.

20. See *Al-Islah* 91 (December 29, 1997).

21. Mansur al-Nuqaydan, "Tafjirat al-ʿUlaya wa qissat al-fikr al-islahi" [The Attacks of al-ʿUlaya and the History of Reformist Thought], *Al-riyad*, May 15, 2003.

22. Al-Hamid's articles have been collected in a series of books: *Li-kay la yatahawwal al-islam ila tuqus* [So That Islam Does Not Become a Mere Ritual] (Beirut: Al-dar al-ʿarabiyya li-l-ʿulum, 2003); *Al-bahth ʿan ʿayni al-zarqaʾ* [In Search of My Blue Source] (Beirut: Al-dar al-ʿarabiyya, li-l-ʿulum, 2003); and *Taʿlim al-qurʾan al-karim* [The Teaching of the Noble Koran] (Beirut: Al-dar al-ʿarabiyya, li-l-ʿulum, 2003). For al-Qasim, see, for example, "Al-nidham al-huquqi al-islami wa azmat al-wasaʾil—Al-dimuqratiyya ka namudhaj li-l-jadal al-fiqhi" [The System of Islamic Law and the Crisis of Means—Democracy as a Model for the Legal Debate], *Al-Watan*, November 21 and 28, 2002.

23. The Islamo-liberals were thus also intent on claiming for themselves the term *wasatiyya* (moderation), which the new Sahwa had already appropriated.

24. www.wasatyah.com; www.tuwaa.com. The second was closed down by the authorities in 2004, while the first, invaded by conservatives, was abandoned by its Islamo-liberal users. Other forums have taken on the role, for example, Dar al-nadwa (www.daralnadwa.com, closed down in late 2005), Muhawir (www.mohawer.net), and Tomaar (www.tomaar.net).

25. J. E. Peterson, *Saudi Arabia and the Illusion of Security* (Oxford: Oxford University Press, 2002), 59ff.

26. Interview with ʿAbd al-Aziz al-Qasim.

27. "Ruʾya li-hadir al-watan wa mustaqbalihi," *Al-Quds al-ʿArabi*, January 30, 2003.

28. Interview with Islamo-liberals.

29. Interview with Matruk al-Falih.

30. "Nidaʾ watani ila-l-qiyada wa-l-shaʿb maʿan—Al-islah al-dusturi awwalan," *Elaph*, December 20, 2003.

31. Interview with Muhammad Saʿid Tayyib.

32. Interview with Saʿud al-Sarhan, who attended the meeting on February 26, 2004.

33. "Bayan al-tadamun ma' al-qiyadat al-islahiyya al-mu'taqala" [Communiqué of Support for the Imprisoned Reformist Leaders], www.metransparent.com.

34. Mansur al-Nuqaydan, "Kharitat al-islamiyyin fi-l-sa'udiyya wa qissat al-takfir" [The Map of Islamist Movements in Saudi Arabia and the History of *Takfir*], *Elaph*, February 27, 2003.

35. Interview with Sulayman al-Dahayyan.

36. "Man huwa Nasir al-Fahd?" [Who Is Nasir al-Fahd?], *Al-Riyad*, December 23, 2003; interview with Sa'ud al-Sarhan.

37. *Al-Islah* 92 (January 5, 1998); "Man huwa Nasir al-Fahd?"

38. "Al-Khalidi al-'a'id min al-takfir" [Al-Khalidi, Who Returned from *Takfir*], *Al-Sharq al-Awsat*, December 14, 2003.

39. Interview with Fahd al-Shafi.

40. Interview with Sa'ud al-Sarhan, who was a former student of al-Shu'aybi. See also the account by the Libyan jihadi Abu Anas al-Libi, "Al-shaykh al-'Uqla 'alam shamikh fi zaman al-inhitat" [Sheikh al-'Uqla: An Eminent Figure in an Age of Decline], www.almuqatila.com.

41. Thomas Hegghammer, *Jihad in Saudi Arabia* (Cambridge: Cambridge University Press, 2010).

42. Such photographs are never found on the sites of al-Fahd, al-Khudayr, and other figures in the movement, whereas global jihadi forums are full of propaganda films celebrating the "great deeds" of the "mujahideen."

43. This comes out in an analysis of the oral and written production of Bin Laden between 1996 and 2005. Gilles Kepel and Jean-Pierre Milelli, eds., *Al-Qaeda in Its Own Words* (Cambridge, Mass.: Belknap Press or Harvard University Press, 2008), 41–77. Since 2005, with the evolution of the situation in Iraq and Lebanon, al-Qaeda has mentioned Shiism more frequently, particularly in statements by Ayman al-Zawahiri.

44. Thomas Hegghammer, "Terrorist Recruitment and Radicalization in Saudi Arabia," *Middle East Policy* 13, 4 (Winter 2006): 49.

45. Interview with Sa'ud al-Sarhan.

46. "Yusuf al-'Ayiri: Shumukh fi zaman al-hawan" [Yusuf al-'Ayiri: Greatness in an Age of Servility], *Sawt al-Jihad* 1 (September 28, 2003).

47. Interview with Sulayman al-Dahayyan.

48. "Bayan fi riddat Mansur al-Nuqaydan" [Statement on the Apostasy of Mansur al-Nuqaydan], January 24, 2003, www.alkhoder.com.

49. Al-Khudayr, *Usul al-sahwa al-jadida*.

50. Yusuf al-'Ayiri, *Munasahat Salman al-'Awda ba'd taghyir manhajihi* [Advice to Salman al-'Awda after He Changed His Methodology], August 16,

2000, www.tawhed.ws. The letters were not made public until the death of al-ʿAyiri in June 2003.

51. Hamud al-Shuʿaybi, *Hukm ma jara fi Amrika min ahdath* [Judgment on the Events in the United States], September 17, 2001, www.tawhed.ws. See also ʿAli al-Khudayr, *ʿAn ahdath amrika wa mudhaharat al-kuffar* [On the Events in America and Compassion for the Infidels], September 21, 2001, www.tawhed.ws.

52. On this debate, see Stéphane Lacroix, "Islamo-Liberal Politics in Saudi Arabia," in *Saudi Arabia in the Balance: Political Economy, Society, Foreign Affairs*, ed. Paul Aarts and Gerd Nonneman (New York: New York University Press, 2005), 47–50.

53. Nasir al-Fahd, *Al-tankil bima fi bayan al-muthaqqafin min al-abatil* [Condemnation of the Errors Found in the Manifesto of the Intellectuals], www.tawhed.ws.

54. Interview with associates of Salman al-ʿAwda.

55. See, for example, Hamud al-Shuʿaybi, "Suʾal hawla sharʿiyyat hukumat Taliban" [A Question on the Legitimacy of the Taliban Government], www.tawhed.ws.

56. See Nasir al-Fahd, *Iqamat al-burhan ʿala wujub kasr al-awthan* [Presentation of the Arguments Showing the Necessity of Destroying the Idols], www.tawhed.ws; interviews with Sahwi militants.

57. See, for example, "Bayan li-fadilat al-shaykh Hamud bin ʿUqla al-Shuʿaybi fi daʿm al-imara al-islamiyya fi Afghanistan" [Communiqué of Sheikh Hamud bin ʿUqla al-Shuʿaybi in Support of the Islamic Emirate of Afghanistan], December 1, 2001, www.d-sunnah.net.

58. "Fatwa fi kufr man aʿan Amrika ʿala-l-muslimin fi-l-ʿiraq" [Fatwa on the Impiety of Those Who Support America against the Muslims in Iraq], www.almokhtar.com.

59. Hegghammer, *Jihad in Saudi Arabia*, 165.

60. ʿAli al-Khudayr, Ahmad al-Khalidi, and Nasir al-Fahd, "Ilaykum ayyuha al-mujahidun (innama hadha ibtilaʾ)" [For You, Mujahideen (This Is Only a Test)]; "Risala ila rijal al-mabahith" [Letter to the Agents of the Secret Police], www.tawhed.ws.

61. Saudi television, Channel 1, November 17 and 22 and December 14, 2003.

62. For more details, see Hegghammer, *Jihad in Saudi Arabia*, 210ff.

63. Ibid., 189ff.

64. Ibid., 220.

65. There are no reliable measurements of Saudi public opinion, but this mixture of indifference and aversion is what came out in discussions with Saudis and from following discussion forums of various orientations on the Internet. The al-Saha forum (www.alsaha.com), the most frequented by Saudi conservatives, gives a sense of the general feeling: messages concerning Islamo-liberals have largely been ignored, those concerning global jihad outside Saudi Arabia have generally been greeted enthusiastically, and those related to AQAP have provoked, beginning in November 2003, anger or perplexity.

66. For an exhaustive study of these reasons, see Stéphane Lacroix, "Les Champs de la discorde: Une sociologie politique de l'islamisme en Arabie Saoudite" (Ph.D. diss., Sciences Po, 2007), 619–635.

67. Although Saudi oil revenues continued to fluctuate after 1995, they experienced no sharp decline and even had a tendency to increase. This increase became even more significant after the American invasion of Iraq in March 2003. Steffen Hertog, "Segmented Clientelism: The Politics of Economic Reform in Saudi Arabia" (Ph.D. diss., Oxford University, 2006), 148.

68. Interviews with ʿAbdallah al-Hamid and Matruk al-Falih.

69. "Bi-tawqiʿ 115 baynahum 15 marʾa bayan li-muthaqqafin wa-mihaniyyin saʿudiyyin taʾyidan li-rafd Sunʿ Allah Ibrahim istilam jaʾizat al-riwaya al-ʿarabiyya" [Signed by 115 People Including 15 Women, a Manifesto of Saudi Intellectuals and Professionals in Support of the Refusal of Sunʿ Allah Ibrahim to Accept the Arab Novel Award], Elaph, November 7, 2003.

70. ʿAbdallah al-Hamid, Li-l-islah hadaf wa-manhaj [Reform Has a Method and an Objective] (Beirut: Al-dar al-ʿarabiyya li-l-ʿulum, 2004), 21.

71. An exception was the liberal Ghazi al-Qusaybi, who, intent on provoking the Sahwi ulema, had assumed the right to speak in the name of Islam. However, al-Qusaybi's initiative did not have the same symbolic value, because it happened in a moment of crisis, and because al-Qusaybi did not have al-Hamid's Islamist credentials.

72. Analysis of the two most popular Islamist forums in Saudi Arabia, www.alsaha.com and www.muslm.net.

73. Nasir al-Fahd, "Al-tarajuʿ ʿan al-tarajuʿ al-mazʿum" [Retraction of the Alleged Retraction], February 17, 2004, www.tawhed.ws.

74. The exception was Abdallah al-Rashud, who had studied shariʿa at Imam University and had become known late in 2002 for organizing a small protest gathering that created a great stir outside the office of Mufti Abd al-Aziz Al al-Shaykh. Al-Rashud died late in 2004. According to some sources, he went to fight in Iraq, where he was killed.

75. Aside from al-Rashud, the individuals in question were Faris al-Zahrani (arrested August 5, 2004), ʿIsa al-ʿAwhsan (killed by the Saudi security forces on July 20, 2004), Abd al-Majid al-Munayʿ (killed by the Saudi security forces on October 13, 2004), and Sultan al-ʿUtaybi (killed by the Saudi security forces on December 29, 2004).

76. Luwis ʿAtiyyat ʿAllah, "Bayan al-muthaqqafin al-saʿudiyyin . . . Asʾila muhimma tahtaj ila jawab" [The Manifesto of Saudi Intellectuals . . . Important Questions That Require Answers], www.yalewis.com. On Luwis ʿAtiyyat Allah, see Madawi al-Rasheed, *Contesting the Saudi State: Islamic Voices from a New Generation* (Cambridge: Cambridge University Press, 2007), 175ff.

77. This logic appears very clearly in the writings of Yusuf al-ʿAyiri. See also Roel Meijer, "Yusuf al-Uyairi and the Making of a Revolutionary Salafi Praxis," *Die Welt des Islams* 47, 3–4 (2007): 422–459.

78. The neojihadis systematically designated the document as "the manifesto of the intellectuals." See, for example, al-Fahd, *Al-tankil bima fi bayan al-muthaqqafin min al-abatil.*

79. Local elections had taken place in the Hejaz in the 1920s and 1930s.

80. This was the case, for example, for the candidate Sulayman al-Salman, who ran in Riyadh.

81. In Shiite areas, Shiite candidates, chiefly Shirazis, won. In the countryside, where the Sahwa is less well established and tribes remain a dominant force, the tribal candidates won almost all the seats.

82. Interviews with activists connected to the *jamaʿat*. A few articles in Arabic have also been published on the subject: ʿAbd al-Rahman Al-Mishari, "Hardlak li-l-ikhwan wa mabruk li-l-sururiyya" [Too Bad for the Brothers and Bravo for the Sururis], www.ala7rar.net; Faris bin Hizam, "Al-intikhabat al-baladiyya naqalat siraʿ al-salafiyyin ila-l-sath" [The Municipal Elections Have Brought the Disputes among *Salafis* to the Surface], February 28, 2005, www.alarabiya.net.

83. Campaign leaflets in the author's possession.

84. Interviews with Sahwi activists involved in the campaign.

85. Gilles Kepel, "Islamism Reconsidered," *Harvard International Review* 22, 2 (2000): 22–27; Olivier Roy, "Pourquoi le 'post-islamisme'?" *Revue du Monde Musulman et de la Méditerranée* 85/86 (1999): 9–30; Asef Bayat, "What Is Post-Islamism?" *ISIM Newsletter* 16 (Autumn 2005): 5.

86. Bayat, "What Is Post-Islamism?" 5.

87. This phenomenon is akin to what Olivier Roy calls "neo-fundamentalism." Olivier Roy, *Globalized Islam* (New York: Columbia University Press, 2004), 117ff.

Conclusion

1. See *Al-Riyad*, December 28, 2008; *Sahb kutub Sayyid Qutb min maktabat al-madaris bi-l-sa'udiyya* [Removal of Sayyid Qutb's Books from School
Libraries in Saudi Arabia] www.islamonline.net, November 25, 2008.

2. On these efforts and the reactions they provoked, see Eleanor Abdella
Doumato, "Saudi Arabia: From 'Wahhabi Roots' to Contemporary Revisionism," in *Teaching Islam: Textbooks and Religion in the Middle East,* ed. Eleanor
Abdella Doumato and Gregory Starrett (Boulder, Colo.: Lynne Rienner, 2007),
170–173.

Acknowledgments

The list of all those without whom I would not have been able to complete this research is long, and the debt of gratitude I owe them is infinite. First of all, I must thank Gilles Kepel for his extraordinary patience and immense generosity. His remarks and encouragement were priceless. At the Middle East–Mediterranean Chair of Sciences Po, I was lucky to be in close contact with a milieu of young, brilliant researchers whose intellectual companionship stimulated me and whose friendship allowed me to overcome my doubts. *Al-mukhlis* Thomas Hegghammer was a fantastic companion in the field and a generous and challenging sparring partner. *Al-'alim* Nabil Mouline was always happy to share his intimate knowledge of the subtleties of Islamic history and the Arabic language. *Al-adib* Thomas Pierret was a superb discussant, allowing me to test my hypotheses in order to improve them. Finally, *al-muhandis* Steffen Hertog offered me his valuable insights on the political economy of the Saudi kingdom. In addition, Carine Abou Lahoud, Lamiss Azab, Joseph Bahout, Laurent Bonnefoy, Aurélie Daher, Asiem al-Difraoui, Amélie Le Renard, Omar Saghi, Claire Talon, and Abdellah Tourabi all provided useful observations or much-needed encouragement.

I also wish to express my gratitude to all those scholars who, throughout this process, enriched my reflection with their informed advice or incisive remarks, especially David Commins, Christian Décobert, Jean-Pierre Filiu, Olivier Fillieule, Gregory Gause, Bernard Haykel, Toby Jones, Brynjar Lia, Laurence Louër, Giacomo Luciani, Gerd Nonneman, James Piscatori, Bernard Rougier, Ghassan Salamé, Jean-François Seznec, Guido Steinberg,

Pierre Thénard, and Mariam Abou Zahab. At Stanford University, where I spent a year finishing this book, I found an extraordinarily fertile academic environment, thanks to the kindness and support of Robert Gregg, David Laitin, Shahzad Bashir, and Marie-Pierre Ulloa. I am also thankful for the help and patience of my editor at Harvard University Press, Joyce Seltzer, whose comments were always insightful.

I must as well pay tribute to the institutions that supported this research: the Middle East–Mediterranean Chair of Sciences Po, and the French Ministry of Research and Higher Education, from which I received a three-year research grant. In Riyadh, the King Faysal Center for Research and Islamic Studies invited me as one of its visiting researchers. I shall never forget the kindness and helpfulness of its Secretary General, Yahya bin Junayd, and of its director of research, Awad al-Badi.

In Saudi Arabia, Yusuf al-Dayni, Sarah Khazindar, Tariq al-Mubarak, and Sa'ud al-Sarhan honored me with their friendship. They opened many doors and made me feel at home during my stays in the kingdom. Naturally, I must also thank all those—shabab, intellectuals, and ulema—who agreed to spend time with me and answer my questions. This research owes them a tremendous debt.

Last, but by no means least, Alexandra supported me during all those long years. Her loving presence gave me the strength to take this project to its end. *Awakening Islam* is dedicated to her, as well as to my parents.

Index

Committee for the Defense of
Legitimate Rights (CDLR), 188,
190, 323n190; Sahwi ulema and,
188, 189, 191–192, 193; "enlightened" Sahwi intellectuals and,
188–189, 191, 192; founding
members of, 189, 323n197;
munasirun and, 189, 191; "Proclamation of the Foundation of the
Committee for the Defense of
Legitimate Rights (CDLR)," 189,
191; Sahwi intellectuals in, 189, 190,
191, 192; Saudi regime vs., 190, 198,
325n226; in London, 192, 195, 204,
205, 231–232, 233, 234–236; as
opposition party, 192; Saudi state
repression of Sahwi protest and,
204, 205; popular mobilization and,
231–232, 233, 234–236
Constitutional monarchy, and
Islamo-liberals, 245, 247
Corporatism, 285n61; Saudi field of
power sectorization and, 23
Council of the Committee of Senior
Ulema, 74, 75, 141, 159, 160, 170,
171–172, 184, 187–188, 190, 208, 210,
219, 222. *See also* Ulema
Countermovements. *See* Sahwi
countermovements
Creed (*'aqida*), 11, 54, 69, 82, 86–87,
105, 111, 123–124, 140, 165, 212,
220, 251; teaching in Saudi
educational system, 47–48; Jami vs.
Sahwi, 215
Cultural supplements (*malahiq
thaqafiyya*), 18, 134; Saudi modernism and, 139, 157

al-Dahayyan, Sulayman, 77, 120, 225,
232–234, 246, 251–252, 336n218

Dar al-Hadith (the House of the
Hadith), 88–89, 300n36; in Yemen,
96, 101
al-Dawsari, Abd al-Rahman, 53, 56–58,
106, 131, 133, 143–144, 152, 171,
293n109
al-Dayni, Yusuf, 102, 146, 220
*Defense of Muslim Territories Is the
First Individual Duty, The* ('Azzam),
110–111
al-Dhayidi, Mishari, 100, 206
al-Dikhna, 23, 24
Dobry, Michel, 28, 32
Does History Repeat Itself? (al-'Abda),
145, 314n145
al-Dubayyan, Ibrahim, 188, 189, 205
al-Dumayni, Ali, 18, 20, 134, 157, 249

Economic capital: in Saudi society,
21, 285n56; social capital and,
21, 22
Economic field: Saudi royal family and,
20, 285n53; in Saudi state birth/
development, 20
Economic recession from oil income
decline (1982): Sahwi uprisings and,
5; overview, 129; Sahwa generation
and, 129–133; Saudi public
employment and, 130–131, 310n24
*Educational Policy for the Kingdom of
Saudi Arabia*, 46–48
Education field, Sahwa internal
competition within, 123, 126,
127–128
Egypt: Saudi state birth/development
and, 12–13; Muslim Brotherhood in,
38–39, 40; Saudi Arabia vs., 41
Elites: Islamist movements/resources
and, 30–31; legitimating resources
and, 30–31; social movements/

field; Intelligentsia; *Muthaqqaf*; New intellectual; Sahwi intellectuals

Intellectual field: in Saudi state birth/development, 15, 16, 17–20, 284n45; literary field and, 18–19; intelligentsia and, 20, 137; Saudi Islamists and, 20; religious field and, 23; religious field vs., 23; Islamist movements/religious field and, 31–33; Sahwa and, 35, 133–134; autonomy, 134; liberal intelligentsia and, 134, 136; Saudi modernism and, 135, 144; Sahwi intellectuals and, 137, 138; Saudi modernization and, 137; Sahwi mobilization into, 149; support of Saudi regime legitimacy, 159–160; Sahwi protest movement and, 177–179, 181; in Sahwa insurrection aftermath, 241, 263; Islamo-liberals and, 256, 257, 258, 261. *See also* Intellectuals; Intelligentsia; *Muthaqqaf*

Intelligentsia, 15, 16, 24; intellectual field and, 20, 137; Sahwa generation vs., 131–133; modernism and, 134; Sahwi intellectuals vs., 136–137. *See also* Intellectual field; Liberal intelligentsia; Liberals; *Muthaqqaf*

Internet forums, and Islamo-liberals, 246, 339n24

In the Shade of the Koran (Sayyid Qutb), 39, 55, 106

Intifada of Burayda, 232–234, 336n218

Intifada of Muharram, 223, 334n171

Intifadat al-Sahwa (Sahwa insurrection), 3. *See also* Sahwa insurrection

Iran, 31, 32, 33, 65, 229; Saudi Arabia vs., 103, 124; Khomeinis and, 222–223

Iranian Revolution (1979), 124, 145

Iraq invasion of Kuwait: American troops in Saudi Arabia and, 2, 158, 316n37; Sahwi ulema and, 166. *See also* Gulf War

Iraq-Iran war, Saudi support of Iraq in, 124

Irja' (postponing judgment), 147, 148, 149

Islah (making something conform more closely to Islam): overview, 176–177; Sahwi protest movement and, 176–177

Islam: Saudi export of, 1; as creed and law, 11; in Sahwi ideology, 60; Hejazi, 221. *See also* Islamism; Wahhabism

Islamic Awakening (al-Sahwa al-Islamiyya), 2, 38. *See also* Sahwa

Islamic cassettes, 140–141; advent of, 143–144; Jami, 216, 219, 332n125. *See also* Sahwi ulema cassettes

Islamic culture (*thaqafa islamiyya*), 46–47, 48

Islamic democracy: "Letter of Demands" and, 181; "enlightened" Sahwi intellectuals and conservative, 245; Islamo-liberals and, 245, 247

Islamic Forum, 125, 154

Islamicized sciences, 47

Islamic literature, 136

Islamic modernization, 43

Islamic recordings stores, 143; Jami, 216, 332n125

Islamic revivalism, influences on Saudi Arabia, 1–2

Islamic Salvation Front (FIS), 175

Islamic solidarity (*al-tadamun al-islami*), 41

Islamic University of Medina, 41, 43, 45, 75, 85, 90, 91, 92, 96, 97, 102, 113, 115, 211–214, 220, 248, 269

Islamism, 1, 281n1; Saudi Islamist movement vs. Middle Eastern, 2; jihadism as new form of internationalist, 109; modernism vs., 140; Saudi Arabia and, 266. *See also* Islam; Islamists; post-Islamism; Saudi Islamism; Shiite Islamism

Islamist(s): disputes over Saudi Islam, 2, 3; vs. Saudi regime over Saudi Islam, 2; non-Sahwa groups in Sahwa insurrection, 199; Saudi state repression of Sahwi protest and foreign radical, 206; in Sahwa insurrection aftermath, 238–264; new insurrection and Saudi Islamists, 270; terminology usage, 281n1. *See also* Non-Sahwi Islamists; Saudi Islamists

Islamist mobilizations, 4, 32, 33; post-Islamism and, 270. *See also* Islamist movements; Saudi Islamist mobilizations

Islamist movement(s): Saudi Arabia religious proselytism and, 1; Middle Eastern Islamism vs. Saudi, 2; ulema/intellectuals and, 29–34; elites/resources and, 30–31; religious/intellectual field and, 31–33; mobilization of, 32, 33; Sahwa vs. rival, 35, 123. *See also* Islamist mobilizations

Islamo-liberals: in Sahwa insurrection aftermath, 241, 245–249, 255, 256–259, 261, 262–263, 342n65; as Sahwa legacy group, 241, 245–249, 255, 256–259, 261, 342n65; "How We Can Coexist" and, 243, 247, 256–257; new Sahwa and, 243, 245, 261; call for political/religious segments union, 245; constitutional monarchy and,

245, 247; "enlightened" Sahwi intellectuals and, 245, 248; Islamic democracy and, 245, 247; political activism, 245, 246, 247–248; political field and, 245, 246, 247–248; field and, 245, 256–257, 258; group incubation in Saudi prisons, 245–246, 249; Saudi regime and, 245–246, 247, 248–249; overview, 245–249, 339n18; Internet forums, 246, 339n24; September 11, 2001 attacks and, 246, 247; *wasatiyya* and, 246, 247, 339n23; Prince Abdallah and, 247, 248; petitions, 247–248; King Abdallah and, 249; neojihadis and, 249, 250, 251–252; movement and Sahwi remobilization aborted attempt, 255, 256–259, 261, 342n65; Saudi society response to, 255, 258–259, 342n65; intellectual field and, 256, 257, 258, 261; Sahwi intellectuals and, 256; ulema and, 256, 257–258, 342n71; *muthaqqaf* and, 257, 258; new intellectual and, 257, 258, 263; global jihadi militants and, 260; Saudi 2005 municipal elections and, 261; Saudi royal family rivalry and, 261

Isnad (hadith transmitters), 82

Jahiliyya (age of ignorance), 39, 53–54, 56

Jahiliyya of the Twentieth Century, The (Muhammad Qutb), 54

Al-Jamaʿa al-Salafiyya al-Muhtasiba (JSM), 89; Sahwa ascendancy resistance/1979 events and, 89–103, 119; Juhayman and, 90, 92, 93, 94–100, 108, 109; Ahl al-Hadith and, 90–91, 100, 101, 102, 103; bin Baz

and, 90–91, 94, 95, 96, 97; House
of the Ikhwan, 91–92; Wahhabi
ulema vs., 92; Saudi state vs.,
93–94, 95–96, 97, 98–99, 100, 103;
Muslim Brotherhood vs., 94;
Letters of Juhayman and, 95–98;
Grand Mosque of Mecca seizure by,
98, 99–100, 102, 103; Mahdi and,
98, 99; militarization of, 98–99,
303n84; Saudi Islamism and, 100;
Sahwa strengthening after Grand
Mosque of Mecca seizure by, 103;
exclusivists and, 108; social
bases of, 119
Jama'at (Sahwa organized networks): as
vanguard of a countersociety, 62–73;
Muslim Brotherhood and, 63, 64;
overview, 63; secrecy around
existence of, 63, 294n127; subgroups/
hierarchy, 63; Saudi Islamist
mobilizations and, 64; origins of,
64–65; mobilizing power of, 71;
youth recruits of, 71–72; incentives
for member attachment to, 72–73;
members break from society, 72–73;
leaders' orders and other Sahwa
circles, 73; extension into social
arena, 78; ulema and, 80; Saudi
institutions control by, 126–129,
310n10; Sahwi protest movement
and, 178; Sahwi mobilization
infrastructure weaknesses and,
226–227, 228–229, 230–231, 234;
Saudi state repression of Sahwi
protest and, 230; place in Saudi
system, 230–231; Saudi 2005
municipal elections and, 262, 268;
Sahwa Islamism and, 266. See also
Saudi Brotherhood jama'at; Sururi
jama'a

al-Jami, Muhammad Aman, 211–212,
216, 225
Jami(s): Ahl al-Hadith and, 193, 212,
213, 215, 216, 220, 225; Saudi regime
and, 211, 212, 213, 215; Saudi royal
family and, 211, 214, 215–216;
Sahwis and use of term, 211–212;
Ahl al-Hadith loyalists and, 212,
213, 220; non-Saudi joiners of, 213,
330n101; participants, 213–214,
330n101; Bani Jam, 214; religious
field war between Sahwis and, 214,
216–220, 225; ulema, 214, 220;
university/religious field replace-
ments for fired Sahwis, 214;
discourse, 215; vs. Sahwi creed, 215;
vs. Sahwi methodology, 215; Islamic
cassettes, 216, 219, 332n125; Islamic
recordings stores, 216, 332n125;
refutations of Sahwi writings/
declarations, 216; confrontations
between Sahwis and, 216–217;
reports on Sahwis to secret police,
217; Sahwi countermeasures to
attacks by, 217–218; Ibn Baz/senior
ulema respect competition between
Sahwis and, 218–219; senior ulema
and, 218–219, 220; war of tazkiyat
from between Sahwis and, 218–219;
Haddadist submovement, 220;
Hanbalism and, 220; Wahhabism
and, 220, 221; Wahhabi ulema and,
220; schisms/movement weakening,
220–221, 225, 333n155
Jami countermovement to Sahwis, 193,
211–221, 225. See also Jamis
Jamism, 213, 225
Janadriyya festival, 137–138, 153,
156–157, 174, 240
al-Jazeera (satellite channel), 240

Military field: Saudi royal family and, 20–21; in Saudi state birth/development, 20–21

Ministry of Hajj and *Waqfs*, 77, 103, 155–156, 208

Ministry of Islamic Affairs, *Waqfs*, Preaching and Guidance, 208–210

MIRA. *See* Movement for Islamic Reform in Arabia

Mobilization: leadership in social movements, 30, 34; of social movements, 30, 32, 34. *See also* Islamist mobilizations; Sahwi mobilizations

Modernism *(hadatha)*, 134; intellectuals and, 134, 137, 138; intelligentsia and, 134, 312n65; Saudi literary criticism and, 135; Islamism vs., 140; Sahwi ulema and, 164. *See also* Saudi modernism

Modernism in the Light of Islam (al-Qarni), 140, 156, 312n68

Modernization: Islamic, 43. *See also* Saudi modernization

Movement for Islamic Reform in Arabia (MIRA), 193

al-Muʿallim, Muhammad, 91, 95, 119

al-Mubarak, Muhammad, 43, 45, 46

Muhammad bin Ibrahim. *See* Al al-Shaykh, Muhammad bin Ibrahim

Muhammad Surur. *See* Zayn al-ʿAbidin, Muhammad Surur

Al-Mujahid (magazine), 118, 308n188

Mujahideen, 30, 109, 113, 115, 194, 196, 254, 260

Al-Mujtamaʿ (magazine), 44, 53, 59–60, 70, 87, 110, 125

Munasirun (traditional Wahhabi ulema who are supporters of Sahwi opposition): in Sahwi opposition

front, 164, 166, 168–172; overview, 168–169; Sahwis and, 168–169; categories of, 169–171; reasons for Sahwi support of, 169–171; Sahwi protest movement and, 175–176, 177, 179, 181, 182, 183, 186–188, 189, 191, 198; "Threefold Response" of, 187–188; ulema vs., 187–188; CDLR and, 189, 191; Saudi state repression of Sahwi protest and, 205

Muslim Brotherhood: arrival into Saudi Arabia, 37, 38–42; Sahwa and, 38, 51–52, 114, 116, 123, 215, 218, 288n1; development of, 38–39; Egypt and, 38–39, 40; Saudi educational system and, 42–51, 290n46; Islamic culture and, 46–47; Islamicized sciences and, 47; *jamaʿat* and, 63, 64; Saudi Brotherhood and foreign, 68–69; Ahl al-Hadith vs., 86, 87, 116; al-Albani vs., 86–87; JSM vs., 94; Afghan jihad recruitment of young members of, 114; pioneers of Afghan jihad, 114–115; Sahwa vs., 123; intellectuals, 136; Sahwa Islamism and, 265, 266. *See also* Saudi Brotherhood *jamaʿat*

Muslim Brotherhood ideology: Sahwi ideology and, 52, 62; Wahhabism and, 52, 53, 57, 59

Muslim reformism, 82; overview, 14

Muslim reformists: overview, 14; Saudi state birth/development and, 14; al-Albani and, 82, 83; hadith reappraisal of, 82; positions of, 82

Muslim world, reaction to Soviet invasion of Afghanistan, 109

Muslim World League, 42, 68, 124, 269

al-Mutabaqqani, Mazin, 77

Non-Saudi: Arabs, 134; joiners of Jamis, 213, 330n101
al-Nuqaydan, Mansur, 105, 107, 109, 143, 225, 245, 246, 252, 339n19

Oil boom (1973): Saudi modernization and, 17; religious field and, 75–76, 78; Sahwa and, 78; Sahwa generation and, 131
Oil income decline: Sahwi remobilization potential and future, 268–269. *See also* Economic recession from oil income decline (1982)
OIRAP. *See* Organization of the Islamic Revolution in the Arabian Peninsula
"Oneness of being" doctrine, 86, 106, 215, 300n26
Organization of the Islamic Revolution in the Arabian Peninsula (OIRAP), 223

Political field, 7; in Saudi state birth/ development, 8–9, 15–16, 19, 21, 282n13; Saudi field of power sectorization and, 25–26, 27–28, 286n77; Saudi field of power sectorization/religious field and, 25–26, 27–28, 29, 286n77; collusive transactions with Saudi fields' dominant elites, 28–29; Wahhabi ulema and, 74, 75, 76; religious field and, 74–76, 207–208; Sahwi mobilizations and, 150; Sahwi opposition front and, 164; changes and Sahwi protest movement, 236; King Abdallah and, 238–239, 240; in Sahwa insurrection aftermath, 238–239, 240, 263; Sudayris and, 239; Islamo-liberals and, 245, 246, 247–248. *See also* Saudi royal family

Popular mobilization: CDLR and, 231–232, 233, 234–236; Sahwi mobilization infrastructure weaknesses and, 231–236; al-ʿAwda and, 232–234; Intifada of Burayda, 232–234, 336n218; demonstrations, 232–235, 336n218; Saudi regime and, 233–234
Post-Islamism: scenario in Sahwa insurrection aftermath, 262–264; Saudi Arabia and, 264, 270; Islamist mobilizations and, 270
"Proclamation of the Foundation of the Committee for the Defense of Legitimate Rights (CDLR)," 189, 191
Public sphere: in Sahwa insurrection aftermath, 241, 245; post-1990s Sahwi organizations and, 268

Qabili (tribal), 21, 22
Al-Qaeda: jihadi identity/network of, 115, 307n168; Osama bin Laden and, 115, 307n168, 340n43; global jihad and, 200; September 11, 2001 attacks, 246; neojihadis and, 253
Al-Qaeda in the Arabian Peninsula (AQAP): neojihadis and, 254; Saudi global jihadis and, 254; attacks/ assassinations, 254–255, 259; global jihadi militants and, 255, 259–260, 342n74, 343n75; members, 255; Saudi society response to, 255, 342n65; Sahwi remobilization aborted attempts and, 255–256, 259–260, 342n65; ulema and, 259. *See also* Neojihadis
al-Qahtani, Muhammad, 94, 95, 98, 99, 303n81
al-Qahtani, Muhammad Saʿid, 56, 162, 204, 249

Repression. *See* Saudi state repression of Sahwi protest

Resources: elites/Islamist movements and, 30–31; elites/social movements and, 30–31. *See also* Legitimating resources; Militant resources

Rida, Rashid, 38, 82–83

Riyadh, 24

Royal family. *See* Saudi royal family

al-Sa'd, Abdallah, 250, 254

Sadat, Anwar, 31, 40, 45, 53, 116

Sahwa: opposition to Saudi royal family and American troops in Saudi Arabia, 2–3, 162; development of, 34–35, 37–38; intellectual field and, 35, 133–134; religious field and, 35, 73–78; rival Islamist movements vs., 35, 123; Muslim Brotherhood and, 38, 51–52, 114, 116, 123, 215, 218, 288n1; emergence of, 51–62; break between rest of social world and, 72; Wahhabi ulema and, 73, 141–150; 1970s favorable growth context for, 73–78; oil boom (1973) and, 78; unifying potential in social arena of, 78–80; Saudi field of power sectorization and, 79, 123; religious field dominance by, 103; strengthening after JSM Grand Mosque of Mecca seizure, 103; jihadism vs., 109, 111–112; Soviet invasion of Afghanistan and, 109; support for Afghanistan, 109–110, 114, 116; vs. 'Azzam fatwa of Afghan jihad, 111–112; movement limits, 118–121; social bases of, 120–121, 309n193; rivalries for social arena control, 122–129; internal competition within education field, 123, 126, 127–128;

internal competition within religious field, 123, 124, 126; internal competition within, 123–129; liberal intelligentsia vs., 133; background of break between Saudi regime and, 152–158; entrance into Saudi cultural institutions, 157–158; three-way split in Sahwa insurrection aftermath, 241, 262–263; Saudi Islamism and, 267. *See also* New Sahwa

al-Sahwa al-Islamiyya (Islamic awakening), 2. *See also* Sahwa

Sahwa ascendancy resistance: Ahl al-Hadith and, 81, 85–89, 102, 118; overview, 81; al-Albani and, 81–89; JSM/1979 events and, 89–103, 119; exclusivist Wahhabism last bastions and, 103–109, 118; by Ikhwan of Burayda, 105–109, 120; by jihadis, 109–118; social bases of, 118–121

Sahwa circles. *See* Sahwa community concentric circles

Sahwa community concentric circle(s): of "committed" *(multazimun),* 62, 130, 229, 234; of "Sahwa generation" *(jil al-Sahwa),* 62, 130, 229; of "affiliates" *(muntamun),* 62–63, 130, 229; *jama'at* and, 62–63; overview of, 62–63; *jama'at* leaders' orders and other, 73. *See also* Jama'at

Sahwa generation *(jil al-Sahwa):* Sahwa community concentric circle of, 62, 130; overview, 129–130; economic recession and, 129–133; Saudi public employment and, 130–131, 310n24; oil boom and, 131; vs. previous generation, 131; intelligentsia vs., 131–133; secularists vs., 131–133, 141; Saudi modernism vs., 141; mobilization into social arena, 149

Sahwi identity: integration and youth camps, 51, 61; construction/ reinforcement through action, 61; ambiguity in formation of, 61–62

Sahwi ideology: Muslim Brotherhood ideology and, 52, 62; Wahhabism and, 52, 53, 56; Qutbism and, 52–53; al-Dawsari and, 53, 56–58, 293n109; al-Rashid and, 53, 59–60; Muhammad Qutb and, 53–56; intellectual fathers of, 53–60; Islam in, 60; Islamist discourse of, 152; political opposition discourse of, 152

Sahwi intellectuals, 135; lay, 136; Sahwi ulema and, 136, 139, 150, 177–178; intelligentsia vs., 136–137; intellectual field and, 137, 138; literary clubs and, 137; Saudi modernism vs., 138, 139, 141; Saudi newspapers and, 139; in Sahwi opposition front, 164, 166, 172–175, 320n118; Wahhabi ulema vs., 174, 321n127; in Sahwi protest movement, 175, 177–178, 179, 181, 182, 183, 185, 186, 188–189, 190, 191, 192, 198; in CDLR, 189, 190, 191, 192; Saudi state repression of Sahwi protest and, 203, 204, 205, 206; Islamo-liberals and, 256. *See also* "Enlightened" Sahwi intellectuals

Sahwi mobilization(s), 151; economic recession and, 149; into intellectual field, 149; mid-1980s, 149; into religious field, 149; of Sahwa generation into social arena, 149; political field and, 150; Saudi regime delegitimization and, 158–159; Sahwi protest movement early, 175–177; Sahwi remobilization aborted attempts and, 255, 342n65. *See also*

Sahwi protest movement; Sahwi remobilization aborted attempts

Sahwi mobilization infrastructure weaknesses, 225; Saudi regime and, 226, 228, 230–234, 235; *jama'at* and, 226–227, 228–229, 230–231, 234; "Letter of Demands" and, 227; Sahwi protest movement leaders and, 227; Saudi Brotherhood *jama'at* and, 227, 228; Sururi *jama'a* and, 227, 228; non-Sahwi Islamists and, 229; rejectionist Ahl al-Hadith and, 229–230; jihadis and, 229–230; Saudi state repression of Sahwi protest and, 230, 233–234, 235; CDLR and, 231–232, 233, 234–236; non-Sahwi popular mobilization and, 231–236. *See also* Non-Sahwi popular mobilization

Sahwi opposition. *See* Sahwi protest movement

Sahwi opposition front: Gulf War wake and, 164; *munasirun* in, 164, 166, 168–172; overview, 164; political field and, 164; Sahwi intellectuals/"enlightened" Sahwi intellectuals in, 164, 166, 172–175, 320n118; Sahwi ulema in, 164–168; heterogeneous nature of, 164–175; three main groups of, 164–175. *See also Munasirun*; Sahwa insurrection; Sahwi protest movement

Sahwi protest movement, 151; Saudi regime and, 155–156, 184–185, 190, 193, 197, 198, 199, 226; Gulf War crisis as catalyst of, 158–164; opposition front's three groups, 164–175; *Memorandum of Advice*, 171–172, 185–188, 195; "enlightened" Sahwi intellectuals in, 175, 176, 177, 185,

188–189, 191, 192; Sahwi intellectuals in, 175, 177–178, 179, 181, 182, 183, 185, 186, 188–189, 190, 191, 192, 198, 199; "commanding right/forbidding wrong" principle and, 175–176, 177; *munasirun* and, 175–176, 177, 179, 181, 182, 183, 186–188, 189, 191, 198; Sahwi ulema and, 175–176, 177–178, 179, 181, 182, 183, 185, 186, 188, 189, 191–192, 193, 198, 240; early organization/mobilizations, 175–177; struggle for reform, 175–193; transformative event, 176, 321n137; *islah* and, 176–177; religious field and, 177–179, 181, 182, 207, 210; religious/intellectual fields coming together in, 177–179, 181; *jama'at* and, 178; salons in, 178, 186; "Letter of Demands," 179–187, 194, 195; subordinate classes and, 182; Shiites and, 182–183; ulema and, 184–185, 186, 187–188, 191; Saudi royal family and, 187, 191; "Threefold Response," 187–188; human rights and, 188–190; CDLR, 188–192, 195, 198, 323n190, 323n197, 325n226; jihadis and, 193, 194–196, 197, 199; Ahl al-Hadith rejectionists and, 193–194, 197, 199; Osama bin Laden and, 194, 195–196, 199, 200, 201; CADLR, 195; ARC, 195–196, 199; 1995 Riyadh attack and, 196, 197, 198, 199; groups' competition and differing goals/interests, 198; call for jihad and Saudi regime delegitimization, 199; Shirazi Shiite opposition and, 223–224; leaders and Sahwi mobilization infrastructure weaknesses, 227; political field changes and, 236. *See also* Committee for the Defense of Legitimate Rights;

"Letter of Demands"; *Memorandum of Advice*; Sahwa insurrection; Sahwi mobilizations; Sahwi opposition front

Sahwi protest movement failure: lack of grassroots networks in, 201; Sahwi countermovements and, 201, 211–225; Saudi regime and, 201–211, 212, 213, 215, 221–222, 223, 224, 226, 228, 230–234, 235, 236; Saudi state repression of Sahwi protest and, 201–211; analysis of, 201–237; lack of reliable mobilizing structures in, 225–236; Saudi state reforms and, 236; summary of, 236–237, 238. *See also* Sahwa insurrection aftermath; Sahwi countermovements; Sahwi mobilization infrastructure weaknesses; Saudi state repression of Sahwi protest

Sahwi protest movement success: at micro/individual and middle/movement levels, 236–237; in religious field, 237; in Saudi social movement field, 237

Sahwi remobilization aborted attempt(s): Islamo-liberal movement and, 255, 256–259, 261, 342n65; Sahwi mobilization and, 255, 342n65; AQAP and, 255–256, 259–260, 342n65; causes of, 255–256, 342n67; neojihadis and, 255–256, 259–260, 261, 342n65; in Sahwa insurrection aftermath, 255–262; new Sahwa and, 260–261; Saudi 2005 municipal elections and, 261–262

Sahwi remobilization potential, 270; potential new Sahwa credibility loss and, 268; future oil income decline and, 268–269; Saudi social liberalization and, 269

Sahwi ulema, 79–80; Sahwi intellectuals and, 136, 139, 150, 177–178; Saudi modernism vs., 139–140, 141; overview, 141; quarrel of, 141–149; religious field and, 141–149, 160, 164, 167–168; Wahhabi ulema and, 142, 144–145, 146–149, 164; social arena and, 143; *fiqh al-waqi'* and, 144–146; critiques of, 144–149; *irja'* and, 147, 148, 149; Saudi regime and, 149, 239–240; denouncement of American troops in Saudi Arabia, 160–161, 317n46; secularists vs., 160–162; modernism and, 164; political conceptions/discourses, 164–166, 168; in Sahwi opposition front, 164–168; religious/moral questions, 165–166; Iraq invasion of Kuwait and, 166; council of preachers, 166–167; fatwas, 167–168; sunna memorization competition, 168; Sahwi protest movement and, 175–176, 177–178, 179, 181, 182, 183, 185, 186, 188, 189, 191–192, 193, 198, 240; CDLR and, 188, 189, 191–192, 193; Saudi state repression of Sahwi protest and, 202–203, 204, 205, 206; in Sahwa insurrection aftermath, 239–240; new Sahwa and major, 243

Sahwi ulema cassettes, 143, 144, 219; banning of, 203

Salafi (faithful to Muslim pious ancestors), 10, 84, 212, 215; movement and Saudi Islamism, 269–270

Salman, Prince. *See* Al Sa'ud, (Prince) Salman bin Abd al-Aziz

Salons, in Sahwi protest movement, 178, 186

al-Sarhan, Sa'ud, 225

Sa'ud, King. *See* Al Sa'ud, (King) Sa'ud bin Abd al-Aziz

bin Sa'ud, Muhammad, 8

Saudi Arabia: export of Islam, 1; Islamic revivalism influences on, 1; religious proselytism/Islamist movements and, 1; as rentier state, 4, 17, 281n4, 282n7; Saudi students co-opted into administration of, 16; Muslim Brotherhood arrival into, 37, 38–42; Egypt vs., 41; Iranian Revolution (1979) and, 124; Iran vs., 124; Shiites vs., 124; support for Iraq in Iraq-Iran war, 124; September 11, 2001 attacks and, 246; post-Islamism and, 264, 270; Islamism and, 266. *See also* Saudi regime; Saudi state

Saudi Brotherhood: foreign Muslim Brotherhood and, 68–69; Sururis vs., 70, 123–129, 142, 309nn1–2, 310n10; in protest movement, 226–229; Saudi 2005 municipal elections and, 261, 262

Saudi Brotherhood *jama'at*: Brothers of al-Funaysan/Brothers of Imam University, 65, 228; Brothers of al-Sulayfih, 65; Brothers of Zubayr, 65–66, 226, 228; Brothers of the Hejaz, 66–67, 113; cooperation amongst, 67–68; Sahwi mobilization infrastructure weaknesses and, 227, 228. *See also* Brothers of the Hejaz

Saudi educational system: Saudi modernization and, 42–43; Muslim Brotherhood and, 42–51, 290n46; religious sciences in, 46, 290n46; Islamic culture and, 46–47, 48; Islamicized sciences in, 47; teaching of creed in, 47–48; Wahhabi ulema and, 47–48; *Educational Policy*

(1970), 48; *taʿlim* in, 48; *tarbiya* in, 48–49, 50; Koran memorization in, 49; student activity Islamicization and, 49–51; youth camps and, 50, 51; Sahwa and, 78; class inequalities in, 120, 309n191; growth of educated population and, 121, 309n194

Saudi field(s): overview, 7; Saudi Islamism and, 7; in Saudi state birth/development, 7–22; Intellectual field and literary, 18–19; economic/social capital of, 21; of women in Saudi state birth/development, 21; Saudi field of power sectorization into autonomous, 22–23, 27–29, 123; Sahwa internal competition within, 123, 124, 126, 127–128; Sahwa internal competition within education, 123, 126, 127–128; various groups competition within, 123; Sahwa and, 133–134; "Letter of Demands" and Sahwi strengthening in, 182; Sahwi protest movement success in social movement, 237; Sahwa insurrection aftermath and media, 240–241. *See also* Economic field; Humanitarian field; Intellectual field; Military field; Political field; Religious field

Saudi field elites: political field's collusive transactions with dominant, 28–29; Saudi royal family's collusive transactions with dominant, 28–29

Saudi field of power: in Saudi state birth/development, 7–22; fields of cultural production and, 20

Saudi field of power sectorization: into autonomous fields, 22–23, 27–29, 123; causes of, 22–23; Saudi sociopolitical system and, 22–29;

corporatism and, 23; fields of cultural production, 23–24, 25, 27; spatial, 23–24; effects, 23–25; symbolic, 24–25; political fields and, 25–26, 27–28, 286n77; religious/political fields and, 25–26, 27–28, 29, 286n77; Saudi modernization and, 25–26; Sahwa and, 79, 123; dismantling of, 139; Sahwa insurrection aftermath and, 263.

Saudi global jihadis: AQAP and, 254; jihad in Saudi Arabia and, 254; neojihadis and, 254; Osama bin Laden and, 254

Saudi government. *See* Political field; Saudi Arabia; Saudi regime; Saudi royal family; Saudi state

Saudi history: contemporary social, 2; of Saudi Islamism and Sahwa insurrection, 3; Saudi state birth/development, 8–22. *See also* Saudi state birth/development

Saudi institution(s), 133; control by *jamaʿat* (Sahwa organized networks), 126–129, 310n10; secularists and, 133; Sahwa entrance into cultural, 157–158; regulations in Saudi state repression of Sahwi protest, 207–210

Saudi intellectuals. *See* Intellectuals

Saudi-Iranian cold war, 103, 124

Saudi Islamism: rise of Sunni, 2; Sahwa insurrection and, 3, 4; Wahhabism and, 4; Saudi fields and, 7; JSM and, 100; golden age of, 193–199; post-, 264, 270; Sahwa and, 267; global context and, 269; potentialities of, 269; *salafi* movement and, 269–270. *See also* Ahl al-Hadith rejectionists; Jihadis; Sahwis; Saudi Islam

Saudi Islamist(s): opposition vs. Saudi regime, 197–198; reconstitution in Sahwa insurrection aftermath, 238; environment after 1990s, 238–239; new Islamist insurrection and, 270. *See also* Non-Sahwi Islamists

Saudi Islamist movement, vs. Middle Eastern Islamism, 2, 265

Saudi Left/nationalistic/opposition organizations: Saudi students and, 16, 17, 284n37; Saudi modernization and, 16–17; Saudi state birth/development and, 16–17, 284n37

Saudi literary criticism, 134; modernism and, 135; Saudi modernism and, 135

Saudi modernism: intellectual field and, 135, 144; literary criticism and, 135; Saudi literary criticism and, 135; social arena and, 135; Sahwi intellectuals vs., 138, 139, 141; cultural supplements and, 139, 157; Saudi newspapers and, 139; Sahwi ulema vs., 139–140, 141; spreading dispute/attacks on, 140–141, 144; Sahwa generation vs., 141; Saudi regime turn against, 156–157, 316n24. *See also* al-Ghadhdhami, Abdallah

Saudi modernization: Saudi Islamist mobilizations and, 5; Saudi state birth/development and, 14–20; Saudi students politicization abroad and, 15–16, 17, 283n35; Saudi Left/nationalistic/opposition organizations and, 16–17; oil boom (1973) and, 17; Saudi field of power sectorization and, 25; Saudi educational system and, 42–43;

dispute over, 133–141; intellectual field and, 137

Saudi municipal elections of 2005, 343nn79–81; Islamo-liberals and, 261; neojihadis and, 261; normalization and, 261; Saudi Brotherhood and, 261, 262; Sururis and, 261, 262; Sahwi remobilization aborted attempts and, 261–262; *jama'at* and, 262, 268; new Sahwa and, 262; ulema and, 262

Saudi newspapers: Sahwi intellectuals and, 139; Saudi modernism and, 139. *See also* Cultural supplements

Saudi political field. *See* Political field

Saudi prisons: Sahwa legacy groups incubation in, 242, 245–246, 249; Islamo-liberal group incubation in, 245–246, 249; neojihadi group incubation in, 249

Saudi public employment: economic recession and, 130–131, 310n24; Sahwa generation, 130–131, 310n24

Saudi regime: vs. Islamists over Saudi Islam, 2; jihadis vs., 116, 196–197, 198; Osama bin Laden and, 116–117, 194–195, 199–200, 325n226; Sahwi ulema vs., 149, 239–240; background of break between Sahwa and, 152–158; Sahwi verbal/written attacks on, 154–156; Sahwi protest movement and, 155–156, 184–185, 190, 193, 197, 198, 199, 226; turn against Saudi modernism, 156–157, 316n24; "Letter of Demands" and, 184–185; CDLR vs., 190, 198, 325n226; Ahl al-Hadith rejectionists vs., 196–197, 198; Saudi Islamist opposition vs., 197–198; U.S. and,

198; Sahwi protest movement failure and, 201–211, 212, 213, 215, 221–222, 223, 224, 226, 228, 230–234, 235, 236; Jamis and, 211, 212, 213, 215; Hejazi Sufism and, 221–222, 224; Shirazi Shiite opposition and, 222, 223, 224; Sahwi mobilization infrastructure weaknesses and, 226, 228, 230–234, 235; non-Sahwi popular mobilization and, 233–234; in Sahwa insurrection aftermath, 238–241; new Sahwa and, 243, 244, 268; Islamo-liberals and, 245–246, 247, 248–249; neojihadis and, 251, 254. *See also* Saudi Arabia; Saudi royal family; Saudi state

Saudi regime delegitimization: Gulf War and, 158; Sahwi mobilizations and, 158–159; Bin Laden's call for jihad and, 199. *See also* Saudi regime legitimacy

Saudi regime legitimacy: religious field support of, 159; intellectual field support of, 159–160. *See also* Saudi regime delegitimization

Saudi religious field. *See* Religious field

Saudi repression. *See* Saudi state repression of Sahwi protest

Saudi royal family: Sahwa opposition to American troops in Saudi Arabia and, 2–3, 162; economic field and, 20, 285n53; military field and, 20–21; collusive transactions with Saudi fields' dominant elites, 28–29; Sahwi protest movement and, 187, 191; political field and, 209; Jamis and, 211, 214, 215–216; Shirazi Shiite opposition and, 223, 224; rivalry and Islamo-liberals, 261; rivalry and new

Sahwa, 261. *See also* Political field; Saudi regime; Saudi state

Saudi social arena. *See* Saudi society; Social arena

Saudi society: economic capital of, 21, 285n56; response to Islamo-liberals, 255, 258–259, 342n65; liberalization and Sahwi remobilization potential, 269

Saudi sociopolitical system: as fragmented, 22–29; Saudi field of power sectorization and, 22–29

Saudi state: JSM vs., 93–94, 95–96, 97, 98–99, 100, 103; Ahl al-Hadith and, 101–102, 116, 117; reaction to Grand Mosque of Mecca seizure and religious field, 102–103, 304n108; Ikhwan of Burayda and, 104–105, 107, 109; Sahwa ascendancy in, 107; Afghan jihad and, 116; control of religious field, 207–210, 268. *See also* Saudi Arabia; Saudi regime; Saudi royal family

Saudi state birth/development: fields/field of power in, 7–22; bin Abd al-Wahhab and, 8, 10–12; Wahhabism and, 8, 10–14; political field in, 8–9, 15–16, 19, 21, 282n13; religious field in, 8–9, 13, 15, 18, 19, 20, 282n13, 284n44; history, 8–22, 282n13; Egypt and, 12–13; exclusivists in, 12–13; inclusivists in, 12–14; Muslim reformists and, 14; Saudi modernization in, 14–20; intellectual field in, 15, 16, 17–20, 284n45; strikes/coup d'état attempts in, 16; Saudi Left/nationalistic/opposition organizations and, 16–17, 284n37; economic field in, 20; military field in, 20–21; field of women and, 21

al-Tawil, Muhammad, 132–133

Tazkiyat (recommendations), 78, 183, 186; Jami/Sahwi war of, 218–219

"Threefold Response":, 187–188

Torture: Saudi state repression of Sahwi protest using physical, 206; Saudi state repression of Sahwi protest using psychological, 206

Transformative event, Sahwi protest movement as, 176, 321n137

al-Turayri, Abd al-Wahhab, 144, 185, 186, 202

al-Turki, Abdallah, 44, 65, 123, 209

al-Tuwayjiri, Abdallah, 170, 178, 183, 186–187, 184, 189

Al-Tuwayjiri, Ahmad, 157, 174, 204, 223

al-Tuwayjiri, Hamud, 104, 107–108, 170–171, 178, 183, 186–187

al-ʿUbaykan, Abd al-Mushin, 171, 175–177, 184, 187, 204, 214

Ulema (religious scholars), 7, 8, 9, 19, 28; intellectuals and, 24; Islamist movements/intellectuals and, 29–34; Sahwa and, 79–80; *jamaʿat* and, 80; "Letter of Demands" and, 184–185; Sahwi protest movement and, 184–185, 186, 187–188, 191; *Memorandum of Advice* and, 186, 187–188, 219; *munasirun* vs., 187–188; Jami, 214, 220; Jamis and, 218–219, 220; neojihadis and, 249, 250, 251, 254, 259; Islamo-liberals and, 256, 257–258, 342n71; Saudi 2005 municipal elections and, 262. *See also* Council of the Committee of Senior Ulema; Religious field; Sahwi ulema; Wahhabi ulema

al-ʿUmar, Nasir, 145–146, 154, 161, 163, 166, 168, 183, 205, 218, 219, 240, 244–245, 247, 253

Umm al-Qura University, 43, 53, 56, 111, 147, 222

United States (U.S.): Sahwi verbal attacks on, 153–154, 156; 1995 Riyadh attack and, 198. *See also specific American topics*

Until There Is No More Fitna (al-Qusaybi), 161–162, 172

U.S. *See* United States (U.S.)

al-ʿUtaybi, Abdallah bin Bijad, 100, 206, 246

al-ʿUtaybi, Juhayman, 3, 25, 101, 246, 304n101; JSM and, 90, 92, 93, 94–100, 108, 109; letters of, 95–98, 301n66, 302nn74–75; on religious field, 96–97; Mahdi and, 98, 99; messianism of, 98, 99, 100; Grand Mosque of Mecca seizure and, 99, 100

bin ʿUthaymin, Muhammad, 78, 111, 144, 148, 158, 169, 172, 183–184, 218, 219, 227, 239, 268

al-Wadiʿi, Muqbil, 91, 92, 94, 95–96, 101, 102, 117, 215, 308n183

Wahhabism: complexity/plasticity of, 4; Sahwa insurrection and, 4; Saudi Islamism and, 4; bin Abd al-Wahhab and, 10–12, 54, 84; Saudi state birth/development and, 10–14; "commanding right/forbidding wrong" principle and, 12; Hanbalism and, 12, 71, 85, 88; inclusivists, 12–14, 66, 103; Muslim Brotherhood ideology and, 52, 53, 54, 59; Sahwi ideology and, 52, 53, 56; Qutbism and, 54, 55, 56; al-Albani vs., 84–85, 219–220,